For Erik, Lov

Terry Sams

Sisters Redeem

Their Grumpy Dad

Terry L. Garlock

"Sisters Redeem Their Grumpy Dad," by Terry L. Garlock. ISBN 1-58939-489-5 (softcover); 1-58939-490-9 (hardcover).

Library of Congress Control Number: 2003114713

Published 2003 by Virtualbookworm.com Publishing Inc., P.O. Box 9949, College Station, TX, 77842, US. ©2003 Terry L. Garlock. All rights reserved. No part of this publication may be reproduced, stored in a retrieval system, or transmitted in any form or by any means, electronic, mechanical, recording or otherwise, without the prior written permission of Terry L. Garlock.

Manufactured in the United States of America.

Table of Contents

Book One – Melanie and Me

Book Two – Waiting for Babysister

Book Three – Kristen Comes Home

Book Four – Dear Kristen and Melanie, From Dad

Appendix

The Children Left Behind

Both of our daughters, Melanie and Kristen, joined our family by adoption, both from an orphanage in China, both at one year old. They have brightened our lives immeasurably.

Melanie and Kristen

Sisters Redeem Their Grumpy Dad

The joy of adoption on each trip to China had a shadow – the children left behind in the orphanage, the ones never adopted. As they grow out of the toddler stage into childhood, time after time they see infants dressed up and taken away to join a family. As they grow into adolescence and struggle with identity, pride, belonging and their own future, they live in an austere setting where they own nothing, not even the modest clothes and shoes they wear.

In 1997 Debbie Bodie and her husband, Al, were waiting anxiously for their own adoption dossier to be accepted in China, and for their turn to come. As Debbie waited, she wondered and worried and hoped about many things, like the age of her child, and something happened in her heart.

Debbie belonged to an e-mail group connecting thousands of families worldwide in the process of adopting from China. There is much discussion on these e-mail groups about how old the child will be when offered. Many implore their agency to make sure their child is no older than eight or ten months, and some prepare to reject a toddler. While experience has shown nearly all the kids who are delayed catch up quickly, there is a practical concern over the cumulative effects of insufficient personal attention and stimulation in the orphanages. More important, perhaps, a mother's desire for an infant is natural, and strong. Older children are understandably overlooked.

In the spring of 1997 Stefanie Ellison told the e-mail group a story upon her return from China to adopt a second daughter. They visited the orphanage, and Stefanie described a little girl in the orphanage about five years old, a friend of the child Stefanie was adopting, who chased after their group pleading in English, "Mommy? Mommy?" She was left behind.

Debbie was captivated by the story of this little girl, and pondered adoptive parents' preference for an infant while older children are overlooked. She was moved to write a poem she called The Waiting Child, and she shared it with the rest of us by e-mail.

On May 25, 1997, Debbie and her husband, Al, adopted their child, 18 months old, from the Leping Orphanage in Jiangxi. They named their daughter Quinn, after a favorite aunt who was never able to have children. Mom, Dad and Quinn are a happy family in Rincon, Georgia. Meanwhile, many people have written Debbie to tell her they were moved to adopt an older child after reading The Waiting Child. Debbie says the words are not her own, but divinely inspired for just this purpose.

The Waiting Child

by Debbie Bodie © 1997
(Reprinted here with Debbie Bodie's permission)

I saw you meet your child today
You kissed your baby joyfully
And as you walked away with her
I played pretend you'd chosen me.

I'm happy for the baby, yet
Inside I'm aching miserably
I want to plead as you go by,
"Does no-one want a child of three?"

I saw you meet your child today
In love with him before you met
And as I watched you take him out
I knew it wasn't my turn yet.

I recognize you from last year!
I knew I'd seen your face before!
But you came for a second babe.
Does no-one want a child of four?

I saw you meet your child today
But this time there was something new
A nurse came in and took MY hand
And then she gave my hand to you.

Can this be true? I'm almost six!
And there are infants here, you see?
But then you kissed me and I knew
The child you picked this time was me.

Of course we are not able to pick and choose a child in the adoption process. But it must seem that way, just as the child thought in the poem, to the older children who watch with envy as groups of infants are adopted again and again.

Like many others, Julie and I were concerned that our child be an infant. Debbie's poem did for us what any writer hopes their work will do – it made us stop and think. I printed and framed this poem, Julie hung it in her office and we talked about it. It made us wonder what is more important, missing the infant cuddling every woman yearns for, avoiding some difficulty as a delayed child catches up, or the life of an older child who never found a home or a family? We refocused our priorities, and though both Melanie and Kristen were 12 months old at adoption, we were prepared to love them just the same if they were older.

Stefanie later reported the little girl in the story was adopted by an American family later that year. But so many older kids are far less fortunate.

On her 2003 adoption trip to China Amy Eldridge met two sisters in the Shantou Social Welfare Institute orphanage, in Guangdong province in the south of the country near Hong Kong. Both sisters have surely been disappointed many times as they hoped for adoption by a Chinese or foreign family, but at least in the orphanage they are together. One girl is named Ling, ten years old in 2003, with crossed eyes that affect both her vision and how she is accepted in China. She cannot go to school, so Ling eagerly gives the little ones in the orphanage her loving care.

Ling

Ling has a biological older sister in the orphanage, Hong, who faces a difficult challenge very soon when she must leave the orphanage as she reaches the age of 16. Hong will leave the orphanage with no possessions, no money, no home and, very important in China, no family, ill prepared for a tough and competitive world. The orphanage staff, with love in their heart for a girl they know so well, pooled their personal money to buy Hong a suitcase. Maybe she will receive a few things to put in the suitcase.

But, as life teaches us whether in China, the US or any other place, hopes and dreams take root in the tiniest crack. Hong dreams of going to college in China, though she was told she could never pass the entrance exams and without funding college would be impossible. Hong studied hard and persisted, the orphanage staff arranged for her to sit for the exams, and she passed! Now she must find a way to pay for college.

(L-R) Ling, Amy Eldridge, Hong

My daughter Melanie is six years old. She asked me about the photos and I explained about Ling and Hong in the orphanage in China. I told Melanie about Hong's dream of a college education, a decent job and the ability to provide a home for her sister, Ling. Melanie asked "Dad, can we help Hong go to college?" Children are so idealistic . . . or maybe we lose too much of our idealism. I told her the small author's royalty for each of these books sold would go into the college fund for her and Kristen. I asked Melanie if she would like to donate part of that money to help girls like Hong in China. Melanie said yes, she would like to share her college fund that way, and beamed with satisfaction at the idea of a book sale helping two Chinese girls in America go to college, and at the same time helping kids in China go to college. Julie and I like it, too.

We can't solve everyone's problems in the US, much less in China, but maybe we can help these older kids just a little. We will donate through AIM-China (www.aimchina.org), a non-profit organization established by John and Jackie Harrah to improve the lives of children in Chinese orphanages. AIM-China can direct donations to assist orphans and children in China from low income areas with elementary, high school, and university expenses. AIM-China is helping Ling obtain corrective eye surgery, and may be able to help Hong in her quest for a college education. Our contribution may be small, but we like the idea of helping these older kids.

You may wonder why we adopt from China instead of in the US, and why we would support Chinese children. Both countries have their problems, like hard conditions that fill orphanages in China, and like a troubled system in the US that often traps abused children in foster care while discouraging adoption. At least in China the foreign adoption system works well and welcomes older parents like us. As Melanie reminds us what we have taught her, no matter our race or national boundaries we are all God's children with hopes and dreams that are very much the same.

All over China, in orphanages like the Shantou Social Welfare Institute where Ling and Hong reside, fine men and women with limited resources generously give their labor and their heart to these kids. We have seen with our own eyes the faces of the orphanage director and staff glowing with joy for their kids as they join a forever family by adoption, and we have seen the tears falling from their face as they give each child one last kiss knowing they will never see them again. We know they ache for the older kids who never find a family. They do what they can but their job is huge, their need is great, and we are pleased to help in our small way.

Inspiration

Julie becomes a Mom a second time

When we adopted a child, my wife Julie morphed overnight from parent wannabe to *mother*, remarkable to witness. She is a superb example of the many selfless near-saints deserving of the exalted title of *Mom*.

On a July 1998 weekend while visiting my mother just a couple of months after returning from China with Melanie, she said to me over morning coffee "Julie sure is a good mother." And she is right.

It seems some magical instinctive metamorphosis occurred about an hour after Julie held Melanie the first time. Melanie immediately became her highest and hottest priority. Endless patience for play and tolerance for kiddie stuff appeared out of nowhere, and she grew a protective side that rivals a mama grizzly.

As you read these stories, you will notice Julie's job requires travel, but not by her choice. Every time she packed a suitcase and hopped a plane while I stayed home to work and take care of the kids, every single time, she would have loved to trade places. I know when she worked late pouring over financial records in a cramped room she was yearning to read Melanie a bedtime story. I know when she had fancy dinners with staff and clients she would have traded Filet Mignon and Baked Alaska in an instant for a hot dog and Tang with the kids.

But we found a way to make it work as well as possible. Melanie quickly adjusted and learned that Mom has to leave *on business* sometimes for a week, and knows based on many such experiences that Mom comes back, every time, just as Mom and Dad have told her. Kristen will soon learn the same.

When Julie is in town, instead of spending time on herself, she selflessly devotes her time to Kristen and Melanie. She has done a superb job of balancing unwanted travel with home life, emphasis on the kids.

To family, friends, and neighbors, you must have known what I didn't, that Julie's virtue would make up for my deficit, and we thank you for your overwhelming support of our adoptions. Even though some of you privately thought we were out of our minds to start changing diapers at our age, you had the good grace not to say so. You have welcomed Melanie and Kristen into your homes and your hearts, and we are eternally grateful.

Read This First!

Some of you will skip this introduction, and as a result will wonder about my mental health as you read the stories about my daughters - Melanie, adopted at twelve months old from China in 1998, and Kristen, also adopted at twelve months old from China in 2003. These stories expose a soft side of me rarely seen, and they are written in a way that begs explanation.

Real Life

I discovered late in life that kids are the world's great equalizer. For example, I have dined in many fine restaurants, but my kids bring back the long lost delight of macaroni and cheese, Popsicles for desert. I left behind potty humor when adolescence faded, but discovered I cannot truthfully tell my girls' tales without the subjects of poop, boogers and the first tiny glimmer of sex, giggles and all. And I discovered that I had to choose between preserving my professional and personal dignity, or writing with candor about my children with words I would never say out loud in public. Dignity lost.

I am most comfortable with the decorum of polite adult company, but getting in the dirt to play with your kids or telling stories with their focus on bodily functions is like an awakening to real life.

The Stress of Adoption

Most people don't get it about adoption because they haven't been through it, they haven't learned the lessons, the lingo, the hot buttons or pressure points. You might assume genetics make you love an adopted child differently than a biological child, and that adopting is the *easy way* to build a family since you don't experience the trials of pregnancy. You would be wrong.

As anyone who has adopted from China can tell you, the year-plus waiting period is a difficult time, full of tension and doubts that it would ever really happen, frustration at having no control, disappointment as hoped-for dates are missed, concerns about the health of the child, worry about parent-child bonding, and jumpy nerves from every nuance of US-China relations until the trip is complete. But that waiting period doesn't even begin until after six months of tedious paperwork. It's a different kind of pregnancy with pent-up tension and it's very own emotional roller-coaster into and out of the clouds.

As anyone who has adopted from anywhere can tell you, adoption doesn't define their children, it's just the way they joined the family at one time. One friend sums it up like this - "Some of my children are adopted, but I forget which ones." Sometimes I forget Melanie or Kristen are Chinese, and that means the same thing.

When Bob Hope died in July 2003 one TV newsman observed just hours after his death that Mr. Hope had four *adopted children,* and wondered in the same sentence whether there would be disputes over the estate. That reporter gave voice to the public's misconception – that adopted children are almost, but not quite, *real* family. We who have adopted know the truth, we know that reporter and many others don't get it. If you read between the lines in this book I am hopeful you will see what we mean.

The Origin of These Stories

During our wait for Melanie in 1997-1998, a vital information source was an e-mail connection to thousands of other couples and singles around the world in the process of adopting from China. The mutual support link is strong among these people as they grapple with ever-shifting requirements and schedules and obstacles, such as the 2003 SARS delay. Those who complete the process share their story by e-mail with others to pass on tips, entertain and encourage them.

When we returned from China with Melanie I wrote a few stories about her as a means of reassuring others by e-mail of what was to come, and to provide a little diversionary entertainment in the process. They asked for more, and so I continued to write stories and as they accumulated it became my outlet of expression of how a child changes your life.

Many of these stories have a message directed to those waiting for their own adoption. I left those messages intact even though they might confuse some readers.

Dads Are Pretty Much the Same

Writing these stories and listening to reader feedback has made me aware of something noteworthy. Some lady readers have actually suggested I could teach their men something about sensitivity. Julie had a near-fatal laughing fit, and these ladies flatter me but they miss the point. I would never say the things I have written in my stories out loud, either. I'm just as much a Neanderthal as their own knuckle-dragger when it comes to talking about deep feelings. Dads everywhere feel the same way I do about their own children, the only difference is I have wrapped up those feelings in story form and let you read them. That's just the way men tick.

These Stories are for Melanie and Kristen

Ultimately, these stories and this book are for Melanie and Kristen, to make sure they know they could not possibly be more loved if they were our biological children. They already know we love them, but some day I want them to read between the lines and see they inspired grumpy old Dad to write tender things about them and tell the world.

Terry L. Garlock

Real Sisters

Melanie with Kristen

"Are they real sisters?" the lady in the grocery store asked Julie while admiring Melanie and Kristen.

Well, the answer is simple, and it is involved. Melanie was born in April 1997 to a Chinese mother in Dayangdian, a semi-rural town north of Hefei, the capital city of Anhui province in the eastern middle of China. Kristen was born in December 2001 to a different Chinese mother nearly a thousand miles south in Yangjiang City, about a three hour drive south from Guangzhou in Guangdong province, near Hong Kong.

Of course the fact they did not share a biological mother or father is what people mean when they ask "Are they real sisters?"

But they don't know that Melanie dreamed about Babysister every day for a year and a half before we met Kristen, or that she set special toys and gifts aside during that time for Babysister, or that virtually every aspect of her life was modified during that waiting period to "whenmybabysistercomes," or that she fantasized every day about the way they would someday play together and how she would teach Babysister to 'aggavate' Dad. They don't know about Melanie's long trip back to China to meet her Babysister, the intensity of her five year old impatience as we waited until the prescribed time, and how her face glowed as she stretched on tiptoes to reach up to touch Kristen for the first time. They don't know that Kristen gave Melanie her first smile, and though she can't say so yet she worships everything about her big sister. They can't know the first question Melanie asks when I pick her up from school is "Where's my sister?" and when she bursts in the door at home she runs to find her, hold her and kiss her hello after the long separation of a day at school.

When people ask "Are they real sisters?" they almost always mean well, and they don't know that we have ingrained into Melanie's thinking that her birthmother and birthfather are in China but we are her *parents* and our family is forever. How could they know their question almost seems a little silly to us, because we wonder how a few genes could possibly make any difference at all in how close and devoted to one another Melanie and Kristen have become, and we fully expect that bond to become tighter as they grow. They have no way of knowing Melanie and Kristen are real sisters in every way that matters, that we will defend them against any assertion they aren't really sisters.

Julie answered "They sure are. All adopted sisters are real sisters."

"That's not what I meant" the lady said.

"I know" said Julie as she walked away, giving the short answer since we're not inclined to explain these private matters to strangers to satisfy curiosity. She didn't want to offend the lady, because it is a natural question and we made ourselves conspicuous when we decided to adopt children of a different race. But most important to Julie were the little ears listening to what was asked, and how it was answered. And maybe, just maybe, the lady will think before asking others while their kids watch and listen. Besides, the nice lady wouldn't understand just how real these sisters have become.

Mar 2003, Melanie 5 yrs 11 mos, Kristen 1 yr 2 mos

Why I Need Redemption

I am not virtuous. In fact, I'm twice a Grump.

First, when I was young I wondered why older people seemed cranky, and now I know though I prefer grumpy to cranky. Maybe, as the years pass and middle age sets our values in concrete while the values of society keep changing, we become less willing to compromise what we believe to be right and increasingly impatient with what seems an increasingly stupid world. Or maybe it's just me.

I know many things have improved in the US since I was a kid, but . . . our society has coarsened, kids no longer respect elders, we're less polite and less trusting, youth has lost its' innocence, sex has lost its' modesty, immorality has lost its' shame, the work ethic is dying, customer service already died, guns are everywhere, births to teen single mothers are staggering, abortion is epidemic, victimhood has replaced personal responsibility, we've divided ourselves into hyphenated groups, schools can't discipline unruly kids but pass them when they fail and teach them self-esteem, OJ got away with murder while a different jury awarded billions to a smoker who said with a straight face he didn't know smoking was unhealthy, we have to worry about drugs in elementary school, TV programming appeals to the worst in us, a pro-white bias is racist while a pro-black bias is not, cable news has a drumbeat, extortion is disguised as litigation, health care costs are insane, alcoholism has become a disease that excuses the misbehavior of its *victims*, Rap is accepted as music, electronic games for kids teach violence, we actually argue about the rights of illegal immigrants while our borders leak like a sieve, truth has been sacrificed to sensitivity, appeasement is a cornerstone of our foreign policy, we give our money to other countries who return the favor by hating us, and we seem to have traded honor, decency, duty and integrity for whatever feels good. Is it just me or is our culture disintegrating? I know for sure it's morphing into something new and leaving me behind, because I refuse to go.

Sisters Redeem Their Grumpy Dad

There, I feel better for a moment. But when some pimple-faced clerk behind a counter ignores me while chatting with his friends my grumpiness is going to re-emerge real fast.

That's just the first side of my grumpy nature. The second side is that I am not a model father. I'm not virtuous like the late Mr. Rogers, who lived for children, or like my wife Julie who devotes every moment at home to Melanie and Kristen with never a thought for herself. Maybe I'm not even as virtuous as the average parent.

Here's my confession, but keep in mind this is sort of good-natured grumpiness, so don't worry about my kids.

By nature I prefer adult company, neatness, cleanliness, order, peace and quiet, though I seldom find it any more. My idea of relaxation involves solitude, an adult beverage, a good book and a cigar, at least as best I can remember. For company I fancy thoughtful conversation with intellectually honest give and take on politics or other topical issues. For leisure I like golf, short trips with other couples, cocktail and dinner parties, cooking for people who share my passion for food and letting them cook for me. I enjoy a manicured yard, but I'm no good at keeping it that way by myself so it's nice to have Julie looking after the flower beds and other fine points.

Kids change things with two busy parents, especially toddlers who need watching every moment. I haven't played golf for three years and gave up my club membership. Adventure in a meal used to mean exotic cooking, now it means macaroni on the ceiling. When I have a client case in process I prefer to ignore the clock and get it done, but now every weekday at 5:30PM I must set work aside to care for the kids until Julie arrives home near bedtime, followed by the bedtime routine. Until the kids pass the toddler stage we are often stuck in the house, and while other parents might relish that time to me it's a little like prison. With a toddler you can't cut the grass without help and a plan.

If you have more than two kids, or if you are a single mother, I can almost hear you mentally clucking at my pathetic complaints, but please know I have learned immense admiration for you.

I almost solved the yard work problem with a little creativity when Melanie was two. I bought a small harness, a leash and a heavy duty steel corkscrew one screws into the ground to hold the leash so I could put Melanie in one spot to play safely on the lawn while I cut the grass. But as I was bending my arm to pat myself on the back for a brilliant solution Julie nearly tore that arm off and beat me with it for even thinking I would stake out our child on the lawn like a dog. Back to prison.

I know the rest of you think it's just darling that toddlers dip your toothbrush in the toilet, drop junk on the floor with each step, pour milk in the toaster, leave jelly fingerprints on the VCR buttons, use the couch for a trampoline, smear spaghetti in their hair, wipe their nose on your slacks and need you to clean their poop. I don't.

The lawn is usually ragged, and the nice trimming is a goner since Julie can't add her touch when she has a kid wrapped around her leg screaming "Mommy-Mommy-Mommy!" And despite all our efforts the house often resembles a chicken coop.

The things that used to be on my short list of what makes life worth living are a fading memory. Even though I could arrange to take the time to enjoy those things with a little planning, it no longer seems worth the struggle. Do I resent the change? I confess that sometimes I do, and sometimes - OK, lots of times - I'm grumpy at the messy house and raucous noise from my own kids.

But, as told in the stories herein, maybe it's kids after all that make life worth living, and maybe we find redemption in the wide-eyed innocence of our children, even an old Grump like me. I am reminded every time I hear "Daddy!"

Book One

Melanie and Me

The stories in Book One were first published in 2001 in a volume titled <u>Melanie and Me: A Chinese Daughter Transforms Her Adoptive Dad</u>.

Hopes and Dreams Fulfilled

When Julie and I married in 1993, we had both been married previously and neither of us had children. I assumed we would remain childless since I was 45 then, and who wants to go to soccer games using a cane with four little stabilizer feet?

A few years later Julie said ". . . I want a child . . ." Though I was pushing 50, I got on the ball looking into adoption. I confess, I was apprehensive about upsetting the comfortable routine of adult life, golf, freedom, etc., and was unsure how an old, fat Grump like me would get along with kids.

Fast forward to May 1997 - all the interviews and paperwork with social workers, agencies, states, Secretaries of State, US State Department, INS, China, the courts, medical exams, financial disclosures, FBI and police background checks and so on . . . were done, with fees paid at every step, and we had been approved to be adoptive parents in the US at long last.

Now the real waiting began - a year or so while the Chinese gears turned. Finally, on March 4 1998 we received a *referral* - Melanie's photo at five months old along with medical reports, and the question whether we would like to adopt this child. How many ways can one say yes?

Do you sense that we were anxious to go? Not so fast! This started another waiting period for Chinese approval for travel to and within their country, another six weeks.

Eventually, Julie and I hopped airplanes for China. After three days sightseeing in Shanghai we flew with 13 other adoptive families to Hefei, about 300 miles west of Shanghai. The next morning, April 22, we were to meet our new daughter.

After breakfast the next day we were gathered in a *disco* ballroom complete with glitter dome. While the officials final-checked paperwork and photos to make sure everything was properly done, the tension of 14 families stressed like piano wire was palpable, each fidgeting in their own way, vibrating to their own tune. And then . . . the babies were here! Chinese officials meticulously organized the nannies holding each child in proper sequence and five minutes later Julie held Melanie for the first time. Neither of them had the slightest idea what to do. I was even less confident.

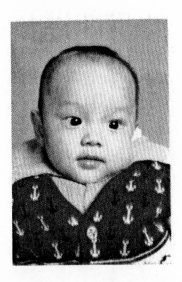

Melanie was one year old, having her first birthday two weeks before. With minimal crying, and a whole lot of curiosity, Melanie seemed more interested than afraid of what was going on. Back in our room we fed her the first time, I held her just a little because she *really* liked Julie, and we let her do whatever she wanted and adjust for a little while before giving her a bath which she did not like at all.

Melanie attached to Julie immediately, and she couldn't stray very far without protests. Melanie tolerated me only when I fed her, and screamed when Julie left the room for a minute or two for necessities. So long as Julie was within reach she was happy.

It turned out that Melanie was the firecracker of the group of kids – loud, curious, wiggleworm, feisty.

We spent a week in Hefei doing tourist things while the local officials completed and translated all the paperwork making Melanie our daughter, legally concluded at that time. We would readopt later in the Georgia courts, but that was our option to ensure that all states would recognize Melanie as our legal heir.

When the adoption was complete in Hefei, we flew to Guangzhou (Canton) in southern China where the US Consulate is located. There we had Melanie's medical exam for entry to the US, photos, visa application, our swearing to support her and contractually committing to reimburse the US government if she required financial assistance, more waiting for that paperwork and more time to explore a Chinese city.

After just one day, Melanie keeps Julie in sight at all times

At long last, all was done, again with fees paid at each step, and we prepared to return home. The flight from Guangzhou to Hong Kong took about twenty minutes, arriving at 9AM. Unfortunately, our flight to San Francisco was to depart at 9PM, twelve hours later. What's worse, we couldn't leave the Hong Kong airport since with Melanie's Chinese visa and passport there was some uncertainty whether she would be able to re-enter the airport, and we couldn't take that chance. Just one more hurdle.

Our good fortune was flying Business Class on Singapore Airline, the absolute pinnacle of luxurious service, and we spent the 12 hours in their Business Class Lounge.

After this final wait, we boarded for a twelve hour non-stop flight to San Francisco - can you say "My butt hurts"? - where we crashed at a hotel for some rest. By the time we crawled into bed, Melanie was *wide awake*! Welcome to parenthood.

The next day we flew to Salt Lake City to visit Melanie's Grandma Shirley Wollschleger and the rest of Julie's family.

Melanie tolerated me when I had food in my hand

Finally, last flight, Delta non-stop first class row 1 to Atlanta, and with a group waiting for us in the terminal the jet landed with broken flaps and with fire trucks chasing just in case. At least in row 1 if we had plowed in we wouldn't have felt much pain! Save the best for last.

At the airport to greet us was my mother Lois Garlock - Melanie's other Grandma - Joann Simmons, neighbors Rhonda Phillips, Dawn Grella and Larry Bowers. We all congregated in the middle of the walkways like every other obnoxious airport family group you see, shuffled out of the way by irritated but nice Delta staff.

Finally, she's ours, the adoption is irrevocably final and we're home.

May 1998, Melanie 13 mos

Life Transformed

We've been home with Melanie now for three weeks, and the way she has adjusted and progressed is truly amazing.

She had no separation problems in China, or thereafter that we can detect. She took to Julie like velcro on the first day, traveled without a hitch, isn't shy and likes to meet new people, eats almost anything although she does insist on eating when we eat no matter how full she is, and just today learned how to hold and drink from a sippy cup.

Melanie could just sit up at first, and even then leaned heavily forward. Now she sits quite easily, walks while she grips two of your fingers, and leans forward into a trot when she wants to go somewhere, like to climb her mother. She has adjusted easily to the car seat on the golf cart, our neighborhood mode of transport, and with a little more difficulty to the car seat in the car.

In the evening after work I try to take her for a walk or a jaunt on the golf cart to ride through the woods or visit friends so Julie can regain her sanity for a little while after a full velcro day. Melanie has a 2.5 year old friend named Katlyn that she calls *Aaaaaahhh*!

We both feed her during dinner. Then at bedtime, after wiggling the little wildcat into her PJs and warming the bottle, I feed her while rocking, and she usually quits before it's empty, rolls over on my belly and rubs her nose into her blankie, struggles a minute or two with the fidgets and goes right to sleep. After the fidgets stop I have it down to a counted 100 rocks before I put her in her crib. I could do 50 but this is not something you want to cut too short.

When I put her in her crib, she rolls over, out like a light, asleep until morning. Occasionally, she'll cry out a little while she's dreaming, but only once did we have to get up with her. I thought we might need to put her in our room for a little while, but she's been in her room from the start.

Yesterday she went to day care for the first time for three hours to start the break-in period since Julie goes back to work June 15. She did great, didn't even cry, although the day care director asked Julie if *she* was alright when she left. Too funny. Tomorrow Melanie goes for her second day care session, and I'm sure she will do fine. Maybe Julie will as well.

Do I sound like a proud father? That's the way of things, although I'm too smart to say we won't have any problems since each day brings new wrinkles. We have to break her from clinging to Julie too much, work on teaching what things mean, and on and on. Life is changed, we're getting by on less sleep but quite content. We wish you all the same.

May 1998, Melanie 13 mos

What a Difference Six Weeks Makes

I am reminded of the remarkable transformation of our travel group just after we received our children. Right up to the magic moment there were 14 sets of stretched piano wires, some of us giving the outward appearance of calm. Next day there were 14 new families spending full time trying to figure one another out.

Now, about six weeks after returning, I am astonished at how things have changed, and I wanted to share a little of that with you as you wait.

When we received Melanie in China, she couldn't crawl, could only sit up leaning forward, and struggled to stand with help after a couple of days. Now she's walking on her own - danger!

In my pre-parent wisdom I told Julie we didn't need a million toys like everyone else, just a few carefully selected ones so she isn't spoiled. She now has a bazillion toys and she needs each and every one. The soft cover I made for the square coffee table is her play surface, and she uses it well, often as an anvil for whatever is serving as a hammer.

Melanie, at 14 months, sleeps through most nights (we're lucky), wakes about 6AM and plays a little before her morning bottle. Before that bottle, she hugs and wrestles with her big, soft white bear as if she hadn't seen him for a month.

She's learned how to feed herself anything she can pick up, so far including one application of applesauce to her hair for that special sheen. She hates grapefruit, loves popsicles cut up so she can pick the pieces up herself. Watermelon is a favorite, and as much as this reflects badly on me and Julie, I'll confess that she also loves a straw full of coke upended and drained into her mouth. We do feed her good stuff as well.

When I hold her up on my shoulders or even the top of my head, or up at arm's length so she can look out the top window, she smiles very big.

She has watched the bluebirds in fascination as they bring grubs to their young in the special house I built to attract them, eye level and close to lawn chairs. I built her a swing, and she giggles at first and falls asleep after 10 minutes most times. In the garage is a rack of bacci balls, and Melanie has selected the small balata as her very own which she snatches on the way out of the house and replaces on the way back in the house. You should see her shriek in nervous delight when I sneak the balata away from her in her swing and let her grab it again on the upswing.

We get around quite a bit on the golf cart and she's well adjusted to the car seat strapped into the front passenger side. But she will not allow my golf balls to sit in their rack, they must be removed. She likes to hold them if there are only two, and will often hand them back to me to hold, but they may *not* be put back in the golf ball rack. Go figure. She knows what *no* means and has tested it several times, but to my surprise has accepted the rules since we stuck to them consistently. I expected more trouble here, and I'm sure we'll get it.

She's adjusted to daycare pretty well, but cries and clings when Julie or I put her down in the infant room. I'd like to tell you how I feel when I go back to daycare at 5PM and when she sees me her eyes light up, she drops what she's doing and holds out her arms for me to pick her up, but the words would be too mushy. Same for Julie.

When Mom gets home Melanie is all over her, and they play and have a giggle fest as girls do.

Melanie knows the evening routine like the back of her hand. Mom bathes her in the big part of the kitchen sink, a back-saver for Mom even if dinner guests might be squeamish if they only knew. Melanie splashes all she wants with her toys. Sometimes when she's hungry she'll climb Mom to get out of the bath to accelerate things.

While Mom is drying her off and wrestling her into PJs, she does an involuntary dance in anticipation of her bottle of warm milk, made frantic by the hum and ding she knows so well from the microwave. If I'm slow and the bottle is not yet in the microwave, she looks at me like I'm El Stupido - girl training 101. This is the only time she struggles out of Mom's arms into mine.

As I rock her to classical music or a lullaby, she drinks as much of her bottle as she wants, then rolls over to be held with her head on my shoulder, now her favorite position after many experiments. Most times she's asleep in three minutes, but when she's fidgety we play a game where she hides her face and I ask "where's Melanie?" and she turns her face up with a big grin as I exclaim "There she is!"

There are many new things to come, and more experienced parents know all these and more. But as you wait, some with patience and some without, I wanted to share with you how remarkable it is that in a short period of time Melanie has come to trust us fully, to naively assume we know just what we're doing, to desperately want to be with one or both of us, and has learned so many new things. So it goes with Melanie, and so it will with you soon.

Jun 1998, Melanie 14 mos

Future Dads Listen Up – Part 1

Future Dads may think they know what's coming. Hah! You don't have a clue. Like my friend Joe Grella used to tell me when I told him having a kid wouldn't affect my golf game, "Just you wait!"

Last weekend Julie was gone Friday AM through Monday PM, and it was a real Mr. Mom test since Melanie was teething, whining, clingy, etc. Saturday and Sunday were long days, with little time for personal hygiene if you get my drift, and despite Melanie's 4:30AM start both days she didn't nap very long, and only so long as I held her so no break there.

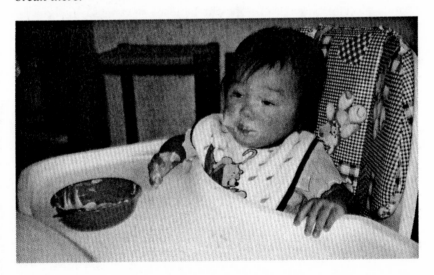

One of our respites is a soothing golf cart ride on paths through the woods. Workmen had just yesterday completed prepping to lay concrete to widen our sidewalk for driving the golf cart into the basement, with a big turnaround area. It had rained yesterday just after they finished digging out the grass and laying the forms. I looked over the situation, wondering whether I could drive the golf cart out of the basement and up the hill. I figured, what the heck I can back out, turn around and make it up the hill, driving inside the forms, without ever touching the forms if I don't slow down in the mud. I was ready for something different so here we went.

I put Melanie in the car seat on the golf cart, backed out and promptly got stuck in the mud. Wrestling the golf cart out of the mud and back into the basement was fun, especially as Melanie would yelp when I stepped more than one foot away from the golf cart. Finally made it, tired, muddy, PO'd, cleaned up, back to where we started. So we went to the store in the car instead.

Melanie also developed a mega-sneeze this weekend, and since it started just after Julie left I suspect sabotage but can't prove anything. It's not that her sneezes were especially loud or frequent, but production was up, way up!

Now, this is just part of the deal when taking care of your darling child, but things weren't going my way that weekend. For example, during one trip to the store in the car, I heard "Achoo!", twisted the rear view mirror and got a good view of Melanie doing her best with two separate and large streams of goo, which means she was seeing how far they would stretch with her fingers. Pull over quickly, scramble for Kleenex, reach around and wipe her clean, pull back into traffic and back up to speed, then "Achoo!" And so the day went.

That evening, after Melanie finally went to sleep, I was looking forward to unsophisticated relaxation in front of the tube with food and drink. Something quick and easy, nothing fancy. I decided on chili dip. That means a can of chili - no beans, in Texas where I'm from beans in chili can be a hanging offense - mix in some cheese and Tabasco when it's hot, get a bowl of dip chips and you're in business. I also had a beer on the tray and headed in to crash in front of the tube to clear my head.

As I sat down, however it happened I dropped the tray, beer went one way, chili dip another, and the chili bowl caught something just right and flipped with maximum leverage to soak my foot, splatter the coffee table, many of Melanie's toys and books, the nearly-white carpet, and all over Julie's nice chair. The good news is it missed the walls and ceiling.

Since I hadn't wasted any time with niceties such as pouring the beer in a glass, I picked up the bottle as it was draining into the carpet, sat back in my chair and drank the rest of it as I dejectedly surveyed the damage. As I was thinking it was a fitting end to this day, the hot chili began to soak through the top of my thick socks sans sneakers, and I began to hop around the living room shouting unmentionables while trying to get that damn sock off. Hop to the pantry, get some Vaseline to rub all over the top of my foot so maybe it won't blister.

After I cleaned up as much as I could, I looked, sort of, for cleaning solution for our carpet cleaner, and was very happy not to find any. What now? What the heck, I made another batch of chili dip, opened another beer, limped to my chair and crashed just as originally planned. By the end of the second beer all thoughts of the carpet cleaner had vanished and I was thankful Melanie slept through, not even an "Achoo!" New Dads have to find their blessings wherever they can get them.

Aug 1998, Melanie 1 yr 4 mos

To Those Who Wait

Monday we discovered that Melanie, twenty months old and adopted in April, has hand, foot and mouth disease. Just an infant viral infection that must work its' way out over a week while she has a mild fever and eats little because of the blisters in her mouth. I just put her to bed and as she cried Da-Da begging to be picked up I told her "Melanie go to sleep now." She rolled over, stuck her butt up in the air, buried her head in her blankie and desperately tried to do so. After a while of my rubbing her back, she sleeps.

Last night Julie was up with her at 1AM, and when she next cried at 3AM, alternately pleading Ma-Ma and then Da-Da, I retrieved her and brought her to our bed over Julie's objections as I told her "I know we're just encouraging her to cry for attention next time, but she's sick." It's a great excuse. I rolled over and went back to sleep, but Melanie was wide awake and began to do and say "tickle-tickle" on my back.

About 3:30 I gave up and took her downstairs to a reclining rocker, and luckily we dozed off while we both struggled for comfortable position, me prone on my back and her face down on my ample belly, covered by her blankie. Sleep blessed us sporadically until I awoke about 7AM, and strangely I thought about you, the countless people waiting to adopt, whom I have never met.

As I was waiting for her to wake, I thought there is nothing sweeter than having your child cling to you, sleeping in complete trust of your care, with her slight breath on your face as you keep one another warm, especially while she is not feeling well. And while so many of you are anxious and worried, impatient for your turn, I know that you will discover the demands of parenthood and will also find this same closeness which words cannot convey.

Please be wise and enjoy the remains of your adult freedom instead of wasting that time with frantic worry. And, when your turn comes, may your life be brightened as much as ours. Happy holidays.

Dec 1998, Melanie 1 yr 8 mos

Bonding - A Sample of One

Many of you worry, as you wait, about bonding with your child. As an a non-expert on the subject of bonding, something Julie and I worried about as we plowed through the process, here's my view based on a sample of one.

Melanie, twelve months old when we met her, immediately attached to Julie. It seemed she was hungry for such an attachment, and when the opportunity presented itself, she held on tight. She tolerated me, but cried when Julie's left the room for necessities.

Our respective roles, or personalities if you prefer, with Melanie have been as follows. Julie is not only Melanie's Mom but also her playmate and best friend. She teaches her to sing songs, play games, reads her books over and over again, patiently tolerates her indiscretions at the dinner table and any other setting, and defends her against all adversaries, principally me as I try to insert a little discipline.

I, on the other hand, play games with her a little differently, tell her "try again, you can do it", "get up you're OK", "show me your Boo-Boo, yea it's OK", "look up into the rain and let it get in your face", "pet the dog, I won't let him hurt you." Julie gives her gentle support and play while I play a little more aggressively, like holding her high over my head to let her ride on my shoulders while she tickles my bald spot and declares "Uh!" which means *up*!

Every night, when Julie is in town she gives Melanie a bath, and on those occasions when Julie is gone I do the bath. But from the day we returned from China I am the one who gives Melanie her evening milk, at first in a bottle and now in a sippy cup, and I rock her to sleep and put her to bed. For me, I think that time is important.

And when Melanie cries in the night, most often I defer to Julie, less often she defers to me, and sometimes we elbow each other out of the way.

This week, Julie has been gone since Sunday afternoon. Taking care of Melanie sometimes disrupts my work schedule, but I control my schedule and I can roll with the punch. Every day this week when I bring Melanie home from day care and we go through the routine of snack, drink, climbing all over me like monkey bars while I lay on the floor, at some point Melanie says "Ma-Ma?" The question is very clear. Now Julie's practice would be to divert her, change the subject, even mislead her to avoid any disappointment. But my way is head-on. I tell her gently but firmly "Mama's not here today" and she seems to accept that and go on. Seems like with me she knows that I tell her one time and that's it. Julie's way is right, and so is mine, but they are different.

Then we do dinner, a couple of cartoons - she loves the *baby* on Dinosaurs - warm milk and rocking to sleep. Frequently, she wakes in the middle of the night and cries "Da-Daaa!" and I can't so I bring her to bed, then for the rest of the night we grunt and nudge as we try to sleep, happy the other one is there close by. Julie lectures me about this, but she does the same thing.

What does all this have to do with bonding? Quite a bit I think. Read on.

When I picked up Melanie today at day care, a little early because Mom was due to arrive, she was having a fine time playing with her friends, and when she saw me she shouted "Da-Daaa!" over and over as she shoved everybody out of the way working her way to me so I could pick her up, and was so happy to see me, waving at her friends and declaring "bye-bye" in a tone that would melt your heart, anyway, does mine.

Then after we got home and she was pressing me for "Ju!" which means juice or milk, I heard Julie's car pull into the garage and I whispered to Melanie "Guess who is home? Mama!" Melanie's eyes got round as saucers, she dropped her sippy cup and went over to the door to the garage and danced because her feet couldn't be quite still. And since Julie has been through this before, instead of just walking in she quietly knocked, and slowly opened the door while Melanie looked like she was seeing Santa Clause, shouted Mama! And ran to her.

While Julie and Melanie played and sang and caught up on girl things, I cooked dinner, cleaned it up, Julie gave her a bath and just a few moments ago I rocked Melanie to sleep and put her to bed.

It seems every adoptive parent worries about whether there will be immediate bonding. For us there was, but I'm not so sure it was terribly important. What does seem clear to me, based on my amateur status and a sample of one, is that our real bonding is tight and seems to be founded on affection and trust, formed over several months and with a routine and consistency of action by me and Julie, even though those actions were very different between us.

Despite everything the experts would tell us, I am sure of two things. First, there are many variables and a few children will unfortunately have difficulty bonding for reasons I am unqualified to describe, whether adopted or biological. Second, and my sample of one and hearing from others has convinced me this goes for most China adoptions, our bonding couldn't possibly be tighter if Melanie were our biological child. And this simple fact has transformed us from two adults and a child to a *family*.

Jan 1999, Melanie 1 yr 9 mos

Another Reason to Exercise

Anyone traveling to China to adopt needs to improve their physical condition before the trip given the strains of carrying a child. And my profile would serve well as a poster for the *need* to get in shape. But this morning I discovered another reason for getting into shape, one you may not have thought of.

Melanie helps organize the Sunday paper

On Sunday mornings Julie usually sleeps in while I take care of Melanie and watch the political talk shows. When Melanie noticed my supine form and my attention focused on Tony Snow of Fox News, she decided to intervene. At first, that intervention was to stand on my chest while I held her hands. Quickly bored with that, she decided to stand on my chest and release her knees to let her butt drop to my stomach, and was delighted at my "*Ooof!*" and look of surprise. So we did it again a few hundred times. But Melanie innovates. Next she discovered that if she first squatted down, then leaped up as far as she could before landing her butt on my belly, my exclamations were that much louder.

When Julie came down after her shower and asked what all the laughing was about, as I limped toward the stairs I told her "Your daughter wants to be an athlete." Be advised - get in shape.

Jan 1999, Melanie 1 yr 9 mos

Charter Member of the Anti-Barney Club

In my pre-adopt world, whenever I caught a brief glimpse of the nauseatingly-sweet Barney and friends on TV, I swore that creep would not enter our home when we had a child of our own.

Melanie with her buddy Katlyn

Before we adopted, Joe Grella invited us to his little girl's birthday party, and asked me if I would wear a Barney suit and put on a Barney act for Katlyn and her friends. I supposed I should have been honored, but in the first place he was just trying to save a few bucks, and in the second place, well, my response was something like "You're out of your #%@*& mind, you @+*$# fool!"

For the first few months with Melanie home, I succeeded in keeping the house Barney-free. But the purple guy cannot be stopped, he's like a relentless rising tide that seeps into every tiny crack and before you know it you're floating. Melanie got Barney toys for Christmas. She sees Barney on TV at her friends house. At pre-school they constantly play with Barney toys and watch him on TV.

I finally gave up, Melanie loves Barney, Baby Bop and the others nearly as much as Elmo, and who am I to tell her no just because he turns my stomach? So she watches frequently. This morning I was cruising with the remote and I swear I flipped past a Barney channel in a microsecond and Melanie shouted "Ba-Baa!" I switched back in defeat and sure enough there he was.

Melanie sat on my lap to watch and repeated every 20 seconds or so "Da-Du Dadee!" ("thank you Daddy" for those of you who need translation). Who can fight it? And to add humiliation to my defeat, when Julie came downstairs she confronted me with "I heard you singing the 'I love you, you love me' song with Melanie and Barney!"

So, those of you pre-adopt parents who dislike Barney and suffer the delusion that you can avoid him, let me give you some advice that will save you from anguish. Embrace the enemy, go with the flow, you *will not* be in charge any more.

The good news is Sesame Street is better. In the video tape "Big Bird in China" when Big Bird first arrives in China he cannot find anyone he understands. He stops people on the street and asks "Do you speak American?" and after repeated failure cries out "Doesn't *anybody* speak American?"

A little Chinese girl responds "I speak English!" Big Bird gives the camera a puzzled look for a moment then declares "Close Enough!"

Look on the bright side. Someone told me compared to Teletubbies Barney and Sesame Street are like Masterpiece Theater. Ain't it the truth.

Jun 1999, Melanie 2 yrs 2 mos

Things That Matter

Once in a while Melanie reminds me of the things that really matter.

This morning while driving her to day care, with thoughts of my morning meeting with clients occupying me, I heard Melanie say from her car seat in the back "Aga, Dad."

What? That's a new one on me.

She said again "Oooh-hoo, Dad! Aga!"

"Melanie, what are you saying?"

She yelled "Aagaa, Dad!" while I turned just enough to see her making a pinching motion with her fingers as she watched the shadow she was making. Then it dawned on me. Of course...Julie had taught her this weekend how to make *alligator shadows* with her hands.

"Are you making alligators?"

"Yeeaah!"

What a trip. And at 25 months old, on Sunday out of nowhere she started calling Julie "Mom" instead of "Mommy" and me "Dad" instead of "Daddy." Julie is not sure she likes that, I'm just holding on for the ride.

The client meeting went fine. But maybe alligators are more important.

May 1999, Melanie 2 yrs 1 mos

Future Dads Listen Up – Part 2

Yesterday we were at Ted & Eileen Reid's house for a cookout, and Melanie was enjoying the pool, first with me, then with Mom, and she commandeered several others from time to time. She's in a real bossy stage - Julie says she's a little girl practicing to be a big girl, don't blame me. Melanie had on a swim diaper, and I knew the time would come. When it did, Julie handed Melanie to me, pointed to the bag and said "your turn!"

Now, it's bad enough at home when you know where everything is. And it's bad enough when the bathing suit is clingy and the swim diaper is so tight you have to roll it off.

But when it's full and near-liquid, and the kid doesn't want to stand still, and you're trying not to ruin the host's new fluffy white bathroom mats, it's a *bitch!*. Thinking quickly, I stopped rolling that toxic waste mess off her and quickly put her in the shower, a brand new three-sided glazed tile and glass and brass beauty installed with care by Ted himself. Melanie freaked when I turned the water on so I picked her up, but not before she backed into the wall and smeared it real good. So I picked her up and gave her a good washing, with my hands and the shower floor the victims. Cleaning that up was the easy part.

Getting the toxic waste swim diaper into a disposal bag was tricky, but getting the shower floor and wall cleaned was a real challenge while Melanie jumped up and down hollering "Mommy-Mommy-Mommy!"

When the damage was repaired I wrestled her back into her swimsuit with a regular diaper, and then soaked up all the water on the new tile bathroom floor with the only remaining diaper in the bag. I mean, they're pretty absorbent, and I couldn't use the fancy white fluffy towels, could I? I don't know if anyone ever uses those decorative towels, but in this circumstance I wasn't going near them.

By the time we were done Melanie was freaking for Mom and I was PO'd. When we returned to the pool Julie put down her cocktail and asked "What took so long?" I dutifully said "Nothing." After all, it was my turn.

And of course I was later informed by she who knows all, too late to be of any use to me, that swim diapers should be torn off at the hip and only a fool would try rolling off a swim diaper full of liquid poop. Give this fool rest.

Don't tell Ted & Eileen, OK?

Jul 1999, Melanie 2 yrs 2 mos

A Few Things I was Wrong About

This morning I was reflecting on how many things I was wrong about when Julie and I were pre-adopt, and thought I'd share a few with you in case some of you are thinking the same sadly mistaken thoughts.

Coffee
Did you know there is a very thin line between the aroma of good coffee and a poopy diaper? I didn't. Whichever one you think it is, the realization it is the other is . . . startling.

Golf
I said to my golf partners "A kid won't change golf for me, we'll just have to be creative about scheduling, and I'll bring her with me on the golf cart if I have to." Hah! I've put my clubs away and it doesn't bother me, there are other things to do with all that time.

Priorities
Julie and I naively promised each other that we just needed to use our heads about including Melanie in our leisure and travel plans, and we can still do the things we like. What a couple of dummies. Last week we had some time off but never even gave a thought to what would be fun for ourselves, we decided to take Melanie for her first train ride in Blue Ridge, Georgia. An hour of clickety-clack through the woods at 15 MPH in an open cattle car to a podunk whistle stop selling the most god-awful trinkets and a quartet on a stage wailing "The Old Rugged Cross" and other favorites I haven't heard for years, a quick face painting then an hour of clickety-clack back to Blue Ridge. To Melanie it was a very big time, indeed, and that's all that mattered to us.

Barney
On the drive back to Atlanta from clickety-clack in Blue Ridge, I willingly played Melanie's (I hate him) Barney tape four times running,

as it kept her happy and comfortable singing with Mom in the back seat instead of a claustrophobic hysterical strain to get out of her car seat.

TV

I'm the one who said no kid of ours is getting overloaded with TV junk. This morning Melanie slept in on the couch while Mom took a shower, and as I read the paper and noticed her stir I automatically said "want to watch cartoons?" Only because when she's overly sleepy that helps wake her up, you see.

Nutrition

We vowed we would feed our child only nutritious meals and no junk. I think I need one of those *Stupid* signs from the country song. Enough said.

Kids Answering the Phone

One of my pet peeves has always been young kids answering the phone before they know how, or without decent telephone manners. No kid of mine . . . The other day a telemarketer called three times for Julie about her Better Homes & Gardens magazine -- I figured if she wants it she'll order it, I'm not giving in to the telemarketer. When he called after Julie got home, I told her who was on the phone and Melanie overheard. Before Julie got to the phone, Melanie picked it up saying "Hayooo!" and started a pretty good conversation for 2 1/2, and Julie and I just stood back and enjoyed it. Funny, nothing but a dial tone when Julie finally took the phone.

Car Keys

I've always thought it just a little stupid to let kids play with car keys, especially when they delight in setting off the alarm. I've asked Julie a dozen times to keep the keys from Melanie, but just yesterday Melanie set off the alarm three separate times. Last week en-route to meet a client I hit a bump and the trunk flew open and slammed shut, the product of key-playing. I'm just waiting for the time when we're in a hurry and we can't find the keys, but you see how much influence I have.

Baby Talk

Like most men, I wouldn't be caught dead using baby-talk. Or so I thought.

It seems that kids get more engrossed in cartoon videos than the TV cartoon of the moment, I suppose because of the familiarity they develop through repetition, and perhaps the depth of the characters. At two years old, Melanie's favorites are Ba-Ba, Poo, Emo, Bi-Buh, and Snow Wipes, translation withheld to avoid insulting your intelligence. And she sure wishes the rest of us would get the pronunciations right!

I must say it is a treat when your daughter starts putting words together in semi-sentences and you can start to talk to each other, albeit each one struggling to understand and to be understood. Melanie has just started to sing herself, without Mom's prompting. Yesterday she held her Mulan doll and sang:

"Bye-babee, tee-top, win-bo, cado-wok."

She makes up nicely for omissions with repetition.

Mimics

I used to think that kids with lipstick or finger nail polish or mock jewelry or a watch etc. was a ridiculous effort on the parents part to *doll-up* their kids long before the proper time. I must have had my head stuck somewhere it doesn't belong. You've never seen a desperate, unstoppable mimic until you have a two year old girl trying to be just like Mom, and if Mom is like Julie her defense is as strong as mush.

Other Stuff

These are a few of the things I was wrong about. If you're waiting for your own adoption and thinking similar thoughts, my advice is forget it, surrender and prepare to enjoy the ride. If you're still dreaming of life like Ozzie and Harriet, you need to talk to a neighbor who summed up parenthood like this:

"The first time she drops her pacifier on the floor, which you haven't cleaned lately because when you can steal a few minutes you doze off, you boil some water and make sure it is sterilized before giving it back to her. But after a hundred drops you just blow it off, stick it back in her mouth and pray for five minutes of quiet so you can catch a Z."

Melanie mimics Dad reading the paper

Of course I wouldn't know. No pacifiers in our house. I think that's the only prediction that survived the kids.

Oct 1999, Melanie 2 yrs 6 mos

Forget About "Parents of the Year"

When you have a kid you have to accept the fact they have a runny nose, cough, cold, etc., almost constantly during the season. Doc says foreign adopted infants are even more susceptible until they've been here a year, and after that they have a little more resistance to the local bugs. And of course day care is a breeding ground and the kids pass bugs back and forth like trading ding-dongs at lunch.

All of which is to say I don't get wound up about Melanie having a cold, especially since I can predict the doc's exact words - "It's a virus, it'll pass if you just give it time." So when Julie said we should take her to the doc, again, since she had a cold, I just rolled my eyes. She said it again a week later, and said she thought Melanie had a sinus infection. I asked why. She said because her breath stinks, it smells like fish. I rolled my eyes again. Repeat doc and rolled eyes for a few more days.

Julie had some time off, and rolled eyes notwithstanding she took Melanie to the doc. When they got home Melanie was trying to tell me something about her nose. Julie said the doc found a big piece of foam in her nose. Make that rotten foam.

She has a Minnie Mouse chair stuffed with foam, and she picks the foam from the bottom and apparently stuffed a big piece into her nose, where it sort of, well, fermented. Suddenly my rolled eyes didn't carry the heavy authority they should, and I covered by saying "See, she didn't have a sinus infection!" It didn't work.

I think I'll have my nose checked since I didn't smell anything, and see what's up there.

Oct 1999, Melanie 2 yrs 6 mos

A Proud Citizen

When we returned from China with Melanie, our paper-chase was hardly over. First we readopted Melanie in the Georgia state courts. This is not required, but very prudent unless she is to rely on China to provide original birth certificates for the rest of her life. Readoption legally changed her name, affirmed her rights to inherit from Julie and I in all 50 states, and provided a Georgia Certificate of Foreign birth. Now her birth certificate will come from Georgia whenever the need may arise.

Once the readoption was complete, with documentation of her new name we applied for her Social Security card and applied to the INS (subsequently changed titles to BCIS – Bureau of Citizenship and Immigration Services – in 2003) for her citizenship. Dealing with the INS is . . . well, how do you . . . um, I guess I'll just give you a little taste.

When we filed the INS I-600A form, the first step in adoption asking our government's permission to adopt a foreign-born child and bring her into the country, the fees were $180 as stated on the instructions attached to the form. But the instructions were wrong, the correct fees were $155, and if we followed their instructions the INS would waste a month or two of our time, return the package in the mail and tell us to start over.

Does that sound a little crazy? Actually it's worse than crazy. The INS built-in errors were so institutionalized that we avoided unnecessary delays by querying others who had recently completed the process, and followed their e-mail advice. That's right, follow the official government instructions and you lose, follow Joe Six-Pack's instructions and it works just fine. If it wasn't so depressing I would suspect the INS errors were intentional to lighten their load.

Of course until you try slugging through a long adoption process you might not appreciate how losing a couple of months is so disappointing. The same inexcusable errors and punitive handling occurred at every step in the INS process, and if you fast-forward to when we adopted Kristen in 2003, the I-600A application fee was increased to $405 to compensate the INS for improved services, but of course nothing had changed. They did make some forms downloadable from a website, but then rejected such forms when submitted because they had not been printed on the salmon color customary for that form, even though the instructions printed with the form said nothing about color of paper for printing. We couldn't call to ask the INS a question, but we could travel to their office, stand in line all day and then ask a question. Chances are, based on my experience and not my cynicism, the answer would be rude and wrong, all wrapped up in a few unpleasant moments. But pardon me, I'm boring you as I become angry again remembering the mesmerizing arrogance of the INS.

If you work for the INS, I offer my condolences. You as an individual might be a dedicated and hard-working person, but after going through multiple steps in adoption and citizenship for Melanie this agency is a shameful slice of my government. I think about all the applicants to the INS from other countries, with the disadvantage of language and perhaps the lifelong suspicion that government agencies are not there to serve you but to take advantage of you, and the INS is their first experience with our government. That cannot be the welcome we would all like to extend to new citizens.

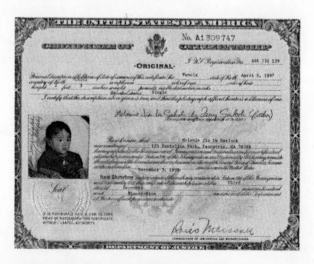

A year after filing the citizenship application, last Friday Melanie became a citizen at the INS in Atlanta, and on what should be a joyous occasion the INS delivered one last little insult. There were many people in the Atlanta INS waiting area for their citizenship – several Chinese girls, families, singles, old and young apparently from all over the world. This had to be for some of them the most important day of their lives, becoming a citizen of the United States of America, and the waiting room had a little magic in the air. That is until a female INS security officer entered the waiting area and bellowed "If I catch any kids running up and down the hall again I'll run this whole group out of the building, and you can apply all over again." Very nice.

On a brighter note, all is finally done, Melanie is now a citizen and we marked the occasion with a party. Melanie had a grand time helping Mom decorate with flags and waited in excruciating anticipation of guests arriving. We had a magician perform for the kids, lots of fun.

Now that it actually is over, with no more paperwork or officials to deal with or hoops to jump through or approvals to obtain or fees to pay, I'll share a couple of thoughts.

Melanie has been with us now for about 18 months. Life is different, she is the center of it, and she is the most beautiful, charming, brilliant, curious, friendly and happy kid in the world.

We really don't think of Melanie as Chinese at all. It's not that we don't want her to be Chinese, that's her origin and we will always honor that, but she's just part of us and we forget that she's adopted and that she's Chinese. She's just our daughter.

And it is a real joy to watch her learn new things every day. At 30 months, she's a giggle a minute in a conversation. Yesterday I gave her a little coke in a cup. After drinking some she set it on Mom's desk and said "Daddy, I'm going upstairs to see what Mommy is doing. Don't touch my coke, that's not fair!"

When she is really frustrated, which only happens so far when she is in the car seat too long and desperately wants out, she tells me and Julie "You not my fren!" This is more of an arrow to my heart than it appears because I am claustrophobic and would be frantic strapped into a seat against my will, and I have pulled over on occasion just to let her out of her car seat a few moments.

But there are compensations. I rock Melanie to sleep every night, and last night she told me with a big smile "You my fren, Daddy, you always my friend." She is the cutest thing in the world, and these are the little things we all dream about before our turn comes.

Of course, this pastoral image would be misleading without just a little of the flip side. A couple of weeks ago I called Julie who was en-route from work and asked her to meet me and Melanie at a restaurant for dinner. Then I was a few minutes late getting Melanie cleaned up and as we rushed out the door she said "Daddy, I need go potty." OK. Long story short, we had a little accident and had poop on her dress, poop on her shoes, poop on the floor, poop on MY pants. Oh well, poop is a big part of the deal. And you're never on time going anywhere with a kid.

Probably the biggest thing I have noticed, besides being unable to do simple things like mow the lawn without help and a plan, is that we are no longer living life for ourselves. Last year we took my Aunt Betty to Callaway Gardens to look at the Christmas lights. Sorry if you disagree, but big, major *yawn* of boredom after five minutes for me, fifteen minutes for the ladies. This year we took Aunt Betty and Grandma Lois to Lake Lanier to see, guess what, the Christmas lights. Lots of fun. The difference was Melanie - I didn't give a hoot about the lights, but I had a blast listening to Melanie say "*Oooooooh Daddy*! Look over here. There's a snowman! Wow, dad, look at the reindeer!"

Life is good with the INS in the rear view mirror.

Dec 1999, Melanie 2 yrs 8 mos

Mom's Christmas Metamorphosis

Did you ever read <u>Metamorphosis</u> by Franz Kafka, where the main character, if you can call him that, went to sleep as usual one night then awoke the next morning as a giant bug?

That's what happens to Julie in early December every year, but instead of a bug she turns into a Christmas Freak.

If we didn't have a large basement, I'd have to rent another house to store all of Julie's boxes of Christmas doo-dads – Christmas trees and decorations galore, a couple thousand strings of lights, wrapping for the stairs, holly of every false description, wall hangings, candles, snowmen, angels, manger scenes, mats, napkins, towels, apparel, door decorations, I'm tired just thinking about it.

But we have an arrangement. I do and say nothing, befitting my attitude and the Grump reputation I need to maintain. I stay the heck out of her way, and it suits us both just fine. Actually there are two things I do, poorly if she told you her deep dark thoughts. First, I carry boxes for her upstairs and down when she lets me, but I have to ask first and I better be quick about it. Second, I hold the ladder while she strings Christmas lights just the way she wants it done around the front door and around a couple of tree trunks. That's a major concession on her part because she would rather do it all herself instead of sharing credit with me. We're just like kids, aren't we?

In 1999 Melanie had been with us 20 months when December rolled around, and she and Mom had a big time transforming our home into a Christmas doo-dad emporium.

We took Melanie to a local elementary school for *Pancakes with Santa* breakfast. She was fascinated by Santa, stayed back and watched a while to make sure he was safe, then sat on his lap and gazed with wonder into his face as she mumbled answers to questions about what she wants Christmas morning. I wonder if she'll remember when she is older?

Then when it was time to send Christmas cards, Julie de-cloaked just long enough to write a Christmas poem based on <u>'Twas The Night Before Christmas</u>. And she did it in no-time, as if her metamorphosis included intellectual superpowers. She won't confirm, but she won't deny it, either. Here's what she wrote, and we sent it with a photo of Melanie to family and friends.

Melanie's Christmas
By Julie Garlock

'Twas months before Christmas
And all through our house
Melanie was stirring,
Not as quiet as a mouse!

Her babies she loved and fed with great care
In addition to giving them the time-out chair.

Our life seemed serene, nothing to dread
While dreams of tranquility danced in our heads.
Terry in his golf shirt and I in my suit
We thought of Melanie as just oh so cute.

When early in April there arose such a clatter
We sprang from our reverie
To see what was the matter
Back to reality we flew like a flash
Tore open our eyes and resolved not to dash.

When, what to our wondering eyes should appear
But a miniature toddler, who all adults fear
Oh what, oh what in the world would we do?
Our own little angel had just turned two!

With a little old temper so lively and quick
We hoped that somehow this must be a trick
More rapid the changes and challenges came
Has anyone ever figured out this new game?

"Now Mommy, Now Daddy, Now Barney and Ollie
Go Wiggle, Go Elmo, Go Big Bird and Dolly

I said time-out! Face to the wall!"
Cries Melanie before pretending to squall.

Then in what seems the blink of an eye
Our little one smiles with a look very sly
Hugs her daddy with a mischievous grin
Says "Let's sneak up and scare Mommy again!"

And then in a twinkling I hear in my ear
A sweet little voice we both hold so dear
"One, two, ... nine, ten. Here-a me comes!"
It's hide'n'seek time I say as I run.

She's rough and she's tumble; growing so fast
She laughs and she sings, just having a blast
We smile and we chuckle, not hiding our glee
As she turns and says "No laughing to me!"

She's pretty, she's smart and learning so quick
Never forgetting bad words that get slipped.
And now after forms and procedures so grand
Melanie's a citizen of this our great land.

We hope you can tell it's been quite a year
Chock full of memories we'll always hold dear
We both look forward to Melanie's adventures
Grown out of this phase before we need dentures.

From Melanie, Julie, Fishy and Terry
We wish you a holiday that's so Very Merry

Christmas 1999

Astonished, cautious, a little afraid,
Melanie confers with Santa before pancakes

Sisters Redeem Their Grumpy Dad

All We Hoped For

For those of you awaiting your first child, I'd like to share a few thoughts with you. Neither Julie nor I had children in our prior marriages, and I was 49 and she 42 when we decided to adopt from China. We both wanted a girl. In my mind's eye, I could envision a dainty person melting my heart with "Daddy," taking a nap on my belly, and eyes full of wonder as she discovered new things, such as Santa. Of course I also envisioned going to soccer games with the aid of a walker.

It has been all I hoped for and more. Since Melanie immediately attached to Julie and only tolerated me, when we arrived home from China I was the one who rocked her to sleep every night, our *special time* designed to reinforce our bond. When she dozed off, and when she wouldn't wake up in the morning or fell asleep on my belly, her breath on my chin was the softest, sweetest thing in the world. Still is.

Melanie loves nothing better than one of us holding her and sneaking up on the other so she can *scare* us - takes a lot of pretending on our part. Well, there is one thing - one of us holding her while being chased by the other like a stampeding elephant herd dominated by the sound of giggles.

It seems like every day brings something new. Yesterday morning I made a rare trip to Dunkin Donuts, and when I walked in the door Melanie yelled "Yaaaay, Mom, Dad gots donuts!" It's the little things that make your day.

She's a wonder to watch as she develops strategy, all on her own. This weekend while I was watching a football game, Melanie crawled up in my lap and said

"What you watching?"

I said "Football" and wondered why since she never asked before.

She said "You like that?"

I said "Yes I do!" She twiddled a minute watching me out of the corner of her eye, at the limit of her patience, and said "Dad, we watch

Frosty?", one of her scads of cartoon videos. And she hit me with what Julie taught her early on as the best weapon to get Dad to do something - "Pweeeeease!" in her tiny-larynyx voice. So much for football.

On rare occasions I pull into my neighbor's driveway to visit with him for a minute, then commit the crime of holding Melanie on my lap so she can *help me drive* about 200 feet to our garage. Big time for her. Then she pesters Mom to "Let me help you drive!" while she's being strapped into the car seat, and Mom gives me the look. That's what Mom gets for teaching Melanie how to say "Pweeeeease!"

"Yaaayy! Dod gots donuts!"

Yesterday, while I was suffering a miserable cold, Julie took Melanie shopping for shoes. Maybe this was a girls rite of passage. It's time I guess, she'll be three in April, after all. They both returned with big smiles and four pair of shoes for Melanie, even "*Red ones, Dad*!" She showed me as she struggled into them, on the wrong feet, of course.

Later, noting my chest cold misery, Melanie rubbed my arm and said "I love you, Dad, you feel better. You watch football, now, OK?" I felt better already, even though the game was over.

Dang, she's smart. Never forgets a thing. Especially a slipped swear word, and her response is instantaneous: "No Dad! You no say #$@*&, you posed to say 'Oh Man!'" She says it loud, of course, just in case there's someone within hearing to embarrass Dad.

Despite all the schedule changes, sleep pattern adjustments and other accommodations, life is good. I know this is pure mush. But for waiting first time parents, just wanted to tell you if your vision was like mine, it will be fulfilled more than you know.

Jan 2000, Melanie 2 yrs 9 mos

Why Do I Look Different, Mom?

Debbie Bodie of Rincon, Georgia, Poetry Editor of Red Thread magazine, wrote this poem about how she would respond when her Chinese daughter Quinn asks her why she is different. I adapted the poem for Melanie and Julie, reprinted here with Ms. Bodie's permission.

Why Do I Look Different, Mom?
by Debbie Bodie © 1998

"Why do I look different, Mom?"
Melanie will ask one day.
"How come I don't resemble
all the kids with whom I play?"

"My hair is inky black and straight,
my skin's a different hue.
So, would you tell me, Mom,
Why don't I look like you?"

"You're an Oriental flower,"
I'll tell my darling girl,
"Your hair and skin and eyes all come
from halfway 'round the world."

"The sun of China warmed your skin
to that exquisite shade.
Your eyes are China's beauty marks,
your hair a silk cascade
the color of a midnight sky unlighted by a star."

"So don't think you look different, dear,
you look like who you are."

Oh, Man!

Melanie helps Mom clean the carpet

I forget who taught Melanie how to whisper, Julie or I. At first she'd grab the top and bottom of my ear and stretch it to the point of pain, and just do some heavy breathing or giggling - she didn't have the concept yet, but loved the idea the other person couldn't hear. Then she advanced to telling a secret, like "Mom's a butthead (family endearment)!" then she'd look at Mom and giggle in my ear. Nirvana. Now she's advanced beyond the cute stage. She grabs my ear, gets real close and blows real hard like she's testing a weak mike. When I yell "Ow!" she says "You hear OK, Dad?" then proceeds with her secret and giggles. I've learned to be alert for new and surprising developments.

The other day Melanie wanted to look at my teeth. That grew into seeing how far she could stretch my mouth at the corners, and me learning that she could pull quite hard! Then she played with how far she could stretch her own mouth, and how far she could stick her tongue out. Routine stuff, but it's fun seeing your kid discover these things.

When I wink at her, she blinks both eyes back. She'll say "Show me how to do it, Daddy." We work on it a little without success, but she is resourceful if anything. The next time I wink she says "No, Daddy, you doing it wrong, do both eyes!"

Poop and potty training humor will become a larger part of your life than you know. When Melanie learned how to stand on her tiptoes and open doorknobs, nobody was safe in the bathroom. To her it's communal. She opened the door and caught me whizzing one day, clapped her hands and yelled "*Yaay Daddy!*" I wondered what the heck she was doing until I realized she was learning praise for going in the potty instead of your pants.

Melanie gets two jelly beans for pooping in the potty, but with some changes she's going through at day care she regressed some lately. So Julie came up with an added bonus - in addition to the jelly beans she gets to blow out a candle. I never would have thought of that, but playing with fire motivates little kids.

The other day after I picked her up from day care I said to Melanie "Want to sit on the front porch with a Popsicle and wait for Mom?" Stupid question. As we sat down on the front steps Melanie held up a very dirty index finger and said "You wipe off my finger, Dad?" I said "Where have you been digging in the dirt?" She looks at me rolling her eyes and says "It's poop, Dad!"

"#$%@&*"

"No, Dad, you no say #$%@&*, you posed to say 'Oh Man!'"

Melanie won't be three until April, but she already plays head games. Maybe every kid does, don't know. When we tell her something new, like "Watch for cars and hold my hand when we're in the parking lot", it's like as soon as the bit stream is loaded in her head she is transformed immediately into the expert and we are all her students. Wagging finger and all she tells us less than a minute later, as if we're dummies "Watch for cars and....."

I love it how she turns things around logically, it's amazing to see girl-thought in infancy. Melanie loves to ride in the golf cart, and there are 70 miles of golf cart paths through the woods and connecting everything in Peachtree City where we live. One house on the path nearby has a mean dog, I mean nasty, held back only by an electric fence. And we have to drive by pretty close. Scares the hell out of Julie, and he's on her side. So when we go by and the nasty dog is in business I give it as wide a berth as I can and try to give a protective arm to Mom and Melanie, and reassure that I won't let the dog get her.

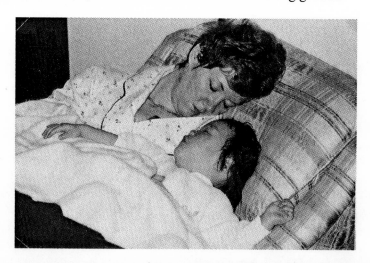

Melanie's eyes get real big and she holds her breath and then says "#$%@&* dog!" Julie gives me a dirty look to which I say "What?" But the funny part is, once we are safely away, Melanie rubs my arm and says "Don't be scared, Dad, it's OK." Now, when we are anywhere in the vicinity of the dog's house, Melanie pats me and says "Don't be scared, Dad, I no let bad dog get you, OK?" I say "OK, sweetie, thanks for looking out for me." She beams with protective pride.

Who needs Michelangelo when you can take a photo of your wife and child dozing together, each hanging on to the other until they fall fast asleep.

Just you wait.

Jan 2000, Melanie 2 yrs 9 mos

Blessings and Passages

By our own adoption experience, I know how anxious many of you are to have your child and all the blessings and challenges that go with it. This is about some of the special joys that come with time.

Tomorrow, Melanie will be three - she's been doing "this many!" for quite a while. Last night she went to bed for the first time with panties instead of a pull-up, successfully I might add. While I was scrambling her egg for breakfast, she asked "You proud of me and happy, Daddy?" More than you know.

On Sunday, we had a birthday party for Melanie at the Atlanta Zoo with her little friends. As our group was led around by a Zoo guide, she didn't whine to be carried or cling to Mom or Dad. Nosir, she was holding hands with her friends in a line of five or six of them, making sure they stepped in every puddle, taking wrong turns, Melanie pulling the group too fast and generally giggling their way to the next animal. There's something magical about camaraderie, and it's a treat to see our three year old and her friends so wrapped up in one another.

Last Friday, one of Melanie's friends, Taylor Darnell, came to bring Melanie a present because she would be out of town and would miss Melanie's Zoo party. During her visit, Melanie said not one word. Despite all my prompting for her to say thank you, she would not speak, would not give her friend a hug, nothing. So the present still sits on top of the fridge unopened until her friend gets back from her trip so Melanie can say thank you so she can open her gift. Julie thinks I'm too strict.

But Melanie deserves a little equal time here, and I'll speak for her. "Sometimes on a sunny day if Dad has time he picks me up early from school so I can play outside in the playhouse he got for me. On Friday Dad picked me up early but he had to make some phone calls while I watched Franklin. While he was on the phone I went potty by myself. My bum was chapped, so I turned over the waste basket for a step and climbed up by the sink to get the Vaseline medicine Mom puts on my bum. When I got it open I scooped out a handful, but I guess it was too much cause I got it all over my dress and shoes and the counter. I tried to clean it up with the towel after I scooped out another handful to play with, but it was all over me and the counter and the floor and the toilet and . . . hi Dad, why you upset, I let you make a phone call, didn't I?"

"Dad said '#$%@&' when he was cleaning up and I told him he's supposed to say 'Oh Man!' Then I watched Franklin some more while he made phone calls some more. The nail polish Mom put on my fingers was chipped and needed a touch up. I would have asked Dad to get it for me but he was on the phone. Mom has this plastic lock on the cabinet doors under her sink, but it gives a little and if I stretch real good I can reach in and get things, and I found the finger nail polish! If you're not real careful when you open it, it spills on your dress and on the floor. I got one of Mom's new towels but that didn't help much. Oh well, better do my nails before Dad gets off the phone. Oops, that skinny bottle tips over easy. Better go tell Dad I made a mess. Daaadeeee! Why you upset, Dad?"

So you see, before Melanie's friend brought the present, she had a bad day.

At her party at the Zoo, she was on fire because these people had come for *her*! She was holding hands and giggling and running, strung out like a piano wire. When we got her calmed down to light the candles on her Batman cake – I didn't know she even knew Batman but she picked it from the picture book - she had a million dollar grin and took three tries to blow out three candles. Then, as she opened each present, she said "thank you" loud and clear to the giver.

Yesterday when I picked her up at school she ran to me excited saying "Daddy, I got 'nother present and I said thank you - you proud of me and happy?"

"I sure am, you're a big girl now, aren't you?"

I know Julie looked forward to a baby and all that goes with it. But this is the stage I wanted, where my little girl talks to me, discovers new things at every turn, raises cute to the power of something, and gives the impression of nuclear power, scooting here and there at full speed till she drops. With constant diaper and poop problems in the rear view mirror, thank you.

Whether *Little Bit* is hugging my neck, kissing my cheek and saying "You a good Daddy, you not a butthead tattletale" (inside joke) or whether she is begging "Pweeeeeeeeeze Daddy!" for something after I said no even though she knows once I say no I rarely give in, I am grateful beyond words for my little girl.

Especially the passage to this stage. May yours arrive soon.

Apr 2000, Melanie 3 yrs

Trying to Get It Right

I'm telling you, my little girl is the funniest kid on the planet. It's a mix of amusement and empathy to watch her struggle to understand something, or to say something, just beyond her language skills so far. One of her biggest struggles in that area has to do with keeping track of the most important person in the world, "*My mom!*"

I have my own estate planning practice and can control my time for the most part. Julie, on the other hand, works on large complex projects which frequently keep her at the office late. It didn't take Melanie long to figure out that sometimes Mom wouldn't be home on time.

So now, every day when I pick Melanie up from school, before we pull out of the parking lot in the golf cart she asks the ritual questions.

"Mom coming home?"

"Yes, Melanie, Mom is coming home."

"Her late?"

"Yes, Mom will be late tonight."

"Her too late?" I didn't understand at first, but the terminology "too late" is *not* a generalization. For Melanie, it has very specific meaning. Yesterday I said, "Yes, Mom will be too late tonight, we'll have to eat dinner while she is still at work, OK?" She used to whine about that, very loud, but now that she's a more mature three she handles disappointment a little better. So she quickly moves past that and focuses on the beany baby chicken in her hand.

So last night while Mom was "too late" Melanie and I were preparing for bed at 9:30 when I heard the garage door open. I thought Melanie would be pleased when I said to her "Mom's home, you can see her for a few minutes before bed." But she gave me *the look*.

Now I know every girl develops the instinctive skill of giving her man *the look*, that's one of her tools to control him, but I didn't think she even knew about the look yet. To Melanie "too late" means Mom will be home after she is asleep, Dad got it wrong, and you could have roasted weenies over the look she gave me before turning away to go downstairs and greet Mom.

She came back a few minutes later before Julie put her to bed, with hands on hips and jaw set to determination, wagged her finger at me and said "You said Mom too late! *She not too late!*" OK, just don't hurt me.

The next day Julie told me on the phone, sorry, will be late again. I said to her, lets get our terminology straight so I don't get lectured again, which of course she thinks is a hoot. So we agreed that she will be "too late" tonight so I can pass the inquisition.

I told Julie maybe Melanie is just following her biological imperative and preparing to control a man someday. Julie, my wife mind you, said "What do you mean someday. She's got one right now!" And I'll keep trying to get it right.

Apr 2000, Melanie 3 yrs

Bubblegum Kisses and Belly Jumps

Melanie has many favorite things. When it comes to *Mydad*, she delights in bubblegum kisses and belly jumps.

Bubblegum kisses are nothing more than her chewing gum and making sure I get a taste when I kiss her, and she loves it for two reasons.

First, because when she asks for gum I always say no, and she says "But my Mom..." to which I interrupt and say "And your Dad is here now and I just said no" since I don't think the gum habit is good for her. When her Mom lets her have gum, she flaunts it to Dad, and I roll with the punch and roll my eyes.

Second, when she has gum and we're doing our goodnight or goodbye kiss, she giggles and puts the gum between her teeth and waits for me to say "Oh no, no bubblegum kisses!" and then breaks up into uncontrolled laughter. And she'll sneak me a taste whenever she thinks she can get away with it. I'll miss this game when she grows out of it.

Belly jumps are a little more athletic, and are best enjoyed by the attacker if stealth is involved. The frontal assault is simple. While I'm sitting in a chair, Melanie talks to me while she sneaks her foot up to a good toehold and counts "One." Then she grabs my shirt and pulls herself up using the other foot to help while saying "Two." From this crouch she leaps straight up into the air while shouting "Three" and lands her butt right in my belly, watching my eyes to see how far they bulge. The bigger the bulge, the louder the giggle and the quicker the turnaround on the next belly jump.

The side assault takes more finesse since she is already up on the arm of the chair, and she has to nearly combine "One" and "Two" since she moves quick. What amazes me, other than how high she jumps and my tolerance for pain, is how she naturally sticks her feet out parallel to the ground in mid-air to hit my belly with her butt. If I were in high school gymnastics I'd have to practice for a week to get that maneuver down.

The other thing that amazes me is how important this is. Remember the girl version of "It'll change your life!" as a mother talks to a prospective mother? The boy version is about the same with a little twist. Many men, like me, are driven by a desire to accomplish big things, to do something important in their life. Some men even get a little carried away with the ego thing, but don't tell anybody. But no matter how long or impressive my list of important things or titles, late in life I've learned the most important thing I can do is be a Dad and get bubblegum kisses and tolerate belly jumps. Soon you'll be doing the same thing.

Apr 2000, Melanie 3 yrs

Blue Not Fast

Three is such a delightful age for a little girl. Potty trained, just barely able to control whining with a little encouragement, insatiable curiosity, tireless in the sandbox, struggling to verbalize with new words learned every day, trying to overcome her innate resistance to sharing when her friends visit on her turf. It's a trip.

And since the affection of your three year old girl will turn you to powerless mush, Dads, you simply must learn to outwit the darling or you'll end up a basket case. A case in point.

Julie and I played golf in a neighborhood tournament Sunday morning. When we returned to relieve the babysitter, our 1992 EZ-Go golf cart died at the foot of the driveway in the middle of the street, stopping oncoming traffic. A driver mercifully stopped and helped me push it up the driveway hill. Turns out the gear teeth on the drive hub wore out, took me 15 minutes to replace once I had the parts. But I didn't know that then, and my wise wife says, "We use the golf cart every day, and this one is taking more and more maintenance. Why don't we get a newer one?"

You don't have to say it twice.

In Peachtree City, Georgia, a town of 25,000, there are over 70 miles of golf cart paths going everywhere, and it's just part of the lifestyle to take a relaxing cart ride through the woods to the grocery store or restaurant or theater, or to visit neighbors. The kids, young and old, love it.

So I said to Melanie, knowing she'll be excited "Want to get a new golf cart?" After jumping and yelling "Yaaaay!" she said "Dad, can we get a blue one, pweeeeeeze?" Uh-oh. Blue is her favorite color, but in golf carts blue is a bit scarce.

Sucker that I am, and under the protective eye of Mom making sure baby gets what baby wants, I started my search for a blue golf cart. Slim pickins. But at my favorite golf cart outlet, a guy named Kevin who rebuilds them in his large garage and sells for far less than *new* prices, I found a recent model in cherry condition with the new Drive Control System that makes it fly. Even though I'm 51, and I'm sure if I make it to 81, power on the pedal makes me feel 16 again. The price was right, all the bells and whistles were there. But it was green.

So I dejectedly continued to look for blue, and found a guy who could rebuild one for me and repaint it blue, although the deal was not as sweet. I decided to consult with the boss.

I asked Melanie "What color golf cart do we want?" She said "Blue. No, red, Daddy. Let's get a red one." And here I thought she was committed. She gave me an opening I could drive a, well, golf cart, through, and I took it. Should have known from the beginning.

I said to Melanie "You know what color golf cart is fast?" She loves speed.

"What color fast, Dad?"

"Green golf carts are fast. Blue and red golf carts aren't fast. You want a green one?"

"Yaaaaay! Mom, we getting a green golf cart. You know why? Green fast!"

That was so manipulative. And it was so easy. I was proud.

The fast green golf cart was delivered the very next day. After the first ride, Melanie quickly instructs strangers, especially if they are driving a blue golf cart, "Blue not fast. Green fast!"

Another lesson learned. If I want reason to prevail, I have to think fast on my feet and shamelessly bend the truth where it does no harm. Dads-to-be, get ready for the games to begin.

May 2000, Melanie 3 yrs 1 mo

What Size Hot Dogs?

Occasionally I am humbled by the daily lesson I learn along life's way. Last week Melanie drove home my lesson with her version of a ball-peen hammer.

We were on the run, Melanie was thirsty and we had neglected to bring a sippy cup on a short errand. So I whipped the car into Krystal, far beneath Julie's dignity on the food scale and scoring a zero on anybody's nutrition chart. "We'll get her a coke" I said as Julie gave me the look from the back seat where Melanie had commanded her to sit beside her car seat.

"May as well get her something to eat while we're at it." I offered.

"Here?" she sneered.

"They have those little hot dogs. She'll eat it." I promised.

"You want a hot dog?" Julie asked Melanie. No answer.

"Melanie, answer Mom." I said. "You want a hot dog?"

"What size hot dogs they got?" Melanie asked.

"Little ones, like you!" I answered.

"I not little, I big!"

"OK, OK, you're big, but their hot dogs are little."

"What size hot dogs they got, Dad?" she asked again.

The drive up line moved and I'm next at the order squawk box and getting irritated.

"Like I said they have little hot dogs, Melanie."

"But Dad, what size hot dogs?"

"*Little ones dammit*"

"*What size hot dogs, dad?*"

"OK, Melanie, that's enough. I'll get you a hot dog, just be quiet."

"*Mom, tell Dad what size hot dogs!*"

Julie and Melanie confer quietly in what appears to be the secret language of girl talk.

Julie says "Oh, you mean what *besides* hot dogs?"

Melanie says "*I been talking over and over!*"

Julie says "Tell Dad you want some French Fries." Nutrition zero, taste 100.

Melanie said "You tell Dad, he no listen to me."

I did what they figured I was qualified to do - pass on their order, drive the car, pay for the food and be quiet. But I'm learning to parse words. When Geppetto's son is "Pochio" you can't assume that "is" means "is."

May 2000, Melanie 3 yrs 1 mo

The Dancer

Some months ago Melanie jealously watched one of her classmates, Darby, enter the glittery and magical world of Dance class with the exotic Miss Carla!

She told me "Darby is potty trained so she gets to dance with Miss Carla and the big girls, but I can't because I not potty trained yet but I will be soon and then I dance with Miss Carla, right, Dad? Huh? OK?"

Mom bought her a tutu and tights, and Grandma sent her tap shoes and a special small bag for dance stuff. And she's almost ready except for an occasional lapse like yesterday's accident.

So every day recently when she gets home from school, she drags out her dance bag and says "Dad, help me take my clothes off so I can put on my dance clothes, pweeeeeeeze! I got to practice." So she wiggles into her tights and tutu and sometimes tap shoes, then I turn on some loud music that inspires movement and she practices the two moves she knows so far, over and over and over again, grinning big when she knows I'm watching. Because soon she'll be able to dance with Miss Carla, and her three year old world will be at peace, at least for five minutes.

May 2000, Melanie 3 yrs 1 mo

Donuts and Sneaks

Each morning when Melanie stirs her first word is "Mom?" But it's nearly always me who picks her up while she's saying "No, I don't want you, Dad, I want Mom" in her pathetic little squeaky sleepy voice. You've must to be ready for toddler brutal honesty or you'll be crushed. I say "I know" and take her downstairs with her special blankie, and we both doze with me in my chair and her on my belly, usually snoring. That's my favorite time.

Probably like many of you in the wait stage, we resolved our child would watch minimal TV and stay off junk food. Duh! So what's the first thing she sees when she wakes up most days? Arthur, a terrific PBS cartoon show for kids. And since she hasn't learned the calendar yet, she always asks right away "Am I going to 'cool today?" She like to get her mind set on playing at school with her friends or staying home with Mom and Dad.

So today, Sunday, the answer is "No, you're staying home with Mom and Dad today."

Melanie says "I want a cookie." OK, so sometimes instead of eggs and toast she gets a breakfast bar called a "cookie," we never applied for parents of the year! But today is Sunday, Mom is sleeping in, and I whisper to Melanie with some conspiracy "Want to go get some donuts?" Her eyes open wide and she says "Dad, put the paper down and get up, we gots to go to the donut store!" Last time we went several weeks ago she protested that she didn't have shoes on, and I told her she didn't need them. She never forgets a thing. This morning she instructed "I don't got shoes, but that's OK."

Now, in my business I wear a suit, but going to get donuts on Sunday morning is another story - shorts, T-shirt, no shoes and hair going in many directions. This is far worse than what your mother was thinking when she advised you to wear clean underwear in case you have a wreck! OK for the donut drive-thru, but I need a hat in case the lady at the window is squeamish. So with Melanie in her car seat I grab my hat off the hat rack in the garage as Melanie watches with great expectation, and I then grab one of my hats for her, and she's happy because it would be tragic for me to have one and none for her. "Look, Dad, we're the same!"

On the way she jabbers nonstop. "Dad there's this many donut stores, right?" as she holds up some fingers in the back seat. "I can't look at your fingers, I'm driving."

"I get a donut with sprinkles, and chocolate for Mom and chocolate for Dad and....."

When I get the donuts Melanie says "Can I hold them, Dad?" She know this is an important job not to be trusted to just anyone, like me. "Sure, but leave the bag closed."

When we get back home she says "I carry donuts, OK, Dad?"

"OK."

She carries the bag with both hands like something important and delicate, walks in the house and shouts upstairs "*Mom, we gots donuts!*"

Melanie eats her donuts like many kids, I guess. She nibbles the chocolate and sprinkles on the top, and when it's a gooey mess with the top eaten away, she says in a condescending way "Here, Dad, I through, you can have the rest." Gee, thanks.

After what passes for Sunday breakfast I retreat to my office to tinker and watch Sunday morning political TV - Fox News Sunday, Meet the Press, Face The Nation and This Week - if my endurance and family patience holds all the way through.

Fat chance. Halfway through the first one I hear heavy three year old breathing. That can mean only one thing: with Mom's active support, Melanie is trying to *sneak on* me. She usually starts by putting her hand over her eyes to hide like an Ostrich, and trying to be quiet which means giggles and heavy breathing.

So I pretend not to hear and focus on what I am doing, and when she rushes me I fake great surprise much to her delight. Then she grabs Mom's hand and drags her from the room saying "Let's 'care Dad again" never thinking that the element of surprise is gone.

What goes on in a three year old mind? I'm still learning, but with simple delights like donuts and sneaking up on Dad, it can't be all bad.

May 2000, Melanie 3 yrs 1 mo

Melanie the Mechanic

Guys will appreciate this. I'm down in the basement on a Sunday morning, pre-shower. I built a golf-cart entry to the basement with auto garage door, and doubled the width of the sidewalk around back and down the hill for the golf cart. Sunday morning I was taking a little time to install three seat belts I bought for the golf cart to make Melanie's ride safer, and for those riding the back seat.

Julie hollers down the stairs "Can Melanie come down there with you?"

"Wellllllllll, I'm working on the golf cart . . ."

"Here she comes, she wants to help you." Mom is ready for some quiet time. Don't fight it, with help it just takes longer is all.

Melanie arrives and says "Wachadoin, Dad?"

It's a rhetorical question, because she quickly concludes that I'm hammerin' on the golf cart.

"Why you hammerin' on the golf cart?"

I'm ratcheting a 9/16" hex bolt 3" long, and Melanie picks up a spare ratchet from the cart seat and says "Hey, Dad, move so I can hammer too."

"That's not a hammer, it's a ratchet."

"How come you gots so many hammers, huh? Why you hammerin'?"

"I'm putting seat belts on the golf cart."

"How come?"

"So you can ride safe beside me and not have to sit on my lap"

"But I like to ride on your lap, Dad, pweeeeeze."

"I know, but you need to ride like a big girl with your seat belt on."

I walk in my workshop room to get another wrench and Melanie hollers "*Are we done?*"

We? I almost laugh out loud, barely caught myself.

Melanie watches me put the wrench on a nut and ratchet a tight fit. She picks up a wrench and pats it on the steel frame "Like this, Dad?"

"Yea, just like that."

Mom yells down the stairs "Melanie, Dragon Tales is on." Melanie's favorite TV show in the world.

Melanie hands me the wrench while she scrambles down off the golf cart and says "Here, hold my hammer, I got to watch Dragon Tales. Can you do this without me OK for a while so I can watch Dragon Tales, Dad?"

"Yea, but thanks for your help."

"You welcome. Bye"

May 2000, Melanie 3 yrs 1 mo

Father's Day with Melanie

For you fathers-to-be, here's a glimpse of fathers day with a three year old.

Of course Mom wouldn't for anything in the world exclude Melanie from the shopping trip to buy Dad a present. But how does a three year old keep a secret? In Melanie's case she grins real big while making a weird suppressed laugh sound, and whispers in Mom's and Grandma's ear, constantly looking my way all the while.

And on Saturday evening, Melanie did a little dance like she just had to pee, Mom judiciously observed that she was at the limit of her wait, and to heck with the calendar go ahead and give Dad his present.

So Melanie grabbed the gift bag - it's a girl thing - and like greased lightning scrambled up in my lap, handed me the bag and said, sort of "...youcanputapictureinit whatpictureyouwant doyoulikeithuhDad?" I wouldn't dream of stepping on my little girl's fun with logical questions like "What?" So in the bag were several things - Julie goes for quantity - a couple of shirts and a small doo-dad wood box with Dad engraved and a place to put a picture on top. I told Melanie "This is just what I wanted!" and she beamed.

There was also something Mom said Melanie refused to leave the store without because Dad would like it. A knitted smiley-face doorknob cover. Go figure.

I wouldn't have thought a three year old could be so, well, involved in things like holidays, but Melanie made sure I enjoyed my day, on her terms of course. She even defended me when the occasion warranted.

Then Julie mentioned that I needed to be in my office at home on Tuesday to receive a delivery, another present. I never told her I knew what it was because the week before father's day when Melanie returned from shopping with Mom and Grandma she whispered in my ear "...webuyyouafrigelator youlikeit whyweneednotherfrigelator Dad?" So I knew Julie bought me a small beer fridge for the garage, especially since I had openly envied my buddy's beer fridge. And I'm very happy with it.

But you know what? The best present for fathers day was the little picture of Melanie they took at pre-school and she glued to Popsicle sticks with a bunch of little foam hearts all over the edge. Just like last year when she made a clay impression of her hand, she said with the pride of Michelangelo "I made this for you, Daddy, you proud of me and happy?" Words fail me.

In fact I have used the clay hand impression in my business. At a couple of seminars on estate planning, trying to impress on the audience the importance of taking action I would ask "Why do you work so hard? What is really important to you? Is it your house or cars or boats or stock portfolio? I'll tell you what's important to me." Then I'd hold up the little clay impression of Melanie's hand and tell them "My little girl made this for me for father's day. That's what important to me. And the reason I do estate planning is to make sure my money goes to HER instead of the IRS."

Today I framed the clay hand impression alongside the Popsicle picture, hung on my office wall. My treasures. Now I need a new seminar prop. Gotta go see if the fridge has the beer cold enough yet.

Jun 2000, Melanie 3 yrs 2 mos

Melanie Learns Goodbye – Part 1

Last week Julie had to be out of town from Sunday PM to Thursday PM. I told her this time instead of sneaking away to minimize Melanie's trauma we should tell her ahead of time that Mom had to go and when she would return. So Julie told her Sunday morning, and marked a calendar with the days she would be gone and posted the calendar on the fridge.

But things don't always go as planned. Melanie stayed much, much closer to Mom all day than a three year old should. All day when Julie took a step away from her Melanie asked, "Mom, you going to business now?" and by noon Mom would roll her eyes and repeat for the thousandth time, "No, dear, not yet." I wasn't allowed to touch Melanie all day, lest it be a sneak attack to divert attention while Mom left in a stealth mode.

After dinner Melanie was fine when we piled in the car to take Mom to the airport, so long as Mom sat beside her car seat and held her hand. She understood the routine we outlined for her, and was dealing with it as best she could. But at curbside baggage check when Mom was leaving, Melanie had a complete no-holds-barred meltdown.

And it is understandable. No amount of explanation or rationale can console a three year old who loves her Mom more than the sun and the moon and the stars while her Mom is leaving for more than a few minutes. Can't be done. And for those of you Moms-in-waiting wondering if your adopted child really will attach to you, be reassured by the relationship between Mom and Melanie, a platonic love affair that burns with white-hot intensity.

So Julie suppressed her tears while strapping a screaming Melanie back into her car seat and a second after the door closed I drove quickly away lest I be arrested for child abuse. Melanie really does listen to me, and my reassurances reduced her to sporadic short breath-sobs by the time we left the airport. She was completely quiet and reflective the rest of the way home, and when I offered to hold her hand she quickly reached out and I contorted to let her hold onto my finger from front driver to back seat rider, but hey it's my little girl.

So every day when Melanie asked about Mom we would study the calendar together, and a couple of times she cried in my arms because Mom was gone. But that's always been part of the deal when Mom travels, and looking on the bright side there is an important lesson she is learning – Mom or Dad might leave for a few days, but they *always* come back.

Every day we would review - three more days, then on Thursday after pre-school Dad and Melanie would drive to the airport to pick up Mom. The calendar really worked, especially when she could mark off the days.

On Thursday morning as soon as she awoke she instructed "Today after pre-school you take me to get Mom, right Dad?"

"Right, dear." And when I picked her up at 5:30 she was so excited she nearly peed her potty-trained pants. On the way to the airport she asked a million questions.

"We have to get on the plane to get Mom?"

"No."

"Why Mom go to the airport, Dad? Her business at the airport?"

"No."

"Her business on the airplane, Dad, that why she get on a airplane?"

"No, her business was in Dallas."

"You sure the airplane not take her to Newtop?" That's how she says Utah, where Grandma Shirley lives. And on and on.

Finally we pull up to the curb where Mom is waiting, and Melanie screams "*Moooooom*! We here to pick you up from business *Moooooom*!" Mom and Melanie are happy kids playing kissy face and sharing the frozen coke I bought for Melanie in a failed attempt to keep her occupied. Life is back to normal, sort of, and Melanie has been broken in by being an informed party on Mom's travel. Maybe next time the trauma won't be so bad. Maybe.

Jul 2000, Melanie 3 yrs 3 mos

Strategy

In our house, on Sunday mornings Mom likes to sleep in till 9. That means Dad has to corral Melanie and watch Sesame Street et al and say "no" relentlessly when Melanie asks "Can I wake up Mom, now?" Melanie has long learned to accept the frustration of Mom sleeping when she would rather snuggle with Mom and play games, well, once a week anyway.

But Melanie has learned that, if she is patient, sooner or later Dad goes to the bathroom. Last Sunday when I emerged I caught her at the foot of the stairs, three year old guilt plain on her face, disappointed to be caught before she escaped upstairs. This morning she must have been waiting, since when I emerged from the bathroom she had already sneaked upstairs and woke up Mom.

When they came down for breakfast I confronted Melanie about disobeying me and sneaking upstairs, and here is how she reacted to the inquiry:

She swung one leg back and forth, nearly losing her balance once, and then with a fake smile interrupted the lecture with "Will you play bounceketball with me, Dad?" She's good.

The men in her life may as well surrender before the games ever begin.

Jul 2000, Melanie 3 yrs 3 mos

Sisters Redeem Their Grumpy Dad

Bullseye and Lipstick

Beware a three year old's taste in movies. Where she got it I don't know but when we passed a movie theater on the golf cart last week en-route to dinner Melanie said "Dad! Lets go see Rocky and Bullseye!" I almost fell out of the golf cart. Long story short, we went to the show, she never watched more than a minute and we left after 20 minutes. Good thing we diverted to the *Dollar Movie* theater.

When I used to see little girls with makeup I'd wonder "What is her Mom thinking?" I didn't know the desire of a toddler to imitate Mom is an *irresistable* force. Yesterday when Mom was ready to take her to pre-school and I was ready for my *kiss-and-a-hug* Melanie crawled up in my lap and gave me a coy look then said "I can't kiss you, Dad, I have lipstick." And she did, a nice, fresh application. Good grief. I caught myself just before making the fatal mistake of shouting at Julie "Why not start with the eye shadow?" So I just kissed her on the cheek and sent her off to pre-school, wondering which will come first, junior high or grandchildren.

Aug 2000, Melanie 3 yrs 4 mos

Knockers and Spinach

Last night for dinner we cruised to the local Chinese restaurant on the golf cart and Melanie had to take her purse with the most prized possessions of the moment.

At dinner she was bored while waiting for our food so she dug in her purse and brought out her binoculars, or "knockers" as she calls them. Imagine the surprise of the people at the next table when they looked up to see they were not only being stared at with each forkfull, but with extreme magnification. I would have apologized if thought I could keep a straight face.

I had no idea until this morning that Melanie's preschool class has ventured into foreign languages. In the car this morning Melanie instructed me, as girls are trained from birth in my house.

"Blue not my favorite color any more, Dad. I like Row-Ho."

"What?"

"Row-Ho, you know, red, Dad."

Oh. Roho.

"You know what adios means, Dad? It means goobye."

"Really?"

"Yep, and Hole-Ah means hello, cause Mom said."

The ultimate authority. I asked her what language that was. She said proudly "Spinach!"

Aug 2000, Melanie 3 yrs 4 mos

Talking to the Fridge

Sometimes no matter how hard you try you just can't be perfect parents. So last Sunday when Julie had to fly to LA we fumbled a bit in preparing Melanie for Mom's travel.

Melanie had a big day because her close friend, Darby, came over with her Mom to pick her up for an afternoon of play. We were going to tell Melanie Mom had to leave just before Julie left for the airport, after Melanie returned from Darby's. But Melanie was late and Mom had to leave before she got home, unaware her Mom was gone. Let me tell you about guilt. While I was chatting with Darby's Dad, I heard Melanie in the house searching from room to room yelling "Mom! Where are you?"

So I said quick goodbyes and sat down with Melanie to explain Mom's trip. I showed her the week's calendar I hastily made and taped to the fridge so she could count the days until Mom comes home. On the Sunday block I drew an airplane, and I explained to Melanie that Mom had to go on the plane for business, that she would be back on Friday night after five more days, and that she left a kiss with me for Melanie.

Melanie took the kiss through her tears, and then lay on my chest and sobbed her sweet little self to sleep. I stayed still for an hour to let her sleep, too guilty to move, and when she woke, she slid to the floor and walked to the kitchen. I heard her talking and went to see what she was doing. She had her cheek pressed to the fridge on Mom's plane talking to her, and every now and then she'd say "Mom, you hear me?" Several times she has talked to Mom through the fridge, and no more tears, just counting off the days.

We have to try harder to do it right next time.

Aug 2000, Melanie 3 yrs 4 mos

Moon Cakes

A couple weeks ago two Chinese ladies from Beijing came to visit, graduate students at Georgia State University. They brought a gift of Moon Cakes purchased at a local Asian grocery in a round tin. They also explained the Autumn Moon Festival is a time of *family reunion* somewhat like our Thanksgiving in the US.

We were grateful for the kind gift, but Julie and I had tasted a version of Moon Cakes before, and the polite comment is - not to our taste, thanks very much. And since we're not averse to sharing, we took some Moon Cakes to Lindy & Ronnie Jennings, who tasted them and summed up with one word, I believe it was "awful."

Now don't mistake this for disdain for the Moon Festival holiday, not at all, but to each their own taste in foods.

Through it all Melanie kept track in her head of the exact day of the Moon Festival. On that day Mom was late home from work and Melanie and I ended up on the front steps, her favorite waiting place for her favorite person in the world. As we walked outside Melanie pointed to the full moon and said:

"Look, Dad, it's time for the Moon spectacle."

"It sure is, look how big the moon is. Do you remember the moon cakes?"

"Sure, you ready to eat some, Dad?"

"No thanks, I'm saving them special for you."

"What's the Moon spectacle, Dad?"

"That's when Chinese families have fun together."

"Cause they're a family forever, like me and you and Mom, right, Dad?"

"That's right."

Melanie walked out on the front lawn close to the street.

"Melanie! Stay away from the street. Remember about cars?" She turned toward me, face to the sky, hands outstretched with palms up as if to say "Sheesh!" She rolled her eyes up and said "Terryyyyyy. I not in the street, Okayyyyyy?"

"Don't call me Terry, I'm your Dad."

Hands on hips. "What else I can call you?"

"You can call me Pop if you want." I always liked that.

"Okay, Poppy!"

"Not Poppy! Just call me Dad."

"Okay, Pops." By pure instinct, she seems to know the secret of compromise – you don't get everything you want but you're satisfied the other guy didn't get everything he wanted either.

She'll be four in April. I wonder if I'll live through the teenage years. Yesterday, a week or so after the Moon Festival, I took Melanie on a golf cart ride past the lake. She wanted to feed the ducks, but I had not brought any bread or crackers. Melanie spotted one of the Moon cakes hiding in a storage area sort of like a glove box. How did that get there?

We agreed to feed the Moon Cake to the ducks. So we broke the Moon Cake into pieces and scattered for the ducks, but after a few tries the ducks rejected our offering. They're not as dumb as I thought.

Sep 2000, Melanie 3 yrs 5 mos

A Credit Card Already?

On the weekends when I sometimes catch up on paperwork, Julie often takes Melanie *shopping*. They both enjoy it, of course, it seems to be in the chromosomes, which is noteworthy in Julie's case since unlike all other girls she has always previously hated shopping. But now she shops *with* Melanie and *for* Melanie.

All of which may help you understand how quickly the chill ran up my spine yesterday when I picked Melanie up from pre-school and she asked "Dad, can I hold my credit card?"

My head snapped around like a spring-loaded trap. "What?"

"Can I hold my credit card, please?"

"What credit card?" I knew this would come, but at age three?

"You know, my credit card!"

"You need to go shopping?"

"No, silly Daddy. *Let me hold the credit card, OK*?" How   stupid do I look? My wallet stayed in my pocket.

When we got to the golf cart to head home I noticed in her little bag an invitation envelope. Uh-oh, another birthday party, in a class of 25 they come steadily. I said "Who's having a party now?"

"On't know. You read my credit card, Dad, OK?"

"You mean this card?"

"*Yeaaaah*" Valley girl style, sounds more like "yah" as she rolls her eyes up in frustration with poor old dumb Dad.

One bullet dodged to live for another day. But I have felt the cold stab of credit card fear, and it is coming, sometime when I least expect, the credit card monster will tap me on the shoulder, just before it eats me.

Sep 2000, Melanie 3 yrs 5 mos

The Plane Lays Down

A couple of weeks ago Melanie and I waited on the front steps after dark for Mom to come home late from work.

"Dad, look, an airplane!"

"Yep, it sure is."

"Is that Mom's airplane?"

"I don't know, it could be."

"Is Mom doing business on the airplane, Dad?"

"No, she gets off the airplane to do her business."

Melanie thinks for a minute, I can almost hear the gears grind.

"How does Mom get down?"

"What?"

"To do her business?"

"Oh, the airplane has to land so Mom can get off."

"Is that how she gets on, too?"

"You're a smart girl! That's just how Mom gets on the airplane, too."

So Friday morning I drove Mom and Melanie to the airport so they could go visit Grandma in Salt Lake City. It's a very busy time for me and a little quiet time will be a welcome break from my daily evening Romper Room duty - don't be a critic, you'll be ready for a break, too.

On the way Melanie says "Dad, you not coming with us cause we're tired of you."

I'm way past being over-sensitive to the brutal honesty of a child. Mom gently corrects Melanie and then she says "Dad, you're not coming with us cause you need a break, right?"

"Right, but I'll miss you."

"We going to eat dinner there and sleep there, Dad." A little mind has to organize thoughts in its' own way - this means they won't be back tonight."

"But you are coming back, aren't you?"

Melanie puts on her adult face. "Sure, we come back, Dad, so you not cry, OK?"

"OK."

As I turn off toward the Atlanta airport, Melanie sees an airplane coming in for a landing.

"Dad, the airplane going lay down?"

"What?"

"Is the airplane going lay down for us?"

"Lay down?" I'm slow, no coffee yet.

"Yeahhhh! Lay down so we can get on, Okayyyy?" I just know she was rolling her eyes.

She'll be home Tuesday. I sure do miss her.

Oct 2000, Melanie 3 yrs 6 mos

More Than a Dry Cleaners

Melanie enjoys our trips to the dry cleaners. The owners, *Roger*, whose real name is Raja Ahmed, and his brother *Tony*, are from India, two of the most kind and gracious men you would ever meet. We most often deal with Roger, who adores Melanie and frequently sneaks a piece of candy to her.

Some weeks ago, after dropping off clothes at the drive-thru window, Roger leaned toward me in the window as if to confide something. He pointed to Melanie's empty car seat in the back and said "The little girl, you adopt her?"

"Yes, we did." I said, appreciating that he had waited until she was not with me to ask. We talk openly to Melanie about her adoption, but when I talk to others *about her* I prefer to do so outside her hearing.

I could see Roger was hesitating to say something, so I waited.

"How long?"

"Two years." I could see the question in his eyes, so I said "She's from China. We went there two years ago and brought her back."

Roger seemed to be moved, and asked "You happy?"

"She's the light of our lives!"

He hesitated for a moment, then confided a special personal affection he has for adoption. Roger reached through the window to shake my hand and said "God bless you, sir. God go with you wherever you go."

Wow, how nice of him. "Thank you, Roger. Good night."

Later on another dry cleaning trip Roger handed me my ticket and said something about a discount, but my hearing is lousy and I said "Excuse me?"

"There's a Best Human Being discount in there."

What? I looked at the ticket, and he had included a 15% discount.

Surprised, I said "Thank you very much, but you don't have to do that."

He bowed slightly and said "God bless you and your family, sir."

This man has class. I expressed my thanks and left. I wanted to tell him that Melanie has blessed us, and that's all the thanks I needed, but I did not want to insult his gesture of generosity.

Some time later, a batch of our clothes was ruined at his cleaners because I left a pen in my pocket, and they missed it. A whole bunch of my clothes and Julie's including favorite slacks and shirts and blouses were ruined, just the kind of incident that prompts many people to go ballistic.

But I have too many miles on me to get excited over an accident one cannot reverse, and I knew that Roger would do the right thing. He took complete responsibility, which was only half his anyway - I left the pen in a pocket and they should have caught it. So he and I had a contest to see which of us could bend over backwards farther to resolve the issue. He offered to buy new clothes and I declined but agreed to take free dry cleaning for a while to offset part of the cost of replacing the ruined clothing.

Roger is such a generous man. It took me a while to convince him to stop giving me free dry cleaning and take my money, and when he did he told me how refreshing it is to deal with me because so many customers try to take advantage when an incident occurs.

Roger told me his father taught him a very important lesson, that the world is full of different types of people, some of them just animals walking upright, and only rarely will you meet a real generous, honest human being. "When you do," his father told him, "make sure to hold onto him and do anything to keep him as a friend." Then he told me he considered me to be one of those few real human beings.

I think Roger and Tony are, too. We are deeply honored to have them not only for our dry cleaners, but as our friends.

Oct 2000, Melanie 3 yrs 6 mos

My Muffin

Yesterday when I called Grandma's house in Salt Lake City, as usual she let Melanie answer the phone. She answered "Hello, Dad?" Wonder how many times other callers were confused during her five day trip.

She said "Dad, today we come home and see you."

"I know, I really miss you."

"Grandma has to take us to the airport then we go up the escalator then get on the plane then get off the plane then go up 'nother escalator then you pick us up, right, Dad?"

She likes to organize events in her mind so she can control them and give everyone orders. "That's right, you're a smart girl!"

"Dad, I make you muffins, OK?"

"OK." I soon forgot about the muffins, but I would later be reminded that Melanie forgets nothing.

Julie and I are so accustomed to flying that we just drop off and pick up at the curb. But I figured she could use some help this time so I met them at the gate. Melanie walked by herself off the plane like a big girl, looking for me with big wide eyes. I snuck up on her and picked her up and she gave me a loooong hug that felt great.

Melanie said "Dad. I show you sumping, OK?" She sat down right in the middle of the Atlanta airport concourse and started opening her purse. I scooped her up before she was trampled and took her to a chair on the sideline to let her "show me sumping."

She took a little baggie out of the new purse Mom or Grandma bought for her and beamed with pride as she presented me with my muffin. "I made it for you, Dad!" The best muffin in the whole world.

So we walked toward the escalator and train, the most memorable part of the airport for her, as she held Mom's hand with her right and mine with her left, every few steps swinging by her arms as she held her legs up despite us telling her not to do that, just like a normal little girl. Every once in a while Melanie would admonish me:

"Daaaad! Slow down. My legs too little, you know!"
I'm glad they're home.

Oct 2000, Melanie 3 yrs 6 mos

Before You Know It

Melanie's friend Taylor is a *big girl*, three and a half I think. For Christmas Taylor's Grandma spent a sizable wad on a motorized two-seater Barbie car. Spending hundreds on motorized cars for kids seems rather idiotic to me.

Last week I was outside reading the Wall Street Journal, my favorite op-ed page, while Melanie pretended to cook me dinner in her playhouse. I heard faint sounds. Whrrrrrr. "Not that way." Whrrrrrrrrr. "Turn the wheel left, come back off the grass." Whrrrrrrrrr. "Stay out of the middle of the street." Whrrrrrr. "OK, turn in the driveway and go show Melanie your car. Don't hit the tree!"

Now Melanie *loves* her playhouse and proudly shows it off to her friends. But she left it like yesterday's dirty socks to go see Taylor's cool Barbie car. Taylor beamed with pride, smiling her pretty smile, and invited Melanie to join her for a ride in the coolest car in the world.

Taylor's Dad, Ben Darnell, said "Let's go for a ride, girls. OK, Taylor, turn it around." Taylor smiled pretty, but had not made the connection between turning the wheel and the direction the car goes. So Ben coaxed and helped and advised and corrected and finally got her turned around and headed down the driveway to the street.

As I stood and watched this spectacle, Julie came out of the house and said "Aren't you going with Ben?" I responded "I'm not chasing that stupid car down the street." She gave me *the look*, like something on the bottom of her shoe.

"OK, OK, but I'll do it my way." I jumped in the golf cart and went to rescue Ben. As I approached he was saying "Taylor, turn it left, no this way!" Whrrrrrr. Stop. Whrrrrrr. "Not up on the grass, stay on the edge of the street." Whrrrrr.

I asked Ben if he'd like to ride and join me in a beer - I figured we could follow the car close with the golf cart and protect them from behind. He didn't have time to answer. "Turn the wheel, Taylor, that's what makes the car go where you want." Taylor turned back to give me her pretty smile, and Melanie grinned at me too, while the Barbie car careened within an inch of a mailbox and Ben scrambled to jerk the steering wheel left and then right to put them on a semi-straight path for at least two feet. "Press on the brake to stop." Whrrrrrrrrrr STOP. "Don't stop now, you're going straight!" Whrrrrrrr.

I thought to myself, Ben I love you like a brother, but this is dumber than a box of rocks. What I said was "Ben, I was just about to buy one of these for Melanie, and you've just convinced me to save my money." Ben gave me *the look*, too, as he took one step, adjusted the steering wheel, took two steps, corrected again, telling Taylor each time to use the wheel to steer the car, but Taylor just smiled her pretty smile, and Melanie smiled her pretty smile, like a couple of Barbies as the car headed aimlessly from one hazard to the next. They were having a big time.

When Ben finally got the Barbie car up their driveway and the kids dashed off to play with frogs or something, I asked him "Doesn't it hurt your back to walk bent over that way steering back and forth?" The nice part of what he said was "Shut up and give me that beer!" Then he said "Just remember I didn't buy that #$@! car, her Grandma did." I asked him if he wanted to borrow a back brace until Taylor learned to steer, but he just growled at me.

A few days later while I was mowing the lawn I saw Melanie start to jump up and down in excitement, looked over my shoulder and saw Ben bent over steering the Barbie car while Taylor smiled her pretty smile. Now that Taylor has Barbie-car status, she is Melanie's *best* friend. I said "Beer's in the fridge, Ben, I'm going to finish the lawn." I took a wheelbarrow full of grass clippings to dump in the woods behind our house. As I approached the woods I heard Melanie's tennis shoes slapping the pavement like a high-speed piston as she ran and hollered "Dad, can I go to Taylor's house?" "Huh? Can I? Huh? Pweeeeze?"

Jeez, I expected to hear this, but not at three years old. "*Daaaad, I'm talking to you!*" With hands on hips! I went to dump the grass while Melanie continued her harangue, and she didn't let up.

"Well, what you say? You hear me talking to you? Can I go to Taylor's, pweeeze, can I, huh?"

I said to Ben "Is this from you, Ben, or is Melanie cooking up her own mischief?"

Ben said "Let her come down, I can watch them for a while. You can watch them both for a while sometime, too, right?" Uh-oh. Zinger. I said "You bet, guess it's my turn." We gave each other *the look*.

When I went to get Melanie in an hour, I took Ben a beer and we lounged and watched them crawl all over the swing-set, and it seems this stuff happens before you know it, while you're thinking it's years away.

And a few months later I bought Melanie a Barbie Car just like Taylor's.

Oct 2000, Melanie 3 yrs 6 mos

The Nag

A couple of weeks ago before Mom was home from work Melanie watched me put on shorts, shirt and tennis shoes.

"Whacha doin, Dad?"

"Dressing for racquetball with Mr. Ben."

"You mean bounceketball, Dad?" A word of her own three year old creation meaning playing ball outside.

"No, I mean racquetball, where we hit the ball with a racquet."

"You mean tennis, Dad?"

"No, I mean racquetball. It's like tennis but with a smaller racquet."

"Sorry, Dad, you can't play racquetball, it's dark outside!"

"We play on an inside court, sweetie. It has lights."

"You gonna get hut (hurt), Daddy." She knows I'm old, fat and out of shape.

"I'll be careful, OK?"

"OK. You going leave me before Mom gets home?"

"No, of course not" I said as I dug in the linen closet for a towel and took two small ones. "I'll wait till Mom gets home."

"Why you need a towel, Dad?"

"I need a towel because I sweat."

"Well, you don need two towels, you getting towel for Mr. Ben, too? Put it back, Dad, Mr. Ben get his own towel."

"These towels are all for me, OK?"

"I tell you only need one towel." Julie never nags, so I can only conclude Melanie gets this by instinct alone. She knows in her bones men need instruction on the most basic things.

As Mom walked in and I walked out a few minutes late Melanie hollered:

"Don' be late, OK? Be careful not get hut, OK? Be sure lights on, OK? Tell Mr. Ben get his own towel, OK? Have fun, Dad."

Jeez, worse than my Mom when I was a kid.

So since I'm old and fat and out of shape, definitely not built for fast cornering, I came home limping with a pulled muscle in my ankle.

Melanie shook her head in disappointment and wagged her finger.

"I tol you be careful, Dad, gonna get hut. I talk and talk but you not listen to me."

In the spirit of loyalty to my gender, if I could send a message into the future it would be "Attention eligible bachelors. Be afraid, be very afraid."

Oct 2000, Melanie 3 yrs 6 mos

Zealot

Whether you are a smoker or not, we all know it's not a good habit.

A lifetime ago I picked up smoking while in Vietnam. I came home on a stretcher and was in hospitals for a couple months where I could not smoke. Then one day I was moved to an area preparatory for out-processing where I could smoke, and although I had broken the habit by forced abstinence, I was 22 years old and far too smart to let them win that one. So on the first cigarette my head spun like a whirlygig and I almost lost my lunch, but I hung in there and eased back into the routine like a real man.

Over the years I quit a hundred times, like some of you have. One time was a stretch of a couple of years but I found a pipe tobacco that felt good inhaling so it was really frying pan versus fire. Then in 1982 I told myself "If you never take that first cigarette, you'll never smoke again." Those who never smoked don't understand the rationalization smokers use to kid themselves when quitting, like "I'll just smoke one or two" and before you know it the routine is back. But I stuck with it and the habit was gone.

Then along came the pleasure of an occasional cigar. When Melanie saw me smoking a cigar the first time, she was amazed at what Dad was doing, then Julie caught her mimicking smoking. Uh-oh. Mom was not a happy girl, and Dad was a guilty boy. She only saw me smoking a cigar once because it's so rare and now a long time ago. But Melanie forgets nothing.

A while back I picked her up from pre-school and said "Lets pick up some ribs and take Mom some dinner!" We often engage in small conspiracies.

"Dinner for Melanie, too, Dad?"

"Yep."

"Dinner for you, too, Dad?"

"Absolutely."

"Can I have candy?"

"No." She'll make a great salesperson, she's always trying. I called in our order with a cell phone on the way.

When we arrived at the Du-Roc Café, we went in to pick up our take-out order. There on the porch was a man smoking a cigarette.

Melanie stopped dead in her tracks and tugged on my pants leg. Looking straight up to me she said:

"Dad, smoking make you sick. You no smoke any more, OK, Dad?"

Dang it, the tough questions aren't supposed to come until later.

"OK, Dad, Pweeeeze?" just like her Mom taught her.
Looking down into those dark, almond, questioning, pleading eyes, I was helpless.

"OK, sweetie, I won't."

And I won't. Because when you have your first child your priorities change. After dinner at home I took the few remaining cigars out of their container and showed Melanie as I put them in the trash can. She said "You a good daddy" as she hugged my leg.

Then a few days later she spotted a cigar in a plastic bag in the golf cart where it sat for a long time - golf and cigars sometimes mix, and I had not yet thrown this one away because, well, sometimes I'm a slob. Melanie, of course, is genetically driven to suspect the male species of infidelity.

"Hey dad, why you gots a cigar?" Hands on hips, again.

Normally I would have been able to make the issue go away with a simple explanation. But my good friend Richard Iorio was visiting, and that morning while we played golf he smoked a cigar - Melanie smelled it on my shirt even though I had kept my promise. She lit into me while instinctively watching my eyes for a flicker of male fear-guilt, that secret signal known only to girls signifying the time is right to go for the throat.

"Dad you not posed to smoke no more, why you smoke?"

Sheesh, what a zealot.

Oct 2000, Melanie 3 yrs 6 mos

State Fair

When we were in the wait stage, my friend Joe Grella frequently summed up the changes we would experience with these words - "Just you wait!" Being inclined to overcome obstacles with a little thought I'd say something like: "Joe, don't be silly, I'll still play golf most Saturdays, we just have to juggle our schedule a bit and trade off to make sure Julie gets some off time, too."

So I've played golf, what, twice so far this year. And I'm not unhappy about it.

I'll bet many of you are kidding yourself like we did. We logically thought we could continue doing the things we liked to do by just applying a little thought and energy to dealing with having a child. But while we were organizing the trees, we didn't see the forest.

You see, our priorities just . . . changed. We are no longer motivated by fun for ourselves, we focus on what would be good or fun for Melanie, and that's what makes us happy. It's hard to explain how much it changes your life. Here's an example.

Recently, I said to Julie "Want to go to the Georgia State Fair?"

"Sure, sounds like fun."

"Not for me. I'd rather dig a ditch than deal with the barkers on the midway. But Melanie would love it."

"Yeah, that's what I said!"

So in the past if I went to the fair I'd search for a comfortable place to sit since my back hurts with too much standing and walking, nurse a beer and hot dogs or whatever. Stay in the shade as much as possible so I don't sweat too much and soil my appearance, be low key and watch all the people do crazy things.

I don't like the animal barns because of the smell and poop piles I can do without. To me it's moronic to play rigged games in search of a worthless trinket, giving up not only your money but your dignity.

And you couldn't get me on the rides at gunpoint, it's a control thing. When it comes to the fair, just call me a Grump and that sums it up fairly, no pun intended.

But Julie and I were eager to get Melanie to the fair so she could have fun. Parked a half mile away. Drug Melanie through the animal barns because she wanted to see them all, dodging poop piles as we went. Sweat like a pig, who cares? Ate when Melanie was hungry, went to the bathroom when Melanie had to go.

Dan and Melanie on the Merry Go Round

We searched the entire midway for rides where she was not too small and where one of us could ride with her. Cram into a kiddie ride in a way that would have mortified either of us pre-kid, Julie on the

Dragon Tales twirl-till-you-puke and me on the merry-go-round. Then with the rest of the parents the non-rider would stand on the sidelines grinning bigger than ever and waving and taking pictures like it was a dear lost loved one returning to earth on a space ship, damn fools all aglow watching their little ones have a thrill. Just the type of geek I used to raise an eyebrow at while in the shade with my beer, being cool. But you can't embarrass me, I have a kid.

We had a great time because Melanie had a great time. She only wanted one thing - cotton candy! She got it and had it smeared on her hands half an inch thick. But I didn't give in to the barkers, I just bought her a stuffed animal. To cap it off we had a hard time finding our car after a half mile walk. If I reviewed the day pre-kid I might say "Gee, I could have saved money by just staying home and pounding my thumb with a hammer!" But it was a good day, one Melanie will long remember.

And that's what matters, now.

Oct 2000, Melanie 3 yrs 6 mos

Drowning in Estrogen

This weekend while riding on the golf cart Melanie gave me a command of some sort and added:

"You better hurry or Mom be mad to you!"

I know how to handle the situation with maturity. "Mom's not the boss of me."

"Oh yes her is!"

"Oh no she's not."

"*Mom's the boss, right, Mom?*"

See? Female logic instinctively at three - ask your own favored side of an argument for an authoritative judgment.

Mom says with an evil grin "Of course I'm the boss." Julie's doesn't nag, but she does enjoy my squirming.

"See, Dad, I tol' you!"

Oh, boy.

"Dad, that's OK. I let you be the boss when Mom's not here, OK? Blah blah blah blah . . . . " How generous. More of the same, over and over, Melanie style but I tuned out, kind of a built-in defense against insanity. I think I'm overdue for some male bonding at the local joint with some baseball, beer, scratching, etc. to take my mind off my oppression.

I am reminded of what a wise old geezer told me on the eve of my first marriage at age 19, I'll never forget. He said "Son, you won't pay any attention to what I'm telling you because you're in love and therefore not very smart right now. But remember for later. Every woman, boy, even your lovely bride, comes out of the womb with a stick in her hand. It's not her fault, just nature. And that stick has a purpose, it's used to make her man do what she wants. Now, son, you got a choice. You can very gently take that stick away from her - we have to be gentlemen with our ladies - or you can spend the rest of your life getting whacked with the stick. Next time I see you, I may not see the lumps on your head, but I'll be able to see them when I look in your eyes." The geezer was very wise.

I can close my eyes and look into the future, look into the eyes of my future son-in-law. I see mass quantities of lumps and a pathetic plea for help.

He better be strong.

Oct 2000, Melanie 3 yrs 6 mos

EELLL

I'm sure most of you know I write these stories with tongue in cheek, with humor as my *deus ex machina* and my shield. I write these not only to help you pass the wait time, but to capture the memories. So . . . here's a little one.

At three and one half, Melanie knows her alphabet and is just starting to learn to spell, trace letters, etc.

"I can spell my name, Dad."

"You can? Show me." She grabs a small banner with her name, "M. . . E. . . ELLL. . . " I didn't hear any more, I was concentrating on how she is training her tongue to say the letter L.

I may be her Dad, but that doesn't prevent me from being selfish. "Start again. Spell your name again, sweetie."

"M. . . E . . .ELLL. . . A . . . N . . . I . . . E" "There, I spelled my name, right Dad?"

"Right!" Incredible. Her little tongue comes out and slides over to the left corner of her mouth every time she says "L."

Now, those of you who haven't had kids may not understand this at all. Those who have know exactly what I'm talking about. How do you take the cutest kid on the planet and raise that cute to the power of 10? It's too intense. I'll almost be sorry when she outgrows the ELLL stage. Meanwhile I'll do my best to hide my reaction, or I'm liable to give her a complex about her speech.

Oct 2000, Melanie 3 yrs 6 mos

Banilla Face Mom & Dad

From the repetition of the slideshow of Melanie's adoption story (see the Appendix), she knows Mom and Dad asked China if we could adopt her for our own daughter, that we were so glad China said yes, that we legally readopted her in the courts to *make sure* she is our own daughter forever. She seems to have a strong sense of *family* and reminds me that I'm too busy from time to time with remarks like "Dad, will you take me and Mom on a golf cart ride so we can be a fambly?"

When she sees an Asian or something Oriental, she says "From China, like me!" And she says it with pride.

So imagine my surprise the other day when out of the blue Melanie asked"

"Dad, why you and Mom gots a banilla face?"

"What?"

"Why you and Mom gots a banilla face?" I realized she meant "vanilla" or white.

"I'll be right back."

I know when I need help. I asked Julie if she had heard this before. Nope. But I brought back reinforcements.

"Melanie, tell Mom what you asked me."

"Why you and Dad gots a banilla face?"

Julie explained to her that we all come from different places and we all look a little different, like Mom's skin is lighter than Dad's. I wanted to know if anyone at school had said something to her to hurt her feelings.

"Where did you hear that?"

"Nowhere."

"Did someone tell you that?"

"No."

"Where did you hear it?"

"*I just asked why you gots a banilla face, okaaaay?*" Back off.

"OK. Your eyes are pretty."

"What, Dad?"

"Your Chinese eyes are very pretty."

"You gots a big nose, Dad." She grabbed it and I gave her the usual "Honk" she loves to hear.

I think she's going to be fine.

Nov 2000, Melanie 3 yrs 7 mos

Therapy

When I've had a trying day, talking with Melanie can be sound therapy. It commands my attention to the point I forget what ails me, even if it is a bit disjointed.

Yesterday we talked for a while as she agonizingly waited for the clock to creep to time for her to visit her friend Elizabeth.

"Dad, is it time to go to Elizibath-es yet?"

"No, sweetie, another hour."

"How will you know when it's time?"

"The clock will tell me and her mom is going to call when she gets home from soccer."

"Why her mom play soccer?"

"She doesn't play soccer, Elizabeth's brother Jeffery plays soccer."

"Elizabeth-es gots a brother named Jeffery and her mom named Wendy and her dad named Dan."

"That's right."

"I can paint by myself, but Jacob, he don't sing so good."

Well, OK?

"Elizabeth my fren, and Darby my fren and Alex my fren but Jacob not my fren."

"I thought Jacob was your friend. What happened?"

"He gots mean frens, Dennis his fren and Jacob says he not my fren so he not my fren any more. Is it time to go yet?"

"No, not yet." Best to stay out of kid squabbles, alliances shift daily. But, gee whiz, a three year old gang! Wonder if they have special colored jackets? But I know by tomorrow they'll be buddies again.

"Do you have a boyfriend?" She gives me a sly grin. "Come on, who is it? Is it Christoff?" Christoff is a feisty young man, frequently in trouble, and he and Melanie like each other a lot. See, the girls start liking the bad boys right away.

Melanie nods and says "Christoff my boyfren and I his girlfren, Dad."

Guess I better clean the shotgun.

After a while the phone rings and Melanie sits straight up with eyes wide as saucers. Yep, it's Wendy, time to go.

"*Yaaaaay. Time to go play at Elizabeth-es.*"

I'll take her on the golf cart, then I'll return to a couple of hours of quiet for me, watching the golf tournament on TV,

maybe fall asleep. Yaaay.

And I can't even remember what was troubling me.

Nov 2000, Melanie 3 yrs 7 mos

Wedding Plans

I'm really proud of Melanie. Since we're honest with her about Mom's travel schedule - no games, no tricks - she's learned to trust what I tell her and accept it even if she doesn't like it. If Mom suddenly has to go for several days or a week, Melanie's brain quickly computes how many days, and usually her emotions overtake for a short session of quivering lip and a few tears, then it's over. Fortunately I've learned to just hold her for a little while until the emotion passes, then she's over it until Mom returns. At 3 1/2, big girl!

When Mom is gone, Melanie talks to me a little more than when Julie is home. Last night Melanie was laying on my soft belly as I watched session 99 of the election free-for-all on TV.

"Dad, Mom coming home tonight?" Julie had been gone all week on a deadline project.

"I don't think so, she has to work this weekend. But tomorrow you get to play with Miss Lindy and Matthew." Diversion until I know Julie's schedule, could be next Friday when she returns. Lindy grew up in England but is now a US citizen, in the process of adopting an infant girl from China. She and her husband, Ronnie, and her son Matthew have grown quite fond of Melanie as they wait for their very own "Gracie" to come home with them.

"What we going play?"

"I don't know, maybe you'll have tea, maybe play with dolls, maybe Matthew can show you things on his computer."

"Will Miss Lindy call you when I want to come home?"

"She sure will."

"Where's the marry place, Dad?"

"What?"

"Where's the marry place where you dance?"

"I don't know." No clue what she's talking about.

"Who I going to marry?"

"I don't know, that's a long, long time away."

"I don't want marry Jordan any more."

"Why not?"

"He mean to me so we not going get married, OK?"

"OK." Reconciliation is likely.

"Can I marry you, Dad?" *The Supreme Compliment.*

"No, I'm married to your Mom, so you can't marry me."
A few Moments of silent reflection.

"Can I marry an uncle?"

"No, can't marry an uncle."

"Then who I going marry?"

"It's a long time away, sweetie, you'll find someone you want to marry."

"Will you and Mom dance at my marry place?"

"We sure will." With a walker and oxygen bottle, no doubt, but so what?

Julie came home after all, after I read Melanie a story and she went to sleep. When Melanie woke in the middle of the night and called for me I brought her back to our bed. When she discovered Mom was there - BOIIIING! - she's awake and clinging and jabbering.

I said "Melanie, if you don't go to sleep I'll take you back to your bed." Instant silence, clinging to Mom, snoring in a moment.

Wedding plans postponed for at least a little while.

Nov 2000, Melanie 3 yrs 7 mos

We Love Melanie Like Crazy Cakes
By Lindy Jennings

This chapter was written by our dear friend Lindy Jennings. We met Lindy when she and her husband, Ronnie, were considering adopting from China. Ronnie was unsure, but he fell in love with Melanie and they decided to proceed. During the year-long wait for Gracie, we arranged for Melanie to spend part of a day with Lindy, and she wrote about it for other waiting adoptive parents. Hers deserves an honored place among these short stories.

Today Melanie Garlock came to play. As we wait for our own daughter we had a little peek of things to come. Matthew found two old dolls in the house for Melanie to play with. They used to be mine, so believe me they're old dolls! Melanie carried the baby doll around while following me. I had to get out of my exercise clothes and put something decent on. Melanie and Matthew followed me and Melanie checked out our walk-in closet.

"Miss Lindy why do you have all those shoes? Mr. Ronnie has not many shoes."

"Quite right!" said Ronnie.

Melanie checked out our wedding photo.

"Mr. Ronnie married to you?"

"Yes, believe it or not that's me in that photo, Melanie."

"My Mommy and Daddy married before China!"

That's good, I thought to myself. The next photo was of me holding Matthew as a new baby.

"Miss Lindy, Matthew grow in your tummy?"

Oh no ,I thought! I just said Melanie could come and *play*!

"Matthew did grow in my tummy," I answered.

"I have a China birth Mommy, don't know her name, I grew in her tummy and a China birth Daddy they loved me Miss Lindy . . ." now

I'm fighting tears and emotions, " . . . they loved me so I could have my Mommy and Daddy forever."

I just hugged her and told her she was loved so much - she just gave me a big Melanie smile, to die for.

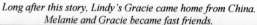

Long after this story, Lindy's Gracie came home from China. Melanie and Gracie became fast friends.

We then said goodbye to Mr. Ronnie and went out. I had to stop by the grocery store and we all went in. As we walked in the door veterans were handing out poppies, so I gave Matthew and Melanie money to put in the jar and collect a poppy. Next question from both Melanie and Matthew was why did we get a red flower - so now in the best way I can I'm explaining Veterans Day and freedom and the men and women that gave their lives for us, in a three year old and seven year old explanation.

Wow, I thought, I hope this day lightens up! The first hour has been filled with very deep conversations.

Matthew, Melanie and I had a wonderful day, playing in the park, and the autumn leaves, having lunch at McDonalds and enjoying a golf cart ride. We love you like crazy, Melanie cakes, come play anytime.

Lindy Jennings

Nov 2000, Melanie 3 yrs 7 mos

Melanie's Proposal

One good thing when Julie is out of town is Melanie talks to me more. And a conversation with a little girl three and one half going on 12 can be a real trip, even if the sudden curves are rough when you're not ready.

After bedtime story reading. "Dad, will you marry me?" Melanie already told me she cancelled her plans to marry a boyfriend who was mean to her.

"No, I told you before I'm married to your Mom, I can't marry you. But I love you."

"I love you, too, Dad. You the bestest Daddy." My head swells while she thinks, chin resting in hand.

"I guess I marry one of my uncles."

"You can't marry your uncles."

"Why not?"

"Well, they're already married, and they're too old for you."

"But I marry them when I get older, OK?"

"Then they'll be older than they are now, won't they?"

A moment of thought. "Yep. You right, you a smart Daddy."

More silence.

"Then who I going marry, Dad?"

"I don't know. You'll find someone you love when you get older."

"*But Dad, there aren't any good boys left any more!*" I didn't think I'd hear that whine until she is 25.

Two minutes later, "Dad, who your birthmom?"

"Grandma Lois is my birthmom."

"But she my Grandma!"

"I know, but she's also my Mom."

"I knowwww." Eyes rolled up, Valley girl style. "But your Mom your birthmom, too?"

"That's right."

She was incredulous. "You grew in Grandma Lois' tummy, Dad?" Uh-oh, getting slippery.

"That's right, I did."

"How babies get out of their birthmom's tummy, Dad?"

Oh no! I know Julie has answered her questions and talked to her about the childbirth process because Melanie is so curious, but I'm not going there, no-way, no-how! But Melanie does *not* let me off the hook.

Grandma Lois Garlock with Melanie

"How babies get out without getting all poopy, Dad?" Now I'm sweating.

"Wait till your Mom gets home and ask her, OK?"

"So what does she know about it, huh, Dad?"

"A heck of a lot more than me." But a short attention span saves me.

"My Mom not my birthmom. My birthmom in China my birthdad, too. What my birthmom's name, Daddy?"

"We don't know her name." Silence, but you can almost hear the gears turning. So I go on.

"We think your birthmom and birthdad loved you, but they couldn't keep you."

"Why not, Dad?"

"You remember Melanie's Story?" This is the Powerpoint slideshow she watches telling her the story of her adoption (see Appendix).

"Yeah, Dad, can we watch it?"

"Not now. Remember how China has too many people, not enough food or jobs or houses, and the leaders made some rules saying families could only have one baby?"

"Yeah, I remember."

"Well, sometimes a birthmom and birthdad have to give up their baby because of those rules. It's complicated, but we know they loved Melanie and they were sad when they couldn't keep you. Then they were happy that you went home with me and Mom."

"They not sad no more, Dad?"

"They're still sad they couldn't keep you because they loved you so much. But they're happy you have a forever family with Mom and Dad."

"I don't want them to be sad."

"But they were sad because they loved you. You want them to love you, don't you."

"Yeah."

"And how long are you and me and Mom a family?"

"Forever and ever like my story says, Dad."

"That's right. Now go to sleep."

Believe it or not, she snores.

Nov 2000, Melanie 3 yrs 7 mos

Cowgirl

*Melanie, in her boots, builds a snowman
with Mrs. Shawn and Taylor Darnell*

Saturday when Julie and Melanie returned from shopping Melanie proudly modeled her new boots for me - white leather cowgirl style zip-ups with tassels, just like a Dallas Cowboy Cheerleader wannabe.

"But I not wear them to school, Dad."

"Why not?"

"Cause my frens laugh to me." Good grief - at 13 I expect this but not at three.

"Why would they laugh at you, those are cool boots, they'll want some, too."

"But these the last ones, not any more, and my frens laugh to me so I not wear them to school."

"When kids laugh they're just being goofy."

"What, Dad?"

"When you laugh at your friends, are you trying to be mean?"

"No, I not mean."

"You're just being goofy. If your friends laugh at you, they're just being goofy, OK?"

"OK."

So she wore the boots to school. When I brought her home yesterday I asked her if anybody laughed at her boots.

"Nope. But Owen lost his Woody." Be careful.

"What's that?"

"He was playing in the sandbox and he lost his Woody and he cried."

"What's a Woody?"

Rolling eyes. "You knowwwww. Like in Toy Story, Dad!"

"Oh. Was he sad?"

"Yup, Owen was very sad. But I don't like to hit the piñata." Hang on for those sudden turns.

"Why not?"

"I like to watch but I don't like to hit it."

"OK, ready for dinner? Lets go to the table."

From the kitchen I asked Melanie "You want something to drink with dinner?"

"Yeah. . . . . Hey, Dad!" I turned around and she smiled big and gave me a big thumbs-up. "Thanks for asking, Dad. Good job!"

Who *is* this kid?

Nov 2000, Melanie 3 yrs 7 mos

Snookering Dad

At three and one half, Melanie loves to scare me by hiding around a corner or hiding behind something and jumping out and roaring *like a monster*. She also enjoys pulling one over on me or getting away with something whenever possible.

The other day in the grocery store with Melanie we hit the ice cream section last. When she sees the popsicles she wants every kind, but we buy the sugarless for sake of her teeth. While scanning the endless possibilities:

"Dad, Dad, lets get these ones!" as she pointed to frozen sugar wrapped around sugar.

"No, those aren't the kind we eat."

"But Dad, I want these ones."

"Here are the ones we always buy, lets, go."

"Dad, lets get these ones, too, OK?"

"Nope."

My miniature Valley Girl rolls her eyes in plain disgust with the male species.

"Well", she says, unfailingly sticking her little tongue out with every "L", "Mom buy them for me and we sneak on you!"

"What?" feigning outrage. Melanie tries to stifle her giggles, but can't help it at the prospect of circumventing Dad's misguided obstruction.

Last night we stopped at the cleaners, where the owner *Roger* Ahmed has shown overwhelming compassion with Melanie and me, touched for some reason by her adoption. I told him once he didn't need to give me discounts, that we are just lucky to have Melanie in our family. But he is delighted every time he sees her, a wonderful man. He gave her candy several times, handing it to her through the drive-thru window as she sat in the car-seat. Now, of course she expects the same each time.

As I turned into the cleaners Melanie said "Dad, the man going give me canny?"

"No, not today."

"Why not?"

"He doesn't always have candy, and you need to eat your dinner anyway."

As I lowered my window for drive-thru service Melanie said "Dad, put down my window, too, OK?"

"Why, you want to say Hi to the nice man?"

"Uh-Huh." So I put her window down knowing she hoped for candy.

So Roger said "Hi, sweetie" and Melanie mumbled her shy hello as we transacted our business. When done he said "Wait a minute" as he fumbled in a drawer looking for a treat and finding none he took a quarter out of the cash register, walked in front of his counter to a gumball-candy machine and bought some banana hard candy. In a little conspiracy with Melanie he droped them one by one into her hand. I think he enjoyed it more than she did.

"Thank you."

Melanie crunched her candy as we drove home and I heard a giggle.

"I snookered you, Daddy!"

"You sure did."

"I like to snooker you, Dad. But you the goodest Daddy."

Even without the leverage of a mouthful of candy, Melanie has taken to spontaneous outbursts lately like "I love you Dad, you the bestest Dad in the whole world." Same for Mom.

It's hard to take.

Dec 2000, Melanie 3 yrs 8 mos

Santa

Snoring, dreaming, fitful slumber,
Stirring, wiggling, fighting daylight,
Grabbing blankie,
Boring under covers,
Eyes squeezed shut,
Leave me alone!

Softly Dad's voice says again "Melanie?" Eyes flutter then close tight again.

"Melanie, do you think Santa came to see you?" Her eyes fluttered then suddenly froze open, not a muscle moving.

Can it be true? Is today the magical, glorious, stupendous day every kid has been fantasizing about for, well, forever by now? Did Santa remember her *Hush Little Baby*? Did the reindeer eat the food she made with oatmeal and glitter at school and spread in the grass with Dad's help last night? Is it possible Christmas is finally here at long last?

She leaped into my arms and squeezed my neck tight. "Did he come? Did he eat the cookies and milk I put out for him? Do I have presents?" We don't put any presents under the tree until after she's asleep Christmas Eve.

"Lets go see." Julie and Grandma Shirley were standing by with cameras ready.

As I carried her down the stairs she usually navigates well on her own, we heard a baby cry. Melanie looked at me with astonished wide open eyes and whispered "Is that a Hush-Little-Baby, Dad?"

"I don't know, lets go see."

It was, indeed, and Santa remembered to put it in a cradle just like she asked. The baby cries until you put a bottle in her mouth then you get a sucking sound until you remove the bottle, then you get a Buuuurp followed by a moment's silence then the crying starts again. Melanie was a good Mom for at least a little while. Then she moved on to the excessive pile of presents I always fight at Christmas, to no avail of course.

You remember Christmas when you were a kid, and if you've forgotten you should get the movie "A Christmas Story." And you probably remember the joy of Christmas transforming from receiving to giving as you grew older. But just you wait. When you have a little one about three years old who is far smarter than you ever thought a kid that age could be, who asks a thousand questions about Santa and Elves and Reindeer and the North Pole, and who looks up at you with big shiny eyes and asks how much longer till Christmas, who tosses and turns on Christmas Eve trying ever so hard to go to sleep, well, just you wait.

Dec 2000, Melanie 3 yrs 8 mos

Aunt Betty at Christmas

Melanie and Me

Melanie is like any normal kid approaching four years, manners and loyalty forgotten in frequent fits of curiosity. She asked me the other day "Dad, how you get fat like a pig?" For a moment, at least, I was without words. But she meant it in the nicest way.

Some weeks ago we passed a stout lady walking on the golf cart path. Melanie whipped her head around to look at the lady again and said "Dad, that lady have a baby in her tummy?"

"No, she's just a little fat, like Daddy."

"Wow, I thought she had *five* babies in her tummy, Dad. You got room for *ten* babies in your tummy, Dad."

Thanks a lot.

Did I tell you what Melanie and Mom gave Dad for Christmas? It's the perfect new Dad present, wireless earphones for the TV/Stereo. I'm in heaven. Melanie can bang and yell and sing and I can still concentrate on my daily dose of Brit Hume's update on politics.

BA (Before Adoption) I opined stupid things to Julie such as (1) our kid doesn't need a big pile of toys, or (2) lets try to raise a kid with just the bare minimum TV and no Barney. But I'm grateful for Melanie's TV tastes - she shares my affection for just one sitcom; she doesn't do the grunt, but if you ask her what time it is she'll say "Tool time, Tim the Tool-Man, Taylor!" When it comes on she asks "Dad, Tim going get hurt this time?" and I just tell her I don't know, let's watch and see. I don't think we're in the running for parents of the year.

Last night while I got my Brit Hume update Melanie colored on her little table and played some kids music loud on her tape machine, and every once in a while picked up the microphone to yell "Hey Dad!" to get my attention through my heavenly earphones. She likes to borrow the earphones, and at one point was listening to Tim the Toolman on the headset while playing her tape machine and at the same time shouting into her microphone "Hey Dad, can you hear me?" You betcha.

But just when I think I'm too old for this, she'll do something like race to bury her head in my belly asking me to hide her when she hears Mom coming. Like an Ostrich, if her head is hidden nobody can see her. And I swear when Mom combs her hair back in a pony tail she must be the prettiest little girl in the whole world - at least until your little girl comes home.

Jan 2001, Melanie 3 yrs 9 mos

Blue

Melanie likes Blue. When I traded golf carts a year ago she yelled "*Lets get a blue one, Dad!*" But I couldn't find a blue one, found a green one that filled the bill, then shamelessly hoodwinked her into believing that blue golf carts are slow while green ones are fast. Now when she sees a rare blue golf cart on the 70 miles of golf cart paths in Peachtree City she is often inclined to shout "*Hey, your golf cart slower than ours!*"

When Mom needed a new car last year, same thing. Melanie wanted blue, ergo Mom wanted blue, no blue car like Mom wanted. Mom got green, Mom hoodwinked Melanie into liking her new green VW Passat with big engine and stick shift just like Mom wants. Mom is an unusual girl.

Now me, I've been conservative and lacking passion when it comes to cars for a long time. I'm a Certified Financial Planner (CFP), and occasionally hauling clients to lunch factors into my choice of cars. But I've secretly harbored a desire for a truck. Not that I really need a truck except for the occasional haul task, but it's a *guy thing*. Alas, a truck has not been practical, so my truck lust has been in my back pocket. Until two weeks ago, that is, when I borrowed Ben Darnell's truck for a haul job and fell head over heels in love. It's a Ford F-150 Super-Crew with a *full* back seat and a shortened bed.

As Melanie and Mom rode in the back seat on my borrowed-truck haul job I looked around the truck at this and that trying to find things I didn't like and try as I might I just couldn't find any. When Melanie sensed my truck lust she yelled "*You buy a blue one, Dad!*" Well, the new truck is in the garage, at least the part that fits in the garage, but that's another story. Actually, I tried to get blue even though I really didn't want that color, and when you get your little girl you'll do foolish things like that too.

But I did make amends, and this is worth telling you about. We had difficulty making a car trip longer than a couple of hours because it's just too much torture for Melanie to be strapped in her car seat for longer than that period of time. So when I saw an option to add to the truck a roof-mounted flip-down TV screen to watch local channels from the back seat, or videos via a player mounted under the seat, I saw a ticket to more travel. It cost $1,200 and that's a lot of money, but I bit the bullet, and now Dad *and* Melanie *and* Mom are in love with my truck.

I brought the truck home yesterday so we've only tripped across town, which in the Atlanta area can be quite a trek. But when I turn on PBS Dragon Tales followed by Arthur, Melanie is focused on her shows and not much aware of her booster seat. And while she listens thru a headset, I don't have to listen. Even though it's pricey, as we say in the south, it's neater than grits.

Yesterday when I picked Melanie up from pre-school, she announced to her teacher "My Dad has a new twuck, and it has a TV in it for me, but it's not Blue." You can't win them all.

Feb 2001, Melanie 3 yrs 10 mos

My Buddy

If you've read much about Melanie, you know she likes her Dad so long as she can always be touching her Mom. This morning I whispered in Melanie's ear expecting she would eagerly join me in the occasional Sunday morning trip to get take-out donuts. She dismissed me with a little wave of her wrists saying "I stay here with Mom, you bring me some chocolate donuts, OK?" Yes, boss.

Later today I needed to make a trip to the Northern store to buy a rope to help fell a tree, and I thought Mom and Melanie would like to get out of the house so I asked Melanie if she'd like to go. Mom told her "Dad's looking for a buddy" and Melanie shouted to me "I be your buddy when you get back, Dad!"

But tonight I lit up her eyes purely by accident. I had not yet given Julie her key to the new truck. I walked in the master bathroom while Julie was in her attached closet and said loudly in no particular direction as I laid the key on the counter "Here's your key to the truck."

I barely noticed Melanie out of the corner of my eye and returned to my office. A moment later Melanie strolled into my office with the key in her hand and said in an almost reverent voice "Thanks, Dad." She mistakenly thought I gave the truck key to her, not to Mom.

I started to tell her those were Mom's keys, not hers, when Mom signaled me from behind Melanie and this one time I actually caught the female vibes and said to Melanie "Would it be OK if Mom keeps your keys to the truck for you?" and luckily she said yes and proudly handed them to Julie.

Julie later told me when I walked out of the bathroom Melanie picked up the keys, walked over to her with great big wide eyes and whispered "Look what Dad gave me." You just never know what's going to happen next.

Feb 2001, Melanie 3 yrs 10 mos

A Hard Rule to Enforce

Some people who learn I'm a Viet Nam veteran start to look at me differently, like "When is he going to snap and start hurting people?" Actually I think I'm fairly normal (humor me), as are most of us unlike the negative stereotype. But I did bring back from that experience a deep dislike for kids playing with toy guns, making games out of casually killing one another ala TV. Few things irritate me more than a little tyke pointing a toy gun at me and pretending to shoot, because of the pure stupidity of what he is learning.

I caught myself looking at squirt guns in a toy store for Melanie the other day and then came to my senses, not that I would criticize any other parent for buying their kid a squirt gun, but because of my belief that kids playing gun games teaches them the wrong thing. I found a squirt toy, so she could delight in squirting Daddy, but it isn't a gun.

Our dear friend and next door neighbor, Ed Pendleton, was Melanie's stand-in grandpa since both of her grandpas are no longer with us. Melanie and Ed were quite fond of one another, and in 2000 Ed died from cancer. That was Melanie's first experience losing someone she not only knew but cared for, and she tried hard to understand.

Ed had a BB gun rifle, and his wife Liz gave it to me. Other than an occasional shot at squirrels eating my attic piece by piece, I'm saving Ed's BB gun for Melanie when she is older. I'll teach her how to use it, teach her about gun safety, about the idiocy of play with guns, and about how to treat it as a serious form of recreation.

I'll tell her about a neighbor kid when I was growing up, how he used to catch a bunch of lizards and hang them with clothespins by the tail on the clothesline so he could go down the line shooting them with his BB gun to see how many he could get spinning at once, and that I still wonder how small a person he must have turned out to be. I'll tell her the most simple truth about shooting living creatures, small or large, that I learned by my own mistakes, best stated in the following verse I never forgot, author unknown:

> The boy killed the frog in jest,
> But the frog died . . . earnestly.

By the time Melanie is an adult and can make her own decisions about whether to have a real gun, maybe she'll choose to be like me and not have one, or maybe not. She may choose to hunt or not, and if she does I hope she'll treat it as a serious endeavor, not just killing for lusty entertainment disguised in the word "sport." Either way, she will have learned that guns are serious, and should have no place in a child's play.

Feb 2001, Melanie 3 yrs 10 mos

I'm Not in Charge

Grandma Shirley and Melanie make cookies

Melanie's almost four now, so mature. Remember last year when I mocked the idiots who spend lots on battery-driven cars for their kids? Now we have two. Remember when I said our kid wouldn't be a TV freak? Melanie becomes horrified when she learns of a video kid movie she does *not* have.

And she keeps close tabs on Mom & Dad - when I arranged a babysitter for Friday afternoons for golf she told me "I know Mom will be at her office when I'm with the babysitter, but where will *you* be, Huh Dad, where, Huh?" I told Julie it's like being married to two women at the same time - she was not amused.

Melanie loves doing Dad-stuff with me in the truck. I had the back filled with bags of leaves, and she went with me to the recycling dump then later told Mom we went "to sell the leaves."

I cleared a few small trees in the back yard to make room for a deck for Melanie's playhouse and sandbox, cut the trees up and put the trash in the truck bed to go to the dump. I was delayed by rain because I didn't want to go to the dump in a mud-mess, and I promised Melanie she could go with me to the adventurous dump.

Next day Grandma Shirley was coming to visit and I told Melanie I'd pick her up early to go to the airport with me. Melanie excitedly asked "Can Grandma go to the dump with us, Dad?"

Well, I was going to get rid of the mess first, but when your little girl asks, why not? So I said OK.

So there we were in the truck when Shirley exited the Delta terminal at the Atlanta airport, like Jethro Clampett in the truck with a big load of trash. Melanie's greeted her by yelling out the window.

"Hey Grandma, you get to go to the dump with us!" Shirley gave me a look and I said "Welcome to Melanie's world, Grandma!" Then we went straight from the airport to the dump, where Melanie was happy because of the adventure.

And Grandma Shirley is happy wherever Melanie happens to be.

Mar 2001, Melanie 3 yrs 11 mos

Evil Dad

Yesterday in the mail Melanie received another video from Grandma Shirley, this one <u>Cinderella</u>, which she watched with rapt attention last night with Mom.

This morning while we were cleaning up, I asked Melanie to pick up two newspaper plastic bags from the floor and put in the trash. She separated the two on the floor so she could pick up just one and headed to the trash can. I said "Hold it, bucko! Come get the other one." Never one to suffer mistreatment gladly, Melanie shouted "Moooom, Dad's making me do *everything*, just like Cinderella!"

Mar 2001, Melanie 3 yrs 11 mos

"To Be A Parent . . .

. . . you must pay attention." According to Melanie. She came home excited from school the other day, reporting on her friend's vacation. "Darby went with her Mom & Dad to London," Melanie said. Hmmm.

"I wonder if they have friends in England" Julie says to me. Melanie quickly interrupted - "Noooo, not Egg-Land. You listen to me, I said they went to London!"

And last night she showed me something new while sitting in my lap. Starting on my neck and walking up my face with her fingers like a spider she sang "Something crawling up on Daddy. . . . " over and over again until I had to tell her to stop. Birthday number four is a few weeks away. I think maybe this will be the very best year.

Mar 2001, Melanie 3 yrs 11 mos

Dad Fails Melanie

The other day when I picked up Melanie from pre-school one of the very young *teachers* said loudly to Melanie "Did you tell your Dad you bit Madison on the hand today?"

Primrose School in Peachtree City has been very good for Melanie. They take excellent care of the kids, but in this case the problem could have been handled better.

Melanie's happy smile melted into a pout as her sparkling eyes darkened to downcast shame - she knows that I won't be happy since biting is a big no-no.

So like a dumbass I made it worse by mildly admonishing Melanie right there about biting, whereupon her friend Madison, the aggrieved party, rushed over to recount how innocent she was and how guilty Melanie had been for biting her, oblivious to Melanie's feelings as kids are.

Melanie melted into tears under this onslaught of disapproval, frozen in her tracks with nowhere to hide, encircled by detractors, unwilling to talk or make eye contact. I picked her up and got her out of there as fast as I could, feeling quite inadequate for not defending her against the world.

At home she laid on my belly for a while but would not talk. After a while I took her for ice cream. As she was eating I asked her:

"Would you like to tell me about school today"

Head-shake no.

"Did you have a fight with Madison?"

Melanie deliberately took an oversized bite of ice cream and pointed to her mouth. Very clever. She took another oversize bite, then another.

I said "You don't want to talk about it?"

"You ask too much questions, Dad."

"You want to talk to Mom when she gets home?"

A very slight nod yes.

So she talked to Mom later, putting a hefty Melanie-spin on the incident, I'm sure.

I don't think she learned much, but I did.

Mar 2001, Melanie 3 yrs 11 mos

Allowance

This week is Melanie's fourth birthday. On Sunday the last thing I remember before falling asleep while watching the Bellsouth golf tournament was Melanie asking me: "Dad, why do dogs chase cats and why do cats chase mouses and why do big bad wolfs like to eat little pigs, huh Dad?"

Next thing I knew I was waking with the sun lower in the sky. I went outside and there was Mom trimming the bushes since the sun was out, even though the wind was chilly.

Mom said "See how much Melanie has helped me trim the bushes?" as Melanie made a show of picking up a stray clipping to throw in the wheelbarrow.

I asked Melanie "Did you work very hard?"

"Yup, I sure did, just like Mom."

"Well, maybe you deserve an allowance now that you're a big girl, you think so?"

"Yeah, Dad, I deserve a 'lowance. Dad, what's a 'lowance?"

"Well, that's where you get some money of your very own every week if you do what Mom and Dad ask you to do."

Melanie dwelled on that for a moment as her eyes grew big at the thought of her very own money. She looked at Mom with a surprised grin and Mom took the opening to tell her "Ask Dad how much your allowance will be!"

Melanie held up five fingers and Mom said "Five dollars! Wow."

I said "How about one dollar for each birthday. That means four dollars."

Melanie looked at Mom and said "Is four dollars a lot, Mom?"

Mom said "It sure is. I think that makes two dollars you can spend, 1 dollar to save to spend on others, and 1 dollar to save for yourself." Thanks to whoever gave us that idea.

Melanie strutted around just a little, proud of her new status.

In just a little while Melanie went with me to pick up fast food, and on the way I handed four dollars to her in the back seat. Her grin took over her whole face as she stared at the bills and her eyes sparkled with anticipation of what she would do with her very own money. On the way home she fell asleep, worn out from her busy day, and three of her dollars fell to the floor. When we arrived home I picked her up out of the booster seat and she woke up, immediately looking around in panic for her dollars, relieved when I handed them to her.

She ran to the door and in the house shouting "Mo-om, look, I got my 'lowance!" and proudly spread the four dollars out on the couch for Mom to see.

She's such a big girl, now.

Apr 2001, Melanie 4 yrs

Dad Hates Mickey

Unlike everyone else, I don't like Disney World. That's the polite version.

When Julie and I married in 1993, I was 45 and she 38 – neither of us had children from prior marriages. We invited Julie's parents, Mel and Shirley Wollschleger, to come to Georgia for Christmas with us, the ultimate attempt to get to know each other, for me anyway. Julie told me how much her dad enjoyed Disneyland in California where he took her countless times, and so we ended up driving from Atlanta to Disney World in Orlando.

We enjoyed one another's company, and just south of Interstate 10 in Florida I suffered an uncontrollable driver's laughing fit when I passed the Fu King Chinese restaurant, had to circle back for the others to see, even stopped to take a few photos of ourselves in front of that sign.

I remembered from a prior visit to Disney World long ago the dense crowds, long lines, long waits, high prices, relentless heat, long walks to the monorail, long trip to the hotel room and constant back pain from an ancient back injury. And of course there was Mickey et al and the constant music and manufactured gaiety of fantasies amidst that suffering, making the whole thing like a very nasty pill coated with candy. I'll pass.

I realize the rest of you love Disney, and I grew up adoring the Disney characters and shows. I remember as a kid, when TV was new and programming sparse, the highlight of the week was on Sundays when Tinkerbell emerged with her magic wand to start the show, and that theme music still puts a warm spot in my heart. But you can have the theme park, I'd be thrilled to never see it again.

So, there I was in Disney World again, years *before* Melanie came along, but I hadn't been there for a long time so maybe I'd enjoy it with Julie and her family. I didn't.

On the second day while the ladies stopped to shop again in EPCOT, Mel and I took a seat on a nearby cement bench. After a moment of silence I said:

"Mel, why do you like this *^&%# place so much?" Mel looked at me like I had just cut the cheese in church.

"Like this place? I hate this *&!% place! I thought you liked it."

I was stunned.

"Well why the heck did we come here, then? Julie thinks you love the place." Mel chuckled and told me how Julie loved it and he suffered through for his little girl, and wasn't she slick since she snookered not only her Dad but her husband, too. Slick, indeed.

Terry and Mel prepare for dinner after a round of golf

But there were compensations from that trip. Mel became my golf partner and buddy, and on that trip he and I found our dream dinner in Orlando – all the lobster you can eat. Maybe enough years have passed that they have forgotten and I can now go back to that restaurant.

On the drive home we had some good-natured wrangling with Julie saying she expected me to take her to Disney World once per year, me saying no more than every ten years and we negotiated it down to five years.

Tragically, Mel was quickly taken by cancer in 1997 just a couple of months after our dossier petitioning adoption had gone to China, and like my own Dad who died in 1996 he would never meet Melanie. Both Grandpas would have loved her dearly, and we named her after Mel.

After that memorable trip with Julie and her parents, I managed to avoid Disney World for seven years until Melanie was four years old. But that's the next story.

Julie with her Dad

Sisters Redeem Their Grumpy Dad

Dad Visits Mickey

Melanie asked Mom to dress her as Cinderella's Fairy
Godmother for Halloween. Mom made it by hand.

Melanie knew all about Disney World from her friends who had already returned from their stupendous adventure, and she talked about her fantastic dream to someday visit Disney World.

Just after her fourth birthday, we made reservations for Disney World and drove the 800 miles in my new truck while Melanie watched movies on the roof-mounted screen, happy and calm. We didn't tell her where we were going, for sake of our sanity, until we were about two hours away. Talk about excited. When Mom told her where we were going she said "Yaaaay. I been dreaming about going to Disney World my whole life!"

The whole thing?

We arrived about 5PM at the Disney Polynesian hotel, selected for its' proximity to the monorail because Dad wanted a quick escape route at any time. As we were walking to our room Mom asked Melanie:

"Do you want to go to the Magic Kingdom, we have plenty of time tonight?"

"No, Mom, we go tomorrow. Tonight you swim with me in the pool, OK?" Very mature.

When we dropped our things in the room I took Melanie to the balcony overlooking the lake with the Magic Kingdom and soaring castle in plain view.

With hushed astonishment she whispered "Dad, is that Cinderella's Castle?"

"It sure is." She tore off running to the room as fast as her little piston-legs would go yelling *"Mooooom, you won't believe it, it's Cinderella's castle for real! We gots to go right now, hurry up lets go Mom, OK?"*

Now I have to admit Disney World is a little different when you take kids, because after all it isn't about my comfort, it's about the kids. That's all I'll admit.

So I went with them to the Magic Kingdom. She saw Mickey and Goofy and Chip and Dale in a performance on the castle steps. She was entranced. When the show ended she was done fooling around and wanted results.

"OK, Dad you go tell Cinderella come down to see us."

"Cinderella's not home now."

"How do you know she's not home, huh Dad?" Merciless.

"She's gone now, I saw a little sign that said she was gone for the day." Nice try.

"Look, Dad, the lights are on in Cinderella's castle. Why the lights on if she's not home, huh, Dad? You go knock on the door, go ahead, tell her I want to see her." Ever feel like a manservant?

We managed to divert her from the castle to ride Dumbo, where she and Julie stood in line long enough for me to go stand in another line and fetch them a snow cone to eat while they waited some more. At least I'm good for something. Finally Dumbo flew and Melanie was in heaven, albeit briefly.

After two Dumbo rides, with a second long line wait of course, we decided to take our line-waiting business elsewhere and waited for the Lion King show. Not bad for kids, cool inside, blessed chairs for sore backs. When Simba came out Melanie said "Hi, Simba!" because she thought he is real. But Scar scared her for the same reason.

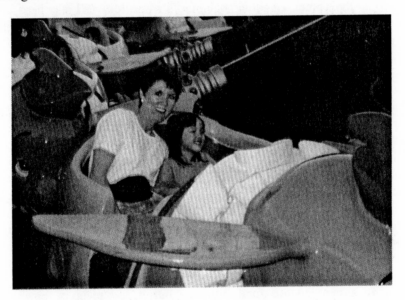

Later we were in the circular area in front of the castle when the nightly electric parade started. By then my back was killing me but I figured we may as well stay and see the parade. Besides, the crowd was so dense I could only move a few inches in any direction anyway. So, with Melanie on my shoulders or in her Mom's arms, she watched the parade with such passion I wouldn't have missed it.

She nearly flipped when Cinderella rode by in the coach, yelled loud at Snow White, the very first celebrity in her life, and said hi meekly to Chip and Dale as their float passed. She hid her face from

Captain Hook and shouted greetings to the three little pigs, but kept her silence when the big bad wolf slithered by.

I thought the parade would never end, and just when I was ready to fold like a church chair it ended and the crowd moved enough that I finally found some relief in a stone wall to sit on. Melanie was fired up. She could not believe all the celebrities she had seen the first day.

I'm a kidder, so back in our room I teased Melanie that Cinderella didn't like her, that's why she didn't come down. I know that sounds mean, but honestly we were just playing. But Dad shouldn't have played around with Cinderella – Melanie kicked me in the belly and told me "Cinderella does too like me, so there!" No mercy for poor suffering Dad.

The second day I lounged by the pool while Melanie and her Mom tore into the Magic Kingdom again. Go for it as long as I stay here and nurse my ailing back. When they returned I stayed in the room with worn-out, napping Melanie while Trooper Mama lounged deservedly by the pool with a book. Melanie woke up with a nosebleed, an occasional occurrence, and saved all the tissues so she could show Mom her "bwood." Dinner was in the Polynesian Kona Café, a small but excellent restaurant I would recommend where each bite was a bit of taste ecstasy.

The third day we went to the Animal Kingdom where the Bug's Life show was pretty good for adults, marginal for little kids, a 10 minute show after an hour plus wait, a wait I might add that was deceptive by design in its' many twists and turns around the big tree, often just short of a claustrophobic squeeze. Typical Disney.

Our last day forces me to concede some merit for the Character Breakfast at the Contemporary Hotel. Of course being a Grump I was immediately on guard when the greeter shuffled us to the photographer for a photo we didn't want, but we were seated quickly.

We assembled our food from the buffet and received beverage service at our table while Melanie watched the characters across the room sitting with other kids, occasionally taking a prompted bite amid her wary observations. Then Chip appeared and sat right by Melanie so she could touch him, food forgotten, followed by Goofy, Minnie, then the Big Guy Mickey himself. The entire trip was worth the look on her face during that breakfast.

Amidst all this the photo guy stopped by to sell us pictures of ourselves and we said no without looking at them. He stomped away in a huff, poor guy.

To this day Melanie believes the characters she had breakfast with are the one and only real thing. OK, so I'll go again, especially to the Character Breakfast. I'll despise many things about Disney World for me, but I'll suffer it for her. Maybe I'll at least get dinner again in the Kona Cafe. And this time I'll have the wisdom to schedule a character dinner with Cinderella in the castle, thereby becoming Melanie's hero.

Apr 2001, Melanie 4 yrs

Bug Hunter

Melanie helps Mom in a flower bed, looking for bugs

One day Melanie found a rolly-polly bug in her sandbox. She put it in a little play teacup and included her new friend in her play, even though I think the new friend may have died, escaping Melanie's notice, from the play.

The next day she went looking for more rolly-polly bugs, and Mom, being totally unable to say "no" when Melanie asks was recruited to help the search for rolly-pollies. I don't know how many they found but Melanie brought them in the house in a little cup to show me, proud as a kitty with a mouse. She kept them in the cup until they died, too, but by then she had lost interest in that group and was on to the next.

Melanie proudly announced *"I'm a bug-hunter, Dad!"* Indeed.

You should see her, squatting down low intensely searching for her next love-victim. Dad couldn't help if he wanted to – I'm no longer built for squatting.

So, Mom bought her a bug-box at the Dollar Store, a plastic box with removable lid, flip-up lid on one side with air holes, and magnifying glass built right into the top. Cool! It even came with a pair of plastic tweezers for picking up bugs.

Melanie really liked the tweezers, so I didn't spoil things by telling her she was squishing the poor little rolly-polly's guts out whenever she picked one up. She'll learn soon enough.

May 2001, Melanie 4 yrs 1 mo

Hello?

One of my pet peeves is calling someone's home and having a child answer with no training on how to handle the phone. So I've instructed Melanie she is not to answer the phone unless Mom or Dad say OK.

Last night Melanie crawled into my lap and said, "Dad, I'm going to answer the phone, OK?"

"No. Not until you can do it right."

"So I say 'hello.' What's so hard about that, huh, Dad?"

"Here's how you answer the phone right - Hello, Garlock residence, may I help you?"

"You don't answer the phone like that!" Just enough indignation.

"No, but little kids answer the phone like that to be polite when adults call, OK?"

"OK, so I can answer the phone, Dad?"

"No. You have to practice."

"Lets practice, Dad."

"All right. Pretend the phone rings, then you say 'Hello, Garlock residence, may I help you?'"

"Hello, Garlockres......." trailing off to an unintelligible mumble.

"Try it again. Say 'Hello, Garlock residence, may I help you?'"

"Hello, GarlockresimenmayIhelp?" Still mumbling.

"Lets try again. Speak clearly and slowly and say 'Hello, Garlock residence, may I help you?'"

"HelloGarlockresidencemayIhelpyou?" barely whispered, caution against embarrassment, you know.

"You have to speak loud and clear, and don't mumble the words, say them slowly. Try it again."

"Hello, Garlock residence, may I help you?" Success! And repeated several times.

Mom heard what was going on and decided to get in the act. So she called Grandma Shirley and asked her to call right back.

"Melanie, Grandma is going to call. You want to answer the phone? Can you do it like we practiced?"

"*Yea, I get to answer the phone. I can do it!*"

The phone rang, and Melanie froze, eyes full of fear.

"Go ahead and answer the phone like we practiced."

Melanie picked up the phone and in a tiny, timid voice said "hello."

Oh well.

Jun 2001, Melanie 4 yrs 2 mos

Gwider

Melanie is like many four year olds with a devoted circle of family and friends to shower her with piles of gifts at every occasion while Dad murmurs ill-concealed obscenities because I don't want her spoiled. So, some time back after playing at Taylor's house on her swing and glider, Melanie returned home to announce "Dad, I want you to make me a gwider, pweeeese" drawing out the pleading just the way Mom taught her.

At the time we were working on her improving on several things, like picking up her toys, and I didn't want to give in and just add it to the top of her pile of *stuff* so I said "We'll see if you're a good girl and do what Mom and Dad ask, and if you can be polite, OK?"

"Okaaaaay" in universal dejected kid-surrender talk.

So after considering several options I decided to build it myself between two trees using a 4x6x10 beam, which when freshly *treated* is twice as heavy as when dry. I picked up a glider and swing from Lowes, along with the heavy-duty lumber.

When Melanie saw what was in the truck she yelled "Yaaay, Dad is building my gwider."

She helped, and it only took me twice as long. I built braces chained to each tree with 4x4s, with small spikes on top to ensure no slippage when I put the beam up there. When it came time to put the beam up, I thought for a nanosecond about calling Julie for balancing help since I'm old and beat up enough to think safety first, but it quickly passed through my head since she was painting Melanie's room, focused like a laser on her project and mean as hell if interrupted.

So I instructed Melanie to go sit on the sidewalk about 50 feet away and *stay there*. Now I have to admit I didn't make this easy because I bolted the glider onto the beam before mounting the beam, and in addition to weighing near as much as my truck it was awkward. I stood the beam on one end and jiggled to find the center of gravity, then with a whoosh of breath lifted it to chest level.

"Dad, can I come out there now, is my gwider ready?"

Huff, puff, *"No dammit, stay there, OK?"*

"OK, Dad, but you hurry up with my gwider, OK?"

So I heaved it up over my head, dancing around like a weight-lifter and tried to slip it onto the top of the 4x4s, but with the little spikes for non-slip I had to lift it over and it was an inch too high. So up I went on my toes. Still not high enough.

"Is it done yet, Dad?"

"Noooo, stay there!" through gritted teeth as my eyes began to bulge.

I was nearing the end of my strength and decided to see if I could get the beam up on my fingertips one side at a time with one final gold-medal effort, and - the beam was up. So huffing and puffing and sweating as an overweight out-of-shape 53 year old should, having just cheated death once again, I told Melanie she could come out now but stay back until I got the beam bolted into place.

I used 18" threaded rods and a 2x6 with holes drilled on each side of the tree on each end of the beam to bolt it into place. Melanie handed me the hammer once and beamed with pride at helping on such an important project.

"Is it done yet, Dad?"

"Yes it is. Ready to ride your glider?"

With an uncontrollable big grin Melanie climbed aboard and away she went, yelling "wheeeee!" I noticed that, as I half-expected, the back side of the glider comes too close to a small tree, and I told Melanie I'd have to take that tree out.

When Mom came out to check it out Melanie yelled "Mom, look at the gwider me and Dad builded. It works real good, but Dad has to cut down a tree whenmybabysistercomes." I told Melanie I would cut down the tree long before that, and that she would likely want to play on the glider with some of her friends before then. She said no, she would "gwide" alone until "mybabysistercomes."

But that's another story.

Jun 2001, Melanie 4 yrs 2 mos

Wizard of August

Melanie in her "slinky" dress

At four yrs old Melanie is already into what's cool like Brittany Spears music and the Backstreet Boys. The other day while I was

Sisters Redeem Their Grumpy Dad

lounging she slithered into view snapping her little fingers, shaking her little "bootie" and singing to me with sly sexy looks and smiles:

"Oops, I did it again

I played with your heart

Ooh baby, baby . . ."

What the heck? She has slinky dresses, plastic high heels, even a feather boa for crying out loud. All she's missing is a leopard skin outfit but I'm not saying it out loud.

But then, just when I think she's turning into the vamp she plays, she reverts to a little girl, climbs up into my lap and starts pulling all six hairs on my chest, keenly alert to my cries of pain and surprise, the sought-after prize.

I was just flipping channels, as guys do, and stopped on <u>Alice Through The Looking Glass</u>, a sequel to Disney's animated <u>Alice in Wonderland</u>. I thought she might like it.

"Dad, what show is this?"

"Watch it and I think you'll recognize what it is." We watched for a little while, but it was a dull part of the movie and Melanie asked:

"Dad, is this the Wizard of August? Is that Dorothy?"

Jun 2001, Melanie 4 yrs 2 mos

Little Butthead, Center of the Universe

Much to the chagrin of child-raising experts, if they ever find out, I've always called Melanie "Little Butthead." That's because Butthead was always a term of endearment between Julie and I, and I wanted Melanie to feel included.

So Melanie wears her title of Little Butthead proudly, sometimes calls Mom Butthead and me Big Butthead accompanied by giggles and some other creative names, and it's our thing just among us. But anticipating trouble since some people are so uptight they would need a tractor to pull a needle out of their butt, I told Melanie we better stop calling each other names since others might be offended.

"But Dad, I like calling you names."

"Most times it's not nice to call people names."

"But we call names just to each other, not other people."

"I tell you what, we won't call each other names when there are other people around, OK?"

"OK, Dad."

"And just to make sure, you don't call names unless I say it's OK, alright?"

"Okaaaaay." A perfected tone of disappointment at gratification delayed.

Later, when Mom was in the kitchen, Melanie crawled up in my lap and said

"Dad, can we call names?"

"OK, little butthead." Always try to get in the first lick.
Melanie giggle-talked "Why you big butthead, li'l poopy head, you cute li'l plumber!" Julie taught her the last one when I was working on something.

I countered with "You're goofy and your feet stink."

"My little feet? Your big icky feet stink real bad and you're a stinky-butt."

From the kitchen "What are you two doing?" Uh-oh. I whispered to Melanie "We better stop calling names now, OK?"

She stretched my ear in a hammer-lock to whisper back "OK, Dad. When can we do it again?"

"Later, not unless I say so, OK?"

"OK. I got some good names for you next time."

Saturday morning while Melanie was watching cartoons and she was singing along with Barney I thought I heard something strange along with her giggles as she gave me a guilty look. . .

"Daddy is a poopy-head, his feet stink . . . Daddy is a moose . . ."

All perfectly sung to the music. My little girl has *talent*! In this day and age I may be prosecuted for letting her call me names, but we're just having fun. She's the center of my universe now, but . . . I wonder at what age she will realize she is not the center of the universe? I am advised that may only happen conclusively when she has a child of her own. Makes sense.

Yesterday Melanie returned from a play adventure with some of her friends with her damp bathing suit on under her clothes. She announced to all as if it were of public interest "I'm going to the bathroom."

It was a hot and oppressively humid day outside, and I guess when the air conditioned air hit her bathing suit she felt cold. Melanie yelled from the bathroom "Mom, get my clothes for me."

But Mom was comfortable in a rare few moments in nap position on the couch, and so the desire to teach Melanie to act independently came easily into play.

"You know where your clothes are, you get them."

"Mom, I'm cold!"

"Well, hurry and get your clothes."

"Mom, run for your life, I'm freezing!"

For now, she's still the center of the universe.

Jun 2001, Melanie 4 yrs 2 mos

Watch It, Mister!

On July 4 we started our day with the Peachtree City Parade. You would have to see this parade, it's hard to describe.

Peachtree City has over 70 miles of golf cart paths going everywhere, and several golf courses. Nearly everyone has a golf cart, even those who don't play the game, because it's a lifestyle thing to scoot around the neighborhood, to the store, or to dinner in a golf cart instead of a car. When we go for a golf cart ride with Melanie through the woods we describe our purpose as ". . . to make the wheels roll and the wind blow . . ."

So every year for the July 4 parade, there's a golf cart traffic jam in the woods as everyone vies for their favorite spot, each cart decorated for the holiday. As far as the eye can see on the parade route past the golf course, golf carts are lined up, many back-end toward the road so one can sit down on the rear-facing seat to watch the parade.

Every group with a purpose is in the parade, every local politician running for office, and anyone willing to decorate their golf cart and line up. This year the highlight for me was a toothless old guy driving his John Deer lawn mower with a big black number 3, obviously in memory of Dale Earnhardt. Norman Rockwell would be proud.

After the parade I did a little work in my office, and when I emerged Julie said to me "Hey, no working today, it's a holiday!"

Now Melanie, a devoted "me-too" follower of her Mom, jumped down from the couch, ran over to me, kicked me in the shin with her soft little bare foot and said:

"Yeah, no working today, it's a holiday, you hear me? I catch you working you in big-time trouble, mister."

Then I contorted my face to a monster and growled at her, and she ran to hide with her little piston-legs pumping in a blur, ready to pop out at any minute and yell at Dad again. But it's all in fun, with a giggle just below the surface.

Jul 2001, Melanie 4 yrs 3 mos

Dance Recital

Melanie feels beautiful in her tutu

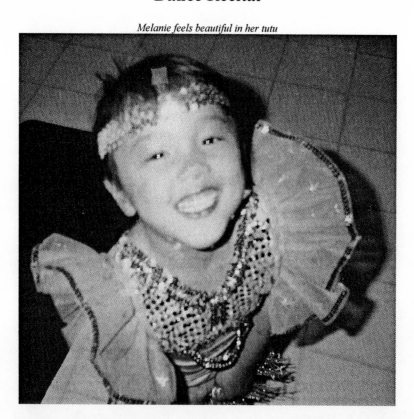

Some weeks ago Melanie needed to attend a practice session for a dance recital, and since Mom was out of town and couldn't be absolutely sure she would return in time, I was to take Melanie to the practice. What the heck do I know about tutus and sparkled headbands and slinky skirts and all the rest? But you do what you must, so we packed all of Melanie's dance paraphernalia in a go-bag and set out to find the school where the practice session was held.

Just as I backed out of the driveway, Julie arrived from the airport, darted her car into the garage and jumped in with Melanie and me. I had two very happy ladies in the back seat, and off we went. About halfway to the school, it dawned on me that I was driving to something akin to a root canal for me, and I didn't even have to be there for practice now that Mom was home. Oh, well, go with the flow.

While Mom helped Melanie change clothes and line up and whatever, I sat in the auditorium seats and watched countless groups like Melanie's try to convert chaos to an orchestrated performance on the stage. In the middle of serious attempts a little one was likely to step forward and wave while yelling "Hi, Mom!" Who in their right mind, I wondered, would choose to do this every day? Reminds me of that TV commercial of the cowboys on horseback, herding cats. But God bless the dance teachers, better them than me.

Darby Smith, Melanie Garlock, Alexandra Ward (L-R)

Like the rest, Melanie waited nervously for her turn, twittering with her friends Alex, Darby, Elizabeth and others, seemingly orbiting one another like mutually-attracted planets. They would run and play until yelled at, Moms repairing damage done to outfits as they waited. Finally they were ON, and this group of 4 year old tykes gave it the most serious focus available to them at that age. They danced and sang and held their little prop-bears, all the while watching Mom and Dad and teacher. Do you remember yourself at that age? I do.

At the end of the practice Mom asked me "Do you know how long we have to be here for the recital on Saturday?"

"No, how long?"

"All day."

"Are you crazy?"

"Well, most of the day, half a day at the very least. They don't want us coming and going as each group performs, so we have to be here when it starts and stay for the whole thing."

Julie knows how, shall we say, *contrary* I can be when others tell me what I have to do according to their rules, so she shut me down by promptly saying "Melanie and I will let you off the hook since you're here for the practice and I know how your back hurts if you have to sit too long."

An escape ticket, on a silver platter. And shamelessly I took it. "OK."

So on that Saturday I did other things while Mom and Melanie went to the recital, relieved but feeling guilty for not going. Now some weeks later, I'm looking over the pictures Mom took of Melanie in her tutu and sparkled headband, commiserating with her buddies, lined up in the hall sweating out the wait, making countless adjustments to the outfit, holding the bears, then on stage under the lights. She was so proud of herself. Almost as proud as Mom and Dad.

There's something about this I cannot explain to you as you wait for your child, but while I watch Melanie growing and spreading her wings, learning to do difficult things, sharing the joy and frustration with her close friends as well as family, my heart is warmed and filled.

She is overwhelmingly beautiful, and I don't mean her appearance. I'm grateful she's ours. May yours come soon.

Jul 2001, Melanie 4 yrs 3 mos

Shove This, Dad!

I vividly recall the adjustment period after we returned from China with Melanie, before she was talking, when everyone seemed to talk through her to me. It's a crutch, and goes something like this.

Mom says, "Tell your Dad we're ready to go so hurry up!"

Grandma Shirley says, "Say I'm hungry, Dad, what's for supper?"

Mom says, "Tell Dad to take us on a golf cart ride."

Its part of a diabolical pattern. Sometimes it's just chatter and giving attention to the kid. But sometimes, when one is hesitant to speak their mind they seem to lose that inhibition by talking, with their own lips, mind you, through the baby.

Grandma Shirley wouldn't say to me, "This place needs to be cleaned up," but she would easily look at Melanie and say "Do you see this mess, tell Dad it needs to be cleaned up."

One day, with two women talking to me through the baby getting to be irritating, I yelled at them just a little.

"If you have something to say, tell me directly, not through the baby, it's driving me nuts!" Of course they did just as they pleased.

Flash forward to now, Melanie is well into her fourth year and talking for herself quite nicely. But this morning Mom and Dad reverted to the crutch of earlier days.

Do you ever act like a child? Of course not, you're an adult, aren't you? But Julie and I do slip ever so rarely, like today.

We had been competing for sections of the Sunday paper this morning, and amidst some good-natured wrangling I said to Melanie "Tell your Mom to bite me!"

"Mom, Dad said to bite him, OK?" Gee, it's a little different when they can talk for themselves.

A few minutes later Melanie delivered a section of the paper to me while I was in the kitchen and deadpanned "Mom says would you shove this, please?" We really must stop this before Melanie realizes she's being used, or perhaps I should say *abused*.

Jul 2001, Melanie 4 yrs 3 mos

Lemonade

The other day I wanted some lemonade, and I like the instant Crystal Light stuff. As I rounded up the Crystal Light package and pitcher, Melanie jumped up and down saying "Let me make the lemonade, Daddy!"

So I picked her up to set her on the counter with legs over the edge so she could be involved. I opened the Crystal Light package, handed it to her and let her pour it in. Then I put the pitcher in the sink and turned on the water to fill it up. When full, I set the pitcher beside Melanie and handed her a long spoon and told her to stir.

"Like this, Daddy?"

"Yep, just like that. Look, you made lemonade, you're a big girl." Her eyes shined with pride, an involuntary grin showing me her teeth. We put crushed ice in a couple of glasses and enjoyed a glass of lemonade. Kids like doing things with a parent. Melanie says so by observing "Look Dad, were the same."

Later when Mom arrived home from work, Melanie ran to the door to excitedly tell her about her latest accomplishment.

"Mom, Imadelemonadeallbymyself, Daddy didn't even help, youwantsomelemonadeitsverygood?"

"Sure, I'd love some lemonade." Mom is very smart, even if she wasn't thirsty.

So Dad didn't even help. Hmmmm. Get used to it.

Jul 2001, Melanie 4 yrs 3 mos

Whenmybabysistercomes

We have succeeded in Melanie's sense of *family* as she reminded me the other day after I had been sequestered in my office too long.

"Dad, can you come with me and Mom on a golf cart ride so we can be a fambly?" Uh-oh.

Now Melanie wants a sister, and Mom, who grew up as an only child, wants a sister for Melanie, too.

So, the paper chase for a second China adoption is under way, and this time Melanie will be old enough to remember a trip to her home country, and will ride the emotional roller-coaster of adoption with Mom and Dad.

Immediately after she learned of our plans she placed herself in charge, instructing us on how old her baby sister should be so that she could hold her. Melanie also insists that ". . . mybabysister will have her own bed, not sleep with me." And the frequent pictures she draws of Mom and Dad and Melanie now include a fourth smaller person, "mybabysister."

Virtually everything involving the future is now modified by the phrase "whenmybabysistercomes."

In anticipation of the difficulties Melanie will go through sharing Mom with a sister, I asked her the other day while Mom did the *dance to the music holding Melanie* routine.

"Melanie!"

"Yes, Dad?"

"How are you going to share Mom with a little sister?"

Melanie shook her head and rolled her eyes at the sheer stupidity of the male species and her Dad in particular.

"I'll hold my Babysister and Mom can hold *meee*! Okaaaaay?"

Stupid me. I thought there might be a bit of a problem during the transition period. But that's a story for much, much later.

Aug 2001, Melanie 4 yrs 4mos

Book Two

Waiting for Babysister

Secrets

I listened to the radio while driving as a renowned marriage counselor held forth that husbands and wives should have absolutely no secrets from one another, that they should tell each other everything about themselves, the kids, etc. Is he kidding?

Should I tell Julie that once or twice a week after lunch at my home office I doze off in my chair for a little bit? I don't think so. She's a really nice person, but jealousy is a slimy critter that creeps through the smallest crack, and I don't want her smoldering while she should be working. She loves naps, but I'm sure she could describe mine as depraved. So I don't tell her because I'm not stupid.

Melanie first learned of secrets when she learned to whisper. The very thought she could cup her hands over Mom's ear and whisper something I couldn't hear made her giddy. Then we progressed to secrets like buying Mom a birthday present, and when we returned home she nearly peed her pants with excitement and blurted out *"Momwebuyyoupresentitsadressandrealpretty"* the day before her birthday. But that's my fault, she was only three then.

When Melanie turned four in April, she and I played a little rough in the living room and in the heat of passion she bit a small spot on my chest, hard, leaving a welt at first then a bruise for weeks. I was immediately angry with her because we don't allow biting, of course, and this was a very rare lapse. I didn't punish her, after all I'm the roughhouse chief, but I did show her what she had done. Her only wide-eyed concern was "Dad, don't tell Mom, OK?" She wasn't afraid Mom would punish her, she was afraid Mom would be disappointed in her. So I promised.

From that moment, it was our secret, and for a couple of days Melanie would look at me with expectant eyes whenever we were around Mom, grateful that I never told her secret. Weeks later Melanie told Mom she and Dad had a secret. Mom asked what it was but neither of us would answer. Tell me I'm crazy, but I think that's important to

Melanie's trust of me, and it's not something Mom needs to know. I later found Melanie and Mom have a secret, too, and I don't want to know what it is, probably "Dad's a stinky-butt" or something fun like that.

Remember in the movie <u>A Christmas Story</u> when Ralphie is tormented by bullies, and he ends up pulverizing them and swearing in a child-level fit of rage as his Mom tried to calm him down and pull him out of the fight? Ralphie just knew his Dad would punish him when he found out he was fighting and swearing, but when Dad arrived home Ralphie's Mom just winked at him and never told. In real life Ralphie would remember that with gratitude forever.

Mr. Marriage Counselor could learn a thing or two from Ralphie's Mom, and from Melanie. He may not have any secrets from his wife, but if she has any sense she has a few. We all need little secrets of some sort, hopefully innocent things because we're wise enough not to keep harmful secrets, but it's a form of privacy. And even Melanie needs a little of that.

Aug 2001, Melanie 4 yrs 4 mos

Sprint to Victory

This weekend as I returned on the golf cart from visiting a neighbor, Mom and Melanie were gone but the car was in the garage. I surmised they were out for a walk, and went looking for them on the golf cart in case they wanted a ride back since Melanie sometimes gets tired and Mom is defenseless against her pleas to be carried. I stopped to talk to a neighbor, and she invited us to go that evening to a Bobby Vinton performance at the local amphitheater. Polite no thank you.

While we were talking my two ladies rounded the corner on their return and I heard Melanie shout "Dad!" They continued walking toward home, and I excused myself to scoot after them. I passed slowly about two houses away from our own, gave Melanie a sly look and said "I can beat you home."

It's fascinating to watch the instantaneous transformation of a kid's eyes from casual to battle mode. Melanie took off running, grunting with effort as I speeded up, and after Mom shouted to her "Cut across Miss Liz's yard!" she took the short cut and I had to speed up some more. I rounded the corner from street to driveway at full speed and pulled up to the garage just after Melanie arrived, huffing and puffing, face flushed with exhilaration and victory.

"I beat you, Dad!"

"You sure did. You can run fast, can't you?"

"Yep."

As Mom passed by she said low enough so Melanie couldn't hear "I see Dad is smart enough to lose by just a little." You can't hide a thing from her, must be that third eye in the back of her head that all Moms grow.

Aug 2001 Melanie 4 yrs 4 mos

The First Bicycle

Melanie's first bike trip all the way to the "Icee Store"

A couple of weeks ago Melanie whined to me:

"Daaaaad, I want a bicycle. Darby gots a bicycle and Alex gots a bicycle so I want a bicycle, too, Okaaaay?"

What in the world would she do with a bicycle, she hadn't even learned to ride her tricycle yet! Now in all fairness to Melanie, there's more to be told. Some months ago my friend Ben Darnell brought his daughter Taylor to visit in her cool battery-driven Barbie Car. When I saw him all bent over, making steering corrections every two feet and explaining with hopeless futility how Taylor should steer, I thought spending a load on a car like that for kids was not too smart.

We had already bought Melanie a tricycle, carefully selected from internet sources for its' special design and safety features - in arrears I have to say to myself "It's just a trike for Pete's sake!" We all lived through it with our cheap little trikes, didn't we? But Melanie didn't figure out how to push one pedal, then the other, and I kept my instruction gentle, there's plenty of time, isn't there? I figured she would at some point by accident push the pedals the right way, have a flash of inspiration like the rest of us and become an instant trike expert. But the modern age intervened.

About a week after the Barbie Car visit, in the Barbie Car section of Toys-R-Us, Melanie fell in love with a battery-driven four-wheeler. It was smaller, $70, and sucker Dad bought it. So why should Melanie get on her ergonomically-designed tricycle and try again to make it go when she could hop on her four-wheeler and push a button on the handle? Duhhh.

Naturally, Melanie's legs grew quickly and she needed something bigger so for her fourth birthday I bought her - you guessed it - a Barbie Car just like Taylor's. So now, even though I said it was dumber than a box of rocks to buy these battery cars for kids, Melanie has two of them. So Dad, with the best of intentions, killed Melanie's motivation to get on that trike.

All of which is to say when Melanie whined to me about a bicycle, I instantly solved the puzzle in my head and said:

"You can't have a bicycle."

"Why, not, Dad, huh, why can't I?"

"Because you haven't even learned to ride your tricycle. Little girls who can't ride a tricycle certainly don't get a bicycle, do they?"

"*Dad, lets go outside, I want to ride my tricycle!*" Dang, I'm smart.

So, Melanie jumped on her tricycle, and now that she had a reason to do so, she figured it out in one minute and was scooting around the driveway.

"*Lets Go Get Me A Bicycle Now, Dad!*"

"Not so fast, you have to ride this trike a bit before we get a bicycle."

"Okkaaaaaay." Dejected kid acquiescence.

So for the next few days Melanie hit the tricycle at every opportunity, but only when one of us was watching, kind of like a politician not wasting his time saying anything unless a camera is rolling.

Yesterday we went to buy Melanie's first bicycle. Instead of the expensive ergonomically-designed, specially painted doo-da version I wised up and went back to Toys-R-Us and bought the 12-inch bike with pink sparkles and pretty plastic strips hanging off the handle bar grips. And it has a cool water bottle, just like Mom's bike. Later, when it matters, we'll spend bigger bucks on better bikes.

But on the way to buy the bike, we almost had a disciplinary delay. Mom and Melanie were in the back seat of the truck and I noticed they were playing a little game where Melanie put a quarter in one hand then Mom was guessing which hand it was in so she could take the quarter. Melanie's little clique of gangsters must have been teaching her the wrong things. When Mom would pick the correct hand, Melanie would covertly but clumsily shift the quarter to the other hand and say, "Nope, you lose, Mom."

"You're cheating!" Mom was, as we say in the south, getting a case of the vapors.

"*No I not, you lose!*"

"I'm not playing with you, you cheat."

"*OK, you're out. Can't play no more.*" She's a tough little kid.

A moment of silence.

"Want to play some more, Mom?"

"Only if you don't cheat." Melanie instinctively knows when not to comment. So she holds her hands out again and Julie picks the correct hand.

"*You're out of the game, you not play no more.*" Brutal.

This is where I intervened with "If that's how you play games maybe you don't deserve a bicycle. Think about that for a minute." In a few minutes they were playing the game in a civilized fashion, so we continue to buy the bike.

Later that day while I worked in my office Mom and Melanie practiced on her bike in the driveway, with training wheels of course. When she *got it* she raced in the house yelling "*Daad!*" stomping out of breath with her little helmet still on, face flushed with excitement, telling me proudly she now knows how to ride a bicycle, big grin and strands of sweaty hair sticking out from under her helmet.

Seeing the shine of pride in your kids eye at discovering new abilities, conquering fears, overcoming hesitations to accomplish simple things, can give you an inner glow. You'll soon find out.

Aug 2001, Melanie 4 yrs 4 mos

Friendship

Melanie, Alex & Darby (L-R)

Last Thursday when I took Melanie to pre-school she received the customary "Melanie!" greeting from a number of her friends, sort of like Norm making his entrance to Cheers. But today Alex, one of her very close girlfriends, looked up at me with expectant eyes, whereupon Melanie remembered something important and announced:

"Dad, Alex is coming to my house tonight, OK?" So, Melanie has progressed to conspiracies planned the day before - sort of makes me proud.

"No, I haven't heard anything from Alex's Mom, and until I do you come home and Alex goes home with her Mom, just like every day." Julie was out of town, but I knew Maria, Alex's Mom, would call me if anything was up. Melanie and Alex powowed with whispers and apparently conspired to have Maria call me to resolve the obstacle of big, bad, uncooperative Dad. They had all day for the problem to be solved, and that is nearly forever in kid-time.

I said "Sorry, Alex, I have to hear from your Mom before you come home with us. What would she do if she came to pick you up and you weren't here?" And off I went to work, not thinking much about it.

At 6PM when I stopped to pick up Melanie, the girl at the front desk said:

"So, Alex is coming to Melanie's house today?"

"No, I didn't hear anything from Alex's Mom."

A second young teacher nearby expressed her sorrow. "Oooohhhhh, no, they'll be so disappointed. They've been telling the whole school all day!" A third teacher emerged from the infant room and said to Alex "Are you going to Melanie's house to play?"

Why do I always have to be the bad guy?

When Melanie saw me she jumped up and said "Come on, Alex, lets go!" It's so easy to ignore Dad's admonition, after all it had been hours ago.

"No, Melanie, I told you until I hear from Alex's Mom we can't take Alex home with us, I'm sorry. Now lets go."

Poor little Alex's eyes looked like her entire little world was caving in, and I felt like a dummy for not tracking down Maria during the workday. In the parking lot I turned on the TV in the truck for a despondent Melanie to watch Arthur on PBS while I sat waiting to see if Maria would show and maybe we could salvage the magic of the day for the kids. But in a little while I gave up and left, needing to visit the dry cleaners before 6:30. We had a busy evening and I didn't get Maria's message until the next morning saying she had *promised* Alex she would arrange play with Melanie, and when could we do it?

Well, Melanie went to play at Alex's house Saturday morning. She didn't return at 4PM as we expected, and ended up on a *sleepover*, her first if successful. We received the expected call about 9PM that Melanie could not pass the night without Mom, and the tired little tyke came home to fall asleep in Mom's arms.

So, dear reader, I told you all of that to tell you this. Yesterday we had a prearranged play day for Alex to come home with Melanie. When I picked them up Alex looked cautious like maybe I would ruin it again, and when I said "Come on Alex, let's go" her little face lit up like a Christmas tree. On the way home on the golf cart the dialogue in the rear-facing back seat went something like this.

Melanie:"We taked a *big* nap today, Dad, didn't we Alex?"

Alex: "Um-Hmmm. And we colored and played outside on the slide."

We passed a house with a new redwood playhouse, an extravagant affair that must cost $10,000.

Melanie: "Wow, look at that playhouse. I asked my Dad to build me one and maybe he will and we can play in it, OK, Alex? Those are made out of big sticks and they're real heavy to carry and if you fall off you might get hurt."

Alex: "My Dad knows how to do things with big sticks."

Melanie: "My Dad cut himself once and there was bwood, lots of bwood all over!"

Alex: "How do you know?"

Melanie: "Because he let me look at it real close, and oh man it was *gross*!"

Alex: "Are you going to show me your new bike?" Melanie is very proud of her big-girl status now that she has a bike with training wheels.

Melanie: "Yeah, sure. Can I ride it Dad, Huh, Dad?" The obligatory showoff.

Alex: "My Dad says when I'm five I can have a big bike."

Melanie: "Dad, can I have a big bike when I'm five?"

Dad: "I think the bike you just got is a big bike, Melanie."

Melanie:"I already gots a big bike, Alex. You're banilla, Alex, am I banilla or black?" They were holding their arms together to compare skin. Melanie's is darker than Alex's and mine, but not too dark. Her recent boyfriend at school is black, so maybe she's trying to sort this out.

Alex: "I think you're banilla, too."

All this time they had been so wrapped up in each other they didn't pay attention to where I was going. When I exited the woods trail and entered the shopping center parking lot Alex remarked I was going to the grocery store, but Melanie knew the Baskin Robbins store was next door, though she didn't know it was my targeted destination all along.

Melanie:"*Dad, can we get ice cream, pleeeeeaaasse?*" Heads turned all over the parking lot.

Dad: "OK."

Both kids: "*Yaaaaaay. We're getting ice cream.*"

Alex: "I want blue."

Melanie:"Dad, can I get what Alex gets?"

Dad: "Sure." Take the simple surrenders when you can. So while we had ice cream at the table I held my arm next to Melanie's then Alex's and we talked about how everybody's skin is a little different but we're all the same inside. But the best was yet to come.

"OK, girls, are you ready to stop to see Miss Lindy and do your Brittany Spears dance for her?" They were and we went. After a little shyness, Melanie and Alex held hands and shook their booties and sang "Oops, I did it again . . . I played with your heart . . . ooh, baby, baby . . ." while doing a little two-step. Lindy Jennings loved it. And no, they didn't learn it at home!

Back home in the golf cart, some BBQ and coleslaw for dinner and the duo colored and played with dolls and played dress-up until it was time for Alex to go home. When we dropped Alex at her house they hugged and said goodbyes until tomorrow morning, and back in the truck Melanie said she missed Alex. The next morning when they saw each other at pre-school their eyes lit up with renewed delight and they held hands and jumped with the tireless passion of friendship.

Aug 2001, Melanie 4 yrs 4 mos

Can Babysister be My Twin?

Last week one night I was reading Melanie her bedtime story. Maybe I should say stories since we read two, as usual, unless she talks me into three. She likes to save her bedtime sippy cup drink until after the stories, to drink just before falling asleep.

When I finished the stories Melanie rested her head on my chest, thinking for a minute then asked:

"Dad, whenmybabysistercomes can we be twins?"

"No, you can't be twins, but she'll be your sister."

"Chas and Shelby are twins, why can't we be twins, too?"

"Twins have the same birthmom. Your sister won't have the same birthmom, but she'll be part of our family so she'll have the same Mom and Dad."

"Why can't she have the same birthmom as me?"

"We don't know your birthmom, and we don't know yet where your baby sister will be born."

"Why can't she have the same birthmom as me, Dad?" Melanie doesn't miss anything.

"Well, maybe she could, but twins are in their birthmom's tummy at the same time and are born at the same time, that's what makes them twins."

Melanie thought for a moment with a look of wonder. "Wow. Chas and Shelby were in their birthmom's tummy at the same time?"

"That's right."

"Their birthmom must be fat like you, Dad, if they have two babies in their tummy."

No comment.

"Do the twins play in their birthmom's tummy?"

"I don't think they can play until long after they are born."

"Maybe meandmybabysister can go back in our birthmom's tummy so we can be twins."

"No, that doesn't work, and besides you don't need to be twins, you'll still be sisters."

"Wellll, I'll be the *big* sister and she can be my little sister, OK, Dad?"

"OK, that sounds good. You ready to go to sleep?"

"Yeah. Goo-night, Dad."

Aug 2001, Melanie 4 yrs 4 mos

Homework for Babysister

Alexandra Ward, Darby Smith & Melanie Garlock, inseparable friends (L-R)

Friday is the big day. On Friday Melanie starts Pre-K, the *Big Kids' Class*. She is convinced this transition to an exalted high level will bring important changes in her life. Last Wednesday was Meet the Teacher night, and we all attended. Melanie and her best girlfriends Darby and Alex were like a triplex weapon, where each component is harmless but when mixed explosion occurs.

At age two Melanie came home with reports about Darbyalex and I thought this person had a strange name for a while before understanding she was talking about two people in the same thought, as in *a unit* sort of like the Three Musketeers, as the three of them are now well known. The school director knows, by bumps and scrapes at this point, that Melanie and Darby and Alex must be together, and any separation will result in outright war. These are not just playmates or acquaintances, you understand, but friends in the deepest sense of the word, where one can always count on loyalty and immediate acceptance, and when you are four it means being intoxicated with one another's company to the point of hysterical jumping at the first meeting every day and a hug goodbye at each parting.

While Darby is a *pistol*, loud and bright with high highs and low lows, Alex is more quiet and steady, always smiling and a little more low key. Melanie seems middle of the road, but I'm her Dad, not objective.

Melanie's unflagging friendship with Darby and Alex has resulted in our families becoming friends, trusted buddies who enjoy one another's company and who cover for each other when schedules and kid-stuff collide. We sometimes party and picnic and swim together, and the girls have started sleepovers, a bit early at four.

At the Teacher meeting, with the Three Musketeers' parents gathered as a group with the teacher, Darby's Mom Tracey Smith said to the new teacher "We apologize in advance for what our kids will do to you this year." I saluted her prediction, as the three kids tore to and fro in the room, bouncing off walls, cutting sharp corners and disrupting little pockets of parents who thought nothing of it, as if they had kids of their own.

One of these other preschool mothers told Julie how she never sent her daughter to school in a dress because the boys would try to get a look at her panties. Now, you have to understand that Melanie has attended this preschool since she was 14 months old, and Julie blurted out "Well, they've been peeing in the same toilet room side by side with no privacy for a long time, who cares if the boys look at their panties?" I guess there's a social lesson in there somewhere - as the kids get older we teach them the difference between boys and girls and all of a sudden the boys want to peek at panties when all along they've been seeing a lot more. Maybe that's where boys start to transform to pigs?

Pigs or not, boys will be in the big kids class, and Friday is the day. And since the two most important upcoming events in Melanie's life are starting pre-K in the big kids class and the expected arrival of her Babysister, her four year old mind wondered if perhaps they would happen at the same time. For weeks now she has been telling all her friends and teachers at school that she will bring home Babysister from China. And she is smart and observant enough to recognize it takes a lot of paperwork by Dad to bring home Babysister. So this morning before school Melanie asked me:

"Dad, will my Babysister be here Friday when I go to the Big Kids Class in pre-K?"

"No, I'm sorry, but it takes longer than that to bring home a baby sister."

"You mean when I'm five and I go to Kindergarten?"

"Yep, that's about how long it's going to take."

So Melanie disappeared to her room for a little while, and when I called her to go to school she emerged with some papers she had been scribbling on and I asked her what she was doing. She said :

"I'm doing my homework, Dad."

"Homework?"

"Yeah, you know, doing lots of homework so Babysister can come home faster."

Sep 2001, Melanie 4 yrs 5 mos

Cutting the Cheese

Thursday after I picked Melanie up from school we stopped on the golf cart to briefly visit Lindy Jennings and her new daughter, Gracie. This time Gracie was under the weather, and Lindy and I talked about the doctor's advice that the first year in the US may bring more *bugs* since many are new to the child, and after a year she will have built up resistance. That's certainly our experience with Melanie. Yet, while Melanie was touching Gracie I was thinking maybe she would pick up the bug herself.

So, just one day later, Melanie didn't feel well, and the pre-school called. When I picked her up early I asked Melanie what was wrong and she said "My stomach was wiggling, Dad, but it's OK now." Melanie's day brightened up considerably with a dish of ice cream and decadent chocolate sauce. Nurse Nancy may cringe, but it worked. My theory is that she picked up the bug, and didn't feel well while her system fought the battle and won.

Later on Melanie's friend Sammy's (Samantha) Mom Tanya called to invite Melanie to play on Saturday. I told Tanya Melanie had felt a little queasy but she felt much better now after ice cream. Tanya said "Well, I usually feel better after ice cream, don't you?" Good question.

So, Melanie played in her room while I finished up some work, and after a while she came to say she was bored and asked if I was done working yet. While I continued what I was doing with Melanie hanging on to my arm she said:

"Crows can pick your skin off."

"What?!"

"Crows can pick your skin off, Dad, they have sharp teeth."

"Where in the world did you hear that?"

"From China."

"What do you mean, from China."

"When I was in my birthmom's tummy, China told me -"

I interrupted her "Wait a minute! Are you sure about what you're saying?"

With a look of guilt mixed with amusement at being caught "Well, OK, not really, Dad."

"Did one of your friends tell you about crows?"

"Yeah."

"OK, but we don't make things up about your birthmom, OK."

"OK, Dad. You finished, now? Can we go wait for Mom to get home?"

Melanie has an active imagination, and I think there are imaginary friends involved. But all was forgotten when we ventured out on the golf cart and intercepted Mom's car on the way home, Melanie's favorite way to watch for her favorite person. On our street I made a U-turn to fall in safely behind Julie's car and Melanie says "*Yaaaay*, Mom's the Hind Leader!" Where she and her buddies came up with *Hind Leader* I'll never know, but she's used it for two years.

Mom was home and dinner was on the table, including a loaf of fresh French bread and some cheese. Since Melanie tummy was no longer wiggling she wanted some cheese and I started to cut it for her but stopped when she intervened with her flatware knife:

"*Noooo, Dad. I can do it. I know how to cut the cheese!*"

She certainly does.

Sep 2001, Melanie 4 yrs 5 mos

Melanie's Office

Melanie decorates Dad with a scarf and helps him work in his office

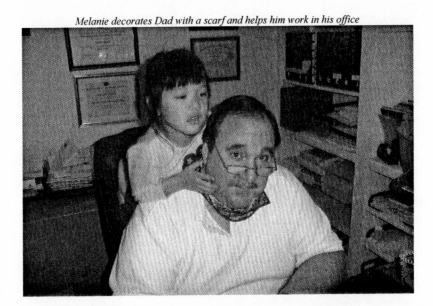

I bought a laptop computer to take on client visits and had the silly notion I would also continue using my desktop computer for daily work. I quickly came to my senses and decided to transfer everything to the laptop and remove the 19" monster footprint from my desk.

That same evening Melanie was sitting in my lap at my desk sharing a game of Pinball with me, manning one side of the laptop flippers, when suddenly she noticed something was missing.

"Dad, where's your old computer?"

"I took it apart. It's in the closet."

If you watched and listened carefully you could witness four-year-old gears turning at lightening speed in her head for a few seconds, followed by a question in a hushed, hopeful tone: "Can I have it?"

Having already made this decision I simply said "Yes."

Kaboom. *"Yaaaaay. I got my own computer. Lets set it up right now, Dad!"*

"No, your Mom and I need to go look for a desk for the computer before we set it up."

Melanie looked at me with astonishment "You mean a desk for *me*?"

"Yep, I sure do." I don't know how a grin that big fit on a face that small. And the next day we bought her a desk at Staples, a little more fancy than we had in mind but big enough for homework plus the 19" footprint, and with 10,000 parts and a 100-page assembly manual.

So, for parents-to-be, here's how it goes. A friend helped me lug the lead-filled desk box into the house, and when I sat down for a breather Melanie inquired:

"What are you doing, Dad? Come on, we gots to set up my desk, hurry up, OK?"

So Dad and Mom and Melanie embarked on a long task together, ultimately resulting in a nice, little two-ton desk for Melanie. As we took a breather Melanie inquired:

"What are you doing? Come on, we gots to set up my computer, hurry up, OK?"

And after setting up Melanie's computer, at her desk temporarily next to Mom's desk while the final destination in my office remains under construction, Melanie said with the most satisfaction I have ever heard:

"Wow. Daddy gots a desk and a computer, Mommy gots a desk and a computer, and now *Melanie* gots a desk and computer!" Sounds excessive, but Julie and I each need our home office and computer for work, and sharing would be ugly.

Mom bought Melanie a little desk chair on rollers in the most intense blue I have ever seen, Melanie's favorite color. While Melanie sits on that chair, feet far off the floor to be raised to desk height, she mimics Mom by hitting the keys with fingers, pretending to type a secret message to her buddies Darby and Alex, occasionally hitting a combination of keys that bring up things like Scandisk, MS Backup, or "Do you really want to format the hard drive?"

But she is learning things on the Little Bear and Reader Rabbit programs, and if we balance computer skills with learning programs and insisting on manual skills, too, we think it will be good for her.

A couple of days later while sitting on my lap gazing at her very own computer, Melanie confided:

"Dad, I don't want to be a grown-up."

"Why not?"

"'Cause if I grow up I have to move away. I want to stay a little kid and stay here with Mommy and Daddy."

Now that's hard to take.

What's even harder is the occasional reminder that this child, not some faceless little one lost among the numbers, but this very person, could have had a much different life, without much laughter or joy, without many of the things that make her the delightful kid she is. When Melanie says something like "Can I save this toy special for whenmybabysistercomes?" it all flashes through your mind in an instant, and sort of takes your breath away.

Sep 2001, Melanie 4 yrs 5 mos

Recycling Presents

Melanie received a present from a friend recently, and she handled it in a graceful way. At least the first part. She went with me to visit Mr. Rod, who supplied her with chocolate pudding and coke while we had a beer and discussed the merits of <u>Oh Brother Where Art Thou</u>, a movie I recorded off the satellite and brought to him.

Melanie told Mr. Rod "It's a dumb movie."

Rod asked "How do you know?"

"Cause my Mom says, and she's the boss."

Rod looked at me for a response, but I'm not riding that horse tonight. I told him to keep an open mind and remember Homer's <u>Odyssey</u> when he watched the movie.

Before we left Mr. Rod gave Melanie a box of chocolate candy, and she said thank you in a very proper way.

When we arrived home Melanie went straight to her little round table where she keeps her writing paraphernalia and colored Mr. Rod a thank-you note in her own unique style. As she always does she sealed the note in one of her little envelopes, then harassed me to take her to Mr. Rod's house *right now* to give him his *good note*. I told her she'd have to wait until tomorrow, which at four years old is like forever, and she finally convinced me to take her in the golf cart to let her put her note in Mr. Rod's mail box while not disturbing him, and our household had a moment's peace before bed. I was proud of her gracious response to Rod's gift.

Of course today things were a little different. After dinner Melanie prevailed on us to let her open the chocolates, which Julie knew she wouldn't like because she doesn't like anything with nuts in it. Just like Mom, wonder how that happened? Much to Melanie's dismay I helped her open the package. Of course I grabbed one and Melanie had a selfish moment in which she tried to take the box from me to protect her stash, but just for a moment. As soon as she and Mom tasted the nuts in the chocolate and found it not suited to their taste, Melanie tried to hand me the remnants of her bitten piece saying "Here, Dad, you can have the rest of it." Just like Mom.

No thanks. She put it in the trash as we told her, and a few minutes later my little darling came over, gave me a kiss, and while batting her eyes with more expertise than I care to think about announced with pride as she presented me with the chocolate box "I don't like it, Dad, now it's your present." I explained how we give gifts of things we *like*, not things we dislike, and that Mr. Rod gave her the chocolates because he liked her and it was a nice gift.

Melanie's said "I know, but I'm recycling the present, Dad."

She gives me chewed up soggy donuts and candy she spits out. At least I know where I stand. And that would be all alone in my house if I watch <u>Oh Brother Where Art Thou</u> again, which I will, however perverse is my enjoyment according to the women I work for.

Sep 2001, Melanie 4 yrs 5 mos

First Dental Exam

We let Melanie have too much bubblegum and sweets. So we were anxious about her first visit to the pediatric dentist for more than one reason. And Melanie knew only one thing - she was deeply afraid of going to the dentist.

So, a few weeks before her appointment I took her with me to my dentist for a cleaning. She stayed with me the whole time, staying just out of the way, peering curiously into my wide open mouth, with the hygienist explaining every step and every tool she used. Melanie was fascinated, and especially wanted to get her hands on the air-water squirter but kept her hands to herself as instructed. But, she was decidedly opposed to one thing she saw in my mouth at the cleaning - "bwood!"

I told her my mouth bleeds just a little when my teeth are cleaned because I'm older than dirt, but that hers would probably not bleed. She believed me.

So, on the morning of her appointment she was not afraid, and I think it's because much of the mystery was removed. But she didn't have much breakfast because we were in a hurry, and her only worry about being late for school was missing snack time. So I followed my instincts and told her "After we leave the dentist we'll get you a donut. Don't tell the dentist, OK?"

Never tell a kid not to tell something, it just makes their brain itch. It's like telling an adult "Don't think about sex." But she didn't tell. She was too distracted.

Dentistry has changed since I was a kid. There was a *theater* as a waiting room. Instead of individual rooms the treatment chairs were in a relatively open area with TV screens built into the ceiling. When Melanie climbed into a chair they laid it back flat, gave her earphones so she could follow the cartoon on the TV over her chair, and put on sunglasses so the dental light wouldn't interfere with her entertainment.

Joleen Cool! She did everything she was told, didn't flinch or complain once, had no cavities, and at the end she picked a trinket out of a bucket for being a good kid.

Mom and Dad were proud of her and she was walking tall. She asked:

"Dad, was there bwood?"

"Nope, no blood, not till you get old."

Now she wanted her donut. We had to waste a few minutes with a trip to the post office to give the fluoride treatment time to absorb before eating, and Julie was getting fidgety about getting to work on something with a deadline so I asked her as I was driving:

"Want to get a donut on the fly?" We could use the Dunkin Donuts drive-up window and Melanie could eat it as I drove her to school.

Julie said "Sure."

But from Melanie in the back seat came a protest "*No!*"

What? "What's wrong?"

"I don't want no flies on my donut. I not eating no flies, OK?"

"OK, we'll tell them to hold the flies on your donut."

Don't much like the taste of flies myself.

Sep 2001, Melanie 4 yrs 5 mos

Fishing

On a recent Sunday Julie needed some concentrated work time at her desk at home, and I needed to remove Melanie from the vicinity or there would be no concentration. So, I decided to take her fishing.

The very idea of the normal struggles of fishing just does not fit a four year old. But we had a better way, which of course is the only reason I considered fishing in the first place.

North of Atlanta, on highway 20 between Georgia 400 and 985 near Lake Lanier, just on the west bank of the Chattahoochee River, is a little place called the Rainbow Ranch: if you're curious, look up their website at www.rainbowranchtrout.com

At the Rainbow Ranch there is no waiting or struggle to fishing because their business is selling you the fish you catch!

At the grocery store the Rainbow Trout that has been lying in the cooler shelf for a week or two costs about $4/lb. At the Rainbow Ranch, where you cannot throw back anything, must buy all you catch, if you have them clean the fish and put them on ice for the trip home the cost comes to . . . just about $4/lb. But I got to drive a long way, have lunch with my daughter at the local upscale IHOP with the rest of the semi-rural Sunday crowd, and Melanie got to catch the fish.

The Ranch supplies the rods and reels already rigged, a water bucket, a net, a cup of worms and a cup of corn, all at no charge but if you get carried away you can spend the truck payment. They have several large ponds to fish from, a 1-lb pond, a 3-lb pond and a 5-lb pond, and at each the kids can watch a few hundred trout cruise the clear water surface waiting for lunch.

We started at the 1-lb pond. I hooked a kernel of corn and threw it out there and within 10 seconds had a 1.5 lb trout on the line. I quickly handed the rod to Melanie who was jumping up and down yelling "Gimme it, Dad, we gots a fish!" and stood behind her helping her hold the rod while she held her tongue sideways out her mouth and cranked the reel like a trooper. She shied away as the fish flopped around on the grass until I flipped it in the water bucket, but she couldn't help squatting to touching it with one careful finger every few seconds to feel the slime of the trout's protective coating.

OK, at 1.5 lbs that's $6 for the first minute, and if you do the math we couldn't afford to stay at the Ranch too darn long. But the second fish took about five minutes to hook after a snag and two smart trout who ate the corn but managed to throw the hook. And of course there's messing around in between like keeping Melanie back from the water's edge where she wanted to use the net to go after the bold trout that cruised right up to the bank. I decided we needed one more fish, and for that one we switched to the 3 lb pond. These older fish are smarter, apparently, because it took a number of tries and a little deeper rig to outsmart them and hook a fish. So Melanie had the excitement of reeling in a 3.5 lb beauty, then off we went to have them cleaned before my wallet gets emptied. But really it was no more expensive than the grocery store, the fish were fresh and she had a blast.

I thought maybe Melanie would freak out as she watched the guy gut and clean the fish she just caught, but she was only curious, struggling to get closer and closer to watch through the screen while she sipped a root beer. When we arrived home Julie had completed her work and Melanie proudly displayed her catch to Mom, and then to Ms. Liz next door since I invited her to come over and take home a fish for dinner. As the ladies marveled over the size of the fish, Melanie and I exchanged the knowing glances that you can only have if you caught these fish your very own self.

Sep 2001, Melanie 4 yrs 5 mos

Melanie Throwed Up

Today I arrived home a little late after stopping at the wine store with a friend to pick up a mixed case of reds. When I dropped him off, well, we got into a bottle for a taste and had to finish it.

When I walked through the door with the case in my hands Melanie shouted "*Dad*!" and ran to hug my leg and made it difficult to walk into the kitchen.

"*Dad, I threw up!*"

"What?"

"Read the note, Dad!"

Primrose school completes an incident note whenever something happens the parents should know about, and this one said Melanie twirled around on a swing too much and then threw up. She was obviously very proud of this passage.

"So, 'twirl-till-you-puke', just like the county fair."

"Yeah, Dad, it was gross. I told Tyler to stop pushing me in a circle but he wouldn't so I threwed up."

"Who's Tyler?" I asked even though I know.

"He's Elizabeth's boyfriend. He wants to be my boyfriend, too but I told Chas you can't marry two girls."

"Well, OK."

I noticed Melanie's Blankie with holes all over it. This is not just any blankie, this is Blankie, a real name, a real character, a real friend who she talks to and has been there since the beginning, the day she arrived home at 12 months. Blankie is so worn by now I kid her I need to bury Blankie in the back yard. Don't have a cow, it's good-natured kidding.

"Blankie's looking pretty rugged. Maybe it's time we bury him in the back yard."

Now Melanie at four and one half is starting to get leggy, and she scooted with little effort from her step to the top of the kitchen counter, standing with hands on hips, bent at the waist to touch her nose to mine and ask with fierce eyes in a threatening way:

"*E X C U S E M E?*"

Don't mess with her Blankie.

Oct 2001, Melanie 4 yrs 6 mos

Good Neighbors

A few weeks ago at a neighbor's house for a dinner party I was reminded how fortunate we are to have such good neighbors. Of course we have known that from the beginning, and it's a good lesson for Melanie.

The day we moved in the new Santolina Park subdivision of Peachtree City long before Melanie, a neighbor named Walt brought over a cooler of cokes while we were humping boxes and introduced himself. Nice guy, weird laugh, a bit strange I thought. Turned out to be my golf partner for years, and he's even stranger than I thought at first but a great friend even though he has now moved away. When we were settled into our house we threw a cocktail party and a bunch of new neighbors had the opportunity to meet us and one another. Someone else threw a BBQ, and the beat goes on and on.

Over the years we have had countless social encounters with our neighbors, block parties, golf tournaments, cookouts, and lots of chance encounters that lead to a gaggle of golf carts gathered on someone's front lawn while we gab and have refreshments on a summer evening. We have even joined one another at four funerals.

On the 4th of July each year there's a morning golf cart traffic jam on the paths thru the woods enroute to the parade, and a jillion golf carts lining the parade route, then another jam on the way home. In the evening on the 4th our neighborhood has an impromptu gathering for the fireworks outing, golf carts lined up and when the time comes we all take off together headed for the golf course # 3 fairway close to the green, where we join a few thousand others.

Last year at the fairway waiting for fireworks I encountered a friend from another subdivision and introduced him to our neighbor group. He asked me later who these nice people were because we seemed pretty close and was surprised we were all neighbors. He said nobody on his block ever does anything together, everybody just stays in their house and to themselves. I asked him if he ever invited a group of them over and he said no, they never invited him so the heck with them. Hmmmm.

In 1997 when we started our wait to adopt Melanie we sent a detailed letter to family, friends and neighbors about our adoption, our hopes and dreams, and by doing so invited them to be part of the process. Our neighbors responded in a most gracious way, with gifts, a baby shower, help while we were gone to China, and when we returned they invited Melanie into their homes and their hearts.

So at the recent dinner party a whole bunch of kids were playing outside and every once in a while Melanie would rush through the house breathing hard with eyes glowing in the excitement of kid play. Because she's younger we watched to make sure she's OK and I asked the kids to make sure she stays out of the street. Strange as it may sound I can trust these kids to watch out for her in the front yard as they kick the soccer ball around, in the back yard as they jump on the trampoline and hold Melanie on the sideline lest she get hurt, and on the swing. They may argue and banter during their play, but they all look after Melanie.

At dinner Melanie sat at the kid table, the littlest one, enraptured to be part of the big kids group, paying not much attention to Mom or Dad as we enjoyed our dinner with friends. Unusual. And later, after the conversation died and we said our goodbyes and yelled outside to Melanie that it's time to go, she started toward us but was stopped as each one of the kids in turn gave her a hug and said goodbye.

Good neighbors. One of God's blessings.

Oct 2001, Melanie 4 yrs 6 mos

Skuffy Did It

I've told you before how Melanie likes to crawl up in my lap and pull all 6 of my chest hairs, watching my eyes closely for the first sign of pain, which is the point. But now she has sort of expanded her horizons. Now she runs her hands down inside the neck of my T-shirt and feels around and then announces *"Mooooom, Dad gots boobs!"*

Now just try to tell a four year old it's not dignified to say that out loud, whether it's true or not, especially while Mom is laughing so hard she cries. And I was sitting down, a position that intensifies your fat as everyone knows.

Not only does she talk about Dad's boobs, she questions my intelligence. At pre-K the kids get a homework folder on Fridays, and Julie and I take turns supervising her homework. If there's any doubt who Melanie likes best it disappears when my turn comes and she whines to Mom:

"But Daddy's too oooold, Mom, he don't know how to do homework!" Thanks a lot, but even I can figure out how to write your name three times. Of course what she really means is she wants Mom to help her because Mom is her best friend. So it's like just an *oblique* stab to the heart, nothing personal. If Rodney Dangerfield needs new material, he should come over for a while.

But if Melanie is merciless, she makes up for it in part by being very clever. I don't know if it's a by-product of being an only child, but Melanie has more than one imaginary friend. Skuffy is the one I know about. The other day while descending the stairs with Mom Melanie pootered - that's kid-talk for fart. Mom looked at her and Melanie said "That wasn't me, Mom, it was Skuffy!"

That's my girl.

Oct 2001, Melanie 4 yrs 6 mos

Picking Mom's Food

Today on the way home with Melanie from the grocery store, I passed a workman at a new building in the shopping center, lowered my window and asked about the new business. KFC, he said. Not even on my food radar screen, sorry I don't like KFC.

Melanie says "What's that building going to be, Dad?"

"Kentucky Fried Chicken."

"Yaaay! Dad, is Tucky Fried Chicken good?"

"Well, some people think so, but not me."

"Dad, lets not eat there. Lets eat at the pick-your-food place."

"What?"

"Lets eat at the place where you pick your food, Dad."

She means the buffet. She's been to two of them and to my surprise she liked being able to browse different foods and select what she wants, especially the dessert ice cream bar.

A friend, who Melanie calls Mr. Rod, likes some buffets, and when it's time to decide where we're going to eat he's enthusiastic about the Grand Buffet (Chinese) in Fayetteville or Morrow, and the Golden Corral, or GC as he calls it, in Newnan, Georgia. Rod can talk longer than you can listen recalling stories of his office crew assaulting the GC at lunch, when constructing dessert combinations was serious competition, and so on until you beg for mercy or give up and say "OK, for Pete's sake, lets go eat at the GC."

Rod and my Dad would have found common ground in buffets. Dad was always eager at the table, and unfortunately my profile testifies to his influence on me in the food arena. Dad loved anything with the whiff of a bargain, and he didn't appreciate it one bit when some wise guy - that means me - pointed out it wasn't really a bargain at all. Just the idea of all-you-can-eat made Dad a little frantic close to mealtime, and in later years when he couldn't even finish a normal plate he still glowed at the thought of a buffet.

When I was growing up, when we had a church group or friends or visiting relatives for a meal excursion, Mom occasionally tried to steer toward a decent restaurant with fine food, but Dad always rushed in to the rescue, eager to share the real food-pile secrets at his favorite spots, strutting proudly the whole way while brushing off protests as if they were insignificant gnats, and anyone who had been through it before rolled their eyes and went along to their fate because there was no debating with Dad when he was right and everyone else was wrong. Critical feedback went right over his head with no effect. Dad apparently assumed anyone who didn't share his enthusiasm had not properly experienced buffets and he committed himself to show them the way with repeated trips. No thanks required, just doing his part for humanity. I rolled my eyes a lot.

Now me, I mostly agree with Alan Stein, a co-worker at Price Waterhouse in Dallas over 20 years ago. One of the other guys loved Pancho's, a Tex-Mex buffet, mostly because it was cheap. Once every week or two he'd round us all up for a group lunch pig-out at Pancho's, and Alan summed it up like this: "It's not worth a *$#%!, but you can have all of it you want!" When you've been to as many buffets as I have when I was growing up you develop code words, and I call buffets "shovel food," meaning quality is an unintended accident, it's all about quantity, which I could do without for, well, the rest of my life. But even I must admit Mr. Rod's two buffets are pretty good, and Melanie is a new convert since she gets to select exactly what she wants on her plate.

All that flashed through my head in two seconds. I answered Melanie: "We can eat dinner where you pick your own food sometime, but not tonight, OK?"

"OK. Can Mom go, too?"

"Well, Mom doesn't like buffets." 'Despise' or 'Loathe' would be better words, but I softened it up for Melanie.

"What's a buffet, Dad? I talking about the pick-your-food place!"

"A buffet is what you call a place where you pick out your own food."

"Ooohhh. Why Mom don't like a buffet, Dad?"

"She likes to be served, she doesn't like to pick out her own food. Maybe you and I can go again with Mr. Rod sometime soon when Mom's working late."

"But Dad, I want Mom to go. She'll like it, you and I can pick out her food for her and she'll be happy, OK?"

With a very satisfied look, Melanie was pleased with herself for solving the problem so her favorite person in the world could be beside her when she once again explored the exotic delights of the pick-your-food place. And if Dad was watching from heaven he would be proud of his granddaughter, not only of her wisdom in food selection, but her instant creativity in squashing any objection to what must surely be God's invention, a buffet.

Oct 2001, Melanie 4 yrs 6 mos

Discovering Poetry

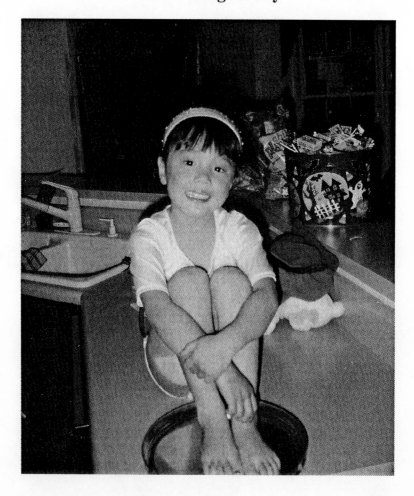

Sisters Redeem Their Grumpy Dad

Last year near Halloween, Melanie at age three learned her first poem from Mom:

Trick or treat,
smell my feet,
give me something good to eat.

Yesterday Melanie, at age four, embellished:

Trick or treat,
smell my feet,
give me something good to eat.
If you don't,
I don't care,
I'll pull down your underwear!

Now I assume she heard this at pre-school, where all manner of noxious and rebellious chants percolate in very receptive pre-school heads. But it is possible, just possible that she embellished on her own. After all, it's a takeoff on the most recent gift she shared with us from pre-school:

I see London,
I see France,
I see Daddy's underpants.
Are they purple,
are they pink?
They just *stink*!

And of course they are convinced this literature is new to the art world, never before uttered, originally crafted within their own little band of budding artists.
Shakespeare, move over.

Oct 2001, Melanie 4 yrs 6 mos

Futility at the Office

Have you ever renovated your house? While you try to work at home? Well, we're adding a room, actually a new office for me to make room for Babysister next year. So while I've tried to get some things done the last week there have been workmen crawling all over the house and each other, beating and banging and commiserating the way workmen do with radios blaring on their favorite station, oblivious to whether they are intruding on the comfort of the owners.

The trash bin in the driveway is literally 25 feet long, 6 feet high and 8 feet wide, delivered and deposited alongside a port-a-potty by a monster truck. I asked the driver if he had a bigger one in case I wanted to haul the house away in one piece instead of two but I think he'd heard it before.

Yesterday they removed the port-a-potty as I requested *before Halloween* since I didn't want a mess when pranksters tip it over, and it was to be a quiet day construction-wise so I planned to get some things done in the office. You can guess my reaction when after just an hour at work Melanie's pre-school director called at 9:30AM to say Melanie had a rash on her belly and had to go to the doctor to see if it was something contagious. Yippee.

The rash looked to me like just some dry skin, but the doctor said keep her home today, if it doesn't spread take her back to school tomorrow. Wonderful. There were a few things I *had* to do so I took Melanie home and sat her down in my old office with me to keep her away from the drywall guys who were tape-and-bedding downstairs in my new office and upstairs in an alcove we're converting to a closet. She watched cartoons while I did what I had to get done in a short time. As I commiserated with a broker-dealer on the pathetic current yield on corporate AAA bonds, Melanie yelled "Hey Dad, turn up the TV, I can't hear Rollie Pollie Ollie!"

So much for business. Wrap it up, give it up, go do something Melanie would like.

"Melanie, want to go see a movie?"

"Dad, you mean at the movie show theater?"

"Yup."

"Yaaay! What movie we see, Dad?"

As I found on the internet, the only movie playing she would like was <u>Shrek</u>. Melanie had seen it before, but that was good news because she likes it better each time she sees a movie because she knows what is happening.

"We'll go see <u>Shrek</u>."

"Yaaaay! I like <u>Shrek</u>, you like <u>Shrek</u>, Dad?"

"Sure, I love <u>Shrek</u>." Why, more than one person has thought of me as an ogre, too, and it fits with my Grump image. He's almost kin.

For lunch we stopped at the malt shop next door to the theater. I figured why not go all the way and ordered Melanie a chocolate milk shake with her grilled cheese, and she sucked it down so hard I thought she might hurt herself or demolish the heavy-duty straw, and at the end while her straw loudly slurped the sound that Julie calls "French for all gone" I tilted the glass so she could get the last little bit. Melanie wiped her mouth, swung her feet, sat back with a satisfied look and pronounced "Dad, I'm having the time of my life!" What do you know?

Melanie marched into the theater, ready for the show. But I've been around long enough to anticipate unpleasant interruptions so I asked:

"Melanie, you need to go potty?"

"No . . . wellll, maybe, OK, yeah, Dad." So I headed for the men's room and picked her up since I want to be in control when I take her in there.

"No, Dad, the lady's room is over there!"

"Yeah, but I can't go in there."

"OK, we'll go in your bathroom."

And once in the stall Melanie told me I better hurry and when I put paper down and lifted her on the potty she breathed a sigh of relief: "Wow, that was close, Dad!"

Another crisis averted.

So we washed our hands and bought some sour wormys and mints, and off to see <u>Shrek</u>. Melanie crawled all over her chair, me, the seats in front of us, fidgeting as kids do, but during scary parts of the movie she was all over me. She clapped when the dragon ate the slimy little king, and all was right in her kid world for just a while.

On the way home she said she was happy to spend time with me but really wanted to see Mom now, thank you very much, and when Mom arrived while we were on the deck, me cooking dinner on the grill and Melanie cooking sawdust dinner in her playhouse, she offered Mom a plate of sawdust which Mom accepted graciously and pretended to eat, capping off Melanie's day of adventure, rash on her belly forgotten, oblivious to the fact that Dad would regroup and try to get a day's work done again tomorrow on a day when in a kids house it will be impossible because, after all, tomorrow is Halloween.

Oct 2001, Melanie 4 yrs 6 mos

The Cinderella Dress

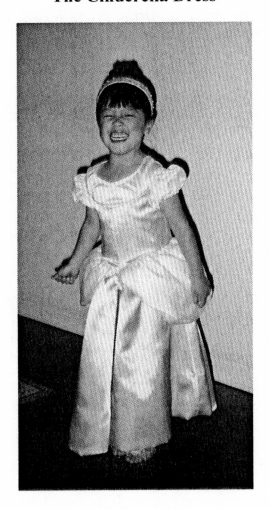

It's November with Thanksgiving approaching, a holiday Melanie doesn't much care for, and she's still chewing on the Halloween stash we let her dip into a piece at a time.

In past Halloweens Melanie has been a clown, a Teletubbie despite my protests, and Cinderella's Fairy Godmother. This year she went all the way, decided early on to be Cinderella herself.

Mom bought an elaborate pattern for the Cinderella dress, dusted off the sewing machine, bought exotic materials and began to spend every waking hour of home time cutting and sewing and measuring and whatever. Early morning, late night, and while Melanie played on weekends Julie focused like a laser on the dress and I knew to stay out of her way because that laser burns flesh if it's crossed.

At one point, from beyond laser range, I told her if she placed much value on her time that dress must be worth a fortune. Julie confided, in rare agreement, that Melanie might have to get married in that dress. But I was proud of her, unfailingly devoted to climb any mountain to deliver on her promise to her little girl.

Of course kids are oblivious to parental sacrifice and Melanie took it all in stride, as if this dress were her birthright. Then one day, after all the waiting and planning, all the whispers and questions and planting goblins in the front yard, as her eyes first opened in the morning while Mom showered and Dad picked her up out of bed, she suddenly startled herself fully awake with the realization that this was Halloween morning. The Big Day.

Julie and I left work early to arrive at the Primrose pre-school at 2:30 PM with Cinderella's new dress for the traditional kids costumed parade in front of parents, a prelude to trick-or-treat. While I talked with other dads in the parking lot Julie put Melanie's hair *up* with a sparkly headband, put on her clear plastic shoes for *glass slippers* and helped her into *the dress*, complete with hand-made matching bows.

At 3:00 PM all the kids in the pre-school started their parade through the parking lot in their Halloween getup. We jockeyed for position to take just the right photo while the kids self-consciously pranced in line following the leader. There were several Cinderellas, but I had my eye on Melanie, stepping carefully, holding her satin dress just so, with her gorgeous hair up in the back like a regal princess showing her tiny porcelain ears, and I wondered if her date for the prom would have a bolt through his tongue among other things and whether I should clean the shotgun. Then a kid in a cowboy suit stumbled and bawled to interrupt the parade and bring me back to the present.

As Melanie finished the course and came over to me, I remembered she had confided to Mom that her skin was darker than some other Cinderellas she knew and she was afraid she might not be as pretty as they are. We teach Melanie that God made each of us different but that all kinds of people are beautiful. But kids are self-conscious, and if they don't have a good reason to be uncertain of themselves they often invent a reason.

So I whispered in her ear:

"How many Cinderella's were there?"

"Lets see, Darby was a Cinderella, and Alex was going to be a Cinderella but she changed her mind to be a clown and that's OK to be a clown isn't it Dad?"

"Sure it is, but there were a bunch of other Cinderella's, weren't there?"

"Yeah."

"Do you know who was the prettiest Cinderella of all?"

She smiled, illuminating a perimeter of 30 feet, knowing my answer, pointed her thumb to her own chest and said "*Me*!"

"That's right, you."

So that evening after a hasty and unwilling meal Melanie suited up in her $100,000 dress for battle. Her friend Taylor Darnell came over from two houses down the street and Julie took them both to trick-or-treat in the golf cart while I sat on the front steps in the balmy weather to hand out goodies. Melanie is a favorite of the older kids in the neighborhood, some of whom serve as her babysitter occasionally, and when they passed in golf carts they yelled "Heyyyy, Melanie!" She had a grand time waving and soaking up the admiration of her friend Taylor because the Big Kids knew her and liked her enough to speak to her.

Now I don't know if this was a strategic success or a fortuitous accident, but as they stopped at a house Melanie would ask Mom who lived there. In front of Dick and Pat Ogden's house Mom said "That's Mr. and Mrs. Ogden's house." So Melanie would ring the doorbell and say "Trick or treat, hi Mrs. Ogden, it's me, Melanie!" So, since we all like the flattery of being recognized by name, Mrs. Ogden would give Melanie an overdose of goodies for her bag, then Melanie moved on to another unwitting victim.

When the many trick-or-treat trips were done, Melanie couldn't quite sit down or stay still, she was on fire, enjoying it all and not wanting it to be over. Finally she brought her loot into the family room and dumped it all on the floor, because Mom had to inspect it to see what if anything to discard before Melanie ate any, and Melanie rummaged through it at double-speed, anxious at what part of her treasure may not pass inspection. Her treasure survived, and Mom let her eat a couple of candies just before she crashed, not a good habit but it's once per kid-year, Halloween over at last.

Which brings me back to Thanksgiving. You see, a kid's year is divided into four parts: Halloween, Christmas, Easter and birthday. Thanksgiving is a good thing since Melanie gets to see Grandma Lois and Aunt Vicki and Aunt Betty and eat turkey along with her favorite food in the whole world - mashed potatoes and gravy. But in Melanie's mind Thanksgiving is just slowing down Christmas, an obstacle, an impediment, and if it were not in the way Santa would surely be here sooner.

So she'll enjoy the holiday but not the wait until it gets here. That's how things are in Melanie's world as she waits for Babysister and makes plans to introduce her to the thrill of Halloween.

Nov 2001, Melanie 4 yrs 7 mos

Melanie's Budget

Last year when Melanie was four, she received her first weekly allowance of $4, $1 for each year of her age. She gets to spend $2 and saves $1 for herself and $1 to spend on others. Needless to say, she likes the Friday evening allowance ritual, though she has to help Mom with chores to earn it. But she's learning something that may be even more important than responsibility for chores.

At first she wanted to buy more than her allowance would sustain because she had no idea how much things cost. Mom is her confidant and consultant since she has learned to ask "Mom, how many weeks do I have to save to buy _____?" When Mom tells her how many weeks Melanie might observe "Wow, that costs a lot, huh, Mom?"

At one point she wanted to buy a silly game called <u>Operation</u>, a battery driven game with a board with an image of a man where you pick organs, like livers and brains, out of little pockets with tweezers. If you are careful and don't ouch the sides, you win, but if you touch the sides it lights up and buzzes, which excites the kids while parents harbor private thoughts about dead patients in the operating room. <u>Operation</u> costs about $15, and it would have been so easy to buy it for her. But since she was shopping with her allowance Mom stuck to her guns and told her how many weeks she'd have to save, and to my surprise she did. I thought it was great she was willing at four years old to delay her gratification, though she strayed to other things as the weeks went by. A kid's memory can only sustain so many things at a time.

One thing Melanie loves to buy and Mom and Dad love to help her buy is a book. Berenstein Bears is her favorite right now, and later she will discover Junie B. Jones. They make good lessons from bedtime story-reading.

Julie and I have both been avid readers since adolescence. I have encountered many people in my life who don't understand that, say

"The last time I read a book was, gee, I forget, but I'm really busy and just don't have the time." They don't understand how we read before sleep every night, no matter how late or tired, because it seems to them like a chore while it's really a source of personal pleasure, a personal indulgence we each refuse to give up. Now Melanie shares our passion.

Sometimes at the grocery store Melanie likes to pull a familiar string by asking "Dad, can I have a treat?" By which she means candy. I sometimes answer "Would you rather have a treat or a new book?" and she always chooses a book. I'd rather spend $5 on a book than $1 on candy. The other option of course is "no" and she gets that sometimes to avoid, as described well in a Berenstein Bears lesson, a case of the 'galloping gimmies.' When we return home Melanie is anxious until one of us reads her new book to her. And with a memory unlike any I've seen, she can then read the book back to you with surprisingly few errors.

Speaking of buying things for kids, Christmas looms on the horizon. It has always troubled me how many goodies kids pile up at Christmas, with ever-escalating expectations and a long list of people scrambling to fulfill their every desire, some eagerly and some reluctantly just because it's expected no matter the budgetary strain. That's why Julie calls me a Grinch. To me the scramble for *bigger, better, faster, more* at Christmas is nothing less than obscene juxtaposed against the specter of families with little, lonely elderly and neglected folks in a nursing home, and others with a real need, while everyone's too busy with the galloping gimmies or feeding someone else's gimmies to care. The excessive indulgence, fueled by encouragement of oblivious parents having fun watching their kids having fun making a Santa list five feet long, pushes me to Grinchdom annually, and I enjoyed the movie with perhaps a unique perspective. All I need is a cave.

A few weeks ago I was quietly disappointed when Melanie emulated her school friends by starting on her Santa's list, dictating to Mom since her writing cannot yet be read by anyone else. To say my admonishment about *gimme lists* was rejected is being overly polite.

But yesterday I was pleasantly surprised. With Julie's complete denial it had anything to do with me, after all I have no influence in some things, like Christmas, Melanie informed me she could only have two things on her Santa list. She started out with a baby doll and playdough. And then it happened. With a stroke of pre-school mathematical insight, Melanie asked Mom how much playdough cost, and finding it was cheap, and that she could buy the playdough with her allowance and stick Santa with a big tab for things her allowance could not buy, she revised her list. I think she might be smarter than me. She already bought the playdough and is consulting with Mom on just the right things to ask for on her Santa list.

Before kids I thought I'd be able to limit the gift deluge on Christmas, birthdays, etc., not to limit Melanie so much as to prevent her character from being sullied by the rot of inappropriate expectations. But I didn't count on the overpowering resistance of Julie and Grandma Shirley, both of whom think I'm merely out of my mind to put a damper on all the fun. I even proposed to Julie letting relatives know how to contribute to Melanie's college fund as an alternative to gifts but she didn't like that idea since others might think we were asking for money and that they'd just write a check *in addition* to buying a gift anyway. Maybe she's right. But while others delight in eye-popping piles of gifts waiting to be unwrapped at Christmas, the bigger the better, I feel a strange urge to haul it all off to a snowy mountaintop cave. What a bunch of Whoos!

I am grateful Melanie's list is limited to two things. She'll be tested as she observes the endless list she sees from her friends, but maybe there's hope. You'll know it got unbearably worse if you hear I've been arrested for stealing presents and trees and ornaments in the dead of night.

Nov 2001, Melanie 4 yrs 7 mos

A Big Heart

Julie and I have a head cold, and last night Julie was drooping and agreed to my suggestion that she hit the guest-room bed early, so she would be undisturbed. Later, I would put Melanie to bed. The wild card was Melanie, who reacts emotionally when Mom is removed from her presence and her routine. She cried for a little while, because she wanted Mom not Dad to help her go to sleep, but mostly just because she loves Mom more than anything in the world and likes to be with her.

A half hour of watching Lulu on HBO made her tears forgotten, and we crept quietly upstairs where I read two books to her while she had her bedtime sippy cup, this time with peach tea. I promised to wait until she was asleep to put her in her bed so she wouldn't be bothered by my snoring or the monsters she swears are under her bed. As she became drowsy she said:

"Dad, sorry I didn't want you I not hurt your feelings I just want Mom."

"I know."

"You know who has a big piece of my heart, Dad?"

"Who?"

"You and Mom and Babysister!"

"That's nice."

"You and Mom and Babysister have a big piece of my heart cause we're a fambly, right, Dad?"

"That's right."

"But not other people, they not in my heart cause they not fambly, right, Dad?"

"Well, what about your two grandmas and aunts and uncles?"

"Oh, yeah, them too, and we going to see Grandma Lois and Aunt Betty and Aunt Vicki in Florida tomorrow!"

"That's right, but we can't see Aunt Betty because Mom and I have a cold and if she catches it she'll be really sick."

"What about me, I don't have a cold, why can't I see Aunt Betty?"

"Well, maybe you can. Maybe I could drop you off to see her for a while?"

"And Grandma Lois, too?"

"Don't know, we'll see."

"So I got room in my heart for other fambly too but not other people."

Aunt Vicki

"What about your friends, Alex and Darby and others friends?"

"Oh, yeah, them too, but not a big piece of my heart or there not any left!"

"There's room in your heart for lots of people. The more friends you have the bigger your heart grows."

"Yeah, but you and Mom and Babysister gots the biggest piece. What will I do when Babysister keeps me awake?"

"Maybe you can help her go to sleep and not be scared of monsters."

"Is Babysister going to sleep in my room?"

"Yep, we'll keep the other bedroom for a playroom, at least for a little while."

"She can play with my toys and read my books and I'll teach her how to go to sleep."

"That's good. Maybe you could practice going to sleep right now."

"OK. Good night Dad, I love you."

"Love you too."

I think her heart has plenty of room.

Nov 2001, Melanie 4 yrs 7 mos

A Cry for Help

Until you have a child, I have discovered, there are parts of you unknown and mysteriously dormant, awaiting to be waked by a genetic tug only your kid can provide. For fathers, the sound of your child saying "Daddy" is apparently a magic code for the release of unique hormones into your bloodstream that supplies a natural high. And until you watch your child's face morph to terror of a real or imagined threat, mixed with a plea of "Daddy!" you cannot know the instantaneous adrenaline infusion that makes you ready to lift cars, rip arms from bodies or stop bullets to protect your little one.

Melanie's terror has come several times from Daisy, a hyper but harmless dog next door, a dog she likes to pet but is scared by when Daisy first tears around a corner running to lick Melanie's face. When Melanie's eyes flash wide open and her mouth twists to fear and she yells "Daddy!" you better not get between me and her or you're going to get hurt.

Now, seemingly unrelated is the fact that I can't hear worth a flip. At the age of 20 on the US Army pistol range firing a .45 I ruined my hearing which has been deteriorating ever since. Even though I can't help it Julie seems to blame me for willful neglect when I don't hear what she is mumbling . . er . . saying to me. And it's convenient if I don't like what is being said to me to pretend not to hear, so maybe that has something to do with it. There are exceptions. I may sleep through various noises in the night, but when Melanie whimpers in her room my eyes pop open, though Julie is almost always already there.

So last night before Mom got home from work I was in my office and Melanie was in the master bedroom watching cartoons and she had pushed the door closed for some reason. Through the concentration on my work I heard a faint noise that set off a subconscious alarm but I didn't know what it was for an instant, then realized it was the very faint tail end of a kid-scream "Daddddyyyy!" finished off with an angry screech at the top of Melanie's lungs to ensure her impatience with my non-response was noted. I tore out of my office and into the bedroom, didn't see Melanie anywhere and yelled "Where are you?" She answered "In here, Daddy."

I found her perched on the toilet, pants around her ankles but feet up in the air. I asked what was wrong and she said she thought she saw a bug on the floor. No ambulance this time. The bug search yielded an all-clear. Melanie finished her business and went back to cartoons. I put my heart back in my chest.

Nov 2001, Melanie 4 yrs 7 mos

Melanie Calls Santa Names

Melanie's Max

Imagine Melanie at four years old, sitting on the front steps holding a bag of canned goods waiting patiently for Santa's fire truck to drive through the neighborhood with siren blaring to collect cans for the food bank. She showed me a piece of paper she had in her hand.

"It's my Christmas list, Dad." Of course it was readable only by her, and presumably Santa.

"What's on the list?"

"A Grinch and a Max and a Shoo-Shoo Baby."

Hmmm. "I thought you could only put two things on your list, that's three."

"Uh-uuuh! Grinch and Max only count one cause they together."

OK, Max is the Grinch's dog.

"How long you going to wait for Santa?"

"Till Mom's haircut."

Julie had a noon hair appointment and Melanie insisted on going with her while I watched Army stomp Navy. When they returned Julie said they ran into Santa at the salon.

"Dad, you know what, Santa's a booger-sneaker!"

"What?"

"Santa'a a booger-sneaker, Mom said."

So I asked Julie about Santa the booger sneaker and she said when Melanie saw Santa in the parking lot *and* in the salon she asked Mom how Santa could be in two places at one time. Julie told her Santa was a sneaky booger.

At four years old, close enough.

Dec 2001, Melanie 4 yrs 8 mos

Melanie the Angel
By Julie Garlock

At our Christmas party for a group of families with adopted Chinese children, Lindy Jennings organized an *Angel Tree* with donation envelopes, proceeds going to Half the Sky Foundation to benefit Chinese orphanages. Lindy reported by e-mail to our group that donations totaled $202.

It gave me a chuckle to read that we had collected $202, but then I teared up and burst with a little bit of pride. I attribute the "$2" to Melanie. Terry and I have been working on teaching her the value of money and to be charitable through an allowance system. She gets $5 per week when she does her chores, but has to save $2 of that for herself or to spend on others. Melanie chose by herself on Saturday to put $2 of her allowance in an angel envelope. Maybe she is learning some of what we're trying to teach her, and we're proud of her.

Julie Garlock

Dec 2001, Melanie 4 yrs 8 mos

Melanie Asks About Boys

If you're sensitive, maybe you better skip this one.

This weekend Mom and Melanie transformed our house into a Christmas emporium with lights, decorations and doo-dads everywhere except hanging off me, but I haven't used a mirror to check my rear so I wouldn't bet. They had lots of fun. My job during holiday decoration time is to stay out of the way and keep my thoughts to myself, which suits me just fine. But Julie graciously permitted me to buy her a stepladder ten feet tall so she can reach higher and can now hang lights on the gutters in front of the house while I silently hold the ladder steady. If we didn't have a cavernous basement for all this stuff I'd have to rent a mini-warehouse.

But there wasn't time to get quite all of it done and Mom and Melanie planned to finish off the tree Monday, or yesterday. And in addition to doo-dad boxes scattered all over, the workmen yesterday tore out our kitchen countertop for the final step of renovation after new room construction, new kitchen floor and new carpet - Julie's sparkly black Silostone countertops are to be installed next week. Since the house is a wreck, when I picked up Melanie yesterday I told her we would buy something to take home for dinner.

"For Mom, too, Dad?"

"Of course, we wouldn't forget Mom."

"Mom never forgets you, Dad."

"That's right, we always remember each other and Melanie, too."

"Dad, why boys have to use a long hose when they go pee-pee?"

Now, here's where most child therapists would lock me up and throw away the key, since my first thought was uh-oh, how do I get out of this, and my second thought was how much fun I could have with that "long" part, but it's way out of bounds with any kid much less your own and the humor would be lost on Melanie anyway. So I went with my third thought.

"Because that's how little boys are made."

"'Cause God made us and we're all God's children, right, Dad?"
"That's right."
"Dad, hurry up, I gots to go to the bathroom real bad."
"OK." So maybe that's what made her think of plumbing.

Dec 2001, Melanie 4 yrs 8 mos

The Pinkie Promise

For us, the holiday season is finally here. Yesterday Melanie was picked up from pre-school by her buddy Alex's Mom, and she had several hours to play at full speed. Meanwhile Julie was working hard and I picked up her mother, Melanie's Grandma Shirley, at Atlanta Hartsfield Airport. I usually pick her up at curbside since she has one bag on rollers and it's easy for both of us, but with new security procedures making it more difficult to wait at curbside I parked and went in to meet her at the baggage claim area.

At the main entrance from the concourses to the baggage area I and a dozen others looking for their party stood waiting where traffic would pass close by, where we would surely be seen if we did not see, like bass waiting for shiners where a creek empties into a lake. I'm pretty hard to miss, so I stood confidently reading the latest wisdom from the best op-ed page in the world in the Wall Street Journal. Something didn't work.

Shirley missed me and I missed Shirley, and by the time I spotted her on my second pass around baggage claim she had been waiting a little while. Back to curbside next time.

Anyway, Julie, Grandma and I arrived at the appointed time at Alex's house and Melanie, wound tighter than a piano wire, met us jumping at the front door, eyes aglow and panting with the exertion of very good play. She jumped right into Grandma Shirley's arms, legs wrapped around her waist, no longer a toddler.

The kids played while we talked to Alex's Mom and Dad over holiday cheer, the kids exchanged small gifts since Alex's family is gone for the holidays and then we said our goodbyes, finally settling in for a night's sleep.

This morning Grandma Shirley wouldn't hear of Melanie, her buddy, going to preschool as planned, she had to stay home to make cookies. And compared to recent shenanigans Melanie has been a good kid today even though she and Grandma didn't get to make cookies because the kitchen has no sink. The plumber showed up as scheduled to hook up the new sink with some re-piping and gave me a price of $518, even showed me his company pricing book as if to prove it must be right - I said no thanks, paid him $50 for a service call and sent him away. I called our maid's plumber-husband, he stopped by and will do the same job tomorrow morning for $200. But back to Melanie.

Making cookies with Grandma Shirley

Melanie stuck her head in my office this morning to do one of her increasingly occasional but still unexpected impressions of a small, obnoxious adult. She said loud enough so Grandma could surely hear "Wow, Dad, you going to have a heart attack cause Grandma Shirley's going to be here for *fourteen days*!" That got a laugh from both of us. But Shirley and I do fine, maybe we'll growl at one another once in two weeks, but I do know this - she'll keep Melanie home and spend every day, all day long with her and never once outwardly show the wear of kids like I would. I encourage her to let Melanie go to school sometime so she can take a break while Julie goes to work and I work at home, but she doesn't and I won't push it because this is her time with Melanie.

So today Melanie was sitting in a chair facing me at my desk, humming and writing her Santa list again, saying each word as she pretended to write it, and making sure to include her buddies Alex's and Darby's Santa wishes to make a combined list, and me sitting here like a dumbass with dead batteries in the video camera. I decided to raise the Christmas ante.

"Melanie, want to know a secret?"

Eyes shining, evil grin. "Yeah, Dad!"

"It's a secret, so you can't tell."

"What is it, Dad?"

"Would you like to help me give Mom a special present for Christmas?"

"Yes!"

"It's a secret, you can't tell Grandma Shirley, because we have a present for her, too."

Melanie's head whipped around to make sure Grandma Shirley wasn't close by and power-whispered "*Yeah, Dad, what is it?*"

"You know how I used to tell you a secret and you'd run right to Mom and whisper the secret in her ear?"

"Yeah Dad, but that was when I was a little kid." Now she's four.

"OK, but this time you have to keep the secret all the way to Christmas morning."

"OK, Dad, I will." Her feet are dancing now, barely able to contain her excitement.

"Pinkie Promise?"

She said "OK, Pinkie Promise!" as we entwined our little fingers in the sacred commitment.

I opened the boxes to show her the presents, gold necklaces of different designs and with different stones, from my annual one-hour Christmas shopping spree at Lord & Taylor with everything marked up so they can make a big deal of marking it down, or so it seems.

Melanie handled the necklaces with awe, whispering to me, excited that I shared the secret. I would have preferred to have her with me when I picked them out, but this is almost as good.

"These are presents for Mom and Grandma from Dad *and* Melanie. Do you like them?"

"Yeah, Dad. I won't tell. We going to wrap them?"

"Yep, we will."

Melanie did a conspicuous routine of being inconspicuous, kid-style. She moseyed over to the door to my office and yelled at Grandma Shirley "*We not doing anything.*" A few minutes later she returned to my office with a roll of wrapping paper. Just like a woman she has to interrupt a man's perfectly good procrastination. I told her I was busy and we'd wrap it later. Just about then Grandma Shirley stuck her head in the door and Melanie hid the tube of wrapping paper behind her back with a foot of it sticking above her head and said "*We not wrapping presents, we not doing anything, Grandma!*"

So Shirley and I stifled our laughs and Melanie exited the room with a conspiratorial nod in my direction. She came back in 15 minutes to con me into opening the box for her to look at the necklace once more.

Now it's true that I set up this tension that, combined with the barely-contained pressure of Christmas, could make a kid figuratively explode. But what the heck. It's one way to introduce her to the thrill of giving rather than receiving, and who knows, she just might make it to Christmas with her Pinkie Promise intact. I'll let you know.

Dec 2001, Melanie 4 yrs 8 mos

Broken Pinkie Promise

Last year when Melanie was three, she was overwhelmed with the magic of Santa, reindeer etc., and quite unwilling to wait. Eye's bursting open with wonder on Christmas morning, she whispered Santa's name with awe, struck by the way he did impossible things.

This year at four was different, and it seems every year must be the best one. Melanie has become quite a giver, giggling with glee when someone opens a package from her, and I started co-conspiring with her at about three to buy presents for Mom even though she couldn't possibly keep the secret at that age. And this Christmas Melanie progressed to the knowledge that we give one another gifts *in addition* to what Santa brings - I was pleased she found an easy way to fit that into the rationalization puzzle in her head that permits her to believe in Santa. When the occasional gift-wrapping started, she got into it too, wrapping various toys or other things and insisting someone unwrap it that very instant because "it isn't really a present," but the process seemed to give her a buzz anyway.

The morning after Melanie's Pinkie Promise not to tell Mom or Grandma about the necklace presents, she came in my office and said "Dad, on a accident I told Grandma 'bout the necklace." Now that sentence is loaded so I have to explain.

First, I'm proud of her for telling me she did something she knew she was not supposed to do instead of hiding it. Second, I fully expected the breach anyway. Third, and most important, "on a accident" is not poor grammar, it is a carefully composed phrase with special meaning for Melanie. It means she did something she knows she shouldn't do, like pee on the floor, but she was totally overwhelmed by circumstances that she could not control and had no other option but to do the bad deed. "On a accident" by definition renders her an innocent victim of her own actions, and by the time she reaches the age of romance it will be a very short leap to concluding that it was her man's fault anyway.

So I knew when she said "on a accident" there was nothing to be done, no guilt on her part was involved anyway, and retribution of any sort would be met by indignant outrage, hands on hips and a shouted challenge "*Hello*! It was on a accident!"

"So why did you tell?"

Shrugged shoulders. "It was on a accident, Dad. But don't worry, it's OK, I didn't tell what color it is."

Well, then, no problem, dude.

And actually it was no big deal at all. Grandma and Mom covered for her masterfully, and since the purpose of Christmas for all three of us was Melanie, who cares?

Christmas morning Melanie was excited to see Santa had eaten his cookies and drank his milk, he even moved the fire screen on the fireplace so he could come and go, and she surprised us with observations we did not anticipate.

"Look, Mom, Santa borrowed our own wrapping paper to wrap my present!" The elasticity of a mind casually stretching facts to fit a belief is a wonder to behold. And we got it all on video.

It goes so fast. Make sure you're ready when yours comes, and don't be afraid to join your little one in the small conspiracies and larcenies that make life worth living.

Dec 2001, Melanie 4 yrs 8 mos

The Holidays

In that down-time between Christmas and the first real business days in January some of us spend "quality time" with family whether we want to or not. But in my case it was pleasant with Mom, Grandma Shirley and of course the spice of Melanie.

Christmas mid-day Melanie surveyed the damage and helped clean up the wrapping-paper mess from the cornucopia of commercial excess that turns my stomach while making the ladies happy. Even now that the financial part can easily be absorbed I can't help but think how much good we could do with the same resources if applied differently and how much harm it can do if kids get the galloping gimmies and an attitude of entitlement. But this year as in all others any such sentiments on my part are lost in the stampede we have come to call Christmas, and Melanie had great fun.

A batch of <u>Melanie and Me</u> books arrived just after Christmas and Melanie discovered celebrity. She wears it well. Envision a four year old asked once again to autograph *her book*. In a businesslike way she stomps to a table, opens the book to the title page, sticks the tip of her tongue out the side of her mouth and begins to write her name with the upside down "e" and with just an inkling that where you start to write and how big you write has something to do with where the signature ends up. It's a scream.

During this same period Melanie, who for a long time has watched Franklin "count by twos and tie his shoes," learned to tie her shoes. No event or crowd or circumstance, it seems, is more important to Melanie right now than demonstrating her new skill, and at the instant an audience of one or more materializes she drops to the floor or ground wherever she may be, like in the middle of a parking lot, and starts tearing her laces apart in order to do the demo with a grin so big you might think something surely will break.

Then came New Year's Day, and maybe the nervous tick in my eye had something to do with being cooped up too long with a house full of women. I had seen advertisements for an IMAX screening of <u>Beauty and the Beast</u> starting New Year's Day at the Mall of Georgia, about 70 miles away. I was smart enough to know every kid in the state was out of school with parents reaching the point of desperation for kid-friendly entertainment, and competition would be fierce on the holiday. So I called the telephone numbers in the newspaper ad to order tickets as instructed, but the same fools who placed the ad told me I could only buy tickets at the box office. I wonder if they used to work at the INS? With visions of looooong lines for show tickets hours in advance, I decided to sacrifice myself and drive up there for the tickets and then decide what to do next. Sort of Terry's dumb adventure. At about 10:30AM I reached the ticket window and the earliest show available was 3PM. Now I needed to drive home and turn around to drive it again. It's astonishing what you'll do to make your kids happy.

On the drive home I had just enough time to stop at Denny's for breakfast. They picked this day to be slooooow on service, so by the time I pulled in the driveway at home it was time to pull out again for lap number two. I had purchased an extra kid ticket and Julie had chased down one of Melanie's friends so she could really have fun. With one Kid in a booster seat on each side of the oversize back seat in my truck, I gave Julie the keys to let her drive and I climbed in between the kids in the back, with the ceiling-mounted video screen staring me in the face since for long drives with kids a movie passes the time. Even though there's plenty of room in the back, I'm a big guy, and if you can imagine Orca being transported in tight straps to a new swimming hole you'll understand how I felt between the two kids. When the TV remote slid out of my lap to the floor and I struggled without success to get it while Melanie hollered "*Dad, turn on the movie*" and claustrophobia began to descend, I had Julie pull over so Grandma Shirley and I could trade seats for a little relief.

We arrived in time for good seats, and with the addition of Gummy Bears, Twizzlers, M&Ms and Milk Duds the show was enjoyed by all. There were a few scary scenes that required a little snuggling with the two girls, but it was a striking production well worth the price of admission, the wait and maybe even a few laps around Georgia.

If I'm smart I'd think ahead to next year and make advance preparations for entertainment to avoid the torture portion of these good times. But that would happen only if I were smart.

Jan 2002, Melanie 4 yrs 9 mos

A Pugilistic Parent

It should come as no surprise that Melanie likes Dad but prefers Mom at least 98% of the time. At any given transition point when she could go to Mom or Dad she might, in brutal kid-speak, say something like "I don't want you, Dad, I want *Mommy!*" In a few moments she is driven by remorse to return for a pat on my arm to reassure me with "I like you, Dad, but I going to play with Mommy, OK?"

During those weekend days with Mom, while I do my own thing on the periphery, Melanie will occasionally look up from what she is doing, startled that Mom has somehow escaped her immediate viewing area, and suspecting that Mom may have escaped she'll whip her head around to me so fast you can almost hear the air snap to demand "Where's Mom?" And she expects a satisfactory answer in microseconds, thank you very much.

It's not that Melanie is totally irrational about keeping Mom under her control, just nearly. But I know sooner or later, usually late in the day after lots of time with Mom, Melanie's focus will shift to me.

Sometimes it comes when those two are in the master bedroom doing whatever and Melanie, standing on the bed will get an aggressive squint in her eye when I walk in the room and shout *"Dad, let's fight!"*

This is a sure sign she's had enough of "gentle" for a while, she's ready for action. So I pick her up and throw her down on the bed for a little faux wrestling, pretending to pound her, rolling over and letting her pin me to the mattress so she can transition to her favorite part of jumping up and down on my belly trying to extract some evidence of pain. Somewhere amid the melee she is sure to try her version of boxing, from girl-slaps to little fists with fingers wrapped around her thumb so if she ever throws a real punch with that she'll break her thumb as I've told her repeatedly.

Now before you judge me as an abusive parent, my key witness for the defense would be Melanie herself and her description of how much she likes this rough play. The only thing missing on the witness stand would be the breathless grin, out-of-breath giggling and grunting and sneers with gritted teeth as she strains to overcome her gigantic opponent, while the total impossibility of throwing me over her shoulder to the floor in no way stops her from trying.

A few minutes of this workout saps her strength, and as she lays catching her breath staring at the ceiling, I think I detect deep satisfaction with her brief stint as a warrior, the fight given at full throttle until she is spent, adrenaline slowly seeping back where it should be for another time, morphing once again to Mom's little girl. And off she goes with Mom.

When she gets big she's going to kick my butt.

Jan 2002, Melanie 4 yrs 9 mos

Sneak Attack and The Dan

Last night at 9:00 Melanie said "Dad, I'm tired, I'm going to bed now." This from a kid who routinely does not sleep until after 10:00 every night, but it helps to know that Julie has been nursing a cold and was lying down reading, and what Melanie really meant was she was going to bed with Mom.

While the two of them turned on the movie <u>Princess Diaries</u> to watch from bed I took the opportunity in another bed to dig into the book <u>Bias</u> by CBS' Bernard Goldberg, all about your highness Dan Rather, "The Dan" according to Bernie, and how and why the media leans left. Whether you're liberal or conservative this is a good read, and I loved Bernie's opening quote from Steven Brill: "When it comes to arrogance, power, and lack of accountability, journalists are probably the only people on the planet who make lawyers look good."

Now for the lawyers and journalists I just offended, come on, you've got to be able to laugh at yourself. I'm a CFP and consultant, so I'll balance it out by telling a consultant joke: "Know what you need to be a consultant? Over 50 miles from home and a briefcase!" Now I've offended the consultants, and I give up.

As I read how Bernie from CBS News committed the unpardonable sin in 1996 in a Wall Street Journal op-ed column arguing the press has a liberal bias, and the ostracism he endured for speaking what he believed to be the truth, I thought I heard a faint scuffle. Then I was drawn to a note Bernie received amid the controversy from CBS' Andy Rooney saying "In the future, if you ever have any derogatory remarks to make about CBS News or one of your co-workers . . . I hope you'll do the same thing again." Another scuffle wrapped in a muffled giggle, and I knew instantly my little darling was sneaking up on me to see how high I would jump when she scared me.

Determined to enjoy my book and play her game, I read on as Bernie described how reporters and network news anchors would regularly point out the conservative or right wing label on someone from the right while rarely using the liberal or left wing label on someone from the left, as if liberal meant normal or mainstream and conservative had to be labeled as some kind of whacko. According to Bernie, who describes himself as a liberal by the way, they don't do it deliberately at all, that it's much worse because they don't even realize they are doing it, but I'm about to be attacked so who cares?

The scuffling and giggling got so bad I thought for a fleeting moment to give Melanie some guidance on stealth but decided not to spoil her fun, so when I could no longer ignore it I looked down from the bed to exclaim "What's going on, here?"

Melanie stood up with something cupped in her hand, and I knew whatever it was I didn't want it, so I said "Go away with that, what is it?" Melanie stood her giggling ground to say "Come on, Daddy, you'll like it."

"No, go away with whatever it is!" Probably half-chewed candy or a really good booger.

So Melanie tried a different approach. She tried to turn off my light so I couldn't see what she was doing, but I'm not dumb enough to let that happen and I stopped her cold. Relentless, she climbed up in bed and on my chest, twiddling with her finger something in her other hand, as if it were alive. Now I'm worried.

"What do you have there?" Just giggles.

"Melanie, what do you have there?" In deep, authoritative Dad-speak since I'm now apprehensive.

Sing-song "A ladybug." The only kind of bug she will actually touch.

"Well, you take your ladybug friend and skedaddle!"

Off she went to return the ladybug to Melanie's torture chamber so she could lovingly keep it handy until it starved to death. Bernie went a little overboard by disclosing to mortals like me CBS had a VP with an unofficial title of "VP in charge of Dan" whose very important job was to make sure The Dan was happy and got what he wanted, that his collection of Savile Row suits were OK, that he had a limo and lunch reservations at the Four Seasons daily, etc. No wonder The Dan is a little out of touch with America, but that's not news, it's my personal opinion.

As I fell deeper into the story, sleepy but determined to finish the book, it would have been a good time to sneak the ladybug into my bed. Thankfully Melanie was now focused on Mom in the other room.

Jan 2002, Melanie 4 yrs 9 mos

Melanie the Baby is Fading Away

I received by UPS a box of <u>Melanie and Me</u> books I had purchased to sign and mail to customers, and on Sunday morning I corralled Melanie to sign a stack of books. She dutifully attacked the books with blue pen, only needed an occasional reminder to slow down as she got into the four year old tempo of slinging those letters around like someone important with a unique scrawl, occasionally running out of page so she stacked the remaining letters vertically.

"Slow down and start out small so it will fit. Your signature is important to each person who bought a book."

"OK, OK Dad!"

She handled it like a pro through the first stack and thought she was done so she could return to her 47th viewing of Shrek. But I pointed to a second stack just as large.

"*Fer criminy sakes, Dad*!" Julie and I muffled our laughs as best we could while she scrawled away with the pen.

Last night as I watched Melanie crawl up onto the kitchen countertop with two steps to fetch a band aid, I could no longer ignore the fact her legs are getting quite long to help her climb anywhere. She's not so little any more. Yesterday I felt compelled to say to her "Don't roll your eyes at me like I'm stupid, you're not supposed to do that until you're 16! Well, at least 12."

I've always been told it goes fast, and it sure does.

So I was thinking I'm glad I wrote stories about Melanie whether a book ever materialized or not. It's kind of like taking a photo, at least for me. Sometimes with camera in hand it seems like a pain in the neck and of questionable value to jockey for position to snap a shot. The value comes later, when the *moment* is gone and what you wrote or the photo you took reminds you of the little things that may have otherwise been forgotten. For those of you with my book, the photo of Melanie bathing in the kitchen sink is one of my favorites for that reason.

So if you have any doubts, write away and snap photos. Because in no-time the baby, like Melanie, morphs from little girl to big girl, and with an attitude!

Jan 2002, Melanie 4 yrs 9 mos

Guess What?

Today is Wednesday, the middle of a week with Mom gone "on business" and Melanie coping in her own way. This time Melanie asked me not to follow through with my offer to drive Julie to the airport early in the morning, because she knows she will cry. So she satisfied herself with brief disappointment when she woke up Monday and I told her Mom was already gone.

Julie's home life is selflessly devoted to Melanie, but she still feels bad when she has to travel, and while she's gone I make an extra effort to scare up playmates to come over for a few hours after school since Melanie would describe Dad as "borrrring." So Monday AM at pre-school I snagged Wayne Smith, Dad to Melanie's good friend Darby and said "Want to trade a pickup this week?" to which he said "Sure!"

For those of you waiting for your child, this is pretty important. I take the two kids for after-school play till 8 or 9PM then drop Darby off. The "trade" part is on another day he picks them up and drops off Melanie at 8 or 9PM. That means I have all day until drop-off time to work or play, so the "trade" part of the transaction has value.

My experience is moms and dads tend to handle this differently. Moms tend to offer ever-so-nicely to pick up the kids, then wait quietly and ever-so-impatiently for reciprocity, getting more PO'd with every passing day when it doesn't come, and would rather be tortured than say "Hey, butthead, how about taking your turn today!" But in guy-talk I took care of that up front with the offer of a "trade." The problem is Wayne didn't commit himself - instead of getting PO'd I'll just call him and say "Yo, it's your turn Friday, you up for it?" Wish me luck.

Monday PM when I picked up Darby and Melanie Darby said:

"Melanie guess what? My Dad's getting a truck like your Dad's." I proudly admit I helped Wayne toward a case of truck-lust.

Melanie said "I bet it doesn't have a TV like *my Dad's* truck."

"No, but guess what? It's black and real pretty."

"Guess what, Darby, I got the movie Princess Diaries."

"Guess what, Melanie. I already saw <u>Princess Diaries</u>." And the conversation continued non-stop.

As I drove them home I wondered to myself how you tell your four year old Chinese daughter you'd rather she didn't imitate a Valley Girl with the cocked head, limp wrists, rolling eyes, inflection and attitude. My better judgment emerged for a rare second and I kept my thoughts to myself.

That was Monday, the girls had fun and only made a little mess. Today was warm like spring and I arranged for the other leg of the trio, Alex, to come play after school. When I picked up Melanie in the golf cart, she and Alex were playing together as usual, as they seem to have a deep comfort with one another's company. Although they had no idea of my arrangement, both of them gave me an expectant, hopeful look, and with a mere nod of my head they both exploded into their individual versions of "Yaaaaay, Alex is coming to my house." Then we emerged to a warm afternoon, with two girls already revved up to a semi-fever pitch and they yelled "Yaaaay, the golf cart." Simple pleasures, remember them?

While I was belting them in:

"Alex, guess what? One time my Dad didn't have my belt on tight and I almost falled out!"

"Guess what, Melanie? I can click my own seat belt."

"Guess what, I almost falled out and I woulda cracked my head open and I'd be dead."

"Wowww."

"Guess what, if you fall on the street it can hurt you real bad."

Alex changed the subject. "Guess what, you need a tic-tack . . ." and at this point Melanie joined in the shouted quote from the movie <u>Shrek</u> ". . . cause *your breath stinks*!"

And as we meandered home through the woods, around the lake on the cart paths Melanie continued:

"Guess what, Alex, here's where I almost falled out, right here, right, Dad?"

"Yep." And the amazing thing is she is right and it happened before she was three. I had strapped her into the seat belt beside me instead of holding her on my lap, and as I whipped around that left turn I approach a woman walking on the path whose startled look made me look at Melanie in mid-turn. She was thrown by the turn halfway out of the golf cart, lying horizontal with a terrified look on her face because the seat belt was not as tight as I thought. I nearly had a stroke, quickly stopped the golf cart to pull her in as the lady passed by glaring at me like pond scum mistreating a child. I never saw that lady again, thank goodness, and since this may be the first time Julie has heard about this incident I may in for a whuppin'.

We arrived home in the golf cart and Melanie told Alex "Guess what, we got chocolate pudding. Dad, can we have some pudding?" Sure. And after pudding they played while I tinkered in my office, one of them constantly talking, giving the impression they could never run out of things to say, with my poor hearing mercifully missing much of what was said right after each "Guess what?"

Sometimes these arranged playdates are selfish because it's easier when they play together instead of hanging on your leg whining "Dad, I'm bored!" But mostly it's for Melanie because having friends over for play makes her so happy she could scream, which she sometimes will do. Since I've had my turn twice this week, maybe reciprocity will come through soon enough for it to be like a two-fer for Melanie.

While Melanie and Alex were watching one of her videos Julie called to surprise me by saying she was at the Atlanta (home) airport, trying to connect from Washington to Detroit without success because of a snowstorm, with her bags checked through but who cares since she'll be home in an hour when we didn't expect to see her for a week. You think Melanie is happy playing with Alex? Wait till I tell her Mom is coming home early.

Guess what? I was going to call that butthead Wayne, but now that Julie is home I think I'll keep what he owes me in my back pocket until I need it, then I know where he lives, I know where he works, I know all his phone numbers and I'm not afraid to use them.

Jan 2002, Melanie 4 yrs 9 mos

The Social Calendar

You remember how I "traded" a kids play date with Wayne Smith, but he hasn't called about his end of the trade? I called him at work Friday and said "Wayne, Julie's out of town this weekend and I'm trying to fill up Melanie's calendar to keep her busy. Is Saturday a good day for you guys?" Wayne said sure, drop her off at 10 and she can play all day. Perfect, even though I'd be home all day.

See? Most ladies would have steamed and stewed in silence, but guys just ask because it's no big deal either way.

So when I dropped her off I saw in Wayne's driveway the distraction that made him forget about trivia like a play date debt - his new truck. I admired his truck with him as only guys would understand and then took off. As it turns out Julie did come home from Detroit Friday night but she had to work all day Saturday and all day Sunday so I kept Melanie's weekend plan in place. Saturday night when Wayne's wife Tracy dropped off Melanie she told Julie all about Wayne's new truck, but the girl version is a little different than the guy version:

The night Wayne brought the truck home Tracy says he asked her :
"You like my new truck?"
"Yeah."
"Want to go sit in it with me?"
"NO!"

So he asked his 1st grade daughter "Chaney, you like my new truck?"
"Yeah, Dad."
"Want to go sit in it with me?"
"No thanks, Dad."
Women!

Melanie returned from her Saturday of play wide-eyed with cheeks flushed and ready for more, running wide open right up until she dropped to sleep like a sack of rocks. Sunday AM she went to church and lunch with a neighbor friend, Taylor, and when she returned she didn't wait one minute to ask "Dad, is it time to go to Elizabeth's house?" It was, and she returned home at 7:30PM after a full day, a good thing for all since Mom was working under the gun again.

Today, Monday, Mom is out of town and when I picked Melanie up from preschool little miss social schedule asked "Who's coming over to play with me today, Dad?"

"Nobody today. Just me."

"*Borrrring, Dad*!" with rolled eyes. "You're so embarrassing sometimes, Dad." I can't wait to see how she deals with me when the teen years arrive.

To distract Melanie from her misery I asked her "Want an icee?" Icee is universal lingo between us for a frozen drink, and since she was two she has called her favorite quick-stop store "the icee store."

"Yeah, Dad!"

So I continued driving past Melanie's "icee store" turnoff since their frozen drinks are sickly sweet and the Tyrone store has simple frozen Coke that Melanie likes. As if that's less sweet.

"Dad! Why you passing the icee store?"

"We're going to a different store."

"Where?"

"Tyrone."

"Dad, where's Tyrone?"

"Just a little way down the road."

"Have I been there before?"

"Yep, lots of times."

"Do I like Tyrone, Dad?"

"Sure you do."

When I stopped at the stop sign Melanie recognized the frozen Coke store and yelled "*Yaaaaay, Tyrone*!"

We took our frozen drink home on this cold day and before long Melanie crawled up in my lap snuggling and shivering. Her eyes sparkled when I offered to make her a fire in the fireplace.

A full weekend of play. Wednesday night to choir practice with Taylor, Thursday evening with Ms. Liz next door, Saturday to a Chinese New Year's party with her Chinese friends, Sunday afternoon to a tea party with Elizabeth. Tuesday and Friday still open but probably not for long. Today it's an icee, a fire and letting her carry the log on the way to the fireplace. Good times are what you make them.

Feb 2002, Melanie 4 yrs 10 mos

Mom's Shadow

With her morning bath twirling down the drain taking all the bubble-bath goop, newly washed jet-black hair wet behind her tiny ears, I thought Melanie must be the prettiest thing I have ever seen. But these images move quickly.

She whined "But Daaaad, I don't want to hold my head under the faucet to wash my hair ooooff."

"I won't let the water get in your eyes, and you can tell me how warm you want the water."

"Arrrgghhh. Parents are so annoying! Mom does it better." Of course. She's super-Mom.

So while Mom is out of town when she'd rather be here I try to keep Melanie busy and today I went all the way. I arranged to bring two, not just one, of Melanie's friends to play after school, thus setting two separate parents free until 9PM, and one of them barely contained her "Yippeee!" To get the most mileage out of my sacrifice I called the school and asked them to let the kids know the drill because kids like to know, and they also giggle and jump all day long so why not milk it?

When I picked them up all three were spring-loaded. The other two tore down the hall ahead of Melanie, who ran to catch up with sneakers flying and hollering "*Hey guys, wait up! I got an idea!*" It hasn't changed a bit since Jeff and Porky ran with Lassie, but most of you are too young to know that.

You're not too young to remember what a three-girl tornado looks like, and we had one. Took only 30 minutes to the first "my foot's broken" which means "I bumped it a little and it's sore for a minute" but you have to go through the pretend emergency anyway. They ate the dinner I made and Melanie said "Mom makes mac-and-cheese, but she's not here so I guess we have to eat what Dad made."

Living in Mom's shadow seems to be something every Dad better get used to. But she's earned her shadow. Even though she's gone without a weekend return this time she left a highly organized Chinese

New Year kit for Melanie's pre-school class, with two videos about the holiday, a bunch of holiday treats for the kids ordered from Chinese catalogs, and a letter to the teacher detailing the holiday and how to use all these things to have the class help Melanie celebrate. Me? I knew how to follow instructions to get the shopping bag to the teacher. And next week I'll help Melanie do valentines since Julie already has all the stuff and step-by-step instructions for me so I'll get it right. She knows I'm only a man and need guidance, no kidding here.

Super-Mom manages Melanie's birthday party

So at the end of the evening Melanie was tired from prolonged intense play, and she missed Mom while Mom missed her even worse, especially at bedtime, but she was tired and dozed off quickly. Super-Mom sets a good example, throws a long shadow, and diverting Melanie with play dates passes the time for a little girl with her 5th birthday approaching, a birthday for which she changes her plans almost daily.

Feb 2002, Melanie 4 yrs 10 mos

I Forgot Melanie is Chinese

Sometimes I forget Melanie is Chinese. While the therapists disapprovingly clear their throat and reach for their notepad and pencil, I think we're doing just fine.

I don't mean we ignore Melanie's Chinese heritage, far from it. I told you about developing a Powerpoint slideshow to teach Melanie her adoption story. We also seek the company of other adopted Chinese girls for Melanie's benefit so she'll grow up with friends from a similar background, and they join us for the Moon Festival and Chinese New Year, and even a Mandarin class last year. We're trying, and as a family we feel strongly connected to the people of China through Melanie.

But at the risk of alarming the international adoption experts here, I don't think the Chinese part is the most important at all. I think what is most important is the knowledge Melanie has deep in her heart that Mom and Dad love her more than the sun and moon and stars, and she returns that love in a way that fills our heart. Today Ms. Liz next door picked Melanie up from school while I continued to work on a case and just 20 minutes ago Melanie snuck away from Liz, in through the back door to come give me a hug ". . . cause I missed you, Dad." See what I mean?

So, sometimes I forget Melanie is Chinese, it just isn't the most important thing about her to me. She is our daughter, with problems like homework and the three boys who want to marry her already. We love her more than our own lives and she loves us back just as much. That, to me, is far more important than Chinese cultural immersion, although we have always honored China and will continually try to do more in that area.

I won't say the experts are wrong that Melanie may have problems at some point related to her adoption. But instead of tying ourselves in knots with angst, I think we'll focus on loving our daughter, because that foundation is the best preparation, in my opinion, for any trouble ahead. And I'll bet you a Dragon Dance Melanie will emerge as a strong young lady without the need for therapy as the therapists predict. I wonder who gets paid for that?

Feb 2002, Melanie 4 yrs 10 mos

Valentimes

Melanie perched on the toilet, pants around her ankles, elbows on knees and chin in hands, humming a tune and tapping her feet in the air to keep the beat. She often sings loudly with the bathroom door closed while she does her business "in privates," but this time the door was open and I was waiting.

"Where you get that marry ring, Dad?" she asked as I urged her to finish so we could scoot to school, late again.

"Mom gave it to me."

"When you got married?"

"That's right."

"Did you give her a ring, too?"

"I sure did."

Melanie took a serious pause, chin still in hands, then confided in me.

"First Tyler wanted to marry me then Jacob and now Jalen. I just don't know who I going to marry. But I not going to marry Jacob any more."

"Why not?"

"Cause we breaked up."

"How did you break up?"

"We just breaked up. I going to marry Jalen, Dad. He's my boyfriend."

"What about Tyler?"

"He'll have to find another girlfriend, Dad. I'll have to tell him we breaked up."

"OK." I'm at least smart enough to stay out of it. These things come and go, but Melanie has liked Jalen for a long time. He's a black little boy, and I think Melanie likes him because he's a sweet and quiet little boy while the other boys are rough-and-tumble. But who knows what really goes on inside that pretty little head? I asked Jalen's dad if he was ready for a *really* interracial family, and he looked kind of stumped but he did take a photo of Melanie and Jalen together.

"Dad, we have to do valentimes for tomorrow!"

"I know, we'll do them tonight."

Off to school she went for another day of Melanie-life with the throttle wide open. And last night we opened the Valentine's Day package Mom had thoughtfully prepared before she reluctantly hopped an airplane for Detroit. With a list of kids from school, I wrote their names and Melanie signed her name on each with her upside-down e's surprisingly corrected as I knew they would be sometime, but just in time for "Valentimes."

"Dad, can I make a Valentime for Mom and Dad 'cause I love them and they 'dopted me?"

"Sure." Sometimes you have to use a word to say what words can't possibly say. I labeled a Valentine from Mom and Dad to Melanie and gave it to her with a tiny box of chocolates wrapped up with a little Snoopy toy.

"For *me*?"

"That's for you from Mom and Dad cause we love you." Her eyes sparkled and she smiled and hugged me tight. Then she had a totally different kind of delight when I helped her open it and she discovered *chocolate* was inside. I have to admit this mushy Valentines stuff has always been lost on me my entire Neanderthal life, proving that little girls can indeed teach old farts new tricks.

We labeled the Valentines and taped a heart-shaped red sucker to each one. To Melanie's delight I had also bought heart-shaped boxes of chocolates for her four teachers, we packed it all up and went to bed.

The next morning just before departing for school, I drug out another Valentine and labeled it "Jalen" since he is in a different class and was not on her list, and asked Melanie to sign her name.

"Why, Dad, who this Valentime for?"

"For Jalen."

Her hands flew to her hips, fire leaped into her eyes. "Why you forget my boyfriend's Valentime yesterday?" Gee, and I thought I'd get an "attaboy" for remembering and saving the day. Just when I thought I had things figured out, I get thumped by surprise.

It figures, she's a girl.

Feb 2002, Melanie 4 yrs 10 mos

Melanie Sits Sideways

Melanie, Alex & Darby, inseparable friends

Sisters Redeem Their Grumpy Dad

"Have you noticed Melanie sometimes sits on the side of the toilet instead of the front?" Julie asked me.

"Yes, why?"

"Do you know why she sits that way?"

"No."

"So when she has a friend over there's room so her friend can join her on the toilet!" Julie giggles at such things because she's always been a little girl at heart.

Melanie's two closest friends, Darby and Alex, have likely found a way to make the toilet a threesome with Melanie since they do everything else together. Last week they had trauma together. Alex's Dad Tom Ward picked up all three from school since her Mom Maria, who had arranged to pick them up for a play date, was running late. When I arrived at their home at 9PM to pick up Melanie, Maria and Tom met me at the door with profuse apologies, saying Melanie was really OK while I had no idea what they were talking about. They showed me her fresh scrapes on face and hand and hip and told about her trauma. Tom had taken the three girls for a ride pulling them in a wagon. As he struggled up a hill with the heavy load he lost his grip, the wagon careened down the hill and crashed and the girls took a dive in the street. I can only imagine a frantic Tom giving chase.

I haven't heard this many apologies since Jimmy Swaggart was caught dead to rights with a trollop in the No-Tell Motel.

The girls were quite proud of their exciting role in the accident, and even more proud of their wounds. Alex had the worst injury with skin scraped off most of her nose and other spots of her face, and had clearly forgiven her Dad who was nonetheless mortified. Darby escaped with little damage and I kidded her that she must have used Alex and Melanie as a skid-shield because she's small, quick and smart. Tom felt so bad I didn't ask the question on the tip of my tongue - "Gee, Tom, you're acting like you expect me to be mad at you. Does that mean if Alex gets a scrape at my house you'll be upset?" I'll save that zinger for when I need it.

And in conspiracy with Darby's Mom, Tracy, I took photos of the kids with their fresh wounds. If the photos turn out well, we'll print them out with a big caption "Tommy's Tender Care Day Care" and make him squirm. We've become friends as a result of our kids' friendship at school, and friends can't let an opportunity like this pass, can they?

Tonight Melanie goes home with Alex to play again. She asked last night "Can I do a sleepover, Dad?" Mom is out of town, or Melanie would surely be asking Mom instead of me.

"No, to be polite you have to wait until you're invited for a sleepover, OK?"

"OK. But Darby and Alex already did a sleepover and I didn't and they say 'you're nana and I'm nana'"

"They say what?"

"They say 'You're fo-ur and I'm fi-ve.'" Said with a sing-song sneer sort of like her favorite taunt "Nanny-nanny-boo-boo."

"Well, you'll be five in April."

"Yeah, but I want to do a sleepover."

When we bumped into Maria at school this morning, she confirmed she'd pick up Melanie and I told her I'd be late, maybe 10:30 - I'm going to a special movie. Maria asked if I wanted to just let Melanie sleep over. Perfect; Melanie witnessed the wait-until-invited routine, she got her sleepover and I don't have to worry about time tonight.

I wonder if Maria knows why Alex sits on the side of the toilet?

Feb 2002, Melanie 4 yrs 10 mos

Sleepovers and the Ia Drang Valley

Thursday morning Melanie was looking forward to going home from preschool with her friend Alex to play. Then we bumped into Alex's Mom Maria at school and it turned into a sleepover. That was good for me since Julie was out of town and I had late business that day, but I needed to bring fresh clothes back to school for Melanie's sleepover.

When I returned Thursday afternoon I found Melanie in her dance class. She saw her clothes in my hand and immediately understood; there is no better detective than a kid keeping an eye on their parents. She grabbed Alex's hands and jumped, yelling "*Yaaaay*! I really am doing a sleepover!"

But a moment later Melanie exclaimed "Dad!" with a pained look and gave my leg a body-hug.

"Are you going to miss me?" I asked.

"Yes."

"I'll miss you too. Still want to do the sleepover?"

"Yes, Dad."

"OK. I'll see you tomorrow. Give me a kiss."

We kissed and she started walking back to her dance class but slowed down and held her hand up to her eye with her back to me, in a posture I instantly recognized as struggling with emotions. Her teacher saw her lip quivering and came over to give her a hug and I stayed where I was for a minute. When she looked back I motioned for her to come and she walked with hand to eye, torn between the prospect of endless play and sleep with Alex versus missing Dad for the night. With a kiss-and-a-hug she went on her way and I knew she'd be just fine even though she may cry a little. After all, at not quite five she's young for sleepovers.

So that evening I went to a private screening of the movie We Were Soldiers, based on the book We Were Soldiers Once, And Young by Lt. Gen. (retired) Hal Moore and correspondent Joe Galloway. This is a true story about the Battle of the Ia Drang Valley in 1965 Vietnam, the first battle between US forces and North Vietnamese forces, a test each side was seeking to assess the strength, strategy and tactics of the other. Maybe this is a good example of the warning *you should be careful what you wish for because you just might get it.*

Moore, who was then a Colonel and portrayed in the movie by Mel Gibson, selected the Ia Drang Valley as a likely spot the NVA would use to infiltrate across the Cambodian border, and he led his 450 men of the 1/7 Cav to sweep the valley. When Col. Moore's helicopter landed with the first group, he didn't realize they would surprise nearly 3,000 hidden, well armed, well trained and battle-hardened enemy. A fierce three-day battle ensued, and reporter Joe Galloway conned his way aboard a helicopter to join the battle amidst the fury. While most reporters were protected throughout the war, Joe always found a way to live with the grunts during the worst times. Col. Moore later said "I looked over and saw Joe Galloway sitting with his back against a small tree, camera in his lap, rifle across his knees. I knew why I was there. I'm a professional military man and it's my job. But what the hell was *he* doing there? Turned out he was doing his job too."

In that battle when a napalm bomb landed too close and burned two of our own soldiers Joe set camera aside to charge with a Medic through enemy fire in a desperate attempt to help one of the wounded. The Medic was killed, the wounded soldier later died, and Joe Galloway was awarded the Bronze Star with V (valor), the only civilian to be decorated for valor in the Vietnam war by the US Army.

We lost 243 young men in that battle while the enemy lost 2,000 and withdrew, so of course our generals declared victory.

Please bear with me while I take my admiration of Moore and Galloway a little further.

At this writing Joe Galloway is a special consultant to Secretary of State Colin Powell. For a long time he was a Senior Writer for US News & World Report, and when our national group of helicopter pilots who flew in that war get together Joe is a favored speaker. Retired Gen. H. Norman Schwarzkopf says "Joe Galloway is the finest combat correspondent of our generation, a soldier's reporter and a soldier's friend." Retired Gen. Barry McCaffrey, a senior commander in the Gulf war said "Joe Galloway has more time in combat, under fire, than anyone wearing a uniform today. He rode along on the 24th Division's tank charge through 250 miles of the western Iraq desert in the Persian Gulf war, and did a splendid job of telling the story."

I was pleased to see Joe honored by having a special award for reporters established in his name. In the spring of 2003, at a ceremony at the Vietnam Memorial Wall in Washington, DC, Jan Scruggs, the Executive Director of the Vietnam Veterans Memorial Fund announced the winner of the first annual Joseph L. Galloway Award, to Alexander Perry, a correspondent for Time Magazine for his coverage of the war in Afghanistan.

Lt. Gen. (retired) Hal Moore is a sought-after speaker because of his role in that pivotal battle, and because he was a leader from the old school – the first to set foot on the field of battle, the last to leave, the last to eat, the first to rise, and committed to never leave a man behind whether dead or alive.

I trust you get the picture I am an admirer of Lt. Gen. (retired) Hal Moore and Joe Galloway. If you mentioned my name to either of them I'm sure they would respond with "Huh?"

Some time before the movie was released, and unrelated to the movie, the Atlanta Journal-Constitution published a column of mine featuring Joe Galloway. Moore, who lives not far away in Alabama, read my column and sent me a note of thanks – I kept his note like a star-struck fan. He also gave his buddy Joe a heads-up and Joe read my column then wrote with thanks for the compliments, and we have swapped some e-mail. When the movie based on their book was released Joe arranged for me to attend a private screening for Vietnam veterans, and he said "Give me a sit-rep." That means "situation report" or feedback without the normal baloney.

I wanted badly to like the movie. Actor Barry Pepper did a fine job of portraying Joe, and while I have never been a fan of Mel Gibson he did a great job in this film. I couldn't help loving actor Sam Elliot's Sgt. Major character. Until now Hollywood productions about the Vietnam war like <u>Apocalypse Now</u>, <u>Deer Hunter</u>, <u>Platoon</u>, and <u>Casualties of War</u> have been more anti-war propaganda than realistic. Galloway and Moore write in the book "Hollywood got it wrong every damned time, whetting twisted political knives on the bones of our dead brothers." Exactly.

There was so much to like in <u>We Were Soldiers</u>. Whereas other films portrayed our soldiers as violent potheads, in this film at last they were accurately portrayed as young idealistic innocents doing their job with honor and courage while their families worried and waited. Like no other film, the heavy burden borne by military spouses enduring anxiously at home was truthfully told.

But like anyone watching a movie about things they know too much about I was a butthead and picked the movie apart. I was disappointed the movie lacked the realism of <u>Blackhawk Down</u>. Our troops looked like cub scouts when they immediately chased an enemy soldier into an ambush. Most of my criticism has to do with helicopters, and I can't help but pick nits, I flew helicopters in that war and I'd like Hollywood to get one Vietnam war movie right. I had hoped it would be this one.

In the movie helicopters leapt off the pad to take off in dramatic twisting turns with a full load of troops, while the reality was we had to nurse them off the ground slowly and gently because they were underpowered, especially in the heat of Vietnam. Rounds were shown ricocheting with dramatic sparks off the helicopter's windshield or body, but the reality was rounds passed through the thin magnesium skin of the aircraft like a paper sack. Gunships were shown hovering close to the ground very near the enemy to blast them, but they couldn't hover like that if they tried with even a modest load of ammo and fuel, and the tactic would make no sense anyway. When Mel Gibson yelled "Broken Arrow" into the radio, seconds later he had fast movers and prop planes dropping bombs and helicopter gunships blasting the enemy. I wish it was that easy, but much of this was obviously for gee-whiz effect on the screen no matter how unrealistic.

The technical flaws distracted from the main point of this movie, to tell the story of good people in a miserable battle.

I didn't arrive home until 11PM. I checked messages on the home phone, found none, figured Melanie survived and I went to bed not realizing my mistake.

Friday morning I wallowed in the luxury of not having to wrestle a wiggle-worm into clothes, getting breakfast, gathering school stuff and rushing off to school almost late again. While reading the paper with coffee in my office I checked my business messages and found two with Maria's voice telling a whining Melanie "See, he's not home." Uh-oh, should have checked both lines. So I called Maria and found that Melanie had cried for Dad a little while before going to sleep, then smooth sailing.

When I saw Melanie on Friday after school she exclaimed "I missed you Dad!" We had a fine reunion. After the bedtime story Melanie said "I don't want to do any more sleepovers until I'm five, no six, no ten, Dad, no sleepovers until I'm ten!"

But as soon as Mom returns from her killer project in Detroit Melanie will latch onto her and leave me in the rear view mirror with no malice at all, and our family will return to the balance that we regard as normal. Mom will be happy to be home, Melanie and I will be thrilled to have Mom home, and Mom and Melanie will renegotiate the sleepover future as only girl talk can do.

Later I e-mailed Joe to tell him I love him like a brother but the movie sucked in some places where accuracy was sacrificed for dramatic effect and gave him a few examples. After all, I couldn't let an opportunity pass to push his buttons now that Joe is a celebrity and I remain a mere mortal. Joe reminded me he is smart enough to know what was Hollywood BS, and that his concern was they got the heart and soul of the story right.

They did, Joe. This movie conveyed the message that America should have been proud of Vietnam veterans. Even after all these years, telling this truth is important to honor the memory of our dead brothers, and important so maybe the country doesn't repeat the mistake of treating the young people we send to war with disdain and neglect.

I will teach my daughters the story of Lt. Gen. (retired) Hal Moore and Joe Galloway. If ever you seek living examples of character to help teach your children, the finest this country has to offer, in my opinion you can do no better than these two men.

At the end of this book I have written down the lessons I learned in that war so Melanie and Kristen can know those lessons even when I am gone – I call it the story of the elephant. But if you wish to find the very best perspective on the Vietnam war, I recommend the five-page Prologue in the book <u>We Were Soldiers Once, And Young.</u> For those of us who fought in Vietnam, these five pages put into words some of the inner turmoil we brought back with us. Though I did not experience the particular battle in the book, as I read these five pages I am strangely reassured to know someone can translate into words what many of us could never explain, and I am reminded of other words Joe spoke at a gathering at the Vietnam Memorial in DC where 58,220 names are etched in the black wall. Joe said he liked to come here between midnight and dawn, when if he listened in the quiet he could hear their voices saying "We are at peace, so should you be . . . so should you be."

Their book helped my peace, which is good because peace is useful when you are in your mid-fifties and your four year old is dealing with genuine crises like sleepovers and friends who are so much more mature because they are five and she is still four.

Feb 2002, Melanie 4 yrs 10 mos

She Gets It

I've told you about Melanie's allowance and budgeting. When you give a kid money when they can't tell a one from a twenty, and she doesn't yet distinguish cost differences between a pencil and a Porsche, you're in for some fun.

Melanie doesn't squander her money on candy, and maybe her very own inventory in the pantry has something to do with that. Her buying preference is books. Mom and Dad are lifelong avid readers, the nightly bedtime ritual has reading at it's core, and Melanie loves her bedtime story. There are a lot worse things than books for a kid to love, and we are pleased she likes books so much. I'll tell you about her most recent purchase.

Melanie learned starting at age two about her birthmother and birthfather in China, that we don't know who they are, that we believe they loved her but could not keep her, how she stayed at an orphanage until her forever Mom and Dad could come take her home. There was a time when she was quite sad for her birthmother and birthfather, she has asked lots of questions, but one thing has worked well - she is not the least bit ashamed of adoption or any discussion of her birthmother and birthfather. The time may come when she has to struggle as she thinks more deeply about her origin and adoption, but I think this positive foundation will help. And I told you all this because what she is learning is the point of this little story.

Yesterday in Kroger there was a new rack of "Winnie-the-Pooh" books. Actually this is one time I talked Melanie into a book because she saw the early Easter goodie display and wanted a fluffy Easter Bunny. I told her to ask her mother about the bunny and she picked out a book for her allowance for the last two weeks.

Last night at bedtime with eyes shining in anticipation of the new story, we read about Tigger noticing he had stripes while his friends did not. Tigger decided to get rid of his stripes to be more like his friends. First he painted himself, but it washed off. Then he covered himself in honey with Pooh's help, but bees chased him into the water. Then he wallowed in a mud pit to cover himself in mud, and while I was describing how he couldn't move because the mud had hardened, Melanie gave me one of her frequent interruption-lectures to inform me how the world works:

"Dad, Tigger should just be himself."

"That's right, I'm proud of you!"

"Everybody should just be themself, Dad, no matter what you look like or whether you're 'dopted or not 'cause that's how God made you, right Dad?"

"That's right."

Out of the mouths of babes. I nominate Melanie for president of the world. Do I hear a second?

Feb 2002, Melanie 4 yrs 10 mos

Melanie's Not Muslim

In the book <u>Melanie and Me</u> I tell the story of *Roger* and *Tony*, two brothers from India who own and operate our cleaners. Roger has a soft spot in his heart for Melanie. Actually Roger has a soft spot for everyone. He was particularly taken with Melanie's adoption, he has his own private affinity for adoption, and has told me he loves his boys but he wishes he had a little girl.

Today while dropping off our cleaning at the drive-thru window I noticed Roger is growing a beard. I grew a beard while in college and I remember the scratchy discomfort before it filled out, so I figured this would be a good time to needle Roger about his beard.

"So, I see you're growing a beard."

"Yes. You like it!" Roger is always open, enthusiastic and smiling.

"I think you should ask your wife if *she* likes it!"

"Yes, but what do you think? What you think is important, too."

Roger hesitates just a moment, then confides. "You see, I am Muslim. The Koran teaches us that all of us are brothers, and what you think is important not because you are a customer, but because you are my brother."

Gee whiz, I just wanted to kid around about his beard. A pregnant pause.

"Did you know, the Koran says when we have a meal we should check with our neighbors' tent on all four sides to see if they have enough to eat. Even the animals, because God made us more capable, it's up to us to look out for them. There's a squirrel always looking around here for something to eat, and I chase him around with a piece of hot dog or something, because God expects me to be kind. I'm not a good man but I try to be."

I'm astonished as always by Roger's open heart, and to tell the truth I'm not comfortable in *God* discussions, that's an intensely personal thing that turns sour as soon as someone tries to push their version on me. But I can't help but love this man.

"You know," he continues, "this terrorist thing going on in the world with people claiming to be Muslim is so embarrassing. That's not God's way, that's not what God teaches us. God teaches us love and peace, and I know God is in your family and watching over your beautiful little girl."

So, what do you say to that? "Thanks, Roger, you're a good man. See you tomorrow."

Later, Melanie is digging through the stuff Mom brought home from the store discovering treasure. She finds some new band aids, although I didn't know it until a few minutes later. Band-Aids are one of her favorite things, so she has to open the package and open a band aid to check it out. Now that she has it open, what to do with it?

So Melanie walks into my office with a band aid unused but sticking to her finger and asks "Dad, you got something that hurts?"

Which makes me think that Melanie is not Muslim like Roger, but she sure is a good person. Just like Roger.

Mar 2002, Melanie 4 yrs 11 mos

Brer Rabbit

This morning before school I corralled Melanie to sign some books; they finally came in and I need to mail them pronto to people who have been waiting. Unlike last time I had her sign a big stack, she didn't say "Fer criminey sakes, Dad!" but she did give me the eye roll. Then just like a trooper she climbed up in my lap, grabbed the pen, stuck the end of her tongue out the corner of her mouth and went to work with her head down. Each signature was a little different, a different mix of five-year old caps and small letters, each succeeding one signed with a bit more flair as Melanie discovers her inner panache.

Then off to school. Today she is happy because Mom comes home and we pick her up at the airport to save her the aggravation of a schlep to the parking lot. As usual Melanie has been good while Mom's gone, and this time we haven't had any friends over to visit, just us. Last night Melanie heard her very first story about Brer Rabbit and how Brer Dog outsmarted Brer Fox when Brer Fox tried to eat Sister Goose and he just got a mouthful of Brer Dog's rolled-up pajamas, that being, according to Uncle Remus, how dogs and foxes came to be enemies.

Which prompts me to thank a friend named Marie for the recommendation of this book:

Uncle Remus, The Complete Tales
as retold by Julius Lester
illustrated by Jerry Pinkney
Phyllis Fogelman Books
1999
isbn 0-8037-2451-9

Melanie complained that there weren't enough pictures. At not-quite-five she likes to look at the pictures while we read to her and it helps her remember the words. I swear sometimes she can sit by herself and go through an entire book pretending to read the words and come quite close to verbatim from memory. But she enjoyed the story and immediately after sat at her desk and drew a picture of Brer Fox and Brer Dog.

Song of the South was a favorite movie when I was a kid, but the video was never released in the US. The many stories of Brer Rabbit and his cronies were written by Joel Chandler Harris (1848 - 1908) who wrote for the Atlanta Constitution newspaper for 24 years, and some of these 263 tales appeared in the paper starting in 1876. But Mr. Harris did not create Brer Rabbit or the other animal characters. His was a faithful attempt to capture the stories told by southern plantation slaves to their children, in the dialect they used, and the result is the largest single collection of Afro-American folktales ever collected and published. Uncle Remus *was* created by Harris as a story-telling character, but he was a composite of three very real former slaves he knew and who had told him some of the tales.

Julius Lester, author of this revised version, is a black man with a love of these tales and great respect for their origin. He disagrees with those who criticize the original works for the reminder of slavery, because it did happen. He does criticize, however, the basic setting of the stories where Uncle Remus tells the stories to the privileged white child of plantation owners. Doing so, Lester observes, loses the importance of these stories, which were told to black children by their parents, thus becoming an important part of their young lives. Mr. Lester's book is a fine one, and he describes the revised language as "a modified contemporary southern black English, a combination of standard English and black English where sound is as important as meaning." The original dialect is difficult reading, but Lester's style make reading the stories out loud more enjoyable.

Lester says these tales are printed into a book only to spread them to as many people as possible, but that "the tales will live only if they flow through your voice. The suffering of those slaves who created the tales will be redeemed (to a degree at least) if you receive their offering and make it part of your life."

Melanie will discover the delights of Brer Rabbit and the rest, and maybe she'll learn from the story-reader along the way something about history, and how wrong it is to treat people differently and cruelly because of their race. And there's more.

I was disappointed to learn Song of the South was never released on video in the US. But Disney did release it just about everywhere else, so go figure. Yesterday I found a new unused version on e-Bay, and I was the lucky winning bidder. It's in England in PAL format, and it has to be converted to run on our VCRs, and when I receive the PAL original and the converted tape it will have cost me nearly $110. That's a lot for a video, but this one is special.

Julie and I will have to watch it to see if there are parts where we need to stop the tape and explain some things to Melanie to make sure she doesn't get the wrong message. I think if treated properly the Uncle Remus stories will be enriching for her.

But before she ever gets to the briar patch story, I know Melanie will feel a close kinship for Brer Rabbit, because she's already been pulling her own version of the briar patch trick on her Dad for years.

Mar 2002, Melanie 4 yrs 11 mos

PS – I didn't like the movie as much as I thought I would, far too little of the cartoons and too much of plantation life with happy slaves and rich, pampered, condescending owners. There has to be more of the cartoons somewhere, but I haven't found them. Meanwhile Melanie loves to hear the stories of Brer Rabbit from the book.

Put Dad in His Place

This winter season, because of the dry air I guess, Melanie has experienced a nosebleed every so often. Sometimes it happens at night and her bedsheets get bloody if it isn't noticed right away.

Most often this minor calamity is self-induced with, um, nose-picking. There, I said it. While Melanie is digging for a good one, she scratches herself instead. So we have become just a little bit expert at twisting a tissue and applying it in the right spot while she sits still to watch Arthur or Dragon Tales and then all is well. All this is to explain at least one reason I ask her not to pick her nose, but to get a tissue and blow it instead.

As you know there is no greater indignation than a kid who discovers an adult in hypocrisy. Let them spot big people doing something they scold the kids for and the fingers wag, the hands go to hips and the sing-song accusations fly at double-decibel. If you don't have kids of your own, page back in your head to your own childhood and you'll remember this well.

I don't mean Melanie caught me digging my own mine. I don't want to scar her forever with such memories, so I'm careful about that. But a while back when my mother was on the phone Melanie insisted on taking her turn and asked Grandma something like "Did my daddy pick his nose when he was little? Uh-huh, OK, *I thought so!*" Then of course came the name tag "Daddy is a nose-picker!"

Of course it didn't stop there. About a week later at the dinner table while we were tugging back and forth about something, Melanie said to me. "You just be quiet, Mister! You picked your nose when you were a little kid, I know cause I asked your Mom!"

And if that doesn't shut you up, I don't know what will.

Mar 2002, Melanie 4 yrs 11 mos

The Big Kid

Melanie's brain is driven by compartmentalization. That's a revelation to me, but maybe it's part of every kid's learning experience. As she learns new facts and rules and other things about life, her little brain builds new compartments and reorganizes old ones with the blinding speed of a nuclear-driven super-computer. And in her case every adjustment is incomplete until she makes an announcement to the world.

Last night I visited a client who is also a friend; when we meet for business I take Melanie so she can play with his daughter, also adopted from China. On the way home, Melanie shared with me her newest spontaneous observation. "I have a mom and a dad, and mom and dad had a mom and a dad, and they had a mom and a dad, and they had a mom and a dad, and they had a mom and a dad, and they had a mom and a dad, and they had a mom and a dad, and they had a mom and a dad, and they had a mom and a dad . . . and, *wow dad*, that's a lots of moms and dads!" Yep, it sure is.

She's almost five. I had forgotten as we all do when we grow up that a kid's world is divided into events preceded by waiting periods - birthday, Easter, Halloween and Christmas. Melanie had a grand time anticipating the Easter Bunny and the magical way he sneaks around like Santa, and now she is nearing the fever pitch of her pre-birthday frenzy. I don't much like all the hoopla, it's one checkbook-party after another for her circle of friends, and her own party is Friday, which happens to be her birthday, at the local Dixie-Land park where they do it all for kids parties. Actually I like the part where they do it all and all we have to do is write a check, but it seems things are too complicated, over-planned, too much expectation, but maybe I'm just a dinosaur. I don't care about the money, but I do remember a simpler time.

I said to Melanie the other day when she prattled on about her birthday party: "You know, birthdays don't always have to mean a big party. How about next year we celebrate your birthday with just you and me and Mom and have a cake and presents?"

Melanie looked at me as if I had just taken out my brain to play with it. Oh well, sometimes it helps to turn off my brain and join the flow with all the morons, um, I mean go along with everyone else.

Melanie has already received birthday packages from grandmas and aunts, and her eyes light up a room when she sees a package arrive in the mail or from UPS. Julie has had Melanie's present for weeks or months, and I'm left to my own devices. Which suits me fine, because I'm going to buy her a pair of walkie-talkies, every kid's dream.

Melanie colors Easter eggs

Today brings a different kind of birthday present. Melanie has for a long time yearned to be old enough to go on field trips "with the big kids on the bus." Some day. Yesterday Julie informed me Melanie's buddies at school were tormenting her because they were going on a field trip today to the local skating rink but she couldn't go [now shift into kid-type sing-song teasing] "because we're five and you're only fooooour!" Well, I was a PO'd man on a mission.

First I asked the school Director about the field trip and she said yes but kids had to be five to go. I told her Melanie's 5th birthday was two days hence and it meant a lot to her so how about arranging for her to go. After the Director hesitated for a moment without realizing I was fully prepared to be extreme she said "Why not?" Shoot, I didn't even get to yell at anybody. So today Melanie embarks on what she has dreamed about for ages in kid-time, and I hope she won't be disappointed. She was delighted that today she could "tell my friends I am too going on the field trip, so there!"

Despite all the anticipation and excess and ceremony surrounding her birthday, sometimes Melanie reminds me she is just a normal kid whose world is developing quite nicely. Last weekend after hours of being cooped up inside as it rained, with the sun emerging and me finishing up the paperwork I was doing so I could play with her as promised, she said "Dad, can we throw the ball at each other and look for bugs?" You betcha. Now I'm off to buy some itty bitty walkie talkies.

Apr 2002, Melanie 4 yrs 11.99999 mos

The Lookout

With the warmth of Spring and extra daylight hours, Melanie's time after school morphs from inside to outside. Stirring mud in her playhouse by the pretend sink and pouring into tiny cups to serve me or anyone else foolish enough to be nearby is a favorite. Hunting bugs, squatting to peer up the rainwater downspouts, watching the bobbing heads and ballooning red throats of lizards and hunting a flower to pick for Mom keep her interested as well.

Yesterday I picked her up from school in the golf cart and drove to the grocery store on the cart paths through the woods. On the way she asked me if she could go to the bathroom in the store, which traps me and she knows it as evidenced by her smug smile, because I can't really say no and she often wants to go just to check out the facilities. As we walked into the men's room Melanie instructed me with her observations:

"This is the men's room 'cause you can't go in the ladies' room, right Dad?"

"Right."

"Why you have to put paper on the toilet seat before I sit down?"

"Well, you know that little hose boys have that you're always talking about because girls don't have one?"

"Yeah."

"Well, they don't always aim very good and they pee on the seat."

"Do you pee on the seat, Dad?"

"Not any more, I learned how to aim."

So she finished her business and washed her hands with soap and water, but on the way out she took a good look around to make sure she didn't miss anything and with some wicked, shameful delight she pointed to the lone urinal mounted on the wall and giggled her way through telling me that's where boys go. All this at five years old, and I know I'm in for an interesting ride in her teenage years.

I needed picked up some pharmaceuticals and splurged to buy her a $10.50 Dr. Seuss book not quite as thick as one of my hairs to keep her occupied in the grocery cart. And when I grabbed 12-packs of soft drinks I relented to her ceaseless begging for nuts in the can, meaning cashews, for which she recently acquired a taste. I selected a can, popped off the top to let her dig in, what the heck. We continued to meats, bread, milk, veggies, oranges, turkey link sausages to try for breakfast, then the last lap down the frozen food lane to get fat-free chocolate Popsicles and mini-cobs of corn.

Melanie used to reject corn, but when we showed her how Grandpa Mel used to roll his hot cob right on the stick of butter and get it all lathered up to eat, well she fell in love. She now enjoys destroying the butter dish and decadently smearing butter all over her face, dripping on her clothes, and generally turning her back on Miss Manners, but some of life's pleasures must be indulged with abandon. And she knows how. I thought about showing her how Grandpa Roy used to butter his cob with a buttered piece of bread, and then eat the bread, but she's already stopping just short of wallowing in the butter dish and I think she has Grandpa Roy beat.

Anyway, all through my grocery shopping Melanie would open the cashew can, take a couple to munch on, close it up, open it again and so on. As we approached the checkout line cooler with cold drinks, I told her as I grabbed an Orange Crush that she shouldn't eat so many cashews.

"Why not, Dad?"

"They'll make your poop sticky." And they will, as a vastly experienced over-indulger, I know. She stopped, but mostly because she now had a bottle of pop to keep her happy.

We loaded up the groceries in a rectangular 10" deep plastic bin I had attached on the golf cart's back seat just for this purpose, and head for home.

Until you've experienced this lifestyle you might wonder how much sense it makes to drive a golf cart everywhere. But Melanie can tell you because she learned from me the answer to the question "Why go you go for a golf cart ride?" Why, to make the wheels roll and the wind blow, of course.

After putting groceries away while Melanie watched Barney, I decided to divert her with a fail-safe offer for the first time this Spring:

"Melanie, want to go up to the bank to wait for Mom?"

"Yeah, Dad, let's go!"

Zooooom, she's out the door and in the golf cart. Since I work at home and control my own schedule, and Julie works in downtown Atlanta 30 miles away, she gets home about dinner time but it varies. Nothing fascinates Melanie more than the search for Mom, and we motor down the street, across a bigger street into the bank's deserted parking lot, up over the curb, around back on the grass, out onto a point overlooking the main drag intersection 30 feet below where Julie will have to turn in to our neighborhood. We sat and watched for Mom, Melanie with patience beyond her five years even though she fidgeted and climbed all over the golf cart, kicking dirt clods, pulling leaves off bushes, flipping the windshield up and down. Of course once you get old and fat like me all you have to do while waiting is move your eyeballs.

We had several false alarms as Melanie would shout "There's Mom!" but it was just a few green cars that look like her stick-shift high-performance VW Passat racecar, not the real thing, and I said some things like "That can't be your Mom, that car had all four wheels on the ground when it turned" but I was just kidding, dear.

After a while I told Melanie that was long enough, lets go. She looked at me like I was a poor suffering slob of a man who just didn't get it, held her hands out palms-up and with shrugged shoulders asked:

"Why? We haven't seen Mom yet." Her rolled eyes added just the right accent.

But I told her to get in, it's time to start dinner and Mom will catch up when she gets here. Off we went, and at dinner Melanie demonstrated her flexibility by digging in to tomatoes, which she had heretofore rejected, but this time she announced she "loves" tomatoes while she ate tomato slices from the inside out.

And as the days go by, she'd like nothing better than a pre-dinner lookout for her favorite person in the world, her Mom.

Apr 2002, Melanie 5 yrs o mos

The Merciless Nurse

With Spring comes a backlog of yard chores. In our case it involves a new and expanded deck and the preparation involved taking out two Willow trees, one of them having grown quite substantial. After removing some extraneous limbs I had a friend help with the chain saw while I pulled with the rope to make sure the tree fell harmlessly as opposed to on my truck. Over several days I dealt with the residue of two felled trees that had to be hauled to the dump except for the trunk, which an eager Melanie helped me stack between two trees as firewood for next winter. The stump of the tree sat about 10" high, no concern since it would be covered by a new section of deck.

Since I'm fat and out of shape and moving slow there are frequent rest breaks involved, and with each one comes an opportunity for Melanie to inspect my bare legs for fresh scratches, because she has a whole box of band aids, you know. A few days ago in the grocery store, wearing shorts as usual even though it's not pretty, I noticed a lady staring at my legs, so I looked down and found a patchwork of band aids that my little nurse had applied with care and they had survived the shower as well as my attention. I thought, oh well, you can't embarrass me, lady, I have a kid.

Friday I finished work early and picked Melanie up early from school so she could play while I continued work on the deck preparation. This time it was digging up shrubs that needed relocation out of the new deck's way. While struggling to pull a shrub loose from imbedded roots I lost my grip and my balance and fell backwards on the small of my back right on that Willow stump.

Nurse Melanie saw me fall and cried "*Daddy!*" and came running. This has to be a Dad's second worse nightmare, getting hurt in front of your child, second only to the child getting hurt. Since I have lived all my adult life with the results of a severe compression fracture of my L1 and L2 vertebrae, removal of disk and insertion of pins to hold it all together, having had paralyzed legs before surgery, I worried through blinding pain whether my legs still worked, and they did. So I struggled to my feet, didn't feel so bad and thought I better sit down for a minute.

Melanie said, relieved, "Dad, you OK now, would you go get me a coke?" and returned to her play. I almost cut myself in half, and Melanie wants a coke. That's parenthood.

Soon I was barely able to walk, used one of Julie's old putters for a cane and when she arrived home I became a patient. I slept until noon the next day, or I should say tried to as Melanie stomped into the bedroom a dozen times to check on me, during which she liked to jump up on the bed and watch my eyes flash wide open in surprise and pain. Never underestimate a kid's ability to hurt you while delivering attentive care.

While I returned closer to normal Saturday afternoon, incapacity combined with pain made me short-tempered and at one point about something inconsequential I exclaimed "*dammit.*" I heard a little nurse's voice from upstairs saying "I heard that bad word. You owe me a buck!" She has a pile of dollar bills in a plastic container on top of the fridge, and it grows.

Sunday was nearly back to normal with some yard cleanup and mowing the lawn while Nurse Melanie played and argued and whined with a visiting friend, then we decided to go for Mexican on the golf cart. I made a deal with Melanie - no whining, good behavior at dinner and I'd buy her a treat. That means a stop at the convenience store and letting her select something with no nutritional value whatever. And by the time she got to the store she was a dollar richer because when I dropped enchilada sauce on my shirt at dinner Melanie caught me and said "You owe me another buck, Dad." And I did.

Melanie and Mom talked a little bit at dinner about Babysister, that we don't know how old she will be, and that she might be scared at first when we meet her in China. Melanie understands, or says she does, that we'll have to be careful to let Babysister get used to us for a while. But one thing she knows for sure and is committed to, as she reminds me with a twinkle in her eye.

"I going to teach Babysister to aggavate you, Dad!" Of that I am certain.

Apr 2002, Melanie 5 yrs 0 mos

Mom, Are You Totally Nuts?
By Julie Garlock

Melanie is very much aware she has a birthmother and a birthfather. She freely talks about them and wonders about them.

The best advice I read about this issue was to choose the appropriate moment and in your own way let your child know it is okay to love and miss their birthmother and birthfather. It lets them open up. She and I have had this discussion many times and I bet Terry has too.

As Terry has told you before, Melanie has two special friends. Sometimes a threesome causes issues because at this age one usually gets left out. They deal with it much better than some grown ups.

However, recently Melanie has become aware and concerned about her being smaller than the other children, particularly her two best friends. Sometimes smaller means she is younger and sometimes it means her height. She is the youngest of the trio and has paid the price. If it were not for Darby, who is about one inch shorter, Melanie would be the smallest in her class.

She constantly asks why she is a little bit bigger than Darby and how can you be bigger if your birthday is not first? I couldn't tell her it was because of good eating habits unless two pounds of candy a day makes the difference. So . . . I said, "Well, Melanie maybe your birthmother was a little bit bigger than Miss Tracy." Tracy is Darby's Mom. Melanie also asks "So, how many eggs do you have in your body, Mom? Why aren't they any good?" Don't ask. I don't know where she got it. Probably the same place she became curious about tickling, by which she means sex. Apparently, she saw something on TV she shouldn't have. Not one of our so-called friends told me I would be having these discussions with her at age five. Just answer the question that is asked, keep it simple and they'll go on. Yeah, right.

On Sunday Melanie went on and on about eggs and how her birthmother's eggs must have been bigger than Miss Tracy's eggs, isn't that right Mom?

"Well, I don't know Mel, maybe your birthmother was just taller or maybe your birthfather was."

"And, hey, Mom what did my birthmother do right after I was born? Did she hold me?"

"Yes, I think so Melanie."

"What about my birthfather?"

"Yes, I guess so. But we weren't there so I don't know for sure. What do you think they did Melanie?"

"*What*? Mommm, are you crazy? Are you totally nuts? I was too little. How would I remember? Geez, Mom. Mom, can Darby come over and play?"

I wonder what Miss Tracy said when Melanie asked about her eggs?

Julie Garlock

Apr 2002, Melanie 5 yrs o mos

Boredom

On a rainy Saturday, one day after the movie <u>Spiderman</u> opened, I suggested to a bored Melanie that we go see the movie. What was I thinking? At 1PM all shows sold out until 7PM. So poor bored Melanie had to endure more hanging out with Mom & Dad. To make things worse, we stopped in a Steak & Shake shop in Newnan and had a waitress who deserved much worse than firing. After a restless Melanie had fidgeted on the edge of trouble far longer than any adult patron should have to wait, much less a child, and the young lady had passed us by a number of times, I finally stopped her to ask "Are we invisible?"

A lady at the next table spoke up loudly to announce "We were, took an hour to get our food. Better ask for your check now!"

With only three mistakes on our order, minor ones, and the need to yell at another waitress for silverware quickly fulfilled, Melanie managed to live through lunch and collected another dollar from me for a bad word. On the way home she engaged Mom in her battle against boredom with the latest version of kid humor. After much wrangling and insisting that Mom answer the questions just right, here's how the joke went:

Melanie:	What's your name?
Mom:	Mary Jane
Melanie:	Where do you live?
Mom:	Down the drain.
Melanie	What's your phone number?
Mom:	Cucumber
Melanie:	Bye

Much five year old hooting and laughter. She gave up on me, I couldn't resist torturing her with strategically incorrect responses. Must be nice to be easily amused.

Maybe boredom does that to her. Melanie's used to action now on warm Spring weekends, and last Saturday she "helped" with general yard work. It only takes twice as long when she helps, but it's fun. She insisted on helping me dig holes for transplanting rosebushes, and barely able to wield the shovel she pushed more dirt into the hole than she dug out. But she stomped on the shovel edge like a trooper, she's proud of her participation and is offended when left out. Mom seems to be most happy when Melanie is helping Dad. I guess she's smarter.

But on Sunday one of Melanie's friends, Darby, was finally able to come over, and boredom disappeared into the forgotten past. They played in the turtle sandbox on our new deck with new clean sand, had a big time with the "talkie walkies" I gave Melanie for her birthday and pretended to be just about everything. After a full afternoon of play, I made some quick spaghetti for them. Spaghetti is part of a food group Melanie simply cannot eat without grated Parmesan cheese - lots of it, we buy it in large quantities. Melanie is basically a pig when it comes to her Parmesan cheese. Darby wanted some, too, and since we have taught Melanie "guests first," she offered Darby first crack at the coveted Parmesan cheese, and they launched in sing-song unison:

"First is worst,
Second is best,
Third is the one with the polka-dotted dress!"

Then they moved on to a sing-song selection that would surely get a rise out of parents, which is the point:

"Johnny ate a bugger,
It tasted like sugar,
He put it in a pot,
And it tasted like snot."

We send them to school to learn about Shakespeare and they bring home vaudeville, just like when I was a kid. We can only hope a little Shakespeare sneaks in here and there. Please.

May 2002, Melanie 5 yrs 1 mo

Parents are *So Embarassing!*

Our beach house for a week

You would think when you rent an expensive four bedroom house on the beach with a panoramic view of the Gulf of Mexico and just 200

feet from the water it wouldn't have a cockroach problem. But it does, indeed, bleed roaches late at night, and if you grew up in this part of the country as I did you would know they cannot be stopped at the beach, it's like trying to keep your kid from seeing Barney on TV. So during the day we don't see them and pretend they aren't there.

Melanie is having a grand time at the beach in Gulf Shores, Alabama, or "Golf Shores" as she says it. Mom plays in the sand with her, splashes in the surf, etc. As for me, I spent much of my kid-life at the beaches from Gulf Shores to Orange Beach to Gulf Beach to Pensacola Beach to Navarre Beach to Ft Walton Beach to Destin. Sun-worshiping, swimming, snorkeling but mostly girl-watching. So it's not new to me, and the truth is if I never have to struggle again to walk in the soft sand that sinks deeper with each step now that I'm old and fat, if I never again splash in the warm, briny water, if I have to enjoy the beach from the dry shaded deck with a cocktail in my hand, Dad will be a happy guy. I've played a little with her in the sand and in the water, and played catch with her new ball and glove, but mostly it's Mom and she gets the credit.

But Melanie did have a bad day on Tuesday. While driving to Fort Morgan she wallowed in a whining fit, one so relentless she ignored parental warnings far too long. Now her giraffe, kitty and bunny are stored away in a box for a week, though Mom gave her plenty of chances to see the error of her ways and back off, but sometimes you gotta do what you gotta do so she plowed ahead and Mom had to take her favorite cuddle toys away for a week. Of course that was after Dad failed to make a dent in her behavior by warning and then imposing a time-out she owed me when we got home, and the poor little dear had to pay up long after it was all over. But I explained why and she understood so she went to the corner and took her punishment. It couldn't have been too bad since she chewed Starbursts through the whole five minutes.

It seems the more you give kids sometimes, the more it turns them rotten for a little while. But Melanie's a good kid, we just have to get her attention and she comes back down to earth.

Yesterday we visited the Chinese exhibit in Mobile, Alabama. Gulf Shores is a barrier island, so we drove to the end at Ft. Morgan, drove the truck onto a ferry and rode across Mobile Bay to Dolphin Island, another barrier island, then across a long bridge and into Mobile. On the ride over while we were watching seagulls and Pelicans search for a meal, Julie and I kissed and Melanie exclaimed "Yuk! You guys are SO embarrassing!" I told her "Of course, that's our job, we're your parents."

Grandma Lois with Melanie

Sisters Redeem Their Grumpy Dad

When we first arrived at the beach house on Saturday, Melanie took her clothes bags into a spare bedroom so that, like a big girl, she can go get herself dressed. Now when she walks into that room she has a routine developed just for Dad - she says, "Toodles, bye-bye, you are SO embarrassing, Dad!" Makes my heart glow warmly since it is irrefutable evidence that I am a parent.

Anyway, the Chinese exhibit is at the Mobile Exploreum Museum, on Government Street downtown near the Convention Center. It's quite an exhibit, with several Chinese artisans doing calligraphy, silk weaving, paper cuts, kite-making and many other items. One astonishing item is a south-facing wagon; it has gears from the wheels attached to a vertical shaft with a face on it, and the gears are intricately calculated so that no matter how many turns one makes, the face will always be facing south. Go figure.

I spoke to George Wilkins on the phone to tell him about our museum visit since he was interested. I told him about the exhibit and in answer to a couple of his questions I said "It was pretty good, but I wouldn't drive from Atlanta for it."

"That's not a ringing endorsement." George said.

"No, but you have to consider the source. When it comes to exhibits, I have the attention span of a fruit fly."

Now envision Mom and Melanie coming in from the beach, having washed feet-sand off with a faucet. Melanie peels off her bathing suit on the run, headed for the bathroom to pee and get a warm bath since the air conditioning makes her cold when she's wet. I hear from the bathroom "Eewwwwww!" as Melanie sees a tiny roach in the tub, and like a hero Mom swoops in and dispatches said roach. Not to worry, there are others.

Then as Melanie is perched on the throne she yells at me in the other room, closed doors or privacy forgotten because, well, she is *on vacation!*

"Dad, know what the princess said when she was on the toilet?"

I resist temptation and simply answer with "What?"

Like a budding poet, brimming with double or triple entendre, Melanie says "Cock-a-raoch-a-doooo!"

This is a time of breathless discovery. Delicacy and sophistication will come later. But I don't know where she's going to get it.

May 2002, Melanie 5 yrs 1 mo

Will Babysister Be Cute?

I have to confess, a cute kid was important to me before we adopted Melanie. It seemed like women never see an ugly child, but I sure had, lots of them.

In our travel group there were a couple of referral photos that prompted Julie and I to say privately "I'm sure glad that wasn't *our* referral." Melanie was cute but a couple of them looked like NFL linebackers. And then they all grew into beautiful kids.

Since our parenting started, I've learned a great deal. At first Melanie was a Chinese girl, and over time the Chinese part is often not noticed. Not that we would choose anything for her other than her

Chinese roots, but once you get past the superficial stage of getting to know your child and begin to love them, something happens that's hard to put into words. How they look helps to identify them in a crowd and remember what they look like, but it isn't who they are, it isn't what you love about them.

What you love is made up of a lot of intangibles, like how her eyes twinkle with mischief just before she strikes, the way she giggles during a frantic pillow fight, the way she loves to twirl her hot corn cob on a stick of butter and let it smear all over her face as she eats, her silent tears on Wednesday when her friends went home from school to play together and she didn't get to go, the way she held hands and jumped with her friend yesterday when I told them I was taking them home to play together, the shout of "Mom!" or "Dad!" with delight as you walk in the door from work, and so on.

These are the things that make her who she is. Ugly is just skin deep, but these things go all the way through.

That's why when we receive the referral package for Babysister, with photo and medical information, I have only one concern - that she be younger than Melanie to preserve Melanie's "first child" place in our family. If Babysister is too ugly, or too tall or too short or has a physical need that we can afford to deal with, it's OK because she needs a home, too. And over time we'll learn about the things that make her who she is, some like Melanie and some different I would guess, and before long we won't notice she's Chinese, either.

May 2002, Melanie 5 yrs 1 mo

Chants

As a five year old sprouts the beginnings of an attitude of independence, it's not necessarily pretty. Melanie had been whining for playmates all last week and this holiday weekend she went to her friend Alex's house all afternoon Saturday. Alex came over here all afternoon Sunday, and Melanie spent yesterday afternoon at Elizabeth's house. Busy and tired girl.

At about 6PM I fired up my brand new Broilmaster grill and prepped baby back ribs then launched the very first grilling guaranteed to slop sauce all over, kiss *new* goodbye. After the ribs had been sizzling for a little while, I took a package of mini-cobs of corn, Melanie's favorite, out of the freezer and started them on the stove inside. I asked Julie when Melanie would be home and she said "after dinner," and I thought that's a shame, Melanie will miss corn, her primary platform for butter.

But five minutes later Elizabeth's mom, Wendy, pulled in the driveway with the van and two kids still spinning at full play. Melanie yelled "*Dad! What you cooking*?" as she saw me on the deck tending to the ribs. Wendy gave me a wide berth since she could see I was sweaty and stinky from mowing the lawn, but Melanie, ever used to sweaty and stinky dad, asked me to lift her up so she could inspect the ribs. When she asked what else we were having for dinner and I told her tomatoes and little cobs of corn she literally licked her lips and said "MMmmmMMmmmMM," a multi-toned expression of hers reserved for occasions when "yummy" is inadequate.

"Hey, didn't you already have dinner?"

"We had some meat and purple ketchup and some milk to drink, but I'm ready to eat *corn*!" What she means is she is ready to eat a stick of butter with the aid of corn, and I never figured out the purple ketchup thing.

When the new Broilmaster completed its' maiden meal under my able and intense attention, we sat down to eat. As I've told you before,

Melanie delights in the corn-buttering method perfected by "Grandpa Mel in heaven," which is simply spinning a hot cob on top of a stick of butter.

I should tell you that Julie finds this pretty disgusting since when it comes to butter or sauces of any kind she is a *minimalist* and even that is understated. A tiny bit of butter or jelly or gravy or sauce spread on whatever is more than enough for her, and most often she passes entirely. You can just look at my silhouette and know my story is different. But Melanie, I am convinced, came by her brand of gluttony with butter honestly, meaning on her own, out of pure love of the tastes of this artery-clogging ambrosia.

So she lathered up her corn and, as usual, I told her "That's enough" and she gave me the look.

"The butter dish is right there beside you, you can have more later." That seemed to do it, at least for a moment. She took a couple of bites, smearing butter all over her face, and then with a look of smug defiance she went for the butter again. Bite then butter, two bites then butter.

Remember on Seinfeld when George was caught at a party "double-dipping" a chip and was banished from that particular group? George can't hold a candle to Melanie.

"Melanie, what if there were other people at the table? Do you think they'd want to use any of that butter after you've destroyed it with your corn?"

"No, and that's OK, Dad, because this is *my butter.*"

Melanie knows when her parents' tolerant mood will let her be silly so long as she doesn't go too far. So when I told her to take it easy on the butter she pushed the envelope.

"*Meaniac!*"

"What?"

"You're a meaniac!" Suddenly she was inspired to expand her verbal fisticuffs with recently learned weapons.

"Meanie-meanie, jelly beanie. Liar-liar, pants on fire, you sat on a wire." Now she's having fun and giggling. Then she unleashes the mother of all her kid-chants, at least for this week because this one is brand new.

"Double-double, loser-loser, get the picture, Duuuuuuh?" I have a feeling how "Duuuuuuh" is said is very important, because it's a multi-tone syllable with an up-tilt at the end to denote a question, accompanied by rolled eyes, Valley Girl style.

I let her know she had to be careful who heard her new ditty because it isn't polite. Sometimes you've got to apply discipline to mold little skulls full of mush into proper behavior, and then sometimes you've got to just chuckle and let it go, while thinking how much smarter she is than you were at her age. Where do you draw the line? Duuuuuh?

May 2002, Melanie 5 yrs 1 mo

Revenge

Last night I corralled Melanie long enough to sign a stack of books. Some customers wanted them for Father's Day, I had just 17 in stock and have to get them in the mail this morning since I promised. Sometimes when she is signing with five year old flair, Melanie gets a little too casual and rushed and I have to remind her to slow down, don't write too big so the letters will all fit. And I must admit that signing a few books is a treat for her, but a large stack seems like an overwhelming chore to a kid.

Last night as she signed and I started a stack of signed books, half way through she remarked "Dad, the first stack is getting smaller and the second stack is getting bigger!" Obvious to me, but a five year old mind is verbal.

This morning I entered and printed address labels before coffee, and then started to sign the stack of books myself. Melanie, seeing this activity that she and dad share, rushed in to climb up on my lap.

"You've already signed these books, it's time for me to sign them."

"I know." Said with a glint in her eye I have come to recognize in the female species as a red flag.

"Go eat your breakfast."

"No, I'll just sit here and watch you sign books."

So, as I grabbed book one, I literally wrote the first letter of my first name before I was stopped by something like a buzz-saw with a microphone, or maybe a Tasmanian Devil.

"*Don't write so big, you run out of room. No, don't start there, start over here. Did you get the letters right, huh, huh. Don't go so fast, you be careful to sign right, people pay hard money for their book, ok Dad?*"

A little astonished at the realization I had been frustrating her with my corrections, and almost physically floored by the assault, I was without words while my bride Julie enjoyed the best laugh of her week. Having slaughtered her prey in a most satisfying manner, Melanie leapt out of my lap and sauntered to her breakfast with the smug look of accomplishment known only to girls.

Women! I asked Melanie last week if she'd like to try playing roller hockey, looks like a good sport.

"Do girls play roller hockey, Dad?"

"Yep, they mix the boys and girls on the same team."

"Will there be any other girls on my team?"

"Probably."

Silence.

"Are you afraid of playing roller hockey with boys?" Wrong question.

"Dad, boys drool and girls rule!" With rolled eyes, naturally.

I guess in her mind, like Jesse Jackson's, if it rhymes it must be true.

And the truth is if she does play roller hockey I feel it's only fair that boys her age should be warned.

Jun 2002, Melanie 5 yrs 2 mos

Melanie Kicks a Grump

Do you remember the despicable creature *Salacious Crumb* that perched on the shoulder of Jaba the Hut in one of the Star Wars films? When the powerful and fearsome Jaba meted out harsh punishment to the unfortunate, this little critter would laugh and poke fun and generally make himself a nuisance under the aegis of Jaba. And when he sometimes awakened to the fact he had wandered outside the protective force of Jaba, his mouth would shut, his eyes would bulge, and he'd quickly scamper back to the place where he could return to being safely obnoxious.

I've been tempted to call Melanie "Mom's Little Salacious Crumb" now and then. When Julie and I bark at each other, rarely, in our original brand of humor, Melanie can be counted on to scurry critter-like from her near-Mom perch to come kick me in the shin accompanied by something like "Yeah, you better listen, Mister!"

So imagine the difficulty in my keeping a straight face when Julie told me she had signed Melanie up for Karate at pre-K summer camp. Of course, what can a five year old kid learn in one hour per week, at an age when a week is so long you forget everything anyway before the next class?

This is just the latest opportunity for me to flex my grumpy side, much as I have done with Melanie's dance lessons. And it's fresh on my mind since last week was Melanie's second recital, an event artificially made into a monumental production. Before you call me names, the fact I am a Grump is already well and widely known, so you might want to save your energy.

In Fayette County, Georgia, south of Atlanta unlike the north side where everything cosmopolitan resides, there are just a couple of well-known kid-dance organizations, and the one that owns Melanie is Carla's Dance Factory in Fayetteville. I like to call it Carla's cocaine corner, in adult company and in jest of course, because it's $35 for the dance lessons, then every week or so it's $35 for the recital, or $35 for the recital video, or $___ for tap shoes, or $___ for ballet shoes, or $___ for the tutu, or $___ for the non-tutu recital dress, or $___ for the spangled headband, and on and on, all of which one must order at - Carla's Dance Factory, of course. If I was told to fork over $350 for dance lessons which are really a happy weekly social encounter for Melanie, I wouldn't be so grumpy, but it's like a drug dealer getting someone hooked by saying "Here, try this!" then coming back for more and more, and it rubs me the wrong way.

Melanie with flowers purchased from . . . Carla

The truth is my grumpiness about the dance lessons is the kids haven't learned much of anything, no real skill, and if Julie were here she'd shush me again and remind me Melanie likes it. But last week during the recital, when Melanie was performing for the masses in her ever-so-cute fashion, I was biting my tongue when Julie said precisely what I was thinking:

"Looks like they're stepping on bugs." So I boldly added my second thought. "Or wiping something stinky off their feet."

Julie retorted with minor indignation "But they're having fun and what do you expect at five years old?" I'm smart enough to not even participate in an argument I have lost before a single word on my side is spoken. But I do expect more, I expect my kid to learn a skill of some sort that adds to her self-confidence, maybe expands her horizons in some way. Something more than stomping bugs, which I could teach her myself if I turn on the deck light in the summer.

Actually, Carla had some excellent older groups at the recital, unlike last year, with some girls showing real promise - so fans of Carla I know you're out there and I know Carla is great, so spare me the rebuttal. Being a Grump, lots of things rub me the wrong way, and it's usually me who objects while everyone else goes with the flow, like sheep I might add, not even aware they are being sheared now and then.

Melanie gets one hour of Karate a week, and I fully expect a command performance at some point where the kids demonstrate they have learned how to hold their hands vertically and yell something like "Yip-Yip" before they slap things. After Melanie's first so-called lesson, Mom asked what she had learned. Sure enough, she scurried over to kick me in the shin, but her wind up was so extreme she nearly fell down before whacking me pretty good and giving her Mom a triumphant smile.

So long as she learns to kick Dad with style, Mom and Melanie will be content with this latest entertainment masquerading as learning, and my complaints will fall on deaf ears. I'm just a Grump.

* * *

Some of this story was more grumpiness than truth, and I hasten to add the first thing Melanie learned in Karate was respect, not bullying. If you don't recognize my writing style as tongue in cheek you should put this book down right now and read something more safe for you, like Strunk's Elements of Style or maybe the dictionary. Nevertheless, my wife feels compelled to rebut, so her version follows.

Grump Rebuttal
by Julie Garlock

Obviously, Terry and I don't always agree about Melanie's activities. Here's my version. Oh, and folks, Terry just likes to be Grumpy so he doesn't have to take Melanie to the rehearsals. Gentlemen, it works.

". . . the kids haven't learned much of anything, no real skill . . ."

Not true. If you really watch you'll see they are performing the more common ballet positions and doing pirouettes. In tap they are doing things like a step ball change and a shuffle step among others. Most notably they are learning to dance together, do a routine and overall becoming more graceful. I admit they are not always in sync and many times struggling not to fall down. They progressed a lot this year. Fred/Ginger/Gene and others were not created in a year or two.

". . . But I do expect more, I expect my kid to learn a skill of some sort that adds to her self-confidence, maybe expands her horizons in some way . . ."

I agree. Let's take Mom's perspective. If getting up on a stage in front of 150+ people, dancing your heart out, feeling down right beautiful in your costume because your Daddy said you were, and showing everyone you can do a routine - albeit a little uncoordinated at times - does not teach a skill that improves self confidence or expands horizons in some way, I'll eat mayonnaise on sandwiches for a year! I *hate* mayonnaise. Gone without a few meals because of it.

Melanie told me several times she was afraid she wouldn't do well. She was nervous and afraid. But she did it! Isn't that what learning is about? Being nervous and unsure but doing it? While it may not be true, she believes that she was the best dancer out there because we told her she was. Her self-confidence and esteem grew from this experience. She has learned new dance steps she is proud of, has learned to work in a team, and is slowly becoming more graceful. She certainly has more grace than her parents do! Well, me anyway. I can't speak for Terry; Papa don't dance.

"So imagine the difficulty in my keeping a straight face when Julie told me she had signed Melanie up for Karate at pre-K summer camp. Of course, what can a five year old kid learn in one hour per week, at an age when a week is so long you forget everything anyway before the next class?"

A lot and she doesn't forget. Heck, she can tell us practically everything that has happened since she was two. Melanie can recount every parenting error we've made in detail with built in guilt. It is not the amount of time spent in the class that matters so much, it's the time spent practicing. For dance, Melanie practiced a little in her room. She practiced a pirouette she could not perform that everyone else could until she could do it, too.

Wasn't she learning perseverance? Seems like a good skill to me. To become more accomplished at the steps she, like the others would require more lessons and studio time. The truth is neither Terry nor I have the desire to take her to dance lessons two or three times a week. It may be inevitable since she seems to like it. Buckle your seat belt, dear, I'm sure I have to go out of town when that happens.

As Terry noted, I believe that skill should be scaled on age. From my perspective, the children are seeking what delights them in life from their own experience level which isn't much. At five life should be simple, and I say let them have fun. Fill them up with love and laughter, guide them, teach them to be respectful and protect them. The real world sets in fast enough. Life should have a good balance of seriousness and fun.

As for Melanie's Tae Kwon-Do class? I have never seen such a large grin on her face. She loved it. I searched for something that is known to build self confidence, self esteem, self control, and self reliance. Everything I heard, read, and everyone I talked to with children in martial arts said these things are the essence of true martial arts. If she gains these things and learns to kick some butt at the same time, so be it. Not to worry, people. This is just our brand of humor. Rough housing with Dad was one of my favorite things as a child and Terry and Melanie do it for fun. She is not a mean child.

Oh, and Dear, I think the sound she made when kicking you was "heeyahhh" not "yip-yip". Hopefully, the respect part sets in quick or your shins will be a bevy of bruises. Don't worry, Nurse Melanie will fix you right up. An ounce of Neosporin and seven band-aids in rapid succession should do it. If not, she'll repeat the torture, I mean nursing, until healed.

Julie Garlock

Jun 2002, Melanie 5 yrs 2 mos

Scaring Away a Dark Mood

Dark moods are unpredictable. Sometimes they seem to hide under the couch and snag your toe as you walk by, then when you sit down to do whatever they wrap around your legs and sneak up your back and up over your head and before you know it you're suffocated by a full-grown funk.

Being a Grump like me is different than wallowing in a dark mood. Being a Grump is half intellectual choice and half evolution. Getting older has nudged me toward these attitudes - a decreasing tolerance for baloney, an escalating irritation that the dips of the world have gained so much power, a hardening unwillingness to accept the petty manipulation served up by daily life as nimrods unqualified to shine your shoes try to guide you like cattle through the gate, up the ramp and in the car because, well, the rules someone designed to manipulate you say so. See, you're feeling a little grumpy already. And I used to wonder about *old cranks*.

But Saturday, in addition to my normal Grump self, I didn't feel good and was wrapped in a dark mood, too. So when Melanie wanted to *fight* I said no. Sometimes five year olds don't hear the frequency of "no" and she persisted because she was ready for some rough play, some wrestling or semi-pretend boxing or pillow fight, but I pushed her away and with Mom's help I was relieved of that burden so I could wallow appropriately in my funk.

In a little while I sat out on the deck being nursed by a cocktail, and Mom told Melanie "Show Dad how you skip rope."

As I looked on with a wrinkled and skeptical brow, Melanie threw the skip rope back over her head, she stooped just a little and strained noticeably with a windup, *heaved* the rope forward over her head, waited a couple of beats until everything stopped moving, and then jumped flatfooted over the wrinkled-up rope lying in front of her feet, followed by a triumphant look of satisfaction.

The dark mood must have scrambled for its' life back underneath the couch because I laughed so hard I could feel my face turn red. Melanie, poor girl, didn't know what was quite so funny but she kept doing her flatfooted jump over a pathetic ribbon of rope lying still on the deck, and I had one of those laughs you feel way down deeper than your stomach.

Dark moods she can sometimes overcome, but she will not dislodge me from my grumpiness, I'm content and cemented in that role.

And for those of you who are concerned that Melanie, and maybe I, need some counseling on rough play, I have a message:

Relax.

Jun 2002, Melanie 5 yrs 2 mos

Snookering Mom

When Melanie was four we started giving her a weekly allowance of $1 for each year of her age, now it's $5.

At first, Melanie's eyes would shine at the very thought of her own money to buy just what she wanted. And she learned to save some to spend on others, save some for her own future, and to save the rest so she could buy things that cost more than she had. If nothing else she learned that things cost money and sometimes lots of money.

Now, at the ripe old age of five her attitude has, well, deteriorated. I think it needs a little maintenance, perhaps a good reminder that parenting is never done.

In the old days, back when she was four, I would remind her it's Friday and watch her glow as I gave her the money. Today she reminds *me* it's Friday and taps her toe with one hand on her hip and the other held out as she demands "Where's my 'lowance, Dad?" So much for gratitude.

One of my perpetual gripes, as you might expect from a Grump, is Melanie's ever-accumulating mountain of toys and dolls. For one thing I foresee a problem when Babysister comes home and develops a desire to have an equal mountain of her own, which is not possible without renting warehouse space. And perhaps a new source of income.

You might think it sounds cute for little darling to say "Dad, let me show you my new baby!" but it wears thin after the 20th time. The other day a friend named Wendy stopped her car in the street to yell at me in my golf cart on a parallel path that her daughter Elizabeth told her Melanie said we had a new baby, and Wendy wondered if we had already been to China to bring home Babysister. I wondered for a moment what the heck she was talking about, then it dawned on me Melanie was talking about her latest doll, which she calls a "baby."

So you can guess my grumpy attitude a few days ago when Melanie once again ran into the house exclaiming "Dad, want to see my new baby?" Yippee. I gave Julie the look, and she shrugged and said "I told her it cost more money than she had, but she got me."

"What do you mean?"

"She said 'No, Mom, I got lots of money.' Then she sat down right in the middle of the Wall-Mart aisle, opened her plastic little purse and started pulling out dollar bills in wads. She had $17 in her purse. I asked her where she got that much money, and she said when I leave money on the counter like I don't want it she sticks it in her purse because she *does* want it. After what I said, since she had the money I let her buy the doll. At least she didn't lie about the money."

So whaddayagonnado? Throw the new doll on the top of the pile, if you can throw that high. But Melanie is happy with the newest addition to her family. Did I tell you she has a double stroller? She couldn't figure out how to attach two strollers side by side so she could push two of her babies at the same time; I helped her with rubber bands.

One of her birthday presents is a *puppet theater* and she immediately and instinctively started a mini-production of Hansel & Gretel beginning with "Ladeeees and Gentlemens" . . . She hasn't thought of it yet, but she will, she has enough babies to line up and make quite an audience.

Jun 2002, Melanie 5 yrs 2 mos

Father's Day 2002

On Father's Day the sun was well up when I was awakened by the stomp of little feet too impatient to wait until after coffee, and the rustle of tissue paper covering something in a gift bag.

"Wake up, Dad! Happy Father's Day!"

Before both eyes are fully opened Melanie has climbed onto me in the bed, thrust the gift bag to me and impatiently waited a few seconds before insisting I open it . . . right now!

So I did, proclaiming my surprise at the package's contents, and Melanie's lust for gift-giving was quenched for a while. It gives me some satisfaction to watch her preparing for and giving things to others. At just five years old she seems to enjoy giving as much as receiving a package.

Well, almost. She knows the UPS truck as the *package man* who delivers things that are either for dad's business, for Melanie from one of her grandmas or aunts, or once in a while for Mom. But she is just five after all and emotions still overtake short memory cells sometimes, and when she discovers a package is for my business she might say something like "I *never* get a package!" with melodramatic disappointment.

The day before, on Saturday, we took the golf cart to our neighborhood bank to open Melanie's very own savings account. Ms. Marshjun at Regions Bank explained how the Junior Banker account worked to Melanie, not to me or Julie though we were allowed to eavesdrop, and she helped Melanie make her first deposit. Now when she gets her allowance for doing her chores, she can set part of it aside to deposit and save.

The bank is next door to the school where Melanie starts Kindergarten in August. Much to my surprise, Marshjun told me on Wednesdays a bank employee sets up shop in the elementary school so the kids can make savings deposits. I asked her what the minimum deposit would be. She shrugged and said "Some kids deposit just a

quarter, but it teaches them to save." What a nice idea. I wrote the bank
president to give Marshjun and her staff a big *attaboy.*

Marshjun Robinson, Customer Service mgr at the Kedron branch of
Regions Bank in Peachtree City, helps Melanie open a savings account

Melanie proudly told her friends about her banking experience. Then on Sunday when I pulled into the bank to withdraw cash from the ATM, Melanie asked:

"Dad, are we going to take some of my money out?"

"No. Your money stays in the bank."

"But what if I want to buy that doll I told you about."

"That's not what you're saving money for, this is for your future."

"But Ms. Marshjun said I can take it out when I want tooooo."

"Ms. Marshjun said you can take it out when Mom and Dad say it's OK, and it's not OK to buy toys."

"It's for college, right, Dad?"

"Right. If we save enough and it grows it will help pay for part of your college."

"OK. What you going to do since it's Father's Day, Dad, you want to play with me?"

"We can play a little while, then I'm going to watch golf on TV."

So we played a little bit, but the truth is it was mostly Mom sunning on the deck and watching Melanie splash in the little pool I filled up for her, and I lazily watched Tiger Woods struggling to protect his lead in the US Open, torn between my loyalty to Woods and Mickelson the underdog in hot pursuit and desperately seeking his first "major" win.

When Melanie came in and wanted to wrestle with just three holes left to play I reminded her I was watching golf. She said:

"Is Tiger winning again?"

"He sure is."

"Sheesh, Tiger win this, Tiger win that. Why Tiger always win?"

"Because he works hard and he beat the other players."

Between then and the end of the tournament she forgot to leave me alone, but only 10 or 15 times. A Father's Day could be worse.

June 2002, Melanie 5 yrs 2 mos

Melanie Learns Goodbye - Part 2

Melanie learned even before she talked much that Mom or Dad have to go away sometimes. Even more important, she learned they always come back. Sometimes it was hard, still is, since what she knows in her brain is overcome for a little while by a heart that really, really, really doesn't want one of us to go away for a few days.

Then when Melanie was three, she learned what goodbye forever means when Mr. Ed next door passed away with cancer. Ed had been Melanie's stand-in grandpa since her Grandpa Roy and Grandpa Mel had died before she could meet them. She tried hard to understand, she went to the memorial service where everyone heard her ask Mom "What's Dad doing up there?" when I said a few words about Ed. She has missed Mr. Ed, who was a kidder with an endless supply of jokes in his pocket, and always a twinkle in his eye for Melanie.

But even before that, her friend Katlyn moved away, then Mr. Keith and Ms. Lynda moved not too far away. I overheard Melanie tell her friend Alex as they rode on the back seat of the golf cart as we passed by their back yard pool: "It's so sad, Alex, Mr. Keith and Ms. Lynda moved away. But don't worry, they said they be back to visit."

Another neighbor, Mr. Bill and Ms. Kim finally sold their house last week and moved back to Vermont, and when Melanie hugged daughters Jennifer and 'Becca goodbye her lip quivered and she didn't know what to say. Exactly.

She later scolded me "Dad, you should have let Jennifer baby-sit me more."

Ms. Liz next door, Mr. Ed's wife, is moving to Virginia to be near her children and Melanie wants to know "When will we see her again, Dad?" Don't know.

And now - Mom and Melanie and I looked at one another in disbelief - Mr. Paul and Ms. Kim and Sarah and Rachel are moving to a new house across town.

"Dad, we sure gots lots of people moving out of our neighborhood, don't we?"

As an earthy friend used to say "Fer a true fact!" Since it seems all our buddies are moving away, maybe it's time to make some new buddies with our new neighbors. Seems like forever since we had a neighborhood cookout or golf tournament. Sure wish someone else would get things organized - but that's what everybody thinks and that's why it never happens. I better get busy.

"But just 'cause they move away that don't mean they die, they not going to heaven yet, right, Dad?"

"That's right, they're still alive and kicking." I dread the day some butthead feels compelled to tell her about hell when she mentions heaven, and their iron-clad version of the stupid rules about who goes where. So far we've escaped that, but it won't last.

While on an evening golf cart excursion with Melanie she was looking up at the sky and asked:

"Dad, can people in heaven see us?"

"I don't know, maybe they can."

"Do they stay there forever?"

"I guess so, but nobody ever called me an expert on heaven."

"When they go to heaven they get to be stars. So Grandpa Roy and Grandpa Mel and Mr. Ed got to be stars, right, Dad?"

"Maybe you're right, maybe they're stars."

"There sure are lots of stars, Dad."

"Yep, there sure are."

Sometimes a conversation with Melanie will cure what ails you.

Jun 2002, Melanie 5 yrs 2 mos

A New Patriot

Melanie's buddy Alex joins us for the parade

Melanie had been anticipating the festivities for days because Peachtree City, Georgia on the 4th of July is a treat for kids of all ages.

The uninitiated are startled at the sight of thousands of golf carts jamming 70 miles of golf cart paths through the woods, each cart decorated to the hilt with flag derivatives, racing one another to the morning parade to pick their favorite spot.

With thousands of golf carts lining the route, huge fire trucks blip their sirens, honor guards march, the mayor and other politicians walk or ride as they greet constituents, then come police officers, high school bands, floats, convertibles bearing selected beauty queens who twist their palms in "the wave," horses followed by poop scooper golf carts, and many others, all tossing bits of wrapped candy to the kids who mix competition and cooperation as only kids can do. Norman Rockwell would be proud.

After mid-day barbeque, Melanie and Alex torturing Mom in the pool, and lazy conversation with friends, we reload the golf cart at sundown for the fireworks show. The golf cart race takes on a different flavor with fading light, and we join hundreds of other carts jamming the Homestead course third fairway at Flat Creek Country Club for a great view of the fireworks.

Kids and parents alike ooooh and aaaaah through the bursts of color and sound, and this year the finale was spectacular.

Melanie forgot her friend Alex and fell asleep on mom's shoulder as I followed the trail of red tail-lights through the woods on the way home. I think she was content.

Melanie is too young to notice, but this year there was something different in Peachtree City, and I imagine in many other towns in the USA.

The flag decorations this year following 9/11 were a bit more intense. As the parade honor guard, fire department and police officers approached our spot a hush fell over the crowd as if they were unsure how to react, and then the crowd broke into applause, loud clapping and cheers. These people who risk their lives to protect us were clearly gratified at the warm reception, and some older ones probably wondered what had kept public support so well hidden for so long.

My own theory is the country turned cynical and jaded long ago when our own cultural revolution and the war in Vietnam divided us, and criticizing or even vilifying our military and "the establishment" became fashionable.

We haven't seen much unabashed US patriotism in the last thirty years until after 9/11, but through it all I do know many have never wavered in their love of the USA and disappointment in anti-US sentiments we have endured at home and abroad.

It is gratifying to see a widespread patriotic awakening, and I hope it endures. I'm reminded of the words of a long forgotten politician named Adlai Stevenson, who said in 1952 patriotism ". . . is not short, frenzied outbursts of emotion, but the tranquil and steady dedication of a lifetime."

For those whose patriotism is recently revived, I'm sure Adlai and the rest of us believe in redemption and extend our welcome. As for Melanie, she is proud to have been born in China, and she is proud to be a US citizen. When she sees a full moon she asks how long until the Chinese Moon Festival. Her hand darts to her heart when she hears the words of the Pledge of Allegiance and she quickly joins in the words she learned when she was three. She waves the flag and admires police officers, firefighters and members of the armed forces. I expect she'll try to grow out of that in her teens, and I'll try harder not to let her.

The USA needs a new generation of patriots, and I think Melanie is a fine example so far.

Jul 2002, Melanie 5 yrs 3 mos

Budding Inhibitions

Melanie knows when I pick her up from pre-K on the golf cart to strap on her seat belt on the passenger side. When she was three she "helped" me install the seatbelts so kids could ride safely.

But yesterday she said "Dad, can I sit in your lap, pleeeeze?" So I knew she missed her nap and was tired, ready to put her arms around my neck, her head on my shoulder, and doze off on the way home, lulled to sleep by the rocking and bumping of the golf cart. One of the revelations to me as a parent was the complete trust your child places in you, such as Melanie's falling asleep while I'm bouncing down the cart path veering this way and that, swaying as I turn and hitting hard on a few deep holes or when I stray off the path as an oncoming cart passes too close. She just knows I won't let anything happen to her and she is completely relaxed.

Melanie is a happy and affectionate child, always has to give a round of hugs when she's leaving school or play, and occasionally blurts out "I love you." When she's tired she is even more prone to say such things, which makes me think at five she is slowly developing an initial layer of inhibitions, a portent of more and more inhibitions as she grows until her spontaneity is suppressed much of the time like the rest of us, with occasional outbursts of honesty.

Not that she suppresses much yet. Just yesterday she told me:

"Daddy, your armpits are hairy and they stink!"

"Well, maybe you should stop sticking your finger in there to take a whiff."

"Alex says her Daddy's armpits are hairy and stinky, too."

"That's comforting. Why don't you check out your Mom's armpits?"

Sometimes diversion is the best defense.

"Her armpits don't have no hair."

"If she didn't shave them she'd have hair in her armpits as long as your legs."

Melanie didn't know whether to believe that, smart girl.

"That's OK, Dad, I love you anyway if you have hairy stinky armpits. Mom says that's how boys are."

"Thanks."

So far I think five is the very best age, but I've said that every year.

Jul 2002, Melanie 5 yrs 3 mos

Girls or Frogs?

Melanie took swim lessons with her buds Darby and Alex a few weeks ago, Mon-Thu in the evening for two weeks. A swim-cookout at Alex's house was dubbed "graduation" and the kids ate it up.

But can they swim? No. They made progress in varying degrees, but Melanie and Darby were a bit reluctant and lagged behind Alex, the enthusiastic frog. Of course Alex has her own pool. And by frog I mean dog-paddling just below the surface with eyes open and no fear.

Of course for kids fear of deep water is a good thing until swimming is instinctive even if imperfect. Which is one reason Julie takes Melanie to the pool at the gym, to continue her attempts to conquer the water. And dang if they didn't do it. Last night is the second night they went to the pool this week, and on Monday Julie reported that Melanie finally *got it* and swam like a fearless frog. Now if we can get her on the surface she'll be good for distance, too.

When my little frog returned last night her eyes were a bit bloodshot, and though I knew she was tired from where she had been I also knew from what she said. Her budding inhibitions must have been down a bit because as she snuggled me and told me about her swimming she said:

"My heart wiggles, Dad."

"What?"

"My heart, Dad. Why my grandpas have to die so fast?"

"I don't know. They didn't want to die."

"But I didn't get to see them."

"I know. And they wanted to see you, too."

Then off to bed where she talked to Mom until she dropped into sleep like a gunny sack of bricks. Melanie reveals her bent to affection when she talks about the grandpas she never knew, the people to whom she has had to say goodbye, her Babysister as she sets aside special gifts to save, and anyone and everyone when they are feeling bad.

Five year old girls might teach lessons to the rest of us.

Jul 2002, Melanie 5 yrs 3 mos

Did Your Team Win?

When you're a parent at first you vow to do all the right things raising your child. But it doesn't work out that way. Remember the country song about getting your *stupid sign*? I have extras if you want one.

And as your kid gets old enough to talk to you and ask innocent questions, maybe they'll be like Melanie and ambush you with questions outside the comfort zone. One day when she was just three Melanie crawled up into my lap and asked:

"Why were you in a war, Dad?"

Uh-oh. "I just was, now do you want to watch Barney?"

"Dad, what's a war?"

"That's where two countries are fighting each other."

"Why?" Good question.

Back pain is a part of my life I've had to accept since I was 21, and since Melanie noticed and asked questions Mom told her I flew helicopters in a war and I was shot down and the crash broke Daddy's back, so it hurts and he has to rest sometimes. Mom did the right thing, you can't lie to your kid without accumulating consequences.

And later that year Melanie met *Mr. John* Synowsky, one of the two young officers who risked their life to rescue me the day I was shot down in Vietnam. So she knows what she calls "the military war" was an important part of Dad's life.

Now that Melanie is five her questions are harder to deflect.

"Did people get killed in your war, Dad?"

"Yes, they did."

"Did they shoot you?"

"I shot at them and they shot at me. Go get a book and we'll read."

"Was there blood?"

"Melanie, that's not something for kids to talk about."

"Did you have blood when your helicopter crashed?"

"No."

"But how come you got hurt with no blood?"

"Sometimes when you get hurt there's no blood. Remember how much it hurt when you bonked your bean the other day?"

"Yes."

"There was no blood then, was there? Show me where you hit your head, was it here?" But diversions don't always work.

"Did you shoot people?" Silent pause. How do I make this go away? If I lie to her and she finds out later she'll wonder what else is a lie. But what do you tell a five year old?

"Did you kill anybody, Dad?" I could write a book about that question, but only guys who were there would understand. I do know this, I'm not taking it any further with a five year old.

"Lets go see what Mom's doing." That diversion worked, but that was weeks ago.

Today when I picked up Melanie at pre-K she said:

"Is Mom taking me swimming tonight?"

"She sure is."

"Did your team win, Dad?"

"What?"

"In the military war, when your helicopter got shot and you got hurt, did your team win?" Good grief, weeks have passed since she asked a question about war, and these come as a bit of a surprise.

While standing in the pre-school hallway my thoughts turned to the faces of friends who died a violent death just when their adult life was beginning, smiling and enthusiastic faces, frozen forever young in my mind, the ones who deserve at least the memory of what happened and why. They deserve better than the disdain so many in the country had at the time for young men in uniform, and they deserve to have their sacrifice noticed, not ignored. I want my girls to know who deserves their admiration, no matter what their revisionist history schoolbooks might say, I want them to know who fought for their country when it was not socially acceptable. I want them to understand that freedom is not free, and that sometimes fighting to help a country defend its' freedom is so hard there are no easy answers. I want them to reflect on the people ready to saddle up and ride into hell to defend freedom. I want them to compare those people to the chattering class at home who protest or critique in comfort and safety, so they can answer my question "Who do you admire?"

But not now. Melanie is too young and Babysister isn't even here yet.

Melanie noticed the faraway look in my eye as I stood there and she repeated "Hey, Dad, did your team win?"

"Yep, my team won. You want some dinner before you change into your swimsuit?"

"OK, Dad."

There will be plenty of time for her to hear the truth about my war later, when she's older. Since I want to make sure she hears the truth from me and I don't know if I'll live a long life, I have written what I want her to know at the end of this book in "The Long Story of the Elephant." When Melanie is older she can read what I have written and ponder the imponderables. And if what I tell Melanie and Babysister prompts them to once in a while say thanks to a young soldier, Dad will rest easy even though the fans left early, the coach was a dumbass, and even though we fought with honor and skill and courage my team did not win.

Jul 2002, Melanie 5 yrs 3 mos

Spinach and Buttermilk in Jail

Yesterday when Melanie kissed me goodbye as she left with Mom for school, she asked if I would bring something to school after lunch, but I don't hear well. What? Candy Kisses? Why? But they were gone.

It had something to do with having enough candy to make sure every kid gets one, something Melanie worries over whenever she is taking something to school to share.

Oh, well. My job is not to know why, just to deliver. So I stopped at Kroger after lunch and they had all kinds of candy but naturally were out of Kisses. With an extra trip to Eckerd I delivered the Kisses as instructed to Primrose school. Melanie interrupted her play to take the package, grinning large. I was in a hurry so I didn't even ask. Later that day when I picked her up from school I asked her if they enjoyed the Kisses.

"Oh, we didn't need them today, Dad, but we might use them tomorrow." OK, my job is just to deliver.

"Dad, when Ms. Maria got stopped by the policeman, why didn't he take her to jail?"

"She was just speeding a little. You have to do something real bad to go to jail."

"When you're in jail you have to eat spinach and drink buttermilk."

"Really?"

"Yeah, Alex says."

Well, Melanie is only five and Alex is five *and a half* so she should know.

Today when Melanie kissed me goodbye she told me she was going on a field trip to the police department - big time! So when I picked her up I asked how she liked the visit to the police department. She said fine.

On the golf cart drive home we passed by a couple of foxes, I mean young women, jogging in their flashy jogging getup. Melanie's head snapped around to watch them and said:

"Boy, Dad, they sure are running hard."

"They sure are."

"Do you want to give them a ride?"

"No." They don't want a ride and I don't want to get beat up by Mom.

"Oh, yeah, I know why. They're *strangers*, Dad, and you have to be careful not to ride with *strangers*, right, Dad?"

"That's right." At least she knows to be careful.

"You know what to do if a stranger grabs you?"

"Yeah, dial 9-1-1, and the police will come help you."

"That's right, but before you dial 9-1-1 you have to get away, so you scream *heeeelp*! OK?"

"OK."

"Dad, *we saw the jail!*!"

"Wow. What do they eat in there?"

"Spinach and buttermilk. *Euuuuuuw, gross!*"

I guess if Alex says so it must be true.

Jul 2002, Melanie 5 yrs 3 mos

Password

Melanie knows things a five year old should not have to know. She knows that five year old Samantha was kidnapped in California by a "bad man" who killed her, even though her friend ran to tell Grandma. It was too late. And she asks if they found Elizabeth Smart in Utah yet. Not yet.

She knows because she catches glimpses on TV and asks questions, but mostly because we talk to her about it. Not because we want to, and in spite of the fact that the media fails in the "perspective" department because you'd never know from TV that child abductions in the US are much less frequent than they used to be. But when you're a parent you discover you'd gladly die a thousand times so long as your little one is protected, and you tend to ignore statistics when they mitigate the abduction and molestation and murder of a child.

So Julie dutifully teaches Melanie through practice and role play how to stand back from a stranger in case he tries to grab her, how to respond if told her mom or dad or grandma told him to pick her up, or if he asks her to help him find his puppy or offers candy or whatever, and in case he grabs her how to kick and scream as loud as she can - "*Heeeeelllllp.*"

So Julie told her we needed a password. That's so if we really do send someone to pick her up she'll be able to ask for the password and feel safe, either that or run like hell! Melanie had to gather the family around to come up with a password. After a couple of false starts I suggested one we all know - "Butthead," and Melanie improved it into "Daddy is a Butthead," and I liked it. Mom rejected it because too many people know Butthead is our family endearment.

Eventually Melanie came up with a good one and we all agreed that our password would be . . . I can't tell you. Too bad a five year old has to know a password.

Jul 2002, Melanie 5 yrs 3 mos

Graduation from Pre-School

Melanie's graduation photo from Primrose Preschool

Sometimes life's milestones slip up on you, even pass you by with no great notice. Noteworthy events don't seem to be so at the time, they take on their importance with the passage of time. But every once in a while I scratch and crawl out of the rut of daily life and actually *forsee* an upcoming event as being important. So it is with Melanie starting Kindergarten next month.

When I talk to Melanie about Kindergarten, her eyes shine with anticipation of the world of the "big kids," and there's something else. Apprehension. The unknown.

Like most kids Melanie is a complex package - happy, smiling, huggy, smart, alert, confident, content, but with new people shy, a little afraid, self-conscious, withdrawn. She usually takes a warm-up period of about five minutes, and then she and her new friend are tearing around the house or yard like little rocket motors.

When Melanie came home from China with us in 1998 at twelve months old, Julie took a month off work to stay with her, then Melanie started full time to Primrose School, a combination day care and pre-school here in Peachtree City, close enough for golf cart trips. I doubt Melanie has thought about it much, but in a few days she is going to be saying goodbye to people, some at least, that she has grown to love, and it won't be an easy goodbye.

When she first started Primrose School, after she settled into the routine and as she grew into a toddler interacting with other kids, I worried that because she is different - Asian and adopted - she might be or feel less than accepted by her peers. We all know how cruel kids can be, and we want to protect ours from that. But Melanie grew to be the darling of the school, seemed to be Miss Popular, and eventually I worried that *she* would be the one who scorned or excluded other kids. But again I learned from her, as her teachers tell us she is the first to help pick up toys, the last to misbehave, sometimes the only one to the rescue of someone being picked on, the one who invites new kids for play. I am quite proud of her. Of course she shows her devilish side now and then and talks too much in school.

Melanie has learned to fend for herself in a group of kids, but when her buddies act a little too aggressive in edging her out or gaining the upper hand you can see the glow in her eyes dim as she pulls back, as if a magic little switch inside all of us called "You don't like me?" turns on and her mood changes in a flash.

When I pick Melanie up from Primrose today I'm sure like every other day she will have to give everyone nearby a hug goodbye, and she will go as far out of her way as needed to give every teacher a hug on her way to the door, sometimes while Dad taps his toes because he's seen this a thousand times. When she says goodbye on Friday for the last time she might have a little bit of difficulty.

As she prepares for Kindergarten I have no concerns about her learning abilities, she has been at the head of her classes' learning level. I do worry about when and where she will encounter merciless teasing about being Asian or being adopted, and I wonder what more we can do to prepare her for that. At some point she has to get beat up by life but I don't want it to happen. She knows her birthmother and birthfather probably loved her but could not keep her, she is proud she is from China, she knows adoption is a very good thing and she knows our family is forever. Now if we can teach her to use that knowledge and belief as a defense when needed, she'll be better prepared for the world.

Maybe something like "I'm sorry you're ignorant about adoption, it's how me and my Mom and Dad became a forever family." Or, "I'm sorry you don't know very much about different races. Maybe you should ask your teacher." Well, I don't know, I sort of favor the drop-kick but Julie keeps me in line.

Saturday Mom took Melanie on a school clothes shopping orgy. I was spared. When they arrived home, *the girls* had to show me each piece, and Melanie would alternately model something with an impish grin, roll her eyes, declare "cool!" or even shake her booty at me. While Melanie was delighting in shaking her booty at me with giggles, and I do see trouble ahead there, I was struck by how comfortable she is with her life, especially so long as Mom is within reach. Here's what I mean.

Melanie doesn't live in our house with us, we three just happen to live here, if you get the difference. Melanie is not a Chinese child in a Caucasian family, she is our daughter and we often forget she is Chinese because, well, race isn't who you are, it's just your outer wrapping, and with family members we move past the superficial stage and don't notice things that outsiders see first. Melanie is very aware she is Chinese and notices other people's Asian features in a heartbeat. But Julie has done a great job teaching her how God made us all different, and it's what's in our heart that matters.

Melanie is comfortable and content in her life, she does not feel in any way out of place in our family, she feels she is where she is supposed to be, in charge in fact, and we are the ones who are supposed to be her parents. When I say we forget Melanie is Chinese some people in this adoption community get their nose out of joint because we are supposed to be sensitive to everything Chinese. That's not the point. The point is when you are racially different and different by adoption, maybe the apogee of human dynamics is when "it doesn't matter" whether you are Chinese.

It will matter to others in Melanie's life, but home is a place to Melanie where it doesn't matter and she can be herself. Completely.

At this juncture in Melanie's life I am very satisfied with a couple of things as parents. Julie is my nominee as Mother of the Decade. While she is no June Cleaver, Julie is either at work, asleep, or doing something with Melanie. If you wanted a picture of the quintessential mother-daughter platonic love affair, you just need a click on Melanie and her Mom. They are inseparable, and drag me along now and then. Those two would rather be doing something together, holding hands or even arguing, than anything else in the world.

When I think back to 1998 we three have come a long way. Writing these stories has been a new chapter in my life. You wouldn't know it but I am really a fairly private person. I would never stand in front of a group and say these things. The anonymity of the keyboard and screen, and your feedback asking for more, has encouraged me to show the world my soft side, in these messages and in my book.

If there's one thing that will bring out your soft side, it's your child, and I'm glad to have had this chapter which needs to close for the sake of Melanie's privacy. I would probably enjoy continuing to write about Melanie forever, it's an emotional outlet to express the father-daughter fondness that too often stays bottled up somewhere. But we have lived in a glass house as I have written these stories about her and our family, and as she starts school she deserves to have the shades pulled down, at least part way, before she's old enough to feel a bit like a zoo exhibit.

I'm glad to have written these pieces about Melanie, to capture the memories and to show her she could not be more loved if she were our biological child. She may not have that conclusion at her first read but as the years pass I think she will value what has been written about her.

She starts school soon. I'll write a story about her now and then, not as many, but now comes Babysister in early 2003. I'll write some about her, but do I want to put her in a glass house as I did Melanie?

We'll find out soon.

Jul 2002, Melanie 5 yrs 3 mos

Waiting for Babysister

Melanie is waiting for Babysister. Mom and Dad, of course, don't wait. While others pull their hair out, bite their fingernails and tear off calendar pages with a hopeful eye on planned holidays, Julie and I just yawn and go with the flow, absorbing the next delay as a routine matter we cannot control, so why raise the blood pressure? Sure, we might drum our fingers or tap our toes privately, but we admit no tension and project outward calm. Why obsess over something you cannot control? You can be stressed or calm, take your pick. We pick calm.

I'm a world-class procrastinator, but the room upstairs that needs painting comes to mind more and more often. Drum-drum-drum. But I'm not waiting or planning holidays or driving anyone nuts.

We learned from a credible source the referral of kids from the Chinese officials was accelerating. But it didn't happen as expected. Drum-drum. Tap-tap. But we're not waiting.

"Mom, when do we go get Babysister?"

"I don't know, it takes a long time, doesn't it?" Tap-tap-tap.

"Yeah." But Melanie occupies her wait by stockpiling little gifts for Babysister. And plotting.

Mom says "Melanie, what's the first thing you teach Babysister?"

"To aggavate *Daad*! Right, Mom?"

"That's right."

But for now she has to satisfy herself by "aggavating" me all by herself. And I take my hat off to her, she's up to the job.

The other day at a Mexican restaurant, our favorite because they have great Texas Margaritas and terrific fajitas, Melanie fidgeted sitting next to Mom as usual, getting herself in a little trouble by talking too loud and came to sit on my side for a moment of peace. She put her arm around my neck and grabbed my ear to tell me a secret, but all I could hear was "sux" and I looked at her and said "What?" She tried again.

"Mom says no drugs, no smoking, no alcohol, and she said no sux till I'm married. OK, Dad?"

"That sounds great to me. But you'll be 35 by then."

"Dad, why did you smoke. It's not good for you, is it?"

"No, it isn't. But I don't smoke cigars any more." But if a good Cuban comes along, you never know . . .

"But I saw you!"

"Good grief, kiddo, cut your Dad some slack. That was three years ago."

"Dad, does your Margarita have alcohol?"

Uh-oh, I don't like where this is going. "Yep, it has alcohol in it."

"Can I have a sip, Dad?"

"No, it's not for kids."

"*But you gave me a sip once, Dad!*"

Guilty. I think Melanie had just turned four, and every time she saw me with a Margarita she'd try to sneak a sip or con me into giving her a sip, and I finally let her take a little sip, since Mom wasn't there to stop me, with the foolish idea it would taste bad and she'd stop driving me and herself nuts with the attempts. But I under-estimated the power of forbidden fruit. She said "Mmmmmmm, that's good, Dad, can I have another sip?" No.

But when we got home and Mom was there, my little darling ran to her saying "Moooom, Dad gave me a sip of his Margarita." You had to be there to know it wasn't sharing a delightful experience, it was an accusation. Whereupon Julie gave me the look, and I stayed out of her way for a little while.

Of course ever since *the sip* Melanie has pestered me for more sips, but without success. Never to be outwitted, the little dear has resorted to the next best thing - she always wants the lime slice perched atop Mom and Dad's Margarita glass. This time Melanie observed my lime slice was half-emerged in the drink. So as I began to scrape the frozen ambrosia off the lime, Melanie declared "Don't wipe it off, Dad!" So since Mom wasn't looking, I didn't, and gave it to her.

After she licked the little bit off the lime slice Melanie said *"Mo-om, Dad's giving me alcohol!"* Loud enough of course so neighboring patrons overhead and I had to endure the look from them. Bad enough I have to suffer the look at home like every other husband, but by strangers?

"&$*#$@!"

"Oh, Dad, you said a bad word, you owe me a dollar."

Caught by the rules of my own making. If Melanie catches one of us saying a bad word, she gets a dollar. And when she misbehaves one of the punishments in our arsenal is taking one or more dollars away from her five dollar weekly allowance, which she earns by helping Mom do chores. Losing a dollar hurts because she already has to save two and can spend three, and losing one or more out of three spendable dollars hits a kid where it hurts.

I got an "aggavation" break when Mom and Melanie visited Grandma Shirley in Utah during the recent school break, but on the drive home from the airport Sunday Melanie was wired, having slept the whole flight, and Julie enjoyed my squirming as Melanie shared everything in her head with Dad at a solid volume level and fever pitch, pausing only to take in a breath. I wondered in a fleeting thought as I sought a moment's refuge inside my own mind whether Julie had remembered to give Melanie her allowance while in Utah.

Yesterday I got my answer. Julie is working on a project in suburban Virginia while the sniper is on the loose and has been most of this whole sniper event, staying indoors unless a shuttle takes her from one building to the other. I gave her orders to that effect, but I'm certain she ignored me and did exactly what she wanted anyway. So yesterday when I picked Melanie up from school I was taking her to our brand new Wall Mart in our town to buy her friend Sammy a birthday present, but I was smart enough to call Julie in Virginia to ask her desires on that birthday present, especially since I don't give a hoot and she does.

While receiving my orders Melanie motioned she wanted to talk to Mom and I handed her the phone. She reminded Mom about her allowance since she was enroute to a place to *spend it*, and gave the phone back to me with an expectant look. Julie told me to let her spend five dollars because she didn't get to spend her allowance in Utah.

"You mean let her spend three and save two?"

"No, let her spend five. She got two extra dollars because she caught Grandma saying a bad word twice."

Grandma Shirley had to pay the piper when she got caught swearing twice. I knew there was something I liked about her. So Melanie reaps the rewards of the transgressions of others, shopping for herself in a way that helps her learn how much things cost, showing her generous side now and then by setting something aside or buying a gift for Babysister.

Now I hear more rumors the Chinese are speeding up the referral process.

Tap-tap-tap-tap-*tap-tap* dammit!

Oct 2002, Melanie 5 yrs 6 mos

and Waiting . . .

I hear drumming of fingers and tapping of toes, the only outward evidence of tension among the quiet ones. Others are more vocal in the angst of waiting, glaring at the calendar and staring at the clock, wondering when the time will come, daydreaming about the magic moment that takes so long to arrive, when all the preparation and planning finally, at long last bears fruit. And of course that magic time is best enjoyed while surrounded by your closest confidants.

I'm referring, of course, to kids at Halloween.

If you're waiting for your first child, you have forgotten much about this kid holiday. Sure, it means they put on a costume and collect candy, but as you'll soon find out, it's much, much more.

Anticipation begins months in advance. You have no control unless your kid is a hermit. First comes the all-important decision "What will I be?" Forget about creative home-made dress-up the way we did it when I was a kid. You have to buy a cool costume or Mom has to labor for endless hours to create a masterpiece, and nothing other than the kid's selected character will do, it having been carefully juxtaposed against your kid's close friends' decisions and having met with their approval. Don't try to stop the freight train.

To avoid trauma you must buy the costume far in advance, like early September, because the cool ones go fast and the freight train decides what's cool, you have nothing to do with it.

Then comes decorating the house with doo-dads and gee-gaws that I never saw when I was growing up, a classic case of created demand marketing. It's all over the front yard, nearly as much candy for the eyes as Christmas, bats in the trees, plastic characters with eerie lighted eyes, and so on.

But most notable is the tension building in the kids, like the skin of an inflating balloon becoming ever-tighter approaching explosion, irritated by interaction with all the other inflating balloons at school every day.

"Dad, how many more days until Halloween."

"Oh, about 15."

"Is that long?"

After giving up the notion that Halloween is just an evening of trick-or-treating, and embracing the notion it is the most anticipated event in the kids life at this age, you finally join the overblown extravaganza.

"How about I pick up you and your two friends early from school on Halloween?" Early means after school is out at 2:30 PM but before the after-school program that normally keeps them until 6 PM.

"Wow, thanks, Dad, that would be way cool." Eyes shining in eager anticipation.

"Are they going to go trick-or-treating with me?"

"Yep, I arranged it with their parents."

"But Dad, we only got one golf cart." Mobility is a big thing in our town.

"Don't worry, well have two golf carts on Halloween."

"But Dad, how will they get their costumes?"

"They'll have to bring them to school." I can almost hear her brain tick with Think-Think-Think-Think.

"But Dad, I won't have *my* costume at school."

"You don't need yours at school, you can get yours when we get home." Thinking logically like a man, big mistake.

"But Da-ad, I want *my* costume at school, too."

"Ask your Mom." Easy escape, she'll cave in a heartbeat.

Later - "Dad, Mom says I can take my costume to school."

"OK. But you can't put it on at school."

"I know, it'll be in my backpack." That means wadded up, to be drug out and admired as she gathers with her friends in dark corners to whisper their conspiracy, planning the biggest evening in their whole lives. It makes no sense to me, but since when did that matter?

And when I picked them up at school they were so excited they wiggled, at home they played frantically, watching for signs of dusk, eager to zip into their alter-ego and take off on a most excellent adventure. These three already have their greeting planned, to be presented sing-song in unison:

"Trick-or-treat
Smell our feet
Give us something good to eat
If you don't

We don't care
We'll pull down your underwear!"

Followed of course by a three-girl giggle.

Last year the kid I liked the best when I answered the doorbell had a Harpo Marx wig and getup, he honked his horn and spoke not a word as he flashed a card saying "Trick-or-Treat." Then before departing he honked again and quietly flashed "Thank-You."

And by the time the little darlings return with malicious intent to gorge on their hard-earned stash, they have to spread it out on the floor so Moms can poke through it to make sure it's all OK and maybe steal a piece of chocolate. After the kids eat their allotted three pieces, already past bedtime, still in their costume and flushed with exertion and excitement, they might fall asleep in Mom or Dad's arms, eyes closed while still quietly wondering "Is it over?" Meaning "Is that all there is?" never dreaming they might wonder the same thing about life in 50 or 60 years.

And you thought it was just about collecting some candy. Get ready.

Oct 2002, Melanie 5 yrs 6 mos

Book Three

Kristen Comes Home

Babysister at Last!

Julie and I don't *wait* for Babysister. Not us. We just live our lives and ignore the calendar and ignore the delays until it happens, because it will. We don't play that wait game. No sir.

In case you don't know, here's how Chinese adoption works in a nutshell. First you spend a frantic few months gathering paperwork and fingerprints and medical exams and social worker reports and on and on until your dossier is properly compiled. Your agency translates and sends the dossier to China, then you wait for a year or so until your turn comes. Then one day your agency calls out of the blue with a *referral,* meaning a photo of a child that China has matched to you along with medical information and the question "Will you accept this child?" If you say no they try again. The referral call is the apex of excitement and emotion, even if like Julie and I you haven't been waiting at all. The last stage is traveling to China to complete the adoption and bring the child home.

Until you have done it you can't know the emotional rollercoaster of the ride, and how foolish it sounds when someone thoughtlessly says "Oh, you're adopting, that's the easy way."

Back when we were not waiting for Melanie in 1997, I asked my agency to make the referral call to Julie whether she was in her office or on the road because I wanted her to have the thrill of hearing it first. But they called me anyway when the time came, and must have wondered about my lack of enthusiasm because I took the info and made notes while thinking about where Julie was and how to reach her. Besides, ditching my dignity and screaming like a hundred dollar winner on *Beat the Clock* is not my style. So I tracked her down and told her what I knew and we called our agency back to play Twenty Questions with both of us on the line.

Flash forward to Babysister. First I will share with you something intensely personal, maybe exposing my shallow side. Melanie has given us new life. It's like half of your heart is unused, on reserve until you have a child, because until it happens you didn't realize you could love something quite that much. Life with Melanie has been full, and good. And because I am in my mid-50s and Julie in her mid-40s, and because Melanie fit so well into our lives, and because I have told the world believing it is true that *one is quite enough thank you,* you could have knocked me over with a feather when Julie told me she wanted a second child. Why? Because Melanie wanted a sister and it would be better if she were not an only child. Recognizing in a flash the impossibility of saying no to my love, being only a man I instantly seized on the opportunity to cut a deal. I promised to start the paperwork ASAP if she would agree to an older child, albeit younger than Melanie's five years, and we settled on a range of two to three years old. Julie hoped for the younger end of the range and I hoped for the older, partially for selfish reasons of not wanting the helpless infant and diaper-changing stage again and partially because I always think of the older kids left behind as they watch batch after batch of infants going to families.

So anyway, how did we not wait? I have called our agency only three times since our dossier went to China in Oct 2001, because I know the time will come, they have plenty to do and we're just not high maintenance waiters like some who call daily for hand-holding. Julie hasn't called them at all. But I did call this Spring to tell them with emphasis that I wanted the referral call to go to Julie, *no mistakes* please, and gave them her phone numbers.

Yesterday Jackie Harrah called from Houston. Jackie and John Harrah own the agency, but Jackie had never called before. I knew John handles inquiries while Jackie gets the plumb assignment of calling families with the surprise referral.

"Jackie, is this a referral call?"

"It sure is, but I can't get through to Julie."

"Do you have an info sheet you can fax to me here?

"I can fax you a referral acceptance form."

"No, I mean info about the child."

"Oh, Terry, I can't do that until I talk to Julie, I have strict orders!"

"Bless you for sticking with the program, Jackie, let me see if I can track down Julie and get you guys connected."

"OK"

"Jackie, how old is the kid?"

"Under a year, she's beautiful."

"Oh man, Julie will be tickled." And so will Melanie, and the transition will be so much easier for our family. Oh man, helpless infant and poopy diapers and . . . but I'll deal with it with as much of a smile as I can muster now and then.

"What about you, Terry, are you tickled?"

"If momma's happy, I'm happy." Jackie probably thought I was a boor.

I found Julie on her cell phone in the Washington DC area, told her what I knew and tried to conference in Jackie without success. Julie yelled at her staff "I'm a new Mom!" They yelled back, knowing the question key to her "How old?" "Under a year" she yelled back. She had to go to a meeting with a gaggle of lawyers and turned off her cell phone. She would try Jackie when her meeting is done.

Babysister

So, while Jackie was calling other and more excitable parents with the news they have been waiting for much of their adult life, Julie met with lawyers and her staff talking through a securities fraud investigation matter, and I am preparing for a "Books & Records Exam" by the State Examiner of Investment Advisors. Meanwhile we don't know her health, what city or province she is in, or whether she is cute or a linebacker. But I'll live, and so will Julie, and before the day is out, we'll know lots more about Babysister. And we'll be able to tell Melanie, who will be so excited to have a baby to cuddle, but for now momma and daddy are pretending to be busy.

* * *

Well, Julie missed Jackie by telephone but talked to Debbie and now that she has the scoop I'm allowed to have it, too. Babysister was born on December 26, 2001, her first birthday is the day after Christmas. Julie got her secret wish for a baby, as did Melanie though hers was no secret.

Debbie e-mailed photos and medical information, and we immediately said "Yes."

I got my secret wish, too, easy travel and easy weather. Well, easier anyway. Since Babysister is in Guangdong province, and our consulate is there in the city of Guangzhou where every US adopting family must travel for the child's visa processing, we could fly nonstop from LA to Guangzhou and back. Some families look forward to a side trip to Beijing after multiple connections, then travel to their adoption city, then to Guangzhou. I chose easy travel, especially with kids. Melanie would get to see her homeland, and there's plenty to see in Guangzhou. The southern part of the country in January would be pleasantly cool. Cool!

We haven't chosen a name for Babysister yet, but we just saw her photo an hour ago. First things first. I get to tell Melanie she has a Babysister.

Nov 25, 2002, Melanie 5 yrs 7 mos, Babysister 11 mos

Big Sister

When I picked up Melanie from her after-school program, I handed her the printed color photos of Babysister and asked her who she thought it was.

Melanie knows quite a few friends also adopted from China, and she thought a minute but didn't recognize her and said "I don't know, Dad." So I told her in a quiet voice since we were standing in the middle of the elementary school hall with people close by "That's your Babysister."

Melanie drew in a sharp breath and looked up at me with an expression that implied "Can this be true? I've been waiting and waiting for so long!" Then she opened the paper she had folded and looked at it again, taking in a long, quiet look, and she looked at me again and smiled very big and said "Dad, she's so cute!"

I nodded my agreement, and Melanie went back for another look. Then she took off from a standing start at warp speed down the hall, sneakers flying almost up to the back of her head, where her best friend sat in a group, shouting "*Alex! Alex! Look, it's my Babysister!*" So Alex and a few other friends gathered around Melanie to look and congratulate and give her a hug, and soon Melanie extracted herself and walked with me to the exit, nearly walking into other people because she couldn't take her eyes off Babysister as she put one foot in front of the other.

I held her photo page while she fastened her seatbelt over her carseat, and she asked if she could turn her overhead light on while I drove so she could look at the three pictures some more. Who could say no? Every few moments Melanie would say "This is my Babysister, my sissy. She's so cute, Dad!"

At home I explained to Melanie why we couldn't bring home Babysister *right now* as she wished, that we had to wait a couple of months until China approved our travel visas and travel arrangements were made. She satisfied herself by gazing at Babysister's photo.

Julie and I had been whittling a name list down to our favorites, and when Julie e-mailed the newest list I showed it to Melanie and let her join in the consideration of names. First Julie and I selected Babysister's middle name of *Jia Li* which means "beautiful jasmine" and has some special connection to Melanie's middle name of *Jia Lu* meaning "beautiful jade". Then we considered the short list of English first names, and with Melanie's participation we settled on Kristen. So her name will be Kristen Jia Li Garlock, and our consideration of names included the assumption that at some point in her life she may choose to use her Chinese name instead of her English name, so it should be a good one. A Chinese friend who knows about such things, Shengmei Di, helped us on name selection with careful advice, and we think her name is a good one.

On Thanksgiving day I installed Babysister's photo on Melanie's computer as the wallpaper, and she was delighted. That evening we visited some friends to toast Babysister, and Melanie proudly showed her photos, and practiced her big sister role looking after younger Gracie Jennings and Liza Eubanks.

This morning I cleaned the Thanksgiving turkey wishbone I had set aside to dry out. I explained to Melanie it is a wishbone, and whoever breaks off the big piece gets to make a wish and it might come true. Melanie's eyes lit up at the prospect of such a game, and while I held the bottom tip of my wishbone leg with the tips of my fingers, she instinctively grabbed hers on the whole leg with several fingers, giving her a most unfair advantage, which was fine with me because I wanted her to win. We pulled, and when she won her eyes bulged like any child's in a moment of triumph.

"Make a wish" I told her.

"You won the wish?" Mom asked her from across the room. "Wish for something good!"

Melanie said "I wish Babysister would come home sooner."

I think she'll make a fine big sister.

Nov 2002, Melanie 5 yrs 7 mos, Kristen 11 mos

The Christmas Box

Yesterday was the first day of December, and the kid-world anticipation of Christmas inches up toward intense. Julie did her decoration-monster thing this weekend, and of course I held the ladder while Melanie helped Mom's every move. Otherwise I stayed out of the way and I discovered something new. Mom is not only a Christmas Freak, she is a Christmas Genius.

This year she somehow found a little box with 24 drawers in it. I wondered what the heck it was, displayed on a table in the hall just outside our bedroom door. And who needs 24 drawers and what for? And what was the big deal about that box that Melanie drug her two buddies up the stairs to show them?

I'm only a man, you know, and since I need my instructions when Julie is heading out of town I learned about the box, and it's pretty important to those who are five years old. Last night, Dec 1st, Melanie got to open the first drawer before bedtime, and found a little wrapped piece of chocolate. Tonight she gets to open drawer number two, and so on, each night getting a small treat. Right up to the big day, the Christmas Box evokes Melanie's wonder each day of what small treasure she will find at bedtime, and it helps her keep track of how long until Christmas.

Out of all the thousands of Julie's Christmas do-dads, I think this may be the very best one. I used to wonder if women really were smarter than men. Must have been the pathetic musing of a lower form of life.

Dec 2002, Melanie 5 yrs 8 mos, Kristen 11.1 mos

Losing a Friend

There have been so many occasions I have refrained from writing a story about Melanie's adventures since she started school and I decided to respect her privacy, but she passed a milestone last night that makes for an exception.

The Discovery

When I arrived home with take-out burgers I heard the whine of a five year old pleading with Mom mixed with the coo of real crying. Being insensitive and impatient about whining I asked Julie "What's wrong with her?"

Julie said her crab died.

I should have known it was more than routine whining, because when Melanie cries with that deep moaning that sounds like no other child it means her heart is breaking and she can't stop even if she wants to stop. And if you're not careful, while you're consoling her and those big tears squeeze out of her eye and drop from her cheek, you'll be crying with her.

So with a shroud of guilt I looked at the footlong plastic box inhabited by the hermit crab Melanie brought home from our trip to Gulf Shores last summer. There he lay, for the first time nearly all the way out of his shell, still and . . . rather dry.

At first when she brought the crab home Melanie couldn't let him touch her, he was too icky like a bug. But after a while she would take him out, let him crawl all over her hands, and once he pinched her pretty good when he mistook her play for an attack on his life.

Dammit, on Monday I noticed his water dish was dry but I forgot. And we hadn't given him fresh food in a while, like a split grape, because he eats very little, and . . . maybe I forgot. Julie forgot, too. Julie carried Melanie into the kitchen and she freaked so I took the crab and his box to the laundry room so Melanie wouldn't have to look at him.

Melanie came to me in a while and I told her I was sorry, that maybe it was my fault he died because I forgot to give him water, and Melanie moaned with big tears dropping on her shirt:

"Noooo, Dad, not your fault. But Mom's going to pull him out of his shell and I'm sooo scared."

Why, I wondered, is it necessary for Julie to pull him out of his shell if that's what is bothering her?

"Well, he won't feel anything if he died, will he?"

"Noooo. Dad, we just had a year together, and that's not very loooong."

Actually it was much less than a year. "I know. I'm sorry."

Before long she went to bed. The next morning Melanie was cheerful, and I went to check to make sure Julie had not disposed of the tiny carcass down the toilet before I made a suggestion to Melanie. Nope, still there. She saw me come out of the laundry room and almost lost it again. I asked her:

"You want me to help you bury the crab in the back yard when you get home from school?"

She thought for a minute, because her good friends Darby and her sister Cheney are coming home with Melanie tonight.

"Can Darby and Cheny come with us?"

"Sure."

"Can we bury him out in the woods where I don't go, Dad?" Tears welling.

"Sure we can."

Melanie nodded her assent while her lip quivered.

"We can put him in a box to bury him with his shell."

"But Mom's going to pull him out of his shell, Dad."

So I looked at Julie and asked "Why?"

"Because Melanie wants to keep the shell!" You have to imagine the word "stupid" or "dummy" in that answer.

"OK, I'll take him out of his shell."

"Be careful, Dad, don't pull too hard, you might get guts."

I looked at her and she smiled real big and playful. I think she'll survive the ceremony.

The Ceremony

When I picked up Melanie, Darby and Cheney from school today, they started talking about playing and having fun. Then Melanie stopped them and said "We're not doing anything until we bury my crab, Poozie." They said OK.

When we arrived they gathered around my desk to look at Poozie, or what is left of him. I had pulled the little critter's foot out of the shell, without guts no less, and placed him in an earring box Julie gave me, wrapped in tissue. I opened it and took out the tissue, opened it up so each of them could have a look while they whispered "Wow" at the deceased.

I re-boxed Poozie and handed the box to Melanie, the honored pallbearer. We went down the stairs, I grabbed a shovel and the kids took off running, decorum for the occasion set aside by the frenzied search for just the right spot. We found a spot but Melanie was still troubled.

"But Dad, what if I come out here sometime?"

"Well, you can say hello to the crab, can't you?"

"Yeah, OK."

With a moment's pause to make sure she was OK with this gravesite, Melanie said to her two friends in a brief transformation from age five to twenty-five, "I know it's silly, guys, but I have to do this."

So I dug a little hole and Melanie placed the box in the bottom of the hole with a solemnity fitting the occasion. I asked her if she had anything she wanted to say before I covered him up.

Melanie gave one wave like Spanky did on Little Rascals and said "Bye, Poozie."

So I covered the hole and before I finished the girls were climbing the stairs, tugging back and forth as to who would play the Mom and who would play the sister.

Life goes on.

Dec 2002, Melanie 5 yrs 8 mos, Kristen 11.3 mos

Melanie Sees the Bright Side

Do you like oysters? I have never overcome my mental objection to eating them raw, but if fried just the right way, meaning with the right seasoning and not overdone, I'd drive a long way for a batch, especially Apalachicola oysters. On the south side of Atlanta, the Farmer's Market restaurant in Forest Park knows the oyster-frying art, and I had a half dozen on Monday.

Now I don't know if it was the oysters or not, but if you'll pardon a little toilet talk that's where I spent most of my life the next three days. Since we depart for China on Jan 2, I was worried that what I had might be contagious, so I visited my doctor yesterday first thing in the morning. When he asked how many trips to the John per day, his eyes bulged when I told him "about forty." So he did a blood test, found it was bacterial, meaning something I ate and likely not contagious, gave me antibiotics and advice to take Imodium. So there was some relief.

When I returned home Melanie was up and said when I walked in the door "Dad, you look nice today." Hmmm, wonder what that's about? Then she added, "You look skinny, Dad."

So that was it. When you're a fat guy, it's noticeable when you spend a few days on the John and the swelling goes down. Especially during the holidays when overeating is constant. So Melanie noticed, and when kids are five years old they still verbalize nearly everything that goes through their head. And she was being nice to poor old sick Dad.

"So instead of two elephants, today I just look like one?"

She thought for a moment.

"No, Dad, you still look like two elephants. But you used to look like *three*!"

Dads have to take their compliments where they can get them.

Dec 2002, Melanie 5 yrs 8 mos, Kristin 12 mos

Melanie's Return to China

I used to fly a lot, but it's been about three years since I've even been on a plane. And since I'm a big guy and a Grump about everything and have back pain from an old injury, I prepared for travel to China in two ways. First, Julie collected a mountain of Delta frequent flyer miles from her business travel so we could fly in style, preferably Singapore Airlines Business Class like last time, and save lots of money.

Second, I was loaded with pain reliever and sleep aids prescribed by Dr. Bill, better living through medication. But I made a critical preparation mistake. When we received our travel notice, I had an immediate choice - get on the phone ASAP or go take care of a business matter and call the airlines later that day. I opted for later in the day, and by the time I called the airlines there were no frequent flyer seats available - our adoption agency's travel agent had blocked out a bunch of seats for sale on China Southern, and all the other frequent flyer Delta partners had no frequent flyer seats left. And when you're flying three over and back plus a lap child on the return, it's even harder to get the seats than for two seats each way.

So I had to buy the seats from the travel agent, and $5,000 you didn't plan for takes some of the shine off the trip preparations. But it didn't bother me much, I bitched about it and that outlet was my relief valve, and that's why I'm a Grump. You do what you must and go on. But since I couldn't use miles for the ticket, and the China Southern tickets I bought were LA to Guangzhou only, I had to then buy the domestic leg. So I tried again to use Delta miles, and long story short had to spend another $800 *and* 80,000 Skymiles to get us into Business Class. But you do what you must and go on.

The good news for the travel-averse like me was no in-country travel; our child was waiting in Guangdong province three hours drive from Guangzhou, and we would spend our entire ten days in China wrapped in the White Swan Hotel's luxury. Fine by me, I've done it the other way.

On travel day, January 2, 2003, Julie and I waited until noon to even start packing, though we had prepared all the important stuff, but we weren't going to do the recommended pre-pack days ahead of schedule. With a 4PM departure time for the airport, no problem! After Melanie's excitement spun in an ever-tighter orbit in anticipation of Babysister, Ronnie Jennings kindly drove us to the airport in their family minivan and finally we were off for a 7PM flight to LA. Ready to rock and roll. While we waited at the gate to board the big plane, Melanie ate snacks and fidgeted while Delta switched out the big aircraft for a smaller aircraft then called us up to let us know with a smile that despite our tickets they had to move us back to coach, thank you very much, and "It's not my fault, I'm doing the best I can." @#$%&! Thank goodness I quit flying when airlines still knew how to at least spell "customer." If not for the soothing nature of the pain killer I might have been in trouble on the flight.

We arrived at the LAX hotel about 9:30PM, crashed and let Melanie's ever-tighter orbit spin around the room until she slept, dreaming frantic anticipation of Babysister. Our flight to China was the next day at 11:30PM, and if you wonder why we didn't just fly in the next day the answer is extra rest for a five year old and besides, I would describe the domestic flight and fare restrictions but I'd probably lapse into profanity.

But the extra time gave us rest for the longer flight to China, rest time Melanie used to get bored and drive us nuts. So we took a $60 round trip cab ride to the Santa Monica Pier where Melanie rode a few kiddie rides, and Dad set a precedent by taking one kiddie ride with her to give Mom a break. Reminded me why I don't do that. You could scrap and burn every kid and adult ride on this planet, and I'd be happy to strike the match. Now you would think after such a generous entertainment overture your kid would be grateful and give you a break, at least those of you who don't have kids yet might think that. But when we returned to the hotel Melanie was wired. Looking out the hotel window at the pool 12 floors below she saw people sunning themselves around the pool and after some badgering Mom gave in and put on her bathing suit while Melanie wiggled into hers in three seconds, and they were off. Perfect reading and nap time for Dad.

After a while I took my book down to the pool to watch Melanie practice swimming to Mom. She shouted "Hey Dad, look, all the people left, where you think they went?" Not a sunbather in sight.

Refuge from the Griswalds, no doubt. But Melanie was happy and when Melanie is happy Mom is happy and when Mom is happy then Dad gets to be happy if he's not being a Grump. And the whole idea was to chew up time, so phooey on the sun-worshipers scared off by Melanie's antics.

Tick-tock, finally time to go.

So there we were at the airport hours early as advised for China Southern, trying without success to keep Melanie awake until wheels up near midnight. At the gate we met Becky and Mike McGinnis, and their four year old live wire named Jeffrey, deep in sleep on Becky's lap recharging his high-output batteries. Becky and Mike were beat, already having run the gauntlet with several connecting flights from Tampa that morning.

We also met Robert and Shelly Hoffman at the gate, who had slept over in LA as we did. We had exchanged photos and other info with the McGinnis and Hoffman and other travel group families long before the trip, and had a good time meeting before takeoff.

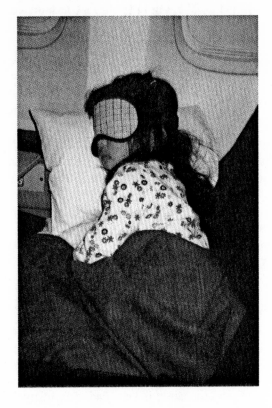

Finally we were able to board at 10:45PM, and parted because a Delta friend had arranged with China Southern for a free upgrade for our family to fly on the way over in Business Class, their highest class. The seats were pure luxury, far apart and reclining nearly flat, but no matter the comforts fifteen hours is far too long in the air in a metal tube, especially for a kid. I was proud of Melanie, however, she slept a lot, fidgeted a bunch but whined very little, a monumental achievement under the circumstances. We landed in Guangzhou on January 5 at 6:00AM local time, losing a day to the International Date Line in the Pacific, sore butts all around.

I had warned our new friends we didn't want to appear to be snobs in Business Class but would not turn down the extra comfort, and that we didn't want to appear to be snobs at the Guangzhou airport but a White Swan Hotel Limo was pre-arranged to pick us up. We never looked back, so I hope they didn't think us snobs. You see, we spent an extra $100 per day in the White Swan to upgrade our room to an Executive Suite, with a living room separate from the bedroom and a number of extra perks like one-way limo transport to or from the airport. Our agency had alerted the other families the in-country rep would meet them at the airport, but somehow I missed that communication and thought we were on our own to get to the hotel. It was just as well because we were ready to get to the hotel ASAP, the limo driver met us with our name on a placard and away we went. Well, almost. The Chinese guy in a bellhop suit who loaded our bags in the trunk was asking me something about going to the hotel and the front seat of the limo, and I couldn't understand him despite several attempts. I didn't think he wasn't asking for money because tipping is uncommon in China. Finally I understood he needed to get back to the White Swan, too, I think he worked there, and since this Mercedes was my hired limo he was politely asking if he could possibly ride along in the front seat. I told him he was welcome to ride with us. He apologized for his poor English and I assured him his English was far better than my Chinese.

Enroute to the hotel Melanie took in new sights warily. I told her a week prior we were arriving in China in the morning, because she wanted to know and prepared her head for morning in China. Now in the limo she wanted to know why it was still dark. Well, in the first place, I told her, China has just one time zone so I can't predict when the sun comes up by the clock. And in the second place, Guangzhou is a very large city of about eight million, without the environmental controls in the US, and the smog is very bad. So Melanie's first glimpse of China didn't meet her expectations, but her hungry eyes took in the motorcycles loaded with piles of whatever, different looking buildings, the early morning stir and thump of the Chinese version of rush hour, and finally the five-star White Swan Hotel complete with uniformed bellmen. Since we were on the Executive floor we had express check-in on our floor even early in the morning, no waiting until afternoon as I had feared.

We were ready to crash with a capital "C," Julie from being awake whenever Melanie was awake because those are Melanie's rules and Mom won't let Dad trump them, and me from sleeping on the flight only in fits and starts because deep sleep was impossible for my miserable body on airplane seats even with the aid of Dr. Bill's medicine.

But Melanie, of course, had slept well and was now wide awake and wired, so we stayed up for a little while and took sleep shifts trying to adjust to the local time. Just you wait till you try to manage a kid's sleep patterns to adjust to local time. This afternoon we meet the rest of our group. Are you tired?

Jan 5, 2003, Melanie 5 yrs 9 mos, Kristen 12 mos

Julia

"When will we get Kristen?" Melanie began to ask as soon as we arrived in China at 6AM on Jan 5. She was undeterred by the response telling her it would be tomorrow, and asked the question again and again, indicating an inability to wait rather than a lack of understanding. For a kid five years old, the wait since we decided to adopt again must seem to span her entire life. She sometimes expressed her deep devotion to her unknown Babysister, though she had progressed to calling her "sissy," and revealing her fear that now we would pay attention to sissy and not to Melanie.

Julie and I took turns with a nap, and somewhere between naps Greg and Brenda Hess arrived in the room next door with their five year old daughter, Julia, who has the cutest dimples you can imagine. Melanie and Julia made fast friends, transforming two benign components into a bionic weapon, delighted to discover relief from the boredom of adult surroundings.

One of the best clothing items I brought was a pair of flimsy gym shorts for lounging in the room. Since they're grey, at first glance they might look like underwear, and that was all Melanie needed. You see, she caught me in my underwear a while back and it struck her as quite funny. She giggled and rolled on the floor muttering something, and I finally persuaded her to tell me. She said I looked like Captain Underpants, a ribald cartoon character. That's not flattering, but what the hey, if my kid's funnybone is tickled then I'll play along. So I did the trumpeting sound of a superhero "Ta-da-da-da-da-*daa-daaa*" and pointed to the sky and declared "*Captain Underpants!*" Melanie loved it then, and now in China I heard her telling Julia in the hallway "My Dad is Captain Underpants!"

Then as I was stirring from my nap Melanie confided to Julie "My Dad's back hurts so he has to rest. He hurt his back in a military war, and if there's another war he don't have to go 'cause he already had his turn." Well said.

So today Melanie and Julia started wearing a path in the hall carpet between our rooms, inventing games, building forts with bedspreads and pillows and chairs and couch cushions, most happy when they were hidden deep in the dark recesses of their habitat away from the prying eyes of big people like me. No doubt they spoke privately of the next day when they both would become big sisters.

Jan 5, 2003, Melanie 5 yrs 9 mos, Kristen 12 mos

Sister Day

Since we received our referral on Nov 25, Julie has been very sensitive to Melanie's inner struggle between joy over anticipation of Babysister, and her frantic worry over losing her spot as the family baby. Mom and Melanie talked frequently about it, in hushed whispers so Dad wouldn't hear, and I reassured Melanie in my own way from time to time.

The day after our arrival in China was the day we would meet Babysister, with a 3PM meeting time for a bus ride to the Guangdong Civil Affairs office, where the babies would be brought to meet us after their own four hour bus ride from the orphanage. For the big day you want to be well-rested, but that's not easy when your five year old is up and wide awake at 2AM. And she was ready for action, for this was her day.

The day before, through the fog of jet-lag that persisted because Melanie was *active,* I had an idea to relieve Melanie's worry about being displaced.

"You guys are gonna pay attention to sissy and not meee." Melanie whined.

After a moment's thought I hugged her and whispered "You know what tomorrow is?"

Her ears perked up, but she was suspicious. "What?"

"It's *Big Sister Day*. And Big Sisters get a Big Sister present. You want to pick out your own present?" I'm not above bribes.

Melanie's eyes instantly glowed and she couldn't help her smile though she wanted to wallow in the whine.

"Mo-om! You know what tomorrow is? It's Big Sister Day, and I get to pick out my own Big Sister Present." Julie whispered to me "That was a great idea." She's tough, so high praise like that is worth a mention. It's not like Kristen, aka "sissy," will know one way or the other, and we turned Melanie's worry into proud anticipation. Of course she also told Julia, and I don't know if I caused the Hess family a problem.

Tick-tock, tick-tock, 3PM took so long to arrive, and we were off with our group. The people were different this trip, but it was the same nervous tension, quick to laugh or giggle and prone to quiet thoughts. On the bus Melanie made herself known to our travel partners.

"This is Big Sister Day" she announced, and realizing like a deft politician that four year old Jeffrey McGinnis is a boy " . . . and Big Brother Day, too. My name is Melanie. I'm in Kindergarten, but I'm off duty now to get my Babysister." Since all were stewing in their own last-minute juices, I'm not sure anyone was listening.

We arrived in a crowded parking lot and walked two blocks, dodging lethal traffic, to an official building that was quite cold, and our guide named Sha-Sha told us none of the buildings in southern China were heated since the winter cold lasted only a few weeks. The building was modern by Chinese standards, the third floor waiting room nicely furnished with a professionally prepared banner proclaiming the loving care of children.

We waited. Tap tap tap went lots of toes. Eyes shifted, stomachs churned, mouths dried, tough guys like me pretending it was all in a day's work. Some of us wondered whether Shelly Hoffman, who was clearly feeling the strain, went to the girls room for the normal stuff or to barf. Finally we heard babies.

Babysister is here. Melanie scooted toward the door, out front on point, eyes wide and shining, not trying to be rude but unable to stand back while her sissy was coming.

The first baby was for Jim Evans and Robin Rosen-Evans. Lots of tears.

Next they announced "Terry & Julie" but I wished they had said "Melanie" and in came little tiny Kristen while I ran the video camera. Julie took her and Melanie stretched up on her toes, reaching to touch her Babysister for the very first time, then Julie kneeled down so Melanie could see her up close. While Melanie smiled with that angelic glow that comes from deep within, her new friend Julia came over to tell her with a buddy's pat on the shoulder "She's just what you wanted, Melanie." Julia would become a Big Sister herself in two minutes.

I continued to catch each family on video as they received their child, and it's a special moment for each one. Every child had on the same red silk-covered down vest for warmth, and they were beautiful. Finally after a couple of moments Melanie asked Mom hopefully "Can I hold her?"

Julie, Melanie and baby Kristen

So we had Melanie scoot back on the couch and put Kristen in her lap, and showed her how to clasp her hands together to ensure she didn't drop the tiny bundle of joy. Melanie's inner glow hit a new high, and her smile showed pride beyond her years. She was now, officially, irrevocably, a Big Sister. Thoughts of a present didn't occur to her now, she was focused on Kristen, whom she had loved even before the little dear was born.

As Melanie held her, Kristen's head flopped to one side and Melanie said "Dad, her head's not stapled. She needs to grow so she don't break her bones." It's never too early for the mother instinct.

Kristen's first birthday had been on December 26, and even for her age, she was small, and quiet. She brought from the orphanage something called the Yangdong Do. That's the funky hair some kids have from the Yangdong Social Welfare Institute in Yanjiang City, Guangdong Province. But funky hair or not, she is finally ours, and Melanie is transformed forever.

Jan 6, 2003, Melanie 5 yrs 9 mos, Kristen 12 mos

An excited Big Sister Melanie meets baby Kristen for the first time

Jim Evans & Robin Rosen-Evans, baby Hannah

Sisters Redeem Their Grumpy Dad

Robert & Shelly Hoffman, baby Judy

Mike & Becky McGinnis, Jeffrey, baby Holley, orphanage Director

Greg & Brenda Hess, Julia, baby Claire, orphanage Director

Indifferent Kristen

Melanie with Babysister Kristen in China

"Did I have a red vest on like Kristen when you got me?" Melanie asked.

"No, you didn't."

"Did I have funky hair, too?"

"No, you didn't have much hair, and it was soft, it didn't stand up like Kristen's."

"Did my head flop like Sissy's?"

"I don't think your head flopped too much."

Back in our hotel room with Kristen, Melanie tried to play with her and asked lots of questions.

Since long before our China trip, Melanie had been comparing her mind's picture of her own adoption to that of her Babysister. And from the adoption story I made for her on the computer, Melanie learned long ago to be proud she is from China, that adoption is a wonderful thing, that we believe her birthmother and birthfather loved her but could not keep her. She talks with us often about these things.

Kristen is about the same age, 12-13 months, as Melanie when we met her. But Kristen is much different. Like most adoptive parents, we worried about the bonding process, and Melanie attached to Julie immediately. She objected when Julie left the room even for a moment, wanted to be held constantly, and tolerated me only when I fed her.

Kristen, on the other hand, is indifferent. In fact she seems most content left to crawl on the floor on her own, and we soon learned the best way to comfort her was to put her down, with a White Swan Hotel washcloth her preferred comforting blankie. She is quiet and a little withdrawn, avoiding eye contact, a slight rattle in her chest.

We brought antibiotics, but decided to take her to the White Swan Hotel Clinic since all the other kids in our group had gone there and had been diagnosed with bronchitis and ear infections. The Chinese lady doctor listened to her chest with a stethoscope and looked in her ear with a flashlight and diagnosed - bronchitis and ear infection! Seemed to be the standard diagnosis, but it fit since Kristen was constantly scratching at her ear. So she got four antibiotic shots over two days, good precaution for $50.

While Kristen liked to be left alone, Melanie the Big Sister was undeterred. She would try to pick up Kristen like a bottom-heavy sack of potatoes, shake a chain of plastic links inches from her eyes, hold up music-playing toys to her ears, and other means of tender torture. We told her repeatedly to back off and give Kristen some space, but she was so excited she soon repeated her kind offense. If you could read Kristen's eyes the first couple of days you might have seen the message

"Someone help me, this big person is trying to kill me!" But she soon responded to Melanie, gave her the first smile and giggle.

Julie and I are not worried that some of the other kids attached quickly while Kristen stayed a bit distant, for three reasons. First, she was sick. Second, she seemed a bit withdrawn, and the change she was going through must be dramatic for a tiny one year old mind trying to understand.

Third, and most important, I am convinced the immediate attachment some kids have to their adoptive parents has nothing at all to do with bonding in the long run. The immediate attachment seems to be matters of who they like because of feeding and play and a familiar face, while real bonding forms over time based on trust and growing, deepening affection. At least that's what I believe, and we're sure Kristen will come around.

If she lives through Melanie's attempt to play with her.

Jan 6, 2003, Melanie 5 yrs 9 mos, Kristen 12 mos

Kristen's Barbie

In 1998 when we adopted Melanie the White Swan hotel was booked and we stayed at the Victory Hotel in Guangzhou. This 2003 trip for Kristen we had the White Swan experience, and I must say it deserves every one of its' five stars. For one small example, the uniformed attendants on each floor listened for a hotel door closing, meaning someone is coming, and they rushed to press the down elevator button. No matter how little you needed such help, when one of the six doors lit up to indicate arrival she would graciously extend her arm and say "This way, please," and she always rushed to put her hand in to hold the door open, just in case, and as the door started to close said "Bye-Bye." Every time. These ladies were very proud of their job, and it showed.

I wonder how many times these ladies were prompted by false alarms as Melanie and Julia ran back and forth between our rooms, slamming doors despite a couple thousand requests to close it quietly?

In our suite's "master bath" there were not one but two toilet paper holders next to the commode with what appeared to be gold plated half-covers, probably a brass alloy. One of those covers fell off under my tender touch, and like in most hotels I thought nothing of it. That day when we returned to the room after maid service the maid came to the door and apologized for the toilet paper cover, asked if it would be alright if it was fixed later that day, and seemed quite relieved when I told her it didn't matter, fix it whenever it's convenient. I hope there's not a tough manager flogging the help.

On Big Sister Day as we arrived at the elevator, on our way to meet Kristen, I saw two boxes on the attendants' desk with Barbie dolls in them and knew what they were. But our minds were elsewhere, me in my typical grump. Melanie had irritated me by begging to be carried like a baby, and since I was lugging the video camera and Julie lugging a soon-to-be-used diaper bag I assumed like an idiot we could leave Julie's camera, but she told me to go back to get it. Since we had two cameras now I assumed it would not be necessary to also bring Melanie's camera. Stupid me, go back and get it. And now that we had three cameras I had no patience left when asked to go back to get the one-use camera someone had given Melanie. As they walked and I stomped down the hall Melanie asked "Mom, why is Daddy pissed off?"

Ooops. My fault for her question, no matter how camera-laden I was, and no doubt my fault for her un-childlike words, better watch it.

We got plenty of photos. And when we returned to the hotel the adoption Barbie was on the desk in our room with a nice note from the White Swan. It's a blond Barbie like you would expect, with a small likeness of a Chinese child rubber-banded between her arms. It's quite sweet, and a generous gesture from the White Swan and Mattel with the best of intentions, and many adoptive families consider it to be a valued keepsake. But Julie and I have never been Barbie fans, and it reminds me of the reporters who have written shallow articles about how common adopting a Chinese baby has become, and how some people adopt a Chinese baby like a fashion accessory. I know, that's my own baggage, not Barbie's fault, but this Barbie had no sentimental value to us despite the generosity of the gift.

So I shamelessly told Melanie the doll was for her, the Big Sister. She was tickled with the doll but wanted to know ASAP whether she still gets to pick out a Big Sister present, and was delighted to hear the answer "yes." So she told Julia "This Barbie is a present from my Dad for me being a Big Sister" and the blessings of a five year old mind is no questions of reconciliation arose when Julia showed her "We got one, too." One of the first things to go when you have a kid is your shame, and I took credit with a clear conscience.

The kids had fun for a while with the dolls, and the next day Sha-Sha took us by bus to a Chinese toy wholesale store, five stories of tiny stalls and big stores, everything from pirate central for electronics to big luxurious stuffed animals. We had a specific mission, Melanie selecting her Big Sister present, limited a little by size since we had to lug it back home. Being a girl, she had to go through *every damn* store before deciding, then we backtracked to buy her selection, a soft stuffed puppy. She named the stuffed puppy Smiley, and for several days I had to step around Smiley's dishes of water and pretend food on the hotel room floor as Melanie played.

Kristen was along for the ride, quiet and content so long as we were walking in a crowd or riding in the bus where new sights occupied her bronchitis-tempered thoughts. She remained in her solitary shell, prompted to whimper or even cry a little by the softest touch to her cheek no matter how affectionately intended. But she was starting to keep an eye on Melanie, whether in wary expectation of the next goo-goo assault where Melanie mercilessly tried to get a smile out of her, or maybe the first glimmer of hero worship. At least she didn't fuss when Julie and I handed her back and forth - some of her peers had already staked out their Mom as their turf.

Throughout these episodes Melanie still had jealousy that emerged in several ways. Sometimes she insisted on being held by Mom when Mom was holding Kristen. Sometimes she had an unexplained meltdown. Sometimes she wanted things she had long outgrown, and would have willingly taken a bottle if we let her. Melanie was getting on my nerves with all this, especially when she wanted to be carried because Kristen was being carried, but Julie was very patient in dealing with her transition. As the days went by she made progress slowly, but her favorite was Mom holding them both, not easy since five year olds are no longer lightweights. A few times I held them both but it's not quite the same, Mom's affection being subject to the most intense competition.

So when Julie and Melanie returned to the hotel from a little shopping with *another* Big Sister present, this time a small battery powered push-button guitar, I didn't grouse at all. Whatever works, bribes and all.

Later, after we arrived back home in Georgia, Melanie brought her guitar to show me a tune that automatically played when she pushed a button. She had seen my guitar hanging in our basement, one I bought over twenty years ago with the thought of learning how to play. I never did. Melanie said:

"Dad, go get your guitar and let's play!"

"No, I don't think so."

"Why not, Dad?"

"Because I don't know how to play it."

Melanie rolled her eyes in a lapse of tolerance for her poor, dumb old Dad.

"Look, you just put this strap over your head like this, and push the buttons, it's easy, I'll show you how, OK?"

If only I had known all these years.

Jan 2003, Melanie 5 yrs 9 mos, Kristen 12 mos

Adopting Kristen

Dispatch from the White Swan Hotel, Guangzhou, China, waiting for Kristen's US visa so we can go home.

Who knew the most valuable thing that should have been among the trove of medications we brought with us, but we didn't think to bring, was child suppositories? Facing a radical change in her life, new parents learning to mix formula and rice cereal in the bottle by trial and error, and not feeling well to boot, Kristen's drain clogged. And we should have known because the same thing happened with Melanie in 1998. Fortunately Greg Hess next door, a physician, brought some suppositories and shared the little tubular treasures with us.

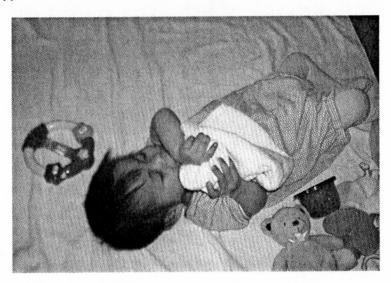

It took us a while to figure out that when Kristen went from quiet play on the floor to a wiggling cry on her back with legs flailing, she couldn't poop. Empty diapers for a couple of days are a clue even to clueless parents. So we helped the little darling when Melanie, who didn't want to miss a thing, would move her head out of the way.

It took two tries, but happy, pooooopy baby! Boy, when you're very young and very old, maybe one of the best things is . . . well, you know.

Kristen likes Melanie, but she's still fragile. She'll twist and wiggle, trying to get away while Melanie is so close her hair hangs down in Kristen's face, tickling under her chin mercilessly, getting her interested in musical toys, goo-goo and the whole works. Julie and I ask her to cool it or back off a hundred times, but Melanie loves her little sister and she came back soon like a cloud of gnats. Sometimes she treated Kristen like a dog, unintentionally I'm sure; she gave Kristen hugs and kisses, and petted her and called her with snapped fingers and whistles.

Someone asked her one day:

"Do you know how to change a diaper?"

"*Ah-Course* I do. I got a little sister!"

And she never missed a chance to "help" with the diaper changing.

I had visions of a tiny tombstone with an epitaph like "Here lies little tiny Kristen, who died from the loving attention of her Big Sister Melanie," but you can't say things like that to anyone or they'll freak out. Which just about describes Kristen when she saw Melanie coming. Until at long last, after endless tender torment Kristen would smile and giggle, a little more this time.

From the moment we met Kristen she had a self-comforting gesture we figured out right away. She holds her left hand up to her mouth, back of fingers, back of hand or back of forearm in increasing degrees of comfort or hiding while she makes a little sucking motion with her closed mouth. She also brings her blankie up to her eyes to hide, and the only blankie that will do is a White Swan Hotel washcloth. We took three of them with us when we checked out, I meant to tell them and forgot but they have my credit card.

Little by little, day by day, as Melanie relentlessly tended to her little sister and Mom held and rocked and played and goo-gooed with her, not to mention the leftover time Dad held and fed her, Kristen started to emerge from her protective shell. She was getting used to us. And I had to sympathize - just imagine having no control and all of a sudden you're surrounded by the Grizwalds.

She more often smiled, occasionally giggled, and started to prefer to be held by Mom. Imagine that.

Now that Melanie had her Big Sister presents and was ever-so-slowly dealing with the adjustment to our family, I told her January 6 would always be Sister Day, not just Big Sister Day. She wanted to know if both she and Kristen would get a present on Sister Day, and I told her that sounded like a good idea to me.

"Mo-om, you know what January 6 is? It's Sister Day and we get presents!"

"That's nice."

Damn, I'm smart! At least once in a rare while.

Melanie seemed never to tire of faux-wrestling with Kristen, and never tired of running her fingers through her Yangdong Do, sticking up pretty much straight.

"Hey, Dad, Kristen's a Hair Dude!"

"That she is."

We took the bus back to the Guangzhou Civil Affairs office where the notary and adoption officials had the legal documents prepared. As Melanie wiggled and Kristen sat still, the notary and adoption officer, high officials in China, interviewed us in two sessions asking questions like:

"Can you treat this child as your own?"

"Yes."

"Do you promise never to abuse or abandon her?"

"Yes, we promise."

"Will you give her an education?"

"Yes, we will."

"OK. When you sign here, she is your daughter, and you must care for her."

We promptly signed, and the adoption was irrevocably final on that day, Jan 8.

Later we went to the Chinese Security Agency, a large room with lots of seats occupied by Chinese people waiting for their number to be called by uniformed officers in little booths behind a low glass partition. Sha-Sha had pre-arranged an appointment, so when the time came our entire group went up to one of the booths and the officer smiled nicely and asked a question or two from each family, compared our passports to our faces and stamped their approval on documents allowing the child to have a Chinese passport to leave the country. One more step done, lots of entertainment for the Chinese people who stared openly at us wherever we went, conspicuous for being Anglos, more so for carrying a Chinese baby.

Kristen took it all in serenely, seldom cried, though she fussed now a little when taken from Mom.

But she didn't seem to hear very well. We guessed it was the ear infection. We started to test her, like clapping two books in a loud noise a few feet behind her head. She rarely flinched, and Julie and I differed, she thought Kristen may be totally or partially deaf, I thought she may just be used to noise around her in the orphanage. Either way, she didn't respond much to loud noises.

Doctor Examining Kristen

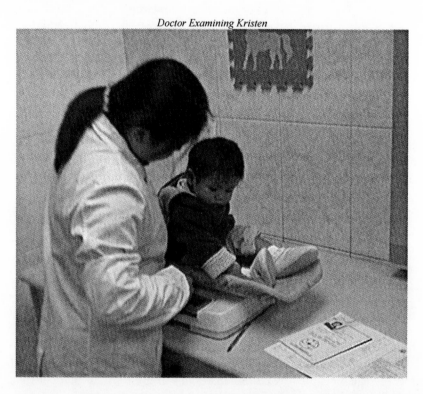

I took Kristen to the medical clinic where they examine the kids as part of the process of the US Consulate issuing them a visa to enter the US. When it came to the hearing test the *doctor* held noisy toys up behind her head on either side, and as usual Kristen didn't respond. The doctor didn't pass her, and our facilitator Sha-Sha was worried, told me the doc said take a seat and we'll try again. We hadn't mentioned Kristen's hearing issue to Sha-Sha, and I think she was now worried that we might not be happy with our child, she might have wondered about the difficulty of a *replacement* child. While we waited to try again I assured Sha-Sha we were very pleased with Kristen, that she was our child now, and if she was deaf, well, she needed a home, too.

In a few moments the doctor called us back in, repeated the tests, and fudged quite a bit to pass her, nudged by Sha-Sha's translation that she was taking medication for an ear infection. I was concerned about Kristen's visa, but I was reassured by one thing I had "in my hip pocket."

You see, the US consulate reviews the home study summary to make sure the child matches what you were recommended and approved for. If you were approved for a healthy child and the child is really *special needs* meaning a medical condition requiring attention and the expense of medical care, the Consulate is likely to decline the visa unless and until they receive a faxed revision to the home study matching the child. So if you were approved for a healthy child and she turns out to be partially deaf at the so-called medical exam, your family is stuck until the conflict is resolved.

We were approved in the home study for a two-three year old healthy child, as we had requested. But Kristen was one year old on Dec 26, 2002, and I had to bring with me to China a home study addendum, with notarized signature for the US Consulate, to cover the child's age. I was smart enough to have the agency add to the addendum their approval for "mild special needs" just in case of a situation like an ear infection appearing to be deafness. So we were covered, but Kristen barely passed the medical test and the issue went away.

Our concern was getting her home, and getting her through the potential ear trauma of airplane pressure changes during ascent and descent, and we'd deal with her hearing issue when the trip is behind us.

Our last official procedure in China was going as a group to the US Consulate with the child. But unlike 1998, this time our facilitator took care of all the paperwork in advance, and I had spent some time with Sha-Sha getting ours together a couple days prior. Each family was called up to an officer behind a window, and they compared our faces to the photos in documents before them, that was it. Then back in the big room with about a hundred adoptive families a Consulate officer came out, got our quiet attention, said raise you right hand, "Do you swear blah blah blah . . ." "I do!" We were done.

Well, not quite. Despite my preparation of documents, and copying critical documents to pack in a second bag just in case, one document turned up missing - the notarized affidavit swearing I understood the US immunization requirements for foreign adopted children and would ensure she gets the shots. I searched high and low but it was gone.

Fortunately, after we all swore "I do" Sha-Sha and I went to the office of the guy who had us raise our right hand, and he nicely put a form in front of me for signature, done in two seconds.

As Madeline says, that's all there is, there isn't any more.

Getting Melanie and the Hair Dude home was starting to sound good. Real good.

Jan 2003, Melanie 5 yrs 9 mos, Kristen 12 mos

Get Ready, Get Set . . . .

If you're quick on your feet as a husband, you might learn a few key tricks before you walk into a buzzsaw by surprise. In general when your darling is intense about something and on the same subject you don't care if snuff goes up to $90 a dip, you better get out of the way before she has to hurt you. And the real trick is knowing what those things are before any blood is spilled.

In our house, packing for a trip is one of those things. I could care less. If it fits, throw it in, if it doesn't, try a little pressure. After all, on the other end what are you going to do but take the stuff out, so what's the big deal? And my way you can pack in no-time.

But Julie, like many women, wants it done just so, and I'm lousy at taking direction when I don't believe in the mission. So when it was time to pack for the 11:30PM China Southern flight from Guangzhou to LA, it took me two seconds to decide I was just going to get out of the way, and you can't embarrass me about not sharing that workload. My contribution was getting Melanie out of the way, too.

I decided to take her to the Guangzhou zoo, a little quality time for Melanie and Dad on a sunny and comfortably cool day. You get spoiled at the White Swan, all I had to do was walk out the front and tell the bellman we wanted to go to the zoo, he whistled up a taxi in three seconds and told him in Chinese where we wanted to go and we were off. You carry your room key card and show to any cabbie for the return, nothing to it though we don't speak one another's language.

The zoo was very respectable, not quite as modern as some but nicely kept and clean. As soon as we paid and entered, an electric open-air bus stopped for us to get on to ride around the zoo, and while I need to walk I love to ride so we got on. Only after the driver started rolling did I realize that one pays for the ride, and it was 7 Yuan, less than $1 for us both. We saw monkeys, tigers, lions, camels, llamas, deer and much more from the comfort of being driven in a comfortably cool breeze. In fact we took off our jacket.

In the zoo is an aquarium complete with jumping dolphin show and a huge tank with a tunnel walkway so you can look up at the sharks and stingrays, pretty neat. We exited the electric bus at the aquarium, and two Chinese ladies yelled to me and pointed until I looked back to the bus - we had left our jackets by mistake, and the driver and several other people were quite concerned about their proper return. Very nice manners, and I bowed slightly in thanks. We enjoyed the aquarium and after an ice cream and warm coke we were done.

Leaving the zoo Melanie saw me raise my hand for a cab and miss it. When the next cab appeared she raised her little hand and behind her I did the same while the crowd turned to stare at us. But she didn't see me wave at the cab. When the cabbie stopped in front of us she looked up proudly and said:

"I called a cab for us, Dad!"

"You sure did, good job."

When we returned to the hotel room Melanie ran to Julie "Mom-Mom, I called us a cab!" Sometimes it's the little things that count.

So the packing general had her silent zip-up and snap-shut troops lined up, ready to go, we just had some last minute shopping to do to spend down our Yuan and top off the pile of stuff we bought in China to bring home. I had purchased an extra suitcase to bring home this treasure, a very large one with rollers and a pull-up handle, big strap around for security, cost me all of $15 down the street from the White Swan Hotel. Now we had three check bags and two carry-ons plus a diaper bag. And of course two kids. No sweat.

We were ready to go home. And then some.

Jan 2003, Melanie 5 yrs 9 mos, Kristen 12 mos

Kristen's Journey Home

Our travel group of seven families met downstairs for checkout and a 5PM bus ride to the airport. Sha-Sha energetically helped each family double-check to make sure all noses were counted and that each family verified all their bags were loaded on the bus, then we were off. We certainly enjoyed this group of five families, plus two more families who adopted from a different orphanage then joined us later. We made some friendships that we hope last into the future with sustained contact.

Goodbye to Sha-Sha

The bus ride to the airport was slow and long at Guangzhou rush hour, slow-and-go just like LA, Atlanta, and Philadelphia. Sha-Sha talked to us by microphone on the way. She is a special young lady. In addition to doing her job taking care of us she went the extra mile many times. When Melanie wanted more attention than she was getting, Sha-

Sha never tired of carrying her or pushing her in the stroller we had borrowed from Sherry's Place. Sha-Sha took us on walking tours of Shamian Island, bus rides to the toy wholesale mart and a museum of sorts that sold keepsakes. That's where I bought a fan carved from Camel bone, and I made the sale ladies laugh when I asked them how many Camels they had to kill to make this fan? Sha-Sha did her job and she did it very well. She did everything for us that could be done on the paperwork, many things I had to do for myself when we adopted Melanie in 1998, and as the days passed one got the feeling she cares deeply about these children, and comes to care for the families she meets on each trip.

Sha-Sha pampering Melanie

On the bus she told us about her own adopted daughter, now two years old, and how she was moved to adopt herself by her involvement with families like ours. She now knows firsthand what we know, that adoption is just another way for a child to come to your family, and the love connection from that point on is just the same as if the child came to your family by birth.

Sha-Sha sang to us on the bus, several songs about mother and child and family and love. I know it sounds corny but it was very moving, not many dry eyes on the bus. Some of us would have liked to bring her to the US with us, but she herded us and our bags all inside, and when she was content all were safely there in the China Southern terminal, she hugged each one of us and our kids goodbye, then rushed off to meet another travel group just arriving so she could do it again. Well done, Sha-Sha.

Stand and Wait

We had a couple hours to stand and wait. China Southern lets one enter the gate area only when the flight is posted at a checkpoint, and we were close to the front, the line growing and snaking back out of sight. We gabbed and talked about a reunion in two years somewhere.

Tick-for-crying-out-loud-tock.

As time for the checkpoint to let us in approached, an American guy in a suit walked up the line and stopped to talk, saying he was looking for a familiar face. Mike McGinnis and I figured out right away he was looking to butt in the line in which we had waited so long, so we ignored him and made sure he headed for the rear. Pinhead. Then he showed up again, with a Chinese associate pushing a cart of bags like the rest of us, inching toward the front to the side of our line, trying to start a conversation to steal a place in line, and since everyone ignored him he waited to take advantage of the Chinese custom of ignoring lines and pushing for the gate, everybody for themselves. The ugly American. Fortunately Mike McGinnis boldly and loudly told him he'd have to go to the back of the line, and he left. I'm glad Mike saved me from losing my temper since everyone already knows I'm a Grump.

Finally we moved through the gate, into another line waiting for luggage x-rays and security strapping on the bags as we pushed our carts, then to another line for the China Southern agent to compete for good seats since none are assigned until check-in. With boarding passes finally in hand, we had to fill out forms for each person declaring our itinerary and also pay about $8 airport tax per person, at long last completing the process, me sweaty and grumpy by now, and we made it through the final security point to the gate area so we could . . . sit down at last and wait for another hour. Are you tired yet?

All Aboard!

At 10:30PM we formed a line again at the gate for boarding, only this time when we made it to the gate agent and showed our tickets and passports for the umpteenth time we then wound around and down stairs to wait in another line for the large stand-up buses that take us out on the tarmac to the huge, brand new shiny Boeing 777, the old ground transport juxtaposed against the newest and finest in aircraft. The stairs we had to climb to board the plane were steep and high, so we had Melanie go first without anything to carry, then Mom carrying just Kristen, then me bringing up the rear with all the carry-on bags and forming a barrier in case anyone fell.

We settled comfortably into our Premium Economy seats at a *late* bedtime, takeoff was right on time at 11:30PM and it didn't take long for people to drop here and there off to sleep until after a while the cabin was dark and quiet, with me wide awake of course because my wreck of a body doesn't sleep in the sitting up position, so I read my book, another Mike Connolly mystery with LAPD Detective Harry Bosch, my kind of grumpy guy.

Through all this, the bus trip and waiting and line after line, Julie held Kristen most of the time, I held her just a little because that's the way Julie and Kristen wanted it. She was sleeping or quiet and content most of the time, just an occasional whine or cry as you'd expect from an infant, an easy kid to travel with. On the flight from Guangzhou to LA, Julie held Kristen, or had her asleep on the floor at her feet, all eleven hours except for a few brief respites with me, and that's the way they would have it. Melanie was a trooper again, didn't whine much at all, played Mom to Kristen when Julie would let her, a super performance for a five year old.

The Little Boxes in Our Head

The Chinese man sitting next to me wanted to talk, though I prefer solitude on airplanes. Flights longer than an hour or two seem to follow a pattern of interpersonal dynamics. Some like to talk, some like to be left alone, the first half hour after takeoff is quiet, the time just before descent loud with chatter.

And the China Southern flight from Guangzhou to LA was certainly longer than a couple of hours. The Premium Economy seats were big enough to comfortably fit my wide frame, but only reclined about half way, not enough for me to do more than cat-nap.

"What state you live in?" he asked after a little conversation.

"Georgia. Do you know where Georgia is?" I replied.

He paused a moment before answering.

"Sure I know where Georgia is. I live in Los Ang-e-les, Cal-i-forn-ia." He punctuated each syllable with emphasis, apparently trying to contain the indignation he felt at my presumption, but just a little seeped through.

Oooooops. "We live in Peachtree City, just south of Atlanta." He nodded as I tried to cover my gaffe.

Of all people, I thought, with Mom holding Kristen, Melanie's new Babysister, with two Chinese daughters I should know better than to make assumptions just because his English is deeply accented, or because he spoke Chinese to the flight attendant, or even because I just finished ten days in China and we were still flying over China.

I have a mental picture of little boxes in our head that hold assumptions based on our life experience that go with what we see. We see a politician and expect a lie. We see a disabled person and see someone who wants and needs our help. We see an Asian child and are surprised when she speaks perfect English, except for the southern accent. And when the little box in our head makes us think of something that actually doesn't fit the image we expect, our mental switch says "Wait a minute!" and we might say something that in retrospect is stupid, like:

"Do you know where Georgia is?"

or "Is that child yours?"

or "Are they real sisters?"

or "Is your husband Asian?"

or "Does she speak English?"

Some gaffes are worse than others, and I'm sure those little boxes in my head will trip me up again. But maybe the realization that we all have preconceived notions, some benign and some not, will help me catch myself before I stumble the next time. And maybe that realization will help me give someone a break when they do it to me or my child.

But only if it's benign.

How Much Longer?

We approached the west coast, after flying against the sun the balance of the night then all day, and finally landed at about 6PM local time. Are you tired yet? Not so fast. As we deplaned and wound our way toward customs, we walked and walked and walked, until about 1/4 mile later we came to a huge room where the INS, now BCIS, processes immigrants. There were about ten officer stations with a line forming at each one, all of us with adopted children were to line up at the last station. We did so, and they collected our paperwork in the sequence we were in line, hundreds of us it seemed, but nothing happened. After nearly an hour, an officer came out to announce the

INS would process all the other people in this huge room at all the other stations, and only then would they *start* on processing adopted children. Welcome home.

So we stood around, and around, and around, and finally they started on the adopted kids. The line was long, and as they had collected our paperwork they stacked it up. When they started working on us they started at the top of the stack, the back of the line. It wasn't a big deal, but seemed like more careless and arrogant treatment by the INS, almost like a deliberate breach to show us we were at their mercy. For Pete's sake we had better treatment and efficiency in China at every stage than from our very own INS. But maybe I was just tired.

We were near the front of the line so we got our paperwork very nearly last, and now we could go find our bags and cross our fingers the customs guys didn't want to strip-search me or something since I was now a Grump plain for everyone to see after our warm INS welcome. But the customs guys were great, we were done in no-time.

I found a luggage cart, kept a grip on Melanie's hand as we crossed the busy street to the hotel shuttle pick-up, negotiated our bags and us onto the hotel bus for the short ride. The driver called ahead by radio to have a bellhop out front to help with our bags and I thanked him and tipped him. While I checked into the hotel Julie stood by our bags on the curb holding Kristen and watching Melanie, and I got a big bill changed so I could tip the bellman $8-10 for five minutes work with our bags, but he didn't show up outside. I looked around and there was the bellman behind his desk, with a nice view of Julie and the kids waiting outside by the bags, standing there with his finger . . . well, I was tired, so I grabbed the luggage cart, wheeled it out, loaded it up, brought it back in the door past bellman Nimrod as he said "I can help you sir" now that I had it loaded, and I'll skip what I said to him because I was tired, you see. But I did call him from our room to explain to him that I wasn't too cheap to pay him to handle my bags, it's just that I was pissed off, you see, because you left my wife at the curb with two little kids and a pile of bags even after the driver called for help with bags, and told him where he could retrieve his luggage cart. Are you tired yet?

We were, ready to crash. But the kids were wide awake.

Julie and I traded off a nap or two, ate room service, relaxed and overindulged with coke in ice. Don't laugh. We had a can of coke from China in a carry-on bag. I asked Julie if she'd like me to warm it up for her. There was a fridge in our room in China with soft drinks and booze and goodies the kids wanted, all way overpriced like $5 for a coke, but even then the fridge was about two degrees above room temperature, like every other refrigerator in China by my experience. And since we could not use ice in China because it is not safe unless the water is boiled before being frozen, we got used to drinking everything in China at room temperature, and we love cold, cold drinks.

Now back in the US, as evening turned into late night, Melanie jumped on the beds until we stopped her, whined and bickered a little, tortured Kristen with kindness a little, but she had been a good kid on a tough trip. Kristen as usual was quiet, crawling around checking things out, wide awake, and whenever she dozed off Melanie was wired.

Nap-awake-nap-awake-nap-awake, tick-freaking-tock, finally time to leave for our 11:30AM Delta flight to Atlanta. This time Delta had a nice big new aircraft, and we had row one in first class. The guy next to me as big as I am said to the flight attendant as soon as he sat down, "Shoot, it's five o'clock somewhere, bring me a *beer*!" Yippee. But after forcing us to listen to his side of his cell phone conversation lecturing his teenage son about responsibility for half an hour, he was OK. The flight was under four hours, and shoot, after the overseas flight marathons we could do four hours standing on our heads. May as well, couldn't sleep. The flight attendant taking care of us took special care of Mom and Kristen, who Julie held the entire flight again, and she told us she had adopted two young girls, showed us their pictures. We talked for a while and I promised to send her one of my books signed by Melanie. I need to do that tomorrow.

We landed about 7PM. At the airport not far from the gate Ronnie Jennings met us walking toward us, coming from his airport office. One thing that happens when you adopt a child is you make new friends. Not just acquaintances, but solid, lifelong friends, and you do things for one another. Let me tell you about friends named Ronnie and Lindy Jennings.

Ronnie had driven us to the airport on the outbound leg. Now he was making sure we arrived, and while we trudged to baggage claim he went somewhere, showed up behind me at baggage claim with a luggage cart, then brought his minivan around to load up. Lindy had collected our mail while we were gone, now stacked on my desk. She had thrown away the newspapers, kept our hermit crabs, checked on the fish to make sure the long-term food was OK, she walked a mile to our house and back every day. What I didn't know was she talked our brand new neighbor into putting our trash bin out and took it back from the street for us, as Ronnie explained on the way home. Ronnie dropped us and our bags off as we admired the welcome home balloons Lindy had tied to our mailbox, and he said no to an invitation for a cocktail since he figured we were ready to crash. Inside we found a big "Welcome Home Kristen" sign with fresh flowers, homemade cookies, a pot roast in a slow cooker, casserole, and an invitation to a shower for Kristen the following week. What magnificent friends, what a touching welcome home, very comforting when you're exhausted.

Ronnie, Lindy & Matthew Jennings

Kristen was crawling and checking things out. Melanie had slept on the flight and was now wired again. I made a cocktail and eased into my chair while kids bounced off the wall.

Are you tired yet?

Jan 16, 2003, Melanie 5 yrs 9 mos, Kristen 12 mos

Kristen's Welcome

With tag-team naps despite Melanie continuing to stay up too late and wake up too early we were slowly getting rid of jet-lag from our Thursday night return from China. Nonetheless, while a few buddies thought we were in need of more rest and help, we decided to have friends and neighbors over on Sunday to introduce Kristen. That kept me busy rounding up snacks and drinks, and maybe that's how jet-lag is best treated - ignore it and stay busy.

Nearly everyone showed up on short notice and we had a fine celebration with a packed house and kids making racket in the upstairs playroom. Tinkling a knife against a beer bottle I got everyone's attention to tell them:

"While in Guangzhou in southern China we visited the Six Banyan Temple, a remarkable Buddhist collection of temples, the first one built in the year 537AD, and at that temple two Buddhist Monks blessed Kristen and Melanie. Not that we're Buddhist or anything. But the very best blessing Kristen could receive is a warm welcome from our family, friends and neighbors, and that's why you're here today. We thank you. Since you were so kind to come we're going to show you the video of the day when we met Kristen."

We showed the video, and it satisfied some curiosities, I think, since some wonder "What must it be like?" A few found it moving to watch and admonished me for not having tissues handy. Maybe seeing the magic moment on video helped make it more real to those who have never been to China. When you only have books and stories about a far away exotic land where there is a long tradition of preference for boys, and where infant girls are sometimes abandoned or worse, it's easy to wonder things such as "What are Chinese people like, that they would do such a thing?" And as you and I know because we have been there, if you want to know what Chinese people are like, look to your left and to your right, and no matter who you are with, Chinese people are just like them. We're all the same in most ways, and however hard the conditions, Kristen's birthmom must have hurt badly in having to give her up. Maybe the video, in which the Chinese caregivers are so clearly devoted to the children, helped them understand, just a little.

Six Banyan Temple Buddhist blessing

While we partied and watched the video, Kristen slept through all the oohs and ahhhs and chatter around her, on her back on Mom's lap with her head hanging a bit down at Julie's knees, a favorite spot so far. Melanie was working up a sweat upstairs playing with friends, leaving Kristen in temporary safe harbor from Big Sister's affections.

We all had a good time, and when most guests were gone I finally sat down and stayed down. A good friend named Terry Morgan started cleaning up in the kitchen and when I asked her what the heck she was doing she said we needed to rest so she was cleaning up. I asked her if she would wash the truck. She said no. It was worth a try.

In fact Terry offered to bring a meal so we didn't have to cook, Julie said no several times because we could easily fend for ourselves, but Terry's insistence overcame Julie's resistance. The next day when Terry brought over a casserole and trimmings I asked her if she was *sure* she didn't want to wash the truck. No luck, but the casserole was good.

It's nice to have supportive friends, like Lindy and Ronnie Jennings and all they did for us, Terry Morgan bringing food even if she wouldn't wash the truck, and Rich Horning who gave us Delta "buddy passes" to use for flights just in case of problems. And I won't forget who meant it when they volunteered to babysit.

So Kristen has been home a few days now, crawling more, exploring just a little, starting to acclimate to her surroundings. Her funky hair is starting to lay down as it grows. Too bad. I like the "Hair Dude."

January 19, 2003, Melanie 5 yrs 9 mos, Kristen 13 mos

The Real Kristen

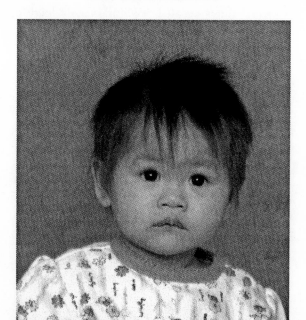

Hiding, lurking, watching, waiting,
Kristen seemed to withdraw from the moment she was handed over to
Julie at twelve months old in Guangzhou by her orphanage nanny,
oblivious to whoever held her, avoiding eye contact and ignoring those
trying to talk to her. Her Big Sister Melanie smiled so big it almost
broke her face after waiting so long for her Babysister, who she could
now touch. Melanie held her just a moment after Mom held her for the
first time, but Kristen was hiding.

Coughing, wheezing, sneezing, dripping,
Kristen was most content, it seemed, when left to lay on the hotel room floor like a slug, alone in her infant misery with bronchitis and ear infection, unable to tell us what was wrong, but I don't think she would have talked anyway. She comforted herself with the back of her hand and a White Swan Hotel washcloth, soon to become her treasured possession. When we held her still for the Chinese nurse to give her bum four antibiotic shots over two days, despite her frantic and strong wiggles away from the needle, her screams didn't last long but I'm afraid it set back any progress we were making in gaining her trust.

Cooing, gooing, laughing, kissing,
Melanie gave Kristen the affections she had been storing in her five year old mind for a long time, undeterred by Kristen's constant turning away and struggle to be left alone. She let Melanie and Mom and Dad hold her to feed her, but she soon wanted down on her own. As Melanie dashed back and forth to the hotel room next door to visit her buddy Julia, she never forgot to kiss Kristen when she was leaving and when she returned, even when it was just a whirlwind stop to retrieve a

toy. Not that Kristen enjoyed the attention, but she did very reluctantly give Melanie her first smile. And Melanie earned it.

Pulling, squeezing, reaching, chasing,
Melanie's mothering torment of her new sister was so relentless, even though always well-intended, that she had to be mildly admonished a few hundred times a day. Between Julie's strategic mothering and Melanie's compulsive mothering, little Kristen must have treasured those moments she had to herself, and I stayed in the background, knowing my time would come. Melanie must be the very best Big Sister Kristen could hope for. I have to give credit to Melanie's persistence for cracking Kristen's shell. Her play seemed to bring the first responses.

Whining, crying, squawking, squealing,
Kristen soon applied those tools available to her to get what she wanted. Like to be carried by Mom. Or to be let down on the floor so she could scoot into her own comfortable position. Or to let everyone know she most certainly did not have her White Swan washcloth in her hand.

Holding, staring, grabbing, sleeping,
Kristen gradually became accustomed to Julie, slept on her shoulder, looked in her eyes, giggled when Julie did the baby-talk things moms do, and sometimes Kristen laughed when Julie tickled her while changing her diaper or trying to stuff errant limbs into pajamas. She came to expect that when we left the room Julie would carry her and make sure she had her White Swan washcloth so she could hide her face to play Ostrich when she wished. And by the time we took the long flight home from China, Kristen had developed a strong preference for Julie.

Scratching, poking, probing, peeling,
Kristen seems to have a mission in her genes to peel off the surface layers of walls, chairs, books, trailer hitches, you name it. She's been a world class scratcher since the day we met. It's not that she has noticeably damaged anything, but we can hear her scratching things with her steel-like finger nails across the room. Today I opened a window in the upstairs bedroom where Kristen was crawling, removed the screen and pulled it inside the room. Julie heard Kristen scratching the screen from outside, one floor below. If there's an Olympic scratching event, she's a contender.

Kneeling, crawling, scooting, standing,
after a few days of subdued exploring and getting used to her new home, Kristen is morphing into a normal kid. She walks with our two-

fingered help, prefers to stand when she is near the now soft-covered coffee table, and gets into everything. We had to remove the small trash can in the family room because one of her favorites is tipping it over and spreading out the contents so she makes sure she sees everything. In my office her favorite is to sneak behind my chair on the floor and probe the network of phone and electrical wires until I see her and quickly remove her. If she hasn't licked her finger and searched for an unprotected electric socket, it's only because she hasn't thought of it yet. Kristen goes everywhere in the house now, even tries the stairs when someone forgets the gate, and scoots frog-like very quickly when she's after something dear to her, like her Mom or her White Swan washcloth. Menace is the word I'm looking for.

Dropping, tossing, smearing, spreading, Kristen upholds the duties and reputation of one year olds. With apologies to lady readers who might have a fainting spell at my admission, this is what I privately refer to as the "Chicken" stage of childhood. Completely oblivious to things other than her momentary focus, Kristen finishes her bottle and then just pushes it away to drop where it drops. She's resisting eating solids so far with a few exceptions, but she did eat dirt out of a planter. Like it or not, kids this age have the sanitary habits of a barnyard animal, and if you don't pick up every 10 minutes your house will soon resemble a chicken coop.

Grinding, gnashing, biting, tapping, Kristen makes sounds with her teeth that your mind tries to deny. Her teeth grinding can be heard across the room. With the TV on. Loud. Maybe we're going to buy a boat for a pediatric dentist.

Standing, frizzing, fraying, straying, Kristen's still the "Hair Dude" Melanie named her. Even though her hair lay down a bit and Julie trimmed it a little, when it's washed it's still the YangDong Do, straight hair sticking in all directions complete with cowlicks. I like her funky hair.

Laughing, giggling, shrieking, scrambling, Kristen greets Melanie's return from school each day with what appears to be delight. Melanie used to rush through the door like any five year old and yell "Mom!" or "Dad!" But now she rushes in and yells "Where's sissy?" Melanie tickles her, shows her how to play with infant toys, tries to show her how to pull the few hairs on my chest to make me squirm, and carries her like a deformed sack of potatoes. Tirelessly. Though at first Melanie's attentions appear to be rough for a one year old, Kristen weathers it well, and if I could capture what she is feeling I would bet Kristen has come to love and admire her older sister, the big scary kid who must know everything. There is a little jealousy as Kristen sometimes objects to Julie giving attention to Melanie, but I see a budding hero worship in her eyes.

Begging, touching, grasping, pleading, Kristen now has Julie trained just the way she wants her. Her indifference about who holds her long forgotten, she keeps her eye on Julie to make sure she has her in sight at all times, her head whipping around if she's turned so you can almost hear the air snap. Being held by Mom is her most favorite thing, Julie's mission accomplished, part one. The first time Kristen held up her arms was an attempt to get Julie to pick her up. And when she feels ignored, she crawls to Julie and taps her foot with her finger. Lucky Julie. When she paid attention to *my* foot, she scraped the top layer of leather off in a big stripe straight down the middle of the toe. Good thing it was a casual shoe. And good thing she's hanging on to Mom. She likes Melanie and me, too, but it comes slowly and naturally.

That's how it goes with Kristen, from indifferent slug to attaching menace in five weeks.

Feb 2003, Melanie 5 yrs 10 mos, Kristen 14 mos

Life With Kristen

What do you call an upside-down smile? No, not a frown, that's Kristen in her favorite position. With Mom it's being held like a sling-load, one hand under her back and one under her neck, not quite in a vertical position while she tries to lay her head back even further as Mom swings her to and fro, trying to wiggle down even further to who-knows where.

With me sitting in my leather chair, which Kristen relentlessly tries to scratch deep past the surface layer, she lays face-up with her head at my knees, scooting down further to lay her head back down over my knees, but that's just preparation for the main event. While Kristen isn't fond of snuggling, she does like when I pat her on the chest, alternating between one hand and the other, very fast in a rat-a-tat-tat, the signal for her to start *talking* in staccato. Melanie frequently joins in for a little light pounding on Kristen's chest.

This kid has a mind of her own. When she is doing something she should not, like shaking the fireplace toolkit so it is bound to bonk her on the head, and we take her away because she doesn't yet respond to NO, she doesn't fuss or cry or resist in any way. But she immediately scoots like Sweetpea in her little frog-crawl back to her point of interest, her exploration not yet completed, thank you.

Kristen is a little behind schedule at 14 months, just recently eating solids but is not yet talking. Mom can't wait for her to start talking.

You see, at first Kristen didn't really care who held her, and she didn't really want to be held at all, her preference was to be left alone while she scanned the room, checking out everything, keeping it all at a distance until she decided to poke her finger into something to see what happens. But Julie's tireless holding and play and cooing and tickling has had a cumulative effect. Now Kristen has Mom trained just the way she likes her, and just as Melanie did at her age she keeps Mom in sight at all times.

Did you ever play with a gyroscope when you were a kid? When you get it spinning fast the gyroscope's inertia resists turning in any direction in three dimensions, and it's easy to balance on a string with that stability. Kristen, just like Melanie, apparently has a gyroscope in her head, activated by the sight of Mom. Focused like a laser beam on Mom, if you turn her away her head snaps around one way then another until the laser reconnects to Mom.

Melanie shows Kristen how to eat her very first donut

And Kristen has discovered the ability to make sounds to communicate to her well-trained Mom just what she wants her to do, like pick her up for criminey sake. But since she doesn't talk yet that sound is kind of a cross between a hum and a whine, a relentless keening that makes Julie wish for the first spoken "mama" to get on with it, please.

Kristen is most happy on the move. Even when it is cold outside, movement and new scenes hold her attention. Lets see, her innate nature is touch-her-not, don't hug her but it's OK if you let her hang comfortably and pat her chest so she can make cool noises, if she's about to bonk herself on the head she'll keep trying until it's a done deed, she's happiest when on the move, and perfectly content with her own company. She sounds just like . . . *me*!

She has met many friends and, sadly, has attended her first funeral.

Some of you know Terry & Susan Flaugher, who adopted Rebecca some years ago and adopted Grace just last year. Terry didn't feel well during the China trip, and long story short he discovered upon their return he had Leukemia. During his battle with the disease Grace had heart surgery with complications threatening her life, but a second surgery solved the problem, and some weeks ago Terry passed away in Ohio where the family had moved for his treatment.

Susan endured a great deal in the past year, and did so with dignity and grace, with the help of loving sisters, other family, and strong faith. Terry's body was cremated according to his wishes, and Susan arranged for a memorial service at the Heritage Christian Church in Peachtree City, Georgia where the Flaugher family had another, extended family, and where Terry had dedicated himself to a special ministry for children.

At the service, a slideshow was played showing many photos of Terry and his family and friends, some narrated by him, and it was a well done and moving celebration of his life, a life that touched many people. Some of those people spoke to us, including his son who said his Dad was his hero, and I think Terry would have been proud of the effect he had on others.

Melanie played in a supervised room during the service, and when it was done and we gathered her to depart, she wanted to know if we had seen Rebecca's Dad's body. Julie told her no, that his body had been cremated, and explained what that meant and how it was different than being in a casket, because a five year old mind must be satisfied.

We took the sleeping Kristen and curious Melanie home, and later that day Melanie asked Julie:

"Mom, when you die are you going to have your bones burned or do you want to be in a casserole?"

Even when life slaps you in the face you have to stop and smile at the beautiful innocence of kids. And when Kristen starts talking, I'll have to be quick to keep up with the conversation.

Mar 2003, Melanie 5 yrs 11 mos, Kristen 15 mos

Giffer-Tickets

Melanie sat on the kitchen floor heater vent to keep warm, with her breakfast plate on the floor beside her milk glass, punching commands into her new Pixter game, cramming a few minutes of play into a tiny slot of time before Mom drives her to school. She doesn't like interruptions from Mom or Dad to tell her to brush her hair and teeth, but when Kristen crawls over to interrupt Melanie gives her a hug, one kiss on the cheek, then a second one square on her left eye, muttering senseless words of affection just like a real mom.

Yesterday Melanie took her family shopping. Aunt Betty and Aunt Vicki had given her Toys-R-Us gift certificates for Christmas, and with the whirlwind of our China trip, not to mention that Julie and I compete for the procrastinators' gold medal, we're just getting around to letting her spend her loot. Of course now is a better time since Christmas involves excessive . . . well, don't get me started.

So Melanie said to me yesterday:

"Come-on, Dad, lets go!"

"Where are we going?"

"To the toy store."

Not willingly, I'm not. "Why?"

"Cause I going to spend my giffer-tickets."

"What?"

"I got giffer-tickets from Aunt Vicki and Aunt Betty for the toy store, come-on!"

So off we go to Toys-R-Us. And it would have been a good lesson for Kristen about the ratchet effect of rising expectations, or at least trading up, if only she understood what was going on. First Melanie picked out a Care Bear with left-over money for more. Then she found a Cinderella nightgown she wanted, but was a few dollars short, so I slipped her five ones for her allowance, and she put back the Care Bear, having traded up. That poured a little sand in Mom's gearbox since

Julie is steadfastly using these spending events to teach Melanie the cost of things we want, but I weakened.

"Mo-om, can Kristen have a Cinderella nightgown, too?"

"No, she's too little."

"Can she have a Care Bear, too, if I don't get the nightgown?"

"No, you don't have enough money." Julie was wisely not letting her spend it all at once.

So Melanie pondered alternatives, and as a girl she was genetically driven to consider every item on the shelves before making up her mind.

Finally, "*Oh, fine, I'll take the gown.*" But Mom wasn't going to let her settle for instant gratification.

"No, we'll look at another store to get something you really want."

"Noooooo, lets look some more here." Kids learn fast to grab it while the grabbing is good.

So Mom and Melanie and Kristen and Dad moseyed over to the book department, my favorite gift for a child anyway. Melanie looked at Rapunsel and Snow White and Cinderella books, needing to examine each page of each book while I was just about out of patience, then she spied the Pixter electronic game. Hold everything! She immediately traded up again, buying something for Kristen with left-over money forgotten.

"Look, Mom, a Pixter. Taylor has one of these."

"OK, you have enough money."

And so Melanie acquired her new electronic game, with Dad conned into buying a $15 carrying case, and Mom & Dad hope that Taylor down the street has some optional plug-in games so we can share more and buy less.

Melanie is still fascinated by the game this morning, which is a long time since yesterday in a kid's world, but she always pauses in her play when Kristen interrupts to give her a hug, and maybe a kiss even if it is on the eye.

Mar 2003, Melanie 5 yrs 11 mos, Kristen 15 mos

Kristen Amuses Melanie

"Heh, Heh, Heh, Heh!"

Melanie laughed the belly laugh I had heard only once before, the kind of mature laugh that sneaks out of her belly a little bit lazy, kind of like an overflow, with just enough grin to add a bit of evil.

"Sor-ry" she said unconvincingly as her grin grew larger, announcing the card she drew, taking her green token from the Sorry game to knock me back to Start.

I bought this game last week, remembering how many times we played it when I was a kid. With her sixth birthday just around the corner she learned the rules faster than I thought she would, and while she sneaks away from the table to pick up Kristen or push her too fast through the kitchen on the little plastic four-wheeler Julie bought, she pays more attention to the game than I would expect from a six year old.

Since I bought the game she has asked to play it every night, and tonight she won for the second time. She's learning to be a good sport, but sometimes when I knock her back to Start she can't help herself and she pulls the hair on my arm. Of course Mom plays mommy rules sometimes, letting Melanie off the hook in the hopes her baby will win, but what do you expect from a Mom?

Kristen started to pre-school this week half-days for a break in period, we'll do another week of half-days then Julie goes back to work and Kristen starts pre-school full time. I didn't realize what zipped through Melanie's head when Babysister started pre-school until Julie and I picked her up early on Monday to visit the ENT doctor.

"Where's Kristen?" Melanie asked from her booster seat in the back seat of the truck.

"She's at Primrose." Mom answered, the same pre-school Melanie attended from age one to five.

"Heh, Heh, Heh, Heh!" Melanie seemed genuinely amused with her brand new grown-up belly laugh, fed by the superior knowledge of one who has gone before, with a bit of smug pity for the poor little schmuck doing the same drill she did so many times before she became a big kid.

Her new laugh was a bit contagious, and Julie and I nearly lost it.

I told the ENT doctor he should take a look at Melanie's tonsils.

"Wow, those are impressive" he said. They need to come out.

I considered not telling Melanie what was coming because she tends to hyperventilate, figuratively and sometimes literally, if left to her own devices in anticipation of something unpleasant. But Mom outsmarted me again, was already telling her, and she asked:

"I'm going to have an *oper-ation*?"

"Yes you are, but it's not too bad, you'll just have a sore throat for a few days, and you'll have to be out of school a few days."

Just like a doctor would have said it. When a doctor says 'This might sting a little' it means it's going to hurt like hell and you'll feel like poking your finger in his eye. But Mom told Melanie about how she'd have to eat pudding and ice cream for a few days, all of which is true. It's a good thing Melanie is so far unfamiliar with Bill Cosby's version of "*Ice Cream, We're Gonna Have Ice Cream*" followed by "Aaahhhhhhh!" from the first taste.

Melanie is cool in anticipation of her oper-ation, and besides she knows quite a bit about these things, she's almost six you know. The other day when she noticed Mom's belly button was lower on her body than Melanie's, the little darling informed Mom with the confidence of certain knowledge:

"You know, Mom, your belly button moves lower and lower when you get old, and when it gets to the end of your big toe you just die."

Well, it's good to know the end can be measured in advance.

And when Melanie wakes up after her oper-ation, I think when she has her first taste of ice cream or anything else, Kristen won't say a word because she doesn't talk yet. But if she did it might be something like "Heh, Heh, Heh, Heh!"

Mar 2003, Melanie 5 yrs 11 mos, Kristen 15 mos

Two is Like Five Hundred

Kristen is now a day care trooper, with two weeks of half days and one week of full days under her belt now that Mom is back to work. So how is life for a working couple getting used to two kids instead of one?

When our dear friend Lindy Jennings was waiting for word about Gracie from China, she was somewhat, well, impatient. During her wait we started our quest for Babysister, and finally Gracie came home from China with Lindy, Ronnie, and their nine year old son Matthew. I am reminded of what Lindy said to me a month or so after her return when we bumped into one another one evening at the Kroger grocery store.

"Just remember," she said, wagging her finger in my face with apocalyptic warning, "one kid is like one, but two is like *five hundred*!"

She exaggerated, it turns out, only a little.

Julie is traveling a few days a week now that she's back to work, and I've discovered what it must be like to hang wallpaper with just one arm. In the morning if I'm lucky I get away with sneaking awake early to shower and dress before the baby cries or Melanie whines for me as she wakens, expecting to be carried downstairs. So it takes two trips to get them both downstairs, then another trip to get their clothes, but I need the exercise. That's the easy part. A bottle for Kristen and breakfast for Melanie and dressing and combing hair and brushing teeth and prepping snacks and school bags and getting them to school within the deadline is routine with one, but about, say, five hundred times harder with two, especially when one of them is just fifteen months old.

By the time I start work, I'm brimming with admiration for single mothers.

No working late, though, and it's a good thing I'm my own boss. I must be wrapped up by 5:30 at the latest because Melanie and Kristen go to different schools, which makes it about, say, five hundred times harder.

Our routine is more pleasant with warming weather. I drive the golf cart to pick up Melanie from the Elementary school nearby, then we both drive to Primrose preschool to pick up Kristen. Melanie rushes to see Kristen first, having been separated from her all day and anxious to reunite. Kristen's face lights up when she sees Melanie, who just cannot keep herself from picking up Kristen. The little one's arms get pinned upward like a referee declaring a touchdown while Melanie struggles and staggers, but Kristen's grin says she is tickled to have Big Sister's arms squeezing her like a sack of flour in a bear hug.

Two different dinners for the kids makes it about, say, five hundred times harder, but the real challenge is synchronizing Kristen's falling asleep with story time for Melanie, and so far the miracles we needed seemed to occur.

Story time just before lights out is the best for me, because Mom usually reads to Melanie while I feed Kristen her evening bottle, change her into PJs and watch her until she goes to sleep. I like reading to Melanie, and it's a time you will discover, if you haven't already, when your kid really opens up and talks to you.

Melanie brings home two books for reading, then she takes a test on the books. So we read about seahorses in one book, and about Maddy's friend, Vincent the alien, in the other. Since Melanie has to take a test, we read them twice.

"Thanks for reading my books, Dad."

"I like reading to you. Some day when you have a daughter of your own, you'll like reading to her, too."

"Yeah, only I get to pick the books."

She thought for a minute.

"But Dad, what if I can't have a baby grow in my tummy, you know, like you and Mom?"

I didn't answer because I knew she would make the leap in an instant, which she did.

"I know!, I can 'dopt a child like you and Mom 'dopted me and Kristen, right Dad?"

"That's right, you can."

"I can 'dopt from China, or from Spain or from Japan or even here in America, right Dad?"

"That's right, you can."

"I know what I have to do. I have to go to the orphanage where they take care of little children whose mommy and daddy can't take care of them, 'cause they are safe at the orphanage, and that's where I 'dopt a child to be my own and part of our family forever, right Dad?"

"That's right." Brilliant and well adjusted, I think, for a kid two weeks from her sixth birthday.

"I'd like to read to my 'dopted little girl like you and Mom."

"Time to go to sleep."

"'Night Dad." She gave me a kiss on the cheek, one like a warm, wet butterfly.

Shoot. This is no sweat. Until morning.

Mar 2003, Melanie 5 yrs 11 mos, Kristen 1 yr 3 mos

Melanie Flips Off Her Mom

While driving to the hospital this Tuesday, Melanie gave Mom The Finger from the back seat.

That's right, the little darling shot her first bird. And while Julie was trying to hide her shaking shoulders as she laughed almost uncontrollably, I shook my head with the thought she is barely six years old.

In fact Melanie turned six just last Saturday. This time instead of a huge production with stampedes of little people, she had three of her buddies come over to celebrate, play games and sleep over in a genuine girl-giggle pajama party. It tested my patience, and since I'm clearly a Grump that must mean they had a great time. By Sunday noon it was over, but after all Melanie's birthday had been going on nearly a week.

When you have family out of town who like to send birthday presents to the kids, something magical happens in the kid world. The mailman brings . . . *packages*. Of course Melanie is so accustomed to the disappointment of packages being addressed to me for some boring business matter, so when a package came last week she sighed and wallowed in self-pity:

"Oh, sure, Dad. It's probably for your boring business!"

But when she recognized her name on it and I told her it was from Grandma Lois and Aunt Vicki her eyes burned into the package like a laser, frantic to have it opened. Waiting to open the package until her birthday was simply not possible. So she opened it and liked it, a musical carousel with a hidden drawer for valuables and a great book. When Mom arrived home from work Melanie rushed her:

"Mom, look, it's a birthday present and it plays the hummingbird song!"

"What?"

Well, close enough for a kid. It plays what I call the "Mockingbird song," you know the one where ". . . Mama's gonna buy you a diamond ring. And if that diamond ring don't shine . . ." The very next day when a package arrived from Aunt Betty, Melanie was all over it because the curse of Dad's boring business packages had been broken. She was on a roll, and she ambushed Mom coming home from work again, this time to show her the bunny.

And on Tuesday, just three days after her birthday, we were driving to the hospital for Melanie to have her tonsil's removed. That gave Melanie just one day, Monday, of the coveted Spring Break, then off to slaughter in the operating room. She was braving it quite well, remarkable, in fact, for a kid her age.

She wasn't tense or mad at Mom or even slightly misbehaving in the back seat when she shot Mom the bird.

"Mom, is this the bad finger?"

Julie turned around to look, and before laughter overwhelmed her she answered:

"Yes, that's the bad finger. It's not nice to do that, OK?"

"Why not?"

"Well, because it means something bad to a lot of people."

"What does it mean?"

"You never mind. Just don't do that. You can use other fingers but don't show your bad finger that way, OK?"

"OK, Mom."

I had to know. "Who told you about the bad finger?" Now I admit, I am a world class contributor to the swearing jar, one dollar for every bad word, but I assure you she didn't get The Finger from me. Innocence is rare for me, so you'll understand if I shout a little loud about it.

"Madison and Bridget showed me the bad finger."

Wow. Kindergarten class is a tough place these days. When I was six years old I was using crayons, round-end scissors and tasting the paste once in a while, but The Finger would have been lost on me. Times have changed.

After Melanie thought about the bad finger for a while she asked in exasperation:

"*Well, if that finger is bad why do we even have it?*"

If you have a good answer, let me know.

At the hospital the nurse gave Melanie some liquid Valium to make her calm before surgery. Calm? She was already calm. This stuff transformed her into a stand-up comic who had to sit down lest she fall down. I can't remember when Julie and I laughed so hard. Melanie first insisted on playing "I spy with my little eye . . ." and as we tried to guess what she had picked out she slurred her words, talked slowly with great pleasure while wearing the smile and twinkle of an adult vixen. Then she would bend over double, folded over Julie's arm in laughter with her head near Julie's shoes and we could hear her saying silly things like "P-U, Mom, you didn't brush your feet this morning." and then laughing with silent glee at her own twist of wit.

I asked the nurse if we could have some of that stuff in a go cup, but I think she'd heard it before a few hundred times.

Melanie came through her surgery just fine, and instead of the whining and crying and pleading we expected since it would be her first experience with pain that would not stop in spite of medication every four hours, she was jumping and playing by mid-afternoon the same day. We had to admonish her to slow down to heal properly.

That afternoon the phone rang and as usual Melanie tore toward the phone shouting "I got it!" to fend off any competitor telephone answerers.

"Garlock residence, may I help you?" she answered as I had taught her, speaking slow and clear. She listened for a minute and then said:

"Mom, it's Doctor Weiss!" and handed over the phone.

The Doctor asked Julie "That wasn't Melanie was it?"

"It sure was."

He couldn't believe it. Her throat hurt and her pain medicine tasted really bad, but she did what had to be done, ignored it and played with her Babysister. What a trooper.

I have a few medals in display cases on my office wall from my Vietnam War days, and they gave me an idea. I found on the net an image of a medal, and I made a small document to insert in a small frame to present to Melanie. It said she was presented the Medal for Bravery for her courage and good humor when she had her tonsils out. She liked her medal quite a lot.

I'm proud of her, she conducted herself better than some adults I know. Me, for example. If I was going to give someone The Finger on the day of my first surgery, I think I'd give it to the Doctor.

Apr 2003, Melanie 6 yrs 0 mos, Kristen 1 yr 4 mos

Kristen Sleeps On Me

As I have told you, Kristen's attitude when we met her on January 6, 2003, was one-year-old withdrawn indifference. For some time, the best way to comfort her when she was unhappy was to put her down, give her a White Swan Hotel washcloth, and don't touch her.

She would not sleep while being held, as if she was uncomfortable, defenses up.

With patience, lots of touching and holding and tickling and goo-gooing, Julie has turned around Kristen's preferences in a couple of months. I take zero credit.

Kristen now follows Julie like a new puppy, arms held in "V' formation on either side for balance as she walks like a monkey, wrapping her arms around Julie's leg when she stops. She does the same to me but only if Julie is not there. She follows the noise, seeking out the company of Julie and Melanie and me, and I don't mind being third place. She used to seek solitude.

When you adopt a child one of the pressing worries bouncing around in your head is all about bonding. In 1998 when we adopted Melanie in Hefei, Anhui Province in China, she grabbed onto Julie right away and never let go. Kristen was altogether different, and we had to restrain ourselves to give her space and time, not crowd her as she adjusted to our family.

In the evening Julie takes Melanie upstairs to read to her and put her to bed while I feed Kristen her bedtime bottle. I take Kristen to bed when she is asleep. She would only sleep after I put her down on the floor with her White Swan washcloth, biting it as she writhed to scratch her back, maybe trying to form a comfortable spot, oblivious to the fact the carpeted floor is harder than her bed. Finally she sleeps.

In the last couple of weeks there has been something new. Kristen fell asleep a few times while I held her. There's something comforting about the soft sleep of a child in your arms, so the change is welcome.

Last night Kristen gave me a little surprise. Just as I recognized the signs of sleepiness and expected her to writhe on her back for a minute before settling in, she toddled over to me with an expectant look, then held up her arms, asking to be picked up. She saved her writhing for my lap, found her comfortable spot and fell into a deep sleep. I think the Hair Dude has decided we're OK.

Apr 2003, Melanie 6 yrs 0 mos, Kristen 1 yr 4 mos

Melanie Reads Dad's Brain

"Will it hurt, Dad?" Melanie asked when I picked her up at school this afternoon for her dental appointment. She had two tiny cavities the dentist said were no big deal but better filled. Her question was almost casual, kind of automatic like asking "Why?" when she asks if she can invite a friend over and I say no for whatever reason.

Melanie with her Hula Hoop, which she believes is a very recent invention

Whenever her dental appointment came up in conversation her knee-jerk question has been "Will it hurt?" Of course your first instinct to comfort a six year old is to reassure her a hundred ways it will be all right, but I didn't do that because Melanie seemed to be handling it well. She was a little apprehensive but boldly ready to do what had to be done, so I told her the truth. "I don't think so."

When the nurse called Melanie's name she jumped to her feet, walked in front of me and asked the nurse "Will it hurt?" The nurse had no trouble lying with "No, sweetie" - she sees this all day every day. She put me in the corner seat, where parents belong, in the drilling room, out of the way within sight of their kid. She helped Melanie settle into the chair, put on her earphones so she could watch Shrek on the ceiling, and gave her sunglasses to minimize the glare of the light.

Then the doc came in (drum-roll, please) to greet Melanie. She asked him "Will it hurt?" He lied, too, then explained to her he was going to have her breathe some funny air to make her feel good, and he strapped on the Nitrous Oxide over her nose and told her to take a few deep breaths. I was reminded of Steve Martin in the movie <u>Little Shop of Horrors</u> as a sadistic motorcycle-riding dentist with a Nitrous Oxide tank strapped to his back and the tubes running to each side of his nose piece and the way he paused to suck in a *seriously* deep breath.

I told the doc she might get goofy because when she drank the magic sauce to prep her for tonsil surgery a couple months ago she turned into Robin Williams. In a few minutes Melanie raised up her legs from the dentist chair to ride her bike in the air, just a mild hallucination, and the doc knew she was ready for business.

In he went for sadistic work, his drill and mirror along with his nurse's water gun and suction hose crammed into her tiny mouth, but she didn't give a flip if they didn't get in the way of Shrek. In no-time they were done, congratulating Melanie on being a great patient. She breathed oxygen for a while, and as her head cleared she picked out a little toy from the basket after examining each and every one, of course.

I was proud of my little trooper. She had been a bit scared but faced the threat head-on. The fact it didn't hurt was a bonus, and I was reminded she's not so little any more. You always hear parents say it goes fast but that only sinks in with your own kids.

The other day with Melanie in the back seat on the way to pick up some dinner on the fly I was reminded of a lawyer and former judge named Frank Holstein I used to work with on professional liability cases. I would share my version of wisdom on investigative techniques with Frank and he would share his version of lawyerly wisdom with me. Sometimes we butted heads and sometimes we mixed in a little self-deprecation to get us closer to honesty, and one day he confessed that his most useful tactic was a knowing nod. I asked him what he meant. He said when he didn't have a clue what was going on he would slowly nod knowingly and say nothing, which gave him time to think while giving others in the room the impression he knew the magic answer but wasn't about to share it with them. I tried it once and Frank was right.

So from the back seat Melanie said "I know where you're going, Dad." Well, I was driving down the street to Wendy's since Julie likes their Mandarin Chicken salad and I can get it at the drive-up window. Melanie said "You're going to Wendy's!" Of course that was the only reasonable possibility in the direction I was driving but why steal a kid's thunder? So I said "That's right, how did you know that?" I looked around at her quickly while driving, and I'll be darned if she didn't nod knowingly with a smirk and say "I can read people's brains, you know."

I thought of Frank and his knowing nod, how we often agreed, while rubbing our sore head, that it was silly to butt heads over conflict between his staff and mine, and what a good thing it was occasionally that neither of us could read brains like Melanie. Frank might think, just because there were a few times we didn't find common ground, that I would reveal he is now a prosecutor in Trenton, NJ, and risk that a clever defense attorney would learn the meaning of his knowing nod. I wouldn't do that to my buddy Frank, would I?

But a kid that reads Dad's brain and instinctively nods knowingly is not a baby any more.

I told Melanie I was proud of her today as we left the dental office and let her choose a treat. She chose a chocolate milk shake with an extra shot of chocolate, any girl's dream. And on the way home she said "590 AM, Dad!" She responded to my look of "What?" with "The Disney radio station, Dad, 590 AM" and couldn't help rolling her eyes. I turned it on.

As she sang along to Backstreet Boys songs she already knows from somewhere and tapped the seat with her foot to the beat I thought to myself I had not planned to clean the shotgun until she was about 14, but I think it's coming sooner than that in today's world. Time goes even faster now.

The Disney station isn't bad, but if rap comes on I'm turning off the radio in my truck. I wonder if she can read that in my brain.

Jul 2003, Melanie 6 yrs 3 mos, Kristen 1 yr 7 mos

Kristen's Learns to "Aggavate" Dad

"But Dad, I wanted to help!"

Melanie was unhappy because the small trees and limbs from overdue trimming filled the truck bed. There's no indignation like a kid seeing what they deem to be unfair, and I had told her she could help me when she came home from her "Dress Up Like A Princess" birthday party at her friend Erica's house. Of course that was routine parental manipulation to stop her from diving into the mess just after her Mom had bathed and dressed her for the party, and to protect my life as well.

"Don't worry, we'll have some more trimming tomorrow." I better not forget. Because she doesn't.

And she doesn't forget her promise, long before she ever met Babysister, to teach Kristen to "aggavate" Dad.

So last night while lounging in my recliner in front of the tube I was attacked. Melanie pushed Kristen into my lap, crawled up herself, and demonstrated how to pull down the neck of Dad's shirt, grab two or three of the six hairs on my chest and yank to make my eyes bulge. The bigger the bulge, the more Melanie laughs. Kristen babbled her nonsense of approval, reminding me she will talk soon, just a little overdue by my measure.

This morning we all piled into the truck pre-shower to head to the donut drive-thru, hats on to hide our messy hair so we didn't frighten the donut lady too much, with a full load of tree limbs in the truck bed, kind of a cross between the Griswalds and the Clampets. On the way Melanie showed Kristen how to make me yelp by reaching over from the back seat to pull the hairs on my arm, more plentiful than my chest.

Kristen was oblivious, but the lessons have only just begun.

Jul 2003, Melanie 6 yrs 3 mos, Kristen 1 yr 7 mos

Kristen's Drama

"Quiet!" I heard Melanie shush Kristen through a whispered giggle, but I pretended to continue concentrating at my desk.

"Arrrgggghhh!" Melanie growled as she charged, swinging the battered couch pillow to give me the opening blow in a pillow fight, not caring that I was unarmed.

Dad with Kristen, both wet from the pool

She was instructing her sissy, you see, and Kristen charged into my office laughing in delight though she didn't know why, with a matching couch pillow held over her head mimicking her big sister. She had no idea what to do. Undeterred, Melanie showed her how to swat me with the pillow, and Kristen took her very first swing, seeming to enjoy my pretending that I felt it.

In six months Kristen has transformed from apathy to a happy kid with a ready smile that quickly takes over her whole face. She's very verbal but no words yet. When I pick her up from preschool she brightens up when she sees me and sometimes runs to raise her arms in the "pick-me-up" position, nearly half the enthusiasm she spends when she sees her Mom. Kristen has developed a startling squeal-giggle-screech to express unabashed glee when she plays with her big sister, when the joy of her golf cart ride is overwhelming, or she discovers something new like distributing parts of the Wall Street Journal to various corners of the room after pretending to read just like Dad.

But Kristen's world is not all smiles, for she has discovered drama. She quickly learned when she heard my voice declaring "No!" to stop what she was doing, like pulling the lamp cord out of the wall to see if her finger would fit in the socket, or rattling the fireplace screen to see how far she could shake it before it fell over. And since she is, well, delicate, when she stops in mid-stride on her way to trouble her expression takes on a little surprise that morphs into a tiny wail of injury. But within the past few weeks her talent has developed further, and a drama queen is spreading her wings.

Now when Kristen is stopped by the "No!" word by me or Julie, she stops in mid-stride, her expression takes on surprise, then she lets her body go limp, collapsing to the floor head down and with butt up in the air, because she cannot go on, it's all over, life is no longer worth living.

I don't know if she'll ever make it on the stage, but the men in her life aren't going to have a chance.

Jul 2003, Melanie 6 yrs 3 mos, Kristen 1 yr 7 mos

Kristen's Crossed Ankles

(L-R) Julie, Terry, Kristen & Melanie Garlock.

"Dah!" Kristen declared with a bright smile when she saw me come in Wednesday night from dinner with a friend.

Julie was spring-loaded to react. "Oh, sure, say 'Dad' but I don't hear you saying Mom or Mommy or Mah!"

Don't ask me why. Like Melanie, Mom has won Kristen's heart as the most desirable and exciting thing on this planet, and she drops everything to run-stomp at the first sound of Julie's shoes stepping through the door when she arrives home from work.

Considering Julie's protest it didn't seem a good time to mention I had heard Kristen say "Dah!" a time or two before but wasn't sure whether it was just babble. So I took Kristen downstairs for her evening milk while Julie read Melanie to sleep, and she sat in her very own spot on the left side of my lap with her legs crossed at the ankles as she always does, sucking down the milk while relaxing every muscle, preparing to doze in the warm comfort of "Dah!"

As I watched her I remembered doing the same with Melanie and wondering how a child could be so beautiful, and now I wonder the same about Kristen. Like Kristen I was indifferent at first, but I guess it's how I'm wired, over a little time I fell in love with the little things that make her who she is.

Like the tiny porcelain fingers with a steel grip, they way she grasps things slowly with thumb and forefinger, the way her funky Yangdong Do hair has morphed into a shiny and heavy mane that curves against her little neck in a way that tempts you to write a poem, her dramatic and fragile collapse when I tell her "No," her smile that lights up her whole face when she sees Melanie coming with Dad at the end of the day to pick her up from pre-school, her complete relaxation in the golf cart car-seat as she enjoys the movement and increasingly familiar scenes on the drive home from pre-school, her energetic lean-back-bounce when sitting in Mom's chair to make it rock, her happy shriek to declare comfort with the din of family noise when we're all together, the way she crosses her ankles when she sits comfortably. As with Melanie it's the little things of her budding personality that you come to love over time, and it's what you see when you look at your child. We have to remind ourselves sometimes Kristen is adopted and Chinese because it's so easy to forget when you come to love your child and know them for who they are and how they act and respond, so easy to not notice things like color of skin until you think about it.

Kristen is still babbling and not talking, but that was probably a good thing as she became involved in an animated discussion I was having with Melanie a few days ago about persistent noise while I was trying to talk on the telephone. Kristen rushed to Melanie's defense with a few things to say to me that might have been spicy if the words had been complete.

Yesterday when Melanie and I walked into the pre-school at 6PM to pick her up Kristen declared "Dah!" Don't tell Julie.

Aug 2003, Melanie Age 6 yrs 4 mos, Kristen 1 yr 8 mos

The Absolute End . . . Maybe

The stories in this book were written as indirect love letters to my two daughters. There are far more stories about Melanie than about Kristen because Kristen has been with us just eight months and I am ending this book here just when she has spoken her first word.

Will I continue writing about Melanie and Kristen? I'm not sure. Julie and I worried a little about Melanie's privacy when she started Kindergarten in a new school, and at that time we were still waiting for Kristen. We didn't want Melanie to be tormented by other kids in school as they discovered her Dad publishes contemporaneous stories about her, and I was concerned she might begin to feel like a zoo exhibit. So I put the brakes on the stories about Melanie with just an occasional exception.

Now I'm wondering whether I should let Kristen become a kid in private like everyone else.

Someone once told me there is nothing quite so certain as a small mind. That's encouraging because I remain undecided.

Sep 2003, Melanie 6 yrs 5 mos, Kristen 1 yr 9 mos

The stories of my daughters end here. You may not wish to read further.

This last book contains my version of wisdom that I want my children to learn. I tell my daughters the truth about my experience in the Vietnam war, however harsh it may be, what it taught me about life, and I give them my opinion and encouragement on several other topics.

If you read past this point you will see opinions that may differ from your own, and if you don't welcome different views maybe you should put this book down now and go have some fun.

You've been warned.

Book Four

Dear Kristen and Melanie,
From Dad

To Tell It True

Dear Kristen and Melanie:

There are many things I want to tell you that I have learned in life so the lessons are not lost, so they do not die with me. But as I write this Melanie is six years old and Kristen 20 months, so the time for telling you my version of wisdom is years away. I could get hit by a truck any day now.

Some lessons are too important to leave to the chance of a truck. To make sure as writer John Steinbeck once said, to tell it true, I have written down here a few of those important things for you to read when you reach an appropriate age. Just in case I'm not there with you.

In my peculiar logic I figure if this is published maybe you will read what I have written and take it seriously.

Consider what I have to say, but think for yourselves.

Dad

The Long Story of the Elephant

During the US Civil War, a new recruit asked an old soldier after the battle of Fredericksburg, "What is war like?" The old soldier thought for a minute and said, "Can you describe an elephant to a man who has never seen one? I have seen the elephant."

Vietnam Service Medal 1965-1973

When I see three red vertical stripes on a yellow background, I know in a heartbeat the one showing these colors is a veteran of the Vietnam war, my brother, my sister. Since our Vietnam war experience was so long ago, why do some still show these colors, and why are some of us quick to greet the strangers who display them? Since these men and women were sent to fight a miserable war and met the cold shoulder of an ungrateful nation upon their return, why are they so overwhelmingly patriotic?

The explanation is important because it involves some of life's virtues like duty, honor, determination, trust, loyalty and courage. Pay attention to this story, for the lessons here go far beyond war, they are about thinking for yourself, finding truth, what you value, who you admire and who you are.

Now I will tell you girls my story of the elephant. Maybe telling it true in words cannot be done, but I'm going to try, and I have to swear just a little to tell it true because once a long time ago I was a soldier.

Soldiers

As I tell you about the elephant I will often use the word *soldier*. The US Army calls their men and women soldiers while the US Air Force calls their own airmen, the US Navy calls their own sailors, and the US Marines calls their own Marines. We all had affectionately insulting names for one another.

When I use the word *soldier* I really mean all of these men and women in every branch of our armed forces. It's a term I use, since I was an Army soldier, of universal respect that you may not fully appreciate because you weren't there with me.

Soldiers are ordinary people, many quite young, doing their duty to prepare for war and fight their country's battles when ordered. In 2003 if President George W. Bush had asked me whether we should invade Iraq I would have said no, lets spend our nation's blood and treasure another way. But he didn't ask me, and soldiers below the rank of General weren't asked their opinion either. They were ordered to launch the strike and they carried out the mission. Talking heads back home on TV argued the finer points of international law and battlefield morality despite the handicap of having no battlefield experience of their own. While the talking heads chattered about not having enough forces, *getting bogged down* after just a few days of battle, and speculated the Iraqi citizens would not welcome us, they did so from the comfort and safety of home while our soldiers took Iraq by force in a surprisingly short time, advancing to Baghdad through enemy fire.

Sometimes we send soldiers to do our dirty work and then ignore them when they come home, perhaps because they remind us of the unpleasant work we sent them to do. The public doesn't want to be reminded of unpleasant things, they want to focus on weekend concerts, getting their kids into the best school and building their 401k.

Soldiers are the ones who defend our freedom when the job is not easy. Or if you have a different viewpoint, perhaps soldiers are the ruffians you want to keep away from your kids because they kill people when unleashed.

In his book <u>Cannery Row</u>, writer John Steinbeck gave us a glimpse how our point of view colors what we think of people. Steinbeck loved the company of common folk as he struggled to write the truth about their life. He studied the bums, merchants, scallywags and illicit ladies on Cannery Row in Monterey, California. He and his friend Ed Ricketts, known as Doc in the book, marveled at the bums' daily conspiracies to secure food, a little wine and a few laughs, and at how these forgotten people were keen to help a friend. Steinbeck wrote that Cannery Row's inhabitants:

> . . . are, as the man once said, "whores, pimps, gamblers and sons of bitches," by which he meant Everybody. Had the man looked through another peephole he might have said "saints and angels and martyrs and holy men," and he would have meant the same thing.

Wherever there are soldiers, there are fine examples of superb conduct, role models for young people like you. Wherever there are soldiers, there are also daily conspiracies by young men to chase women, drink anything made of alcohol, gamble, swear, tell dirty stories, and have fun in ways that keep them in trouble while the women do their version of the same thing. These are the same ones who are ready to walk into hell to face the devil when the country calls to defend your freedom. You must choose who you admire, the critic or the soldier.

As for me, when I look through Steinbeck's peephole at soldiers I see saints and angels, martyrs and holy men.

Why did the USA Fight in Vietnam?

On the other side of the world, just south of China is the country of Vietnam where competing forces have been killing one another with enthusiasm for hundreds of years. How did we get involved?

At the end of WWII when Vietnam was liberated from Japanese oppression, the country was divided between North Vietnam and South Vietnam. North Vietnam was influenced by Russia and became a Communist dictatorship while South Vietnam was a client state of France and remained free. The Communists in the north dedicated themselves to the violent overthrow of South Vietnam to make all of Vietnam Communist.

If you become interested in this history you should study the spread of Communism after WWII starting in the 1950s, and understand how Communist countries were slowly succeeding in their efforts to overthrow free countries. Some of the most fascinating brutality of Communism occurred during the *Cultural Revolution* under the leadership of Mao Tse-Tung in your home country of China.

You might have to read some real history to understand this struggle, maybe with some help at the library because I wouldn't trust your history books at school. Schoolbook publishers are in business to sell books, and their customers are local school boards who want to *feel good* about what is in the books instead of how accurately they tell what really happened. Publishers *adjust* the contents of schoolbooks to keep their customers happy, so your schoolbooks don't always tell the truth. To learn about good intentions run amok, please read <u>The Language Police</u> by Diane Ravitch, who describes those who filter *offensive* words or images out of textbooks as *The Keystone Cops of American Education.* Welcome to the real world.

In the 1950s the French withdrew from Vietnam after struggling with a tough Communist enemy from North Vietnam for years. In the early 1960's the US decided to step up our support to help South Vietnam defend their freedom, because the fear was if South Vietnam fell to Communism then other free countries in the region would subsequently be overthrown in what was called *The Domino Effect.* So over a decade we sent massive amounts of troops and equipment and weapons to help South Vietnam keep the Communists out.

Critics of North Vietnam would describe it as a brutal dictatorship, while critics of South Vietnam would describe it as chaotic and corrupt, and both critics would be right.

The Communists from North Vietnam invaded the South through the Ho Chi Minh Trail, a road network they built in Laos and Cambodia to the west of Vietnam. The Laotian and Cambodian governments were unable or unwilling to resist.

The Ho Chi Minh Trail is a fine metaphor for the Vietnam war. Starting in North Vietnam they poured in manpower, trucks, food, ammunition, weapons and support materiel, with much carried by soldiers on their back or their head or pushed on a bicycle, for a march of hundreds of miles through jungle, mountains, and tortuous terrain in horrendous heat and humidity. One sack of rice at a time, one mortar shell at a time. We bombed them on the Trail in Cambodia and Laos when we could find them and publicly denied doing so because the US policy was to contain the war to Vietnam, and sometimes we dealt them serious setbacks. But they knew if they kept pouring in up north, what arrived at the end in the south would feed their war machine. Seldom has an enemy been as tough and determined as our enemy in the Vietnam war.

The NVA (North Vietnamese Army) recruited the disaffected in the south, and forced others to join an indigenous force called the Viet Cong (VC). The NVA and VC fought fiercely, sometimes with inferior weapons, and while we killed one another they earned our respect.

In 1946 Ho Chi Minh, the Communist leader of North Vietnam, told the French in the South "You will kill ten of our men, and we will kill one of yours, and in the end it will be you who tire of it."

The elephant is a fitting metaphor for war in view of another Ho Chi Minh observation: "If the tiger ever stands still, the elephant will crush him with his mighty tusks. But the tiger will not stand still. He will leap upon the back of the elephant, tearing huge chunks from his side, and then he will leap back into the dark jungle. And slowly the elephant will bleed to death. Such will be the war in Indochina."

We can't say we weren't warned.

What the Heck is a Limited War?

One thing you never want in a war is a fair fight, you want overwhelming force to overpower and defeat your enemy as quickly as possible. That way fewer of your own people die, the objective is accomplished more quickly and maybe even fewer of the enemy die.

But President Johnson was worried if we used overwhelming force in Vietnam the war would escalate out of control as other countries like China might become involved. And so President Johnson decided to fight a "limited war" to prevent its' spread.

That meant our military didn't have the freedom to fight an unrestricted war to win, they had to follow a bunch of rules. For example, our forces couldn't cross the borders to Cambodia or Laos where the Ho Chi Minh Trail was the primary source of enemy re-supply and rest and training camps. The NVA infiltrated across the South Vietnamese border, hit targets and then retreated back to Cambodia and Laos where they knew we could not attack them.

Our targets often had to be approved before we could attack, and sometimes the targets of bombing in North Vietnam were selected in the White House in Washington, DC instead of by the commanders in the war. With separation by time, distance and battlefield common sense, target selections or restrictions were sometimes just plain dumb.

When we saw the enemy we had to have clearance to fire on them, and sometimes that clearance had to come from a Vietnamese province chief. The enemy sometimes escaped while we waited for clearance, other times we could use our own judgment in *free fire zones.*

Our enemy was fighting a strike-and-hide guerilla war. While we had bases and strongholds the enemy could strike, they held no territory or infrastructure that we could hit. They hid in the jungle, like the tiger hiding from the elephant, until we found them or until they would strike and return to hiding.

When we won a battle and the enemy returned to hiding, we withdrew and later might have to take that same territory by force again and again. The only point, it seemed, was to kill more of them than they killed of us.

We certainly did that.

Did We Lose the Vietnam War?

Yes, we lost the war. But it matters how we lost it, and your schoolbooks will never tell it true.

Our soldiers fought with skill and honor and courage, and we won every significant battle in the war against a very tough enemy. But micromanagement from Washington did not help.

In 1972 the public support and political will to continue the war evaporated, our politicians negotiated a "peace with honor" agreement to withdraw US forces in exchange for North Vietnam's promise not to invade South Vietnam. Our negotiators must have wanted badly to believe North Vietnam's promise, and the US brought our troops home in 1973.

In 1975, two years after our forces were gone, the North Vietnamese attacked South Vietnam in a massive armored assault down National Highway One. They met light resistance because the South Vietnamese troops knew without the Americans it was hopeless, the country panicked and Saigon fell in short order. With the few resources we still had in Vietnam we got as many of our South Vietnamese friends as possible out of the country, but most were left to face their conquerors. The North Vietnamese brutalized the country and murdered countless thousands in their zeal to rid South Vietnam of all resistance.

Even though our forces had been gone for two years, the news media painted the picture as a US military defeat when North Vietnam violated their agreement and invaded in 1975. It was not. It was a political defeat, an ironic end since politicians had been screwing up the war for a decade.

Some Vietnam veterans like to argue that we didn't lose the war. I understand what they mean because we did constantly defeat the enemy, and it was the politicians who tied our hands and ultimately folded, not the military. But the truth is the US goal was to maintain the freedom of South Vietnam, which we did while we were there. But whatever the reasons we withdrew, the US abandoned an ally to an inevitable fate and they fell to Communism.

The anti-war/anti-military left might argue our military lost the war. They were wrong then, and they are wrong now.

How Did Your Dad Get Involved?

In the 1960s when I was in high school and the draft targeted every eighteen year old male because of the demands of the Vietnam war, the art of draft deferral became a cottage industry. In those days not everyone went to college, and the College draft deferral gave an extra measure of protection to wealthier families with college plans and funding. Some students seemed to study forever without graduating if you can imagine that! Some graduates became teachers not because they wanted to teach but because teachers received a draft deferral. Some faked health problems or homosexual tendencies to fail their draft physical, some fled to Canada.

Terry Garlock as a young Warrant Officer

When world champion boxer Muhammad Ali was drafted he refused to serve, telling the world on camera in semi-English "I ain't got no quarrel with them Viet Cong." Well, neither did I. While the media and the rest of the world now worship Muhammad Ali, I certainly do not because he preferred risking a jail cell to serving his country. The worshipers seem never to consider he could have been a medic or other noncombatant as many conscientious objectors have done. Muhammad Ali was a magnificent boxer, but when his country called he said no.

While war loomed and our friends scrambled for any angle to dodge military service, many of us joined voluntarily or answered when our country called for a simple reason. We learned from our parents the meaning of duty, honor and country. As our fathers had done in WWII, we considered it our job to serve the country we loved. Friends asked "Do you really want to fight the Viet Cong?" That wasn't our decision to make. "Aren't you afraid you might get killed?" We all hoped we would not be killed. While others dodged and slithered, many never saying they were afraid but declaring their moral objections to war a bit too loudly, we left our families behind to do our duty.

Maybe this is what Texas ex-Senator Phil Gramm meant when he said people can be divided between those willing to pull the wagon, and others expecting someone else to give them a ride.

Snake Driver

The US Army trained me to be a helicopter pilot, a Warrant Officer at twenty one years old. Since I worked hard and graduated from flight school near the top of my class I was given the option to receive advanced training, and I chose to fly Cobra gunships, otherwise known as *Snakes*. The AH-1G Cobra was the first helicopter designed specifically to attack the enemy, and it had just arrived in Vietnam.

The Cobra's primary weapon was 2.75" rockets with 10 pound or 17 pound warheads. The standard rocket was HE (high explosive) that detonated upon contact. We could also use an anti-personnel proximity fuse that detonated above the ground so the shrapnel would scatter in a downward cone-shaped kill zone. Even more effective against enemy troops were Flechette rockets, or "nails" as we called them. The Flechette warhead was like a shotgun shell with a charge behind a container of thousands of pointed little nails with fins crimped in the tail so they would fly pointed-end first. When we fired nails the rocket would fly half-way to the target then the charge blew out the nails high above the target, marking the discharge point with red smoke and scattering lethal nails toward the enemy.

Sisters Redeem Their Grumpy Dad

Rockets fired in pairs, one from each side to keep the aircraft balanced. We had a dial that allowed us to fire one pair at a time, so we would fire a pair and then adjust aim to fire again, or any number of pair at one time for more desperate circumstances.

The turret under the nose carried a minigun, a fearsome 7.62mm six-barrel electric gatling gun with fire rates of 4,000 or 2,000 rounds per minute. That's up to 66 rounds per second if you do the math, and with every 5th round a tracer firing the minigun was a bit like aiming a garden hose, but with deadly results. The minigun fired so fast it sounded like a loud burp. We normally used the lower rate of fire to conserve ammo and reduce the risk of jams.

The turret also had a 40mm grenade launcher with a fire rate of up to 400 rounds per minute. These were the same rounds ground troops fired with the M-79, which looked like a large-barrel sawed-off shotgun. These rounds flew slower than bullets in a pronounced arc since they were heavy, and had no penetrating power so were only useful as an anti-personnel weapon, used most often to force the enemy to keep their head down and suppress their fire. I wasn't fond of the 40mm because the risk of hitting friendly troops was too high for my comfort. Would a young man be able to hit a stop-sign 50 feet away by throwing a baseball? Probably so, and that's analogous to firing the 40mm. But it becomes much harder to hit the target when you're flying by at 100 MPH and climbing and turning at the same time, and the delay from slow flight of the projectile makes adjusting fire problematic. So I didn't like firing the 40mm too close to our guys.

Terry Garlock, helping the ground crew reload 40mm grenades

The Cobra was slightly underpowered with a full load of fuel and ammo. Helicopters have to deal with *density altitude* since the air is thinner when hot or at higher elevations, providing diminished lift. Vietnam was hot. We sometimes had to nurse it into a low hover and to that magical change called *translational lift* when a helicopter transitions from hovering to flying. Sometimes we had to take on less fuel, but we always fully rearmed. Most often we carried 19-rocket pods inboard and 7-rocket pods outboard because that second pair of larger pods was just too heavy.

The UH-1 Huey was the workhorse helicopter of Vietnam. We called them *Slicks* when they hauled troops or the various "ash & trash" that needed hauling, and Huey's had even more difficulty than the Cobra with a heavy load. Huey C (Charley) Model gunships had rocket pods and guns mounted on either side, and had the toughest power problem with a full load of rockets, ammo, fuel and crew. The Vietnam war movies you have seen showing helicopters leaping off the pad in dramatic twisting takeoffs are pure Hollywood baloney.

Dick Butler tells the story about flying C-Model gunships out of Camp Holloway at Plieku, and how he never could hover with a load of ammo and fuel. To take off he would have to get the aircraft light on the skids and slide it along with the crew chief and gunner out of the aircraft walking and then jogging alongside, and they knew when to jump in as he was about to take off. Dick said one day the tower radioed him as he was climbing out: "Avenger 4, uh, I think you, uh, left something on the runway." He turned back to see his crew chief lying still on the runway. It turned out that he had stumbled while jogging before takeoff, the minigun apparatus had hit him in the helmet and knocked him out cold. Since Dick's gunship was still loaded and couldn't hover, he made a running, sliding landing to pick up his crew chief.

I flew with the 334th Attack Helicopter Company, 145th Combat Aviation Battalion at Bien Hoa in III Corps near Saigon. Our platoons were the Dragons, Playboys and Raiders. I was a Dragon. We were a Cobra gunship company, on call to support allied units in a wide area. Gunslingers, we thought of ourselves.

Cobra and Slick, on our way to people-sniff some jungle

We usually had one fire team of two Cobras on emergency standby, with the preflight inspection done and the aircraft ready for startup and takeoff in five minutes. When a ground unit needed gun support fast, they radioed for help and we scrambled.

We flew gun cover for medevac missions to take our dead and wounded out of the field and jungle.

We covered combat assaults, firing on either side of the LZ (landing zone) or PZ (pickup zone) to keep the enemy's head down while our Slicks landed to insert or extract ground troops, or engaged the enemy if we had contact.

The people-sniffer mission was very boring, we just covered and guided a low-flying Slick in a back-and-forth pattern over a map grid so the machine they carried could detect ammonia traces, meaning there were probably people, frogs or monkeys in the area. This imperfect process helped identify the movement of enemy units concealed in the jungle.

We flew a hunter-killer mission with two Cobras covering a "Loach," an OH-6 LOH Scout (Light Observation Helicopter) snooping around to find enemy campfires, trails or weapon caches. Scouts flew low and slow to snoop and to draw enemy fire to expose their position.

OH-6 LOH Scout

We covered Special Forces (Green Berets) and LRRPS (Long Range Recon Patrol), small teams inserted into hostile territory to sneak around in extreme camouflage for a week or so to complete their covert missions, sometimes within touching distance of the enemy. LRRPs were very effective making the enemy's life miserable, as evidenced by a substantial and standing bounty on the death of any US LRRP. Covering LRRPs always made me nervous because they were astonishingly bold, and they often whispered radio instructions to guide our fire at the enemy because they were "danger-close" to the enemy. I always feared I might hit them instead of the enemy.

Whatever mission we had for the day, we usually flew in light fire teams of two Cobras, rarely in heavy fire teams of three. When we were doing what the Cobra was designed for, firing on known or suspected enemy positions, we typically used rocket runs, shallow dives to stay on target longer than steep dives so we could fire a pair of rockets, adjust and fire a few more pair. At the bottom of the run we were vulnerable as we pulled out and slowed down to climb around for another run, and the front seat would lay down minigun or 40mm fire from the nose turret to *cover the break.* Our sister ship would be at altitude, also covering our break with minigun fire just before starting their own rocket run while we climbed to do the same. We did this in racetrack patterns, varying our approach direction to keep the enemy off balance. Some hot situations called for innovation instead of this established tactic. When we used heavy fire teams of three, one could go for rearm/refuel while two remained on station and covered one another.

Some missions were uneventful without a shot being fired, in others we had firefights with the enemy, and our motivation was always doing our job and protecting our brothers in the air and on the ground. When you haven't been in a war you might think of it as constant battle, but it was not that way at all. Many missions were routine patrols, searching for the invading enemy who eluded contact until the time and place of their choosing. There was a lot of boredom with scattered specs of terrifying firefights.

Though we and our enemy were trying to kill one another, this job was not devoid of fun. We were testosterone-laden young men living in dangerous adventure, flying cool machines with mean weapons that went boom in several ways when we used electronic sights and pushed buttons, and as girls know boys like that. Just kidding, but not much. We typically flew above 1,500 feet, out of small arms range, or below 100 feet so we flew by too fast for the enemy to aim and shoot. Flying low level at 150 MPH was a kick, dodging and weaving to stay low, sometimes clipping trees with the rotor or skids. There is a river north of Bien Hoa with very high trees on either side, maybe 150 feet tall; as we flew a few feet off the river surface we would gently lay the aircraft on its' side and slide up the tree line to follow the river's turns, more of a thrill than any theme park ride.

The juxtaposition of beauty and misery in Vietnam was striking. Some parts of the country were stunningly beautiful. When I saw a picturesque village surrounded by palm trees and lush rice paddies, I knew it was a good bet at some point in the war crossfire from us or our enemy left innocents in that village dead, their family maybe watching them die.

One of the prettiest sights I have ever seen is a white phosphorous (WP or "willy pete") artillery airburst, a small intensely white cloud with drooping trails, sometimes at eye level from the cockpit, fired to mark the first shot for on-target confirmation. One of the most gruesome sights I have seen was flying cover over a wounded soldier who had triggered a *willy pete* booby trap and discovered that pretty stuff burns right through flesh.

With engine and rotor noise, helmet and the shroud of a Cobra canopy we rarely could hear gunfire on the ground unless we were flying very low. For the uninitiated a group of twinkles like stars in the daytime from a treeline or hillside is curious to look at until you realize those are the muzzle flashes of someone shooting at you.

A firefight in the distance at night is mesmerizing. The tracers seem to float a bit slow from one side to the other, careening wildly when they ricochet and burn out. Scenic flashes of artillery or rockets or other munitions with showering spark trails send delayed and muffled thumps of sound amidst the tiny pops of gunfire. It sounds harmless so far away, but you know that while you watch the brilliant show piercing the darkness, you are really watching young men on one side or the other struggling and fighting and dying in agony. Sometimes it was me pushing the button to fire into the show. I have never watched a fireworks display since then without these thoughts.

Do We Have to Know This, Dad?

Does it seem gruesome to tell you about the weapons we used and the missions we flew? Is it really necessary?

I want you to know the truth, because too many people get their sanitized view of war watching movies where dying soldiers dramatically clasp their wound and make eloquent speeches to soft background music. Too many get their war news and opinion from TV talking heads who have never been near a battlefield. In this modern day things have taken a strange twist, where getting war's brutal job done has taken a back seat to treating the enemy in a tender way that cannot be criticized. Today some are offended to hear in the Vietnam war so long ago we had derogatory nicknames for our enemy. I guess to some it might be OK to kill one another so long as you respect race, religion, sex, age and national origin. Stupidity has arrived in a cloak of sensitivity.

As I write this the talking heads are focused on the war in Iraq, and the hair-splitting and second-guessing is endless by people who have never been under fire and think of war as an intellectual exercise. They babble on in makeup and coifed hair under the lights about how our soldiers should conduct themselves in war, having no clue of the chaos unleashed when the shooting starts.

Here's reality without the sugar coating. War is killing each other as fast and furious as possible with the weapons most effective at tearing men apart. The quicker the guys on the other side are dead, the better chances your favorite soldier and his friends will live to see their family again.

Dying in war is often the province of the young, and it isn't pretty. Some scream for their mom or flop around in agony, or maybe squeeze anyone's hand as their life quietly slips away. Some are violently mangled into unrecognizable remains like the roadkill we see on our highways.

Here's more brutal reality. Our enemy named the Cobra *Whispering Death* because our weapons were so lethal, and they hated gunship pilots. We heard many reports of the special treatment our enemy gave captured gunship pilots, like our troops finding a pilot's body strung up, skinned alive, genitals cut off and stuffed in his mouth, apparently while he bled to death. We carried .38 pistols and knew they were good for just one thing - killing ourselves if capture was inevitable.

War is about violently overwhelming the enemy, it's about kill or be killed, a return to the law of the jungle. For those who find themselves in the fight, it is a stark reminder the world remains a very dangerous place, and that the safety we assume every day in our civilized life back home is in some ways an illusion, a result of being temporarily removed from the malice of real life by a strong protective curtain and by telling the masses what they want to hear about being safe. If the protective curtain falters, the brutality of the natural world will quickly sneak through.

When we are provoked to military force, we should squash our enemy like a bug to get it done quickly and decisively.

I hope you recognize the talking heads as the dumbasses they are when they prattle on TV about rules and sensitivity in war. I hope you see the young people we send into this hell as deserving our gratitude and respect when they come home. That's why I'm trying to tell it true.

The Finest Men I Ever Knew
In such a miserable war with no immediate prospect of victory, you might expect troops to be unenthusiastic, disinterested, demoralized and unreliable. But they were not. These young men became tough, dedicated and capable warriors. They won every major battle in the war, and we learned incredible things about the guys we knew and about ourselves.

The men I knew best in Vietnam were AH-1G Cobra pilots like me, or *Snake Drivers* as we called ourselves. I also knew many UH-1 Huey gunship pilots and *Slick Drivers*. We gun pilots kidded our Slick brothers with a takeoff on an old breakfast cereal commercial by saying "Slicks are for kids," but beneath it all we had loads of respect for them. On a routine day *Slick Drivers* would overload their aircraft with ground troops, called *grunts*, fly in dangerously tight formation so they could land in an LZ (landing zone) together, wait for the offloading and take off from the LZ as one, never knowing on their approach, landing, waiting or takeoff when the treeline would erupt in enemy fire eager for a helicopter kill. Even if the LZ were hot, sometimes they had to reload with grunts and do it again and again.

Some of these bold young men flew UH-1 *Dustoff*, the medevac crews who landed in an LZ or hovered over jungle to use a hoist, often under fire, to whisk our dead and wounded to hospitals, so desperately rushed in the extraction the Medic and crew behind the pilots did their triage work in-flight to advise the pilots because some wounds required a specialized hospital. I owe *Dustoff* a personal debt of gratitude as I will tell you later, and I remember with pride giving them gun cover in a Cobra.

I always kidded LOH *Scout* pilots when we flew a hunter-killer mission that they must have to carry their balls in a wheel barrow since their job was to get down low and slow near the enemy to draw their fire and expose their position.

Some were *Hook* pilots, flying CH-46 tandem rotor Chinooks to lift artillery pieces or other heavy loads, or the huge CH-54 flying Crane to lift the heaviest loads of all, including a hospital operating room pod.

Whether they flew Snakes, Slicks, Scouts, Hooks or other aircraft, helicopter pilots in Vietnam inspired this prayer, author unknown:

> God grant me the eyes of an eagle,
> the judgment of an owl,
> the quickness of a hummingbird,
> the reflexes of a cat,
> the radar of a cave bat,
> the heart of a bull, and
> the balls of an Army helicopter pilot.

Whether they were pilots, crew chiefs, gunners, ground crew, LRRPs, Special Forces or the grunts who had to do all the dirty work on the ground, the folks back home living their lives in comfort and safety never knew the remarkable things these young men were doing and enduring for their country.

They were bold, skilled in their work and calm under fire though some were not old enough to buy a beer. I learned by watching those who came before me the true meaning of loyalty and courage and trust.

We learned to trust our brothers on the ground and in the air to do the right things, even under fire. We came to deeply value the same trust they placed in us, and that mutual trust would form a bond that cannot be explained in words. We quietly feared dying in battle, but there was something we feared even more. We knew if we should panic under fire and fail to do our job, we might lose our brothers' trust or we might lose their lives, and this we feared more than anything.

At this writing my brief part in the war was over 33 years ago, and yet I think of these men all the time. I am proud to be one of them. When I see a politician or celebrity posturing for the camera, I can't help but compare them to the guys who served with me, guys who are still working at their jobs, ordinary guys who stand head and shoulders above politicians and celebrities by my measure.

But the story of the elephant isn't really about me or the guys I served with or even my war. It's about serving your country, doing the right thing even when it's hard, putting others before yourself, learning to think for yourself, deciding what you value, who you admire and who you are.

There's much more to tell. I hope you're both still listening.

Aid and Comfort to the Enemy

While the war ground on and on in Vietnam, the nightly news at home reported the daily body count of enemy dead and our own killed in action (KIA). A large ratio of our KIA to theirs seemed to be our insane method of keeping score. As weeks and months turned into years and our KIAs mounted, news reports reflected an increasing objection to the war.

In this setting, an anti-war movement took root, and ultimately became an anti-military and anti-America movement both openly and covertly supported by Communist and other leftist forces. Many good people and faithful citizens opposed the war on moral grounds and did not know their vocal opposition served an anti-American purpose. Others knew but did not care. Some took an anti-war position as part of dodging the draft.

Many were college students who seemed to follow the crowd to rebel against their country at the same time they were rebelling against their parents. I always thought it must be rather stupid and liberating at the same time to feel no responsibility whatever to do the hard things, to contribute something or defend your country, but free to take its' benefits while you rip apart its' flaws and encourage its' enemies. The flower children culture of anti-establishment, anti-war, free love and drug experimentation always struck me as naïve and self-indulgent. That culture grew strong in the 60s and 70s. Some of its' participants outgrew these attitudes and emerged into responsible adulthood, but I worry that many did not and currently occupy influential positions on our university faculties.

While nearly three million of us served in the Vietnam war in some capacity, over sixteen million draft age males found a way not to serve by college deferments or other means. Some of those sixteen million were honorable people willing to serve their country if called, some were self-indulgent draft dodgers with no sense of duty.

The worst part of the anti-war movement was the aid and comfort they gave to our enemy while that enemy was killing America's sons. It was not unusual to see a demonstration where our enemy's flag was flown and the US flag was burned. One of our enemy's slogans was "We'll win this war on the streets of New York." Maybe they did just that.

Tet is the Vietnamese New Year holiday, a very big event. Out of respect for their holiday as Tet approached in 1968 we negotiated a cease-fire in the war for the holiday period. Our enemy was planning all along to strike during the cease-fire to surprise our forces and the civilian population. When they had promised a period of peace, on the holiest night of their year, they attacked when least expected all over the country. Our forces counterattacked and battles raged all over South Vietnam. The tone of press reports suggested this treachery was a failure of our own military, apparently because the press had tired of war and were disappointed hostilities had escalated.

The ancient cultural center of Hue was overrun by the enemy, who brought with them a list of Hue doctors, nurses, teachers, business owners, elected officials and others. They rounded up and executed over 3,000 of these "enemies of the people." Our Marines were brought in to fight house-to-house to retake the city in a horrendous battle. A high school buddy of mine named Ken was one of those Marines, and his life was forever changed when it was over. Ken shot and killed a boy less than ten years old when the boy surprised Ken as he was searching a house for the enemy. The kid looked like the enemy and Ken saw something that looked like a weapon, he reacted in a split second and the kid was dead. While you read this Ken likely still thinks about this every day. It doesn't help him to know that kids far younger had routinely been used to lure our soldiers into booby traps or toss grenades that killed them.

All over the country, and eventually in Hue, we won every battle. The enemy surprised us with their treachery and had the upper hand for a short while, they succeeded in killing great numbers of their own countrymen in the South but our counterattacks were so successful the enemy VC forces were decimated. But if you read press accounts at the time in the US, there was little mention of our victory. Rather, our military seemed to be blamed for escalating the war, and the anti-war demonstrations spread like wildfire.

Had it not been for critical accounts in our own press about these nasty battles, had it not been for the anti-war movement tearing the country apart with marches and flag-burning and demonstrations leading to violence at home, the enemy might have withdrawn from the war for a considerable time because their ability to fight had been dealt a serious blow.

Long after the war, interviews with our enemy's leaders confirmed their Tet 1968 losses were devastating, but that they were so invigorated by the US press and anti-war movement in the US they redoubled their efforts to rebuild their forces and continue killing Americans and South Vietnamese. How many US soldiers died because our enemy was encouraged by the anti-war actions at home? We'll never know.

In early 1970 the NVA invaded Cambodia and Laos in force, captured the Plain of Jars, defeated the Hmong army and created the Khmer Rouge, which was destined to murder millions of Cambodians in coming years. They used the Ho Chi Minh Trail to build up more and more forces for the war in South Vietnam.

On April 30, 1970 President Nixon gave the order to attack our enemy's strongholds in Cambodia and Laos. Finally a presidential order made some sense. Over 32,000 US troops crossed the borders to attack areas known as the Fishhook and the Parrot's Beak for two months, destroyed NVA supplies, fortification, equipment and personnel, setting back the enemy's war plans an estimated two years. It was a solid military victory.

But it was a political disaster. The anti-war left went crazy when we attacked our enemy across the border. It seems it was OK that our enemy killed America's sons by hiding their supply lines on the other side of the border, but according to our brilliant military strategists amidst the flower children, the US military was out of line taking the battle to the enemy. Protests erupted a few days after our attack started, and the violent protests and deaths at Kent State University brought the anti-war movement to fever pitch.

Jane Fonda in Hanoi, pretending to fire at American jets

Later, in 1972 Jane Fonda handed our enemy a propaganda victory during her visit to Hanoi as they snapped photos of her on an anti-aircraft gun pretending to shoot at US jets. How many US soldiers died as she broadcast radio messages from Hanoi to our own troops telling them our president and pilots were war criminals and the troops should disobey their commander's orders and refuse to fight? We'll never know for sure.

It was Jane Fonda's right to oppose the war in Vietnam, and her right to protest. But she forgot about her *responsibility* to not jeopardize the lives of our own troops by giving *aid and comfort* to our enemy. For her actions in her trip to Hanoi she should have been charged with treason, but there was no political courage on the matter because the war was so controversial.

As I write this in 2003, our forces recently deposed the Saddam Hussein regime in Iraq and we now occupy that country. As we prepared for war many outspoken critics protested war plans, characterized our president as evil, and some even traveled to Iraq to have televised conversations with Iraqi leaders to show the world they are human just like us. As if we didn't know.

I, too, was against the war with Iraq. Unlike the talking heads on TV I felt removing Saddam Hussein's regime was entirely justified with or without the aegis of the UN. But that does not mean we were *compelled* to war, we had choices. My first concern was spending much on Iraq at a crucial economic time. My second concern was that, after our inevitable conquest, having control of Iraq might be like riding the tiger - difficult and dangerous to get off. My third concern was we would become the sheriff, mayor and governor of Iraq, and we would be viewed as responsible when food was short or electricity failed or the water didn't flow or the economy didn't work or whatever the Iraqis or the Arab world wanted to gripe about. I thought we might tear ourselves apart with hysterical and endless political finger-pointing while TV cameras rushed to every violent incident for replay again and again on cable news, and our hyper-sensitive country would not be strong enough to simply turn off the TV cameras in Iraq until the hard work was done. I hope in the end I was wrong, but I fear I was right.

Despite my disagreement with President Bush about war with Iraq, I felt it was my *responsibility* to remain silent. From the time our nation was first squared off against Iraq and seeking the help of other nations, it was my responsibility to not encourage our enemy and critics, therefore I should not speak out publicly against the President's war plans. After all, he's elected to make the tough decisions, I am not. I can exercise my rights to oppose the war in the voting booth if I choose when the time comes, and in the meantime I can write letters to the White House and my representatives in Washington if I wish. Unlike me, protestors predictably acted like self-indulgent children, bleating about their right to speak out and ignoring their responsibility to not encourage an enemy determined to kill our soldiers. And the media covered the protestors well to send the message around the world our own country was divided on the issue, a division that aided our enemy.

With the image of protestors in your mind, I will tell you about a few soldiers then ask you a question: "Who do you admire?"

John Synowsky

Capt. John Synowsky, from Butler, Pennsylvania, was the 334th Co. Dragons Platoon Leader. At 21 years old, he led his men with quiet confidence beyond his years, and he would one day risk his life to save mine.

I learned a lot from John about flying in the war, tactics on shooting at the enemy and keeping our own risk as small as possible under the circumstances.

Capt. John Synowsky

One day a friendly ground unit was losing a firefight with a superior enemy force and feared being overrun, meaning they would all likely be killed or captured, which could be worse. They radioed an emergency call for gunship support and John scrambled his light fire team of two Cobras. The firefight was west of Cu Chi, near the Cambodian border, not far from the Ho Chi Minh Trail.

With little information on the enemy force, John was caught in a *helicopter trap* where the enemy places anti-aircraft guns at the three points of a triangle surrounding their position, then when we fire on them and pull out of a rocket run, at least one of the big guns will have an easy broadside shot.

The enemy's .51 caliber anti-aircraft gun was a helicopter pilot's worst nightmare because the slugs are so big and heavy if it hits you in the hand it might pull your arm off. At night .51 tracers glowed so big we called them *basketballs* and as they reached up toward us they looked like they would hit us right between the eyes no matter how far they missed.

John Synowsky (left)

Have you ever heard a pilot talk about the pucker factor? That's when your mouth instantly dries up, your skin flashes cold no matter how hot it may be, your heart tries to leap outside your chest and the cheeks of your butt reach down and clench the seat real tight because you're scared as hell. When we ran into .51s, the pucker factor was high.

That day John took .51s through the cockpit. One round went through his chest protector plate, or chicken plate as we called them, penetrated his chest and burned him real good because rounds are hot when fired. John was lucky it bounced around the cockpit first because it didn't go through him, and he's lucky it was hot because it burned the wound enough to slow the bleeding. John's co-pilot was hit too, but they ignored their wounds, the aircraft held together and they continued the mission, attacking the enemy again and again through .51 fire because if they didn't our brothers on the ground would die.

Their attack forced the enemy to withdraw, and the families of those young men on the ground would never know their loved one lived that day because John stayed with the job under heavy fire. For that mission John received the Silver Star for *gallantry*.

The Silver Star

John went on to serve a second tour in Vietnam. For his service in Vietnam he received the Purple Heart, the Bronze Star three times, the Distinguished Flying Cross, the Soldier's Medal and the Silver Star.

John Synowsky, Christmas 2000

John now lives with his family west of Ft. Worth, Texas where he is doing what he loves, raising cattle.

Who do you admire?

Graham Stevens

Pilots come in many sizes, and I was quite a bit taller than Graham Stevens, from Ft. Walton Beach, FL. When I met Graham in 1969 at the 334th, he was a fun magnet - wherever there was beer, cards or grab-ass of any sort, you could bet he was in the middle of it. But in the cockpit he was all business.

Graham Stevens, brand new pilot in Vietnam
Clean clothes, looking mean and cool!

One day Graham had his light fire team of two Cobras on the ground near Tay Ninh, ready to scramble when someone had trouble and radioed for help. He and the young men he led were playing a new version of grab-ass, shirts off and throwing rocks at a smoke grenade they set up so it would pop if it was hit. Finally someone hit it but instead of smoke they got a full dose of tear gas. Just as their eyes stung so bad they couldn't see, the radio called for emergency help near the Cambodian border.

They cleared their eyes enough to climb in the aircraft, crank them up and take off to the west while ground contacts told them the enemy was everywhere, infiltrating again from Cambodia. Graham had Johnnie Allmer in his front seat, and his wingman Larry Pucci had Wayne Hedeman from Hawaii in his front seat.

Johnnie Allmer (L) and Graham Stevens (R)

Wayne Hedeman

They flew toward Cambodia and as they approached the friendly position red and green tracers came at them from every direction. Graham confirmed the friendly position, spotted an enemy anti-aircraft position and dove in firing rockets. As he pulled out and Johnny *covered the break* with suppressing minigun fire Graham spotted a second enemy anti-aircraft gun that had him cold, and the pucker factor went through the roof. Graham took anti-aircraft rounds through his canopy and took hits in vital places but neither pilot was hit. Warning lights flashed telling Graham he was losing the hydraulics that made the flight controls work, and Larry radioed to tell Graham he was on fire. This is what you call being shot down, and Graham hurried to find a spot to put it down because the aircraft would very quickly become uncontrollable.

Larry Pucci

Graham put it on the ground and he and Johnny ran from the aircraft at Silver Medal speed. They dove into a bomb crater with one survival radio but no weapons because the urge to *un-ass* a dying helicopter as the enemy is desperately trying to nab you for their evening entertainment will make you move rapidly without much thought. Luckily they spotted a friendly position about 100 yards away and took off, this time scoring the undisputed Gold Medal speed with boots on, no doubt about first place.

Now Graham was able to radio Larry, who had been circling in the wing ship nearby to see how he could help, and Graham helped him locate the enemy anti-aircraft position. Larry lined up for a rocket run to take it out. This time when he fired rockets and the 17-pound warheads slammed dirt, trees and enemy into the air Graham got the experience most pilots never have, seeing and hearing the destruction dealt by our own gunships at ground level, not far away. No wonder the enemy hated Cobra pilots! But the suppressing minigun fired from the front seat to cover the break abruptly stopped too soon, and Graham radioed to ask:

"Everything OK?"

Silence for a moment. Larry responded "Front seat is hit."

"How bad?"

"I don't know. All I can see is a hole in the back of his neck."

So nineteen year old Larry Pucci broke away and flew as fast as the aircraft would fly to the hospital at Tay Ninh, but it was too far and Wayne Hedeman died on the way. They took his body, patched the bullet holes, and washed out the blood because the aircraft had to return to the Cambodian border where our brothers on the ground were in trouble.

This was one day in Graham's life as a combat Cobra pilot. He went on to serve a second tour in Vietnam flying Cobras, and years later he flew his last combat missions in the invasion of Granada. For his service in Vietnam Graham received the Bronze Star two times, the Distinguished Flying Cross three times, and the Soldier's Medal. For service in Grenada he received the Air Medal with V (Valor).

Graham now lives with his family in Williamsburg, Virginia.

Who do you admire?

Graham Stevens, 2000

John Synowsky and Graham Stevens Rescue Your Dad

On Sunday, December 17, 1969, we were on emergency standby, sitting around the ping-pong table waiting for the emergency buzzer. When it buzzed we scrambled, John Synowsky and Graham Stevens in the fire team lead ship, Ron Heffner and I in the wing ship. The enemy had ambushed an allied convoy near Lai Khe in III Corps not far from Cu Chi in a region replete with enemy tunnels. This was a notorious enemy infiltration route from the Ho Chi Minh Trail in Cambodia to Saigon, the capital of South Vietnam. We were on the way to help.

When we arrived at the ambush site we engaged the enemy with rockets, 40mm grenades and minigun fire, and they hit us many times with small arms and automatic weapons. As we pulled out of a rocket run we took hits and lost our tail rotor, very big trouble. As fire team leader, John urged us by radio to pick up airspeed to keep it flying but it didn't work.

Graham Stevens, at home in the cockpit

You know, sometimes you learn new things at the most inopportune moment. I knew, of course, without the tail rotor we would spin in the opposite direction as the rotor blade spin. But even in a deadly situation I was fascinated to see the slipstream working against the tail fin and the narrow body of the Cobra with the tail rotor gone to prevent the spin, nose cockeyed to the right and straining against the wind to flip around, and as airspeed bled off with reduced power to try to prevent the spin, it finally snapped around to the right so fast in a 360 degree spin I was thrown out of my seat against the shoulder straps until the slipstream caught it again, straining to the right again until it snapped around again and again and again, out of control with the ground rushing toward us. At a time like this I guess a lot of people pray, but I was not inclined to begging. I do recall thinking it was a sadly stupid way to die so young, and hoped it wouldn't hurt too much. Strange what little things are burned into your brain forever.

John Synowsky (standing) and Graham Stevens
The Thousand Yard Stare

The crash and rotors disintegrating didn't kill us but it did knock us both unconscious, and when I roused the aircraft was on its' side with my front seat escape door pressed against the ground. I didn't know it at the time because my body was in shock but I had a broken back and paralyzed legs, the turbine was still running and fuel was leaking all over. We were in grave danger, and while I groggily grabbed the break-out knife provided for just this purpose and weakly tried to punch a hole in the canopy to get out, I didn't know my brothers were coming to help.

John and Graham broke away from the enemy before we hit the ground, radioed a Mayday message with our map coordinates, ignored the rules about keeping their aircraft in the air and boldly landed nearby. They were at risk of being killed or captured by a determined enemy with a record of torture-killing gunship pilots, and our wreckage was apt to explode any second.

Even in a tense situation like this there is sometimes comic relief. I always carried my .38 pistol with the hammer on an empty chamber for safety, and I once suggested to Graham he do the same. But he said that might be the last round he needed, so he loaded all six rounds. When John and Graham landed near our broken Cobra, John put their Cobra in idle mode while Graham jumped out and ran to my aircraft lying on its' side trapping me in the cockpit. I was weak and making no headway with the breakout knife, just scratching the canopy. Graham had just one thing he could use to break open the canopy, his .38 pistol. So he took his .38 out of his holster, swung it and when he hit the canopy the round under the hammer fired through the cockpit. It missed me. And we didn't explode. Graham knew he had to hammer quickly so he aimed at the ground to the side and fired the remaining five rounds pow-pow-pow-pow-pow to empty the pistol, and when John heard the gunfire as he was stepping to the ground his pucker factor went way up because he thought the bad guys had arrived.

Graham hammered through the canopy while John shut down the turbine and helped Ron Heffner, who was dazed and injured but able to walk. Graham hammered so hard on the canopy with his .38 he knocked the wooden pistol grips off both sides and later had to exchange it for another pistol.

Though I was bigger than Graham, he drug me by my collar out of the cockpit and away from the wreckage in case it blew, and I remember as I lay in that field waiting for the medevac helicopter, unable to move my legs and my back hurting like hell I sang "I'll be home for Christmas" because surviving after being certain you will die is a powerful narcotic, and I knew I was hurt bad enough to go home.

Instead of getting airborne ASAP for their own safety when the Medevac helicopter arrived, John and Graham stayed to help load us on stretchers and into the helicopter.

Standing guard over their injured men in the middle of a hostile area, in the open with no cover, just pistols for weapons and a dangerous enemy nearby - that's the last time I saw John and Graham in Vietnam. They were 21 years old.

The medevac helicopter took me to a field hospital at Lai Khe. They quickly determined I needed surgery so I was flown to the larger hospital at Long Binh. Later that day as I was prepped for surgery a compassionate young doctor gently told me he didn't know if I would walk again but he would do his best. His best was superb. I had a serious compression fracture of my L1 and L2 vertebrae, the surgery removed bone splinters and a disk and inserted metal pins. I would later find that I had lost one inch of height by compression, and that I was very lucky, indeed, not to have been paralyzed for life.

Meanwhile, back at the 334th, after the Commanding Officer chewed out John and Graham for risking themselves and their aircraft, they were awarded the Soldier's Medal for heroism that day. Both of them earned a number of decorations for their courageous service over two tours in Vietnam, but they both consider the Soldier's Medal to be *special*. Perhaps that's because amidst all the killing and dying, I was one they were able to save.

The Soldier's Medal

While I spent a few months recovering in hospitals and then recuperating, John and Graham continued to fly combat missions every day.

Who do you admire?

Capt. John Synowsky receiving Soldier's Medal and Purple Heart

Warrant Officer Graham Stevens performing his preflight inspection

Jim Teaches Me About Small Stuff

My legs quickly regained feeling and function after surgery, and over some weeks the bowel and bladder control I had lost slowly returned. I was on a metal bed that was specially designed to allow patients to be flipped over with their spine immobilized to prevent further injury, turning every few hours to prevent bed sores from being in one position too long.

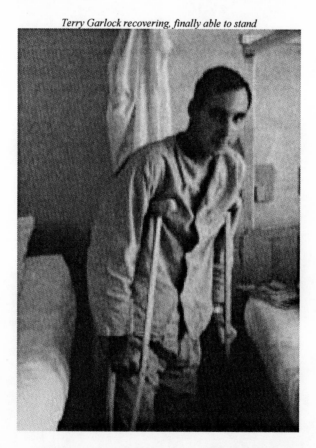

Terry Garlock recovering, finally able to stand

Since I came out of surgery about a week before Christmas I had hopes of being home for the holidays. I missed it and was flown on a hospital C-130 on a stretcher to a hospital in Japan where Vietnam war casualties were treated. I stayed for two weeks, and the day I arrived I slipped into a funk, feeling quite sorry for myself.

As I wallowed in self-pity, I was startled when Jim screamed, and during my stay in Japan I would learn from him an important lesson about small stuff. After a pause Jim screamed again, and a young guy with no legs below the knees zipped past me in a wheelchair yelling "Hang on Jim, I'm coming," and that's how I knew his name.

The nurses were showing a John Wayne movie projected on the wall, but pretty soon Jim's screams drowned out a lot of the dialogue.

Nobody in the hospital ward complained.

I called to a nurse and asked about the guy screaming. She told me his back was ripped to shreds by a grenade, and when they changed the dressing on his wound, or when his pain medication wore off before they were permitted to give him more, he hurt so bad he couldn't help but scream.

I heard guys talking to Jim, many from other beds so they had to shout. "Go ahead and scream, Jim." "Give-em hell, Jim." "Dammit, nurse, can't you give Jim more of that magic needle?" One of the resident hustlers in the ward hobbled by on crutches yelling "Hey, Jim, want to play poker and get some of your money back?" Others tried to distract him from his pain by asking "Jim, where you from, Chicago?"

All around me young men, black and white and Hispanic and Asian, officers and enlisted men, missing limbs or eyes, with all manner of injury received in violence, set aside their own problems as small stuff and joined together to help one of their stranger-brothers get through an unbearable time.

Pretty soon the nurse announced she was preparing Jim's pain shot, and the clamor arose. "Yo, my man, help is on the way!" "Hang in there, Jim, it'll be better soon." "Nurse Nancy gonna make you feel better, Jim." And soon after Jim's shot he slept, at least for a while, because Jim went through this about five times a day.

I had a conversation with myself in my head about counting my blessings, and not being a damn fool about the small stuff in life. I was hurt and bored and wanted to go home, but I'd get through it with little permanent damage. I was among the lucky ones.

Since that day 33 years ago when I see someone become frantic with worry and anger about a missed appointment, a flaw in the paint job on a new car, a delay in the delivery of furniture or other small stuff I think back to a guy I never saw because I was stuck in a bed, and the lesson I learned from him about life.

Sometimes when I need a reminder, I think about Jim and the generous young men around him who instinctively knew about small stuff.

Who do you admire?

Pete Parnell

At the 334th in Bien Hoa I had a roommate for a while named Pete Parnell from Lee's Summit, MO. Pete and I never flew together because he was with the Raider platoon while I flew with the Dragons, and we were together because the bunks were available and we were all in the same small area anyway.

Pete drove me nuts sometimes talking about his wife and the baby they were expecting. We all talked about our girlfriends and wives but Pete never stopped.

Pete Parnell

I was shot down and hospitalized on Dec 17, 1969, so I didn't know it at the time but Pete received a telegram the next day, Dec 18, informing him he had a son named Thad. That makes Thad 33 years old now as I write this. Pete found a way to send his wife some roses, wired instructions somehow from Vietnam.

Four days later on Dec 22 Pete was the Cobra front seat when his Raider fire team was supporting the 3rd Mobile Strike Force (Green Berets) at the village of Bu Dop, west of Song Be and about five miles from the Cambodian border. There had been enemy .51 fire in the area and Pete's fire team of two Cobras was called to destroy the enemy anti-aircraft position. We don't have details of how it occurred, but Pete and his back seat Harry Zalesny from Plymouth, MI died when their aircraft went into trees, 150 to 200 feet high, at a high rate of speed. The aircraft burned high in the thick jungle trees.

Three Green Berets immediately volunteered to rappel down from a hovering helicopter to recover the bodies, and while they were able to recover Pete's body they were not able to recover Harry's because the heat of the fire was intense and the rockets and grenades and 7.62 ammo began to cook off. The Green Berets willingly sustained burns in their effort to recover the bodies of their brothers.

Back in the USA, while protestors insulted soldiers returning from Vietnam, the Parnell family received word of Pete's death on Christmas Eve, and the flowers Pete had sent arrived days later. Pete died doing his duty at 21 years old and never saw his son.

Who do you admire?

Women in the War

You should know some of our women served in the Vietnam war, and some of them died doing their duty. Most of our women I saw in Vietnam were nurses, and I owe them many thanks for how they helped me as I recovered. The pressure nurses and doctors felt must have been overwhelming as they struggled to care for a relentless stream of broken young bodies.

In 2000 CSPAN broadcast a panel discussion by women who were journalists in Vietnam during the war. The discussion gave an interesting different view of events, and I'll describe it as best I can remember.

Several individuals told of their primary frustration, overcoming the *handling* they faced since the military tried to manage reporters anyway, and since women in the 60s were still treated in a way that pushed them to *soft news* stories. They found themselves again and again confined to protected areas by the military, and assigned by their own news bureaus to human interest fluff pieces one might find in the Sunday newspaper People section, but nothing like the hard news they wanted to report about the war.

Those who did break out of the mold to do what they called *real* reporting had to fight and stand their ground to get there. They wrote about battles and they wrote about the impact of the war on our soldiers and innocent civilians. Several said as they watched the war over time their heart broke at what we were doing to our "beautiful young men" who were being slaughtered while there appeared to be no coherent plan to win and end the war.

It's too bad, it seems to me, these women were not as free to report the hard news as their male counterparts, because if ever there was a need for fresh perspective it was the Vietnam war.

Like those of us who fought the war, these women said it changed them. But they were rarely able to share that life-changing experience when they returned home.

At the end of the discussion the moderator asked the panel if they thought this conversation had been worthwhile. They all said yes, some emotionally. One said "Thank you. Thank you for asking." Then with tears streaming down her face she told the story that when she arrived home nobody in her work life discussed the Vietnam war, it wasn't a suitable topic, and the political mood of the newsroom was anti-war anyway. Friends treated her as if they pretended she had been on vacation for a year and nothing had happened that changed her. Like many who return from war she had things bubbling inside her but nobody wanted to know. Her mother and father, who she thought surely would want to listen to the things she had seen and done and how those things had changed her into a different person, were a disappointment as well. When she would open the conversation they changed the subject to talk about things like baking cookies or the upcoming church social as if she were still in high school.

"So thank you for asking" she said through her tears. "Thank you, because after all these years it's nice to know it actually matters to someone, because it was terribly important and it should matter."

Who do you admire?

Did You Kill People, Dad?

It seems that those who have not been to war ask two questions that cannot or should not be answered: "What was it like?" and "Did you kill people?"

I think most of us answer the "What was it like?" question by mumbling something inane that rolls easily off the tongue because, well, how do you begin, where do you end, and what can you possibly put in the middle to help someone understand? That's why it's taking me so long as I try to tell it true.

When someone asks a combat veteran "Did you kill people?" I am tempted to counter with questions of my own. Should the soldier feel remorse over doing the unpleasant job we sent him to do? Does he owe an explanation of the things he has seen and done and endured while the folks back home continued their lives in comfort and safety? Does every dumbass who wants to crawl inside his head and root around like a hog to find out how he *feels* get an entry ticket? Does the glimmer of titillation in the query about people killed tell you something about the person who asked?

But you are my daughters and it's a natural thing to wonder, especially about your Dad, so I will tell you. Yes I did kill people, that was my job, to fire on the enemy. I did my job with enthusiasm when our own guys were in danger, though most of the time we were shooting at a jungle position with the enemy well-hidden and it was often hard to know the result. I don't take any particular pleasure in knowing that I killed people, and I don't have any regrets about doing the job I was sent to do.

But here's something to think about, for the future and for other soldiers you meet. If you wanted to be respectful of a soldier, instead of asking questions that intrude into that private place most of us have walled off so we can live a normal life, you could say something like "Thanks for serving your country." In 2000 I was stopped at a light waiting for it to turn green when I noticed the driver of the car next to me motioning for me to lower my window. I did and he asked "Is that your Purple Heart on your license plate?" I nodded my head yes and he said "Thank you." I asked "For what?" because I was confused. He said "For what you did." And he drove away because the light was green. I'll never forget that.

Try it sometime. If you feel a little gratitude for what our soldiers do, offer your hand and your thanks. You'll feel better about yourself, you'll set an example for others and you may be the only one to ever say thanks to a soldier who may forever remember your small gesture of support.

How hard is that?

When We Came Home

Conventional wisdom says that you will experience discrimination in your life because of your Chinese features, but that since I am a white male I cannot know what discrimination feels like. The truth is discrimination is the ugly side of human nature whether it is based on race, religion, where you live, your social status, your occupation or whatever, and nobody is immune from thoughtless treatment. The welcome we received when we returned home from Vietnam is just one example.

Maybe if you've read carefully so far you can imagine how anxious we were to return home. In the Vietnam war we counted not the days served but the days until DEROS (Date Estimated Return from Overseas Service). Here's how it worked. When you departed the US the days you had left on your one year tour was 364 and a wake-up, because on that 365th day the plan was to wake up, grab your stuff, get on the freedom bird and fly home, or back to the world as we said. So when you hear short-timers talk about 45 and a wake-up you know they are getting nervous about going home. Everyone had the unspoken fear he might still be killed so close to the end.

At the 334th in Bien Hoa once in a while at night a siren would alert us to an attack, and we knew who was *short* because they scrambled to the bunker with their helmet on and chicken plate on their chest, not willing to risk anything so close to returning to the world. The rest of us usually walked over to a fence to watch 122mm rockets hit the Air Force base across the way since the jets and runway were usually the enemy's target.

In my case I forget how many days I had left, it was a bunch and I was nowhere near *short* when I was shot down. I came home on a stretcher in a hospital aircraft, with a two-week stopover in Japan to give the fractures in my vertebrae and pins from surgery more time to heal while I was immobilized. So I didn't experience the normal flight home.

Our reception was usually warm from our family, but cold from America. I remember TV news reports of protestors meeting planeloads of returning soldiers in California, shouting things like *Babykiller!* and sometimes spitting on soldiers or throwing packets of urine or animal blood to splatter their uniform. I'm not sure which was worse, these rare incidents of overt hostility or being greeted by silence, turned backs or looks that clearly conveyed our presence was not welcome.

At cocktail parties years later when the conversation turned to my role in the war there would sometimes be a sudden embarrassed silence, people would slowly and politely excuse themselves to seek other company, stepping away from the stink emanating from me, the foul odor of a war they despised. Once a young lady wrinkled her nose and quietly exclaimed "Eeuuuuw!" At least she was bold enough, or perhaps unwitting enough under the influence of her drink, to say exactly what she thought.

B.G. Burkett tells in his book <u>Stolen Valor</u> about his return trip from Vietnam. He had a layover at an airport waiting for the final flight to his home city:

> At the dinner hour, the airport restaurant was half empty. I threw down my duffel bag, sat, and tried to catch the waitress's eye. "Miss, Miss," I said. The waitress, a woman in her thirties, was only a few feet away. But she pointedly ignored me and began waiting on people who

had come in after me. Finally a younger waitress came over. "Oh, don't mind her," she said. "She's got this anti-war thing. She won't serve anybody in uniform."

There was a time we were advised not to wear our uniform off the base for our personal safety. In the country we were serving.

The anti-war crowd pushed the myths that minorities fought and died in the war in disproportionate numbers, exacerbating racial strife, and that Vietnam veterans were violent and disturbed with vast numbers of us suffering from Post Traumatic Stress Disorder. The mainstream media repeated this baloney until everyone seemed to believe it. Over time the accepted image of a Vietnam veteran became a bearded, burned-out bum ready to snap at any second.

In Dallas, Texas, on Veteran's Day 1989 a memorial honoring the memory of our brothers who died doing their duty in Vietnam was dedicated with President George H.W. Bush in attendance. This memorial was made possible by years of tireless work and fundraising by a group of successful businessmen who were Vietnam veterans. After a moving ceremony these proud patriots in coats and ties prepared to answer questions by the press in attendance, but reporters and camera crews brushed them aside to interview a few ragtag attendees wearing uniform remnants and unit patches, guys who fit the stereotype, guys who had no role in the memorial and who may or may not have served in the war. These were the faces on the evening TV news reports about the ceremony in Dallas, the event marred by the image of Vietnam veterans as losers. While good people had worked hard for a worthy cause, they had been portrayed once again as wild-eyed bums with fried brains. The lie became accepted as the truth.

Having Vietnam veteran on a resume was a sure way to not be considered for a job. TV drama and sitcom shows had an occasional angle for a Vietnam veteran, usually someone who killed unexpectedly or was apt to go ballistic at small things. And of course Hollywood churned out Vietnam war movies like Apocalypse Now, Deer Hunter, Platoon and Casualties of War. They were not only a far cry from reality, they were little more than anti-war propaganda.

When we returned from Vietnam to a nation far less than grateful for our service, we wondered "Don't they realize they sent us to that miserable war? Don't they know we didn't want to go?" We went back to normal life, had families and jobs, and didn't talk much about the war, nobody wanted to hear about it. Besides, some of us didn't want to talk about it because some memories just can't be reduced to words and are best left alone. Some of us kept it to ourselves to shield loved ones from the dark side of life we hope they never know.

We didn't need the public's acceptance to feel good about ourselves; there is no better school than combat to build inner strength and self-reliance. Nevertheless, rejection by the public had a sting to it for a couple of reasons. First, many of us hated the war, too, but we bit our lip and did our duty. Second, the lies told about us were also lies about our brothers who died young serving their country.

So Vietnam veterans share something unique. We know the American people never did get it about the Vietnam war, but we know the truth. Part of the truth is that our country should have been proud of its' Vietnam veterans, and the country lost something by not knowing the difficult things we had done with skill and honor and courage under fire. We know.

When two men meet and discover they are both Vietnam veterans, even after all these years you might hear them say to one another "Welcome home, brother!" because many were never welcomed.

In May 2003 I met a group of fellow Vietnam helicopter pilots at the Air Force museum in Warner Robbins, just south of Macon, Georgia, to have lunch and then tour the museum. One of them named Dave told us that just last year he met a fellow Vietnam veteran who greeted him with "Welcome home, brother." Dave told us nobody had ever said such words to him in all the years since he returned, and he couldn't explain why but he stood there with his perplexed wife by his side and cried like a baby.

Welcome home, Dave.

Forgetting and Remembering

My own return home was complicated by many weeks in hospitals, and with a little rehab work I returned to stateside duty and finally returned to flight status. My flight school Tac Officer job didn't require daily flying and I flew just the monthly hours required to meet my pilot minimums because the vertical vibrations were painful.

A little over a year after I returned from Vietnam the US Army offered all Warrant Officers a choice – either sign up for an indefinite enlistment or leave the Army. I chose to leave, and I left behind not only the Army but flying and the memories of the Vietnam war. It wasn't that I was traumatized by the war, I just wanted to get on with life and that part was over. I didn't seek out those I knew in Vietnam because I wanted to forget it instead of continually reliving it. Forgetting worked better than I had planned.

I worked on Wall Street in New York City for two years, then took advantage of the GI Bill to complete my Bachelors degree and MBA. After college I was working in Dallas, Texas when the phone rang, seven years after I returned from Vietnam.

The guy on the phone said he was "Ski" and I had no idea who he was. He reminded me his name was John Synowsky from the 334th in Vietnam but I still didn't remember clearly and we agreed to meet for dinner at his home in Ft. Worth. I couldn't rely on photos because when I was medevaced out of Vietnam all my photos were lost. When I saw John's face at his front door it all came back in a flash, and I was ashamed of myself that I had forgotten the one who had rescued me. I didn't know many post-impact details of our crash in 1969 since my body was in shock at the time, but that night John and I got drunker than skunks and he filled me in on a few things I didn't remember, including the part where Graham nearly shot me. But Graham was rescuing me and he meant well!

I talked to John once in a while over the years but I didn't know how to find Graham Stevens. I knew him in Vietnam as "Steve" the fun magnet, so with a common last name and no first name I had no luck finding him. A few years ago John and I collaborated over the phone, used internet resources and found Graham in Williamsburg, Virginia. In our first telephone conversation in 30 years Graham told me now that he is a civilian he wears a lapel pin version of just one medal, the Soldier's Medal he received for rescuing me, and so he thought of me every day for years when he dressed for work. Imagine that.

In December 2000 near Christmas, John's family and mine met for dinner. Melanie, you were not quite four years old then, and as the evening ended John gave you a farewell kiss. You said to him with no prompting from me "Thank you for saving my Daddy, Mr. John." I couldn't have said it better myself.

Some day I want both of you to meet John and Graham, and I want you to always remember them as living examples of two great virtues - loyalty and courage.

For many years I avoided Vietnam veteran gatherings, and though I visited Washington, DC many times I always passed by the Vietnam Veterans Memorial, I didn't stop. Some co-workers who knew I was in Vietnam asked sometimes when I returned from a DC trip if I had visited the memorial, and when I said "no" I could see in their eyes the wonder if I were too fragile and suffering from PTSD, or maybe they were puzzled why I didn't pay my respects. They didn't know I have no need to go to a special place to honor the memory of friends who died, and they never knew I avoided the memorial for the same reason I avoided veteran gatherings. I didn't like what I saw driving by the memorial, long-haired and bearded guys hanging around in uniform remnants, selling trinkets, handing out pamphlets about the war, perpetuating the myth Vietnam veterans are losers and victims. I wanted no part of that and I didn't owe anyone an explanation.

But one day I did stop to look up a few names and discovered the genius in the memorial's design. To find a name among the 58,220 on the wall you have to look them up on an alphabetic index to find the panel. Then you have to search for their panel and on that panel the names are in order of date of death, but the dates of death are not listed so you have to look through all the names. As I searched for the names I first wondered why in the world they didn't alphabetize them to make them easier to find because there were so many names, and I began to be overwhelmed because there were so many names, and by the time I found the names I searched for I realized something emotionally I had previously only known intellectually, that there are so many, and each one is a loved one. The numbers just don't tell the story.

To the memorial designers, well done. I'm glad I overcame my reluctance.

Now I'm in touch with John and Graham and others including some I didn't know in Vietnam, but they flew helicopters like me. There's nothing cathartic for me about spending time with them, I just enjoy their company because they are the finest men I ever knew.

Who do you admire?

Common Virtue

Read this well, girls, for here is the essence of the elephant.

In 1945 Adm. Chester Nimitz coined the phrase "uncommon valor, common virtue" as he marveled at the brutal punishment taken by US Marines fighting for control of Iwo Jima. There is a famous photograph of our men raising the flag on Mount Suribachi on Iwo Jima as the battle still raged far below, and the Iwo Jima monument at Arlington National Cemetary depicts the photo.

Iwo Jima Monument, Arlington National Cemetary

James Bradley's father was one of those men who raised the flag. Bradley wrote the book <u>Flags of Our Fathers</u>. As he interviewed the *heroes* of Iwo Jima in search of Adm. Nimitz's *uncommon valor*, he was frustrated as they each told him the same thing. "I didn't do anything special", they each said, "I just did my job like the other guys." Bradley finally understood the meaning of Adm. Nimitz's observation, that instead of looking for heroes he should have seen the *common virtue* of these ordinary people doing extraordinary things.

These Marines suffered together through brutal battles when they wanted nothing more than to go home, they came to love one another, and they fought desperately to keep one another alive. When some of the survivors were singled out as heroes, they didn't want to stand apart from all the others, they took enormous pride in being just one of the guys they grew to love and admire.

That's how it was for them in war, and I believe that's how it's always been. When I thanked John Synowsky and Graham Stevens for risking their life to rescue me, they brushed it off, saying "Any of the other guys would have done the same thing." And the remarkable thing is, they were right, and that's what Adm. Nimitz meant by *common virtue*.

I have told you several stories in which ordinary guys did their job while facing extreme danger. The astonishing thing about these stories is not just the courage and determination of these young men and the loyalty that bound them together, it is how common these stories are. There are thousands of stories that tell how day after day these young men faced danger, just doing their job, and virtually all of them were prepared in an instant to risk everything to protect one another. That's what Adm. Nimitz meant by *common virtue*.

You have seen on my office wall several medals from my time in the Vietnam war. The ones I display are the Purple Heart, for when I was shot down and injured; the Bronze Star for a day when a ground commander said we saved their skin; and the Distinguished Flying Cross with a citation that says "For heroism . . ."

Does that mean your dad is a hero? No, I just did my job like the other guys. I often read well-intended words about heroic soldiers "giving their life" but I never knew anyone who willingly gave up his life. I do know some who died a terrible death trying to do their job and protect one another. There is something rather honorable about that, I think, that has nothing to do with medals, but I think it has much to do with Steinbeck's ". . . saints and angels and martyrs and holy men."

Terry Garlock receiving a medal in Vietnam

Veterans with fancy medals are sometimes sought after as somehow more virtuous than the others, but only by those who don't understand *common virtue*. Those who have seen the elephant know that medals are nice recognition, but we don't pay too much attention to them. Here are a couple of examples to illustrate the point.

Soon after I arrived in Vietnam I attended my first awards ceremony and saw a captain, who I later came to privately refer to as Capt. Dipshit because he was a jerk, having an award pinned on his chest. I knew he didn't fly so I asked another pilot why he was receiving a medal. It seems Capt. Dipshit walked in front of a forklift as he was crossing the flight line at night, and he had minor bumps and scrapes. But even though he never came close to combat it was a war zone and he received the same Purple Heart I received when I was shot down and injured. Go figure.

Woody McFarlin tells the story about his Scout pilot buddy, who shall remain nameless to protect the guilty, flying a LOH in the Mekong Delta area. It seems he was having fun flying aggressively low level at dusk one day when one skid caught the dike of a rice paddy and that tough little helicopter rolled itself up into a ball of spare parts. The lucky and now dizzy pilot was miraculously unhurt, but when he crawled out of the destroyed aircraft he wondered how in the hell he was going to explain this. So he pulled out his pistol and shot a few holes in the remains of the aircraft so he could sell the story he had been shot down. Things got complicated when an enthusiastic awards officer put him in for a medal, and he couldn't decline without making trouble for himself. He now has a V device for *valor* on an Air Medal to remind him of the misadventure. But don't tell anybody.

A pilot named Skip Davis refused to accept the Purple Heart when he took a bullet in a tender spot and didn't want harassment from his fellow pilots about a medal. And Skip didn't receive a medal when he lost an aircraft to enemy fire three times in one day. Skip was leading his platoon by flying the tail ship on a flight of eight Slicks in a combat assault, the most dangerous position because often the enemy would wait until all the aircraft settled into the LZ (landing zone) to open fire, and the tail ship was the last one out after unloading troops. This LZ was just across the Cambodian border, and the enemy was waiting.

When Skip's ship was hit many times in the LZ and rendered unflyable, he and his crew scrambled onto the ship to his front to get out. When they arrived back at the PZ (pickup zone) for the second load of troops Skip rounded up another aircraft because he would lead his Slick platoon back to the same hot LZ. Skip tried for a replacement co-pilot and crew, too, since he thought his men deserved a break, having just survived serious enemy fire. But his men said no way, they were a team and Skip wasn't going back in without them. So they returned to the hot LZ together and lost a second aircraft to enemy fire, then returned again and lost a third aircraft. I don't need to see any medals to admire Skip Davis and his loyal men, and a chestfull of medals won't make me admire Capt. Dipshit.

Flight of Slicks, Combat Assault into a cold LZ

Sometimes medals carry profound meaning, sometimes they do not, but the *common virtue* of men who fought together under fire never goes away.

When I meet with a group of Vietnam veterans, even when we don't know one another I am among close friends because we share the brotherhood of once having been at the top of our game, putting everything on the line for our country and for one another. What matters to us is not medals, what matters is the affection and admiration we have for one another, the recognition of *common virtue* in one another, seeing in one another what is best about ourselves.

What We Learned From the Elephant

You don't have to go to war or even serve in the military to be a faithful citizen. But those of us who have seen the elephant learned some things many people will never know.

We learned that courage is not the absence of fear, courage is getting the job done while you're so scared your hands shake.

We learned that once the shooting starts we're not fighting for the flag, we're fighting for one another.

We learned that we admired our fellow soldiers, our young brothers, because we saw in them virtues our parents taught us to admire, like duty, honor, determination, loyalty, trust and courage. We learned to like ourselves because we came to act the same way, and we learned these virtues are more important than money, fame or celebrity.

We learned that heroes are not larger-than-life and fearless, they are the ordinary people who do extraordinary things when their brothers are in danger.

We learned that we loved our brothers even though we never said it out loud.

We learned that our country may sometimes send soldiers to war and then fail to support them with a commitment to win.

We learned that war is a terrible, sad, unforgiving, unfair, chaotic and brutal affair devoid of the glory Hollywood pumps into war movies.

We learned that military commanders must have the freedom to use overwhelming conventional force to accomplish the war mission, and that half-measures will only feed our soldiers to the elephant. Many years later the country came to understand this vital lesson about war.

We learned that even though we didn't want to go to war, the citizens who sent us would blame us for the war they hated, and we would return to insults instead of parades. We resolved that would never happen to our soldiers again while we are alive. In 2003 there were some encouraging signs of the public's recognition of sacrifice. On a Delta flight from Atlanta to Mobile, Alabama, the Captain announced to passengers they had the privilege and honor to be escorting the body of US Army PFC Howard Johnson, killed in Iraq, to his home in Mobile for burial. The cabin became very quiet. At the gate upon arrival, the passengers left the aircraft but remained at the gate, lined up at the window and waited to quietly watch the coffin, draped with an American flag, transferred to a hearse surrounded by PFC Johnson's family members. At about the same time the body of Marine Cpl. Mark Evnin, killed during the spearhead to Baghdad, arrived at his home in Vermont. The funeral posed a problem for his family as they planned for a large group of cars to drive 50 miles to the cemetery on the busiest highway in New England. To their surprise they found the highway cleared by volunteer state troopers, and citizens standing by their parked cars with hands over their heart as the procession drove past. I hope increasing frustration in Iraq does not diminish the public's support of families who pay the ultimate price.

We learned the loss of young friends dying a violent death. We learned that casualties get lost in the numbers while each one was someone's son, or bother, or husband or friend. We remember their faces, frozen forever young in our mind.

We learned that we did not depend on public support for our own self-respect. We knew what we had done together and have always been proud to have served our country.

We learned there are great numbers of dumbasses who take their freedom for granted, assuming it must be someone else's job to serve their country to defend that freedom.

We learned there is real evil in this world. While we helped the Vietnamese people by building roads and schools, digging wells, donating money to orphanages and hundreds of other civic actions, our enemy routinely murdered their own countrymen for the effect of terror. Public beheading or worse was used to bend villagers to their will, and they frequently tortured prisoners, executed our wounded and enthusiastically shot at unarmed medevac helicopters in violation of the Geneva Convention. Our side sometimes violated the rules of war, too, but we prosecuted our own for atrocities, like the Lt. Calley trial for the My Lai massacre. Our enemy, by contrast, trained their soldiers to use atrocities as a strategy and rewarded them for doing so. Some dumbasses oppose the use of force against enemies who threaten us, believing all things can be resolved by talking, love and understanding. These dumbasses cannot conceive someone would enjoy killing them and their family. We wish they were right, but we learned they are wrong.

We learned it is the responsibility of *all of us* to protect our country, though many in the public and the media are willfully or passively ignorant of the threats we face. The USA was suddenly awakened on September 11, 2001 to the realization there is real evil in this world aligned against our country. While others rested comfortably in the blissful ignorance of the threat, we have always known, we learned from the elephant. The USA has now elevated the priority of national security, but it is still subordinate to the prevention of *profiling* and other matters of sensitivity, our borders are still unsecured, and America's dumbasses are nodding slowly back to sleep. We are watching and waiting because we know the threat will always be there.

We learned that when a conflict arises, even though protestors march and scream in childish self-indulgence, we have a *responsibility* to conduct ourselves in a way that withholds aid and comfort from our enemy whether we agree or disagree with our country's current policy.

We learned that our pop culture encourages trashy values and worship of celebrities undeserving of our admiration. Seeing the elephant changed us, and now we considered ordinary people with sound character to be far more worthy of admiration than the rich, famous and powerful.

We learned that reporters sometimes slant stories to their own agenda, because the war they reported was not the same war we fought. We learned to look for a reporter's or network's agenda on any particular issue, to question whether they are digging to tell it true or grinding their own ax.

We learned when our country is threatened and young soldiers do their job amidst killing and dying, the protected ones at home may take little notice of the sacrifices made to keep them safe. We learned the professional chatterers can talk endlessly about war without realizing the ones who know what it is like, the ones who have earned the right to tell it true, are ordinary soldiers who have faced the elephant.

We learned to treasure the gift of our citizenship and freedom, purchased with the risk and blood of those doing their duty. We learned if soldiers are bold enough to face danger for our country, our citizens should be bold enough to thank them for their service. We learned such thanks are rare.

We returned home from our encounter with the elephant just a little older but not quite the same. We no longer had an impulse to follow the pop culture crowd. We were not overly concerned with what others thought of us because we had learned to like ourselves and trust our own judgment and distinguish between the trivial and the substantial. We watched daily news reports with a little skepticism because we had learned to think for ourselves. We knew what we valued, we knew who we admired and we knew who we are.

* * *

Dear Kristen and Melanie, I have tried to tell it true. If you are strong enough to seriously reflect on these issues, you can learn important lessons of life from the elephant without going to war, without the heartbreak or the risk of being trampled.

I wanted to tell you the long story of the elephant in hopes that you might remember some of these lessons, and I wanted to tell you that young, ordinary soldiers are the finest men I ever knew.

Mel Wollschleger and the Elephant

The lessons of the elephant are known to all those who have fought for our country, but especially so in WWII. It is important that you know, and that you tell your children, about the sacrifice of these young men who took a trip through hell to save the world. Some of them were part of our family.

First I will tell you about your Grandpa Mel Wollschleger. He died in 1997 so we can't ask him about what he saw in WWII, but we know just a little.

Mel Wollschleger, soldier

Grandpa Mel, from Salt Lake City, Utah, joined the Mountain Ski Patrol unit of the Army, hoping that his training would be in Colorado, not too far from home. If you had known Grandpa Mel really well you would think that is just like him, quietly trying to outsmart the Army. But the Army rarely does what common sense leads you to predict, and they shipped him out to Europe right away.

He served with the Mountain Ski Patrol and fought the Germans in the mountains of Italy. Grandpa Mel wore the coveted Combat Infantry Badge (CIB), a musket on a blue background.

Since 1943 every US Army soldier who fought in combat on the ground has worn this badge. Those who wear the CIB are highly respected because it symbolizes the infantryman who bears the brunt and misery of war. The infantry is known as "The Queen of Battle" because the battle is never won until tired, hungry, dirty foot soldiers arrive to complete a dangerous job at the point of a gun.

A grenade that killed some of his friends in a foxhole injured Grandpa Mel's hand, and the shrapnel and one of his fingers were finally removed in Bushnell Hospital in Brigham City, Utah. Grandpa Mel received the Purple Heart for his wounds.

Who do you admire?

Roy Garlock and the Elephant

Roy & Lois Garlock, wedding photo

Your Grandpa Roy Garlock died in 1996, but we have some records of when he saw the elephant in WWII. Grandpa Roy served in the US Navy aboard the small aircraft carrier *Fanshaw Bay* in the Pacific. In October 1944 a huge fleet of over 700 allied ships prepared to retake the Philippines, a key stepping stone to defeating Japan. Adm. "Bull" Halsey commanded the fleet and was desperate to find and destroy the Japanese Central Force, the most fearsome collection of huge battleships afloat.

Fanshaw Bay was part of Task Unit 77.4.3, nickname Taffy Three, a battle group of several small carriers, destroyers and escort ships. Taffy Three was just one of many task forces of warships organized on the periphery of this gigantic invasion force to protect the troop ships.

As the invasion force approached the Philippines, Adm. Halsey was notified scout planes had identified several Japanese carriers to the north, and thinking this was the Japanese Central Force Halsey took his primary carriers and battleships to the chase. They were 300 miles north by the time they realized they had taken the bait of a diversionary force of old and near-empty Japanese carriers, and they turned around to steam back to aid the invasion force.

While our big battleships and aircraft carriers were north with Halsey, at dawn on the morning of Oct 25 the Japanese Central Force steamed from behind a group of islands, through San Bernardino Straight, sort of a left hook to surprise the invasion force. With them were the *Yamato* and the *Musashi*, among the largest battleships ever built. Taffy Three, a tiny David to the Japanese Goliath, stood in the way. The battle was huge and furious, the shells thrown by the Japanese battleships were as heavy as trucks and for the first time the Japanese used Kamikaze suicide bombers against ships. Taffy Three fought desperately and stood their ground against all odds, and the Japanese ultimately withdrew to fight another day.

What happened that day was briefly recounted in a Presidential Unit Citation given to Taffy Three. Read it carefully and show it to your children, for it is just one of many stories of extraordinary sacrifice in WWII.

Who do you admire?

Destroyers lay protective smoke screen, enemy shells splash

The President of the United States takes pleasure in presenting the
PRESIDENTIAL UNIT CITATION to:

TASK UNIT SEVENTY-SEVEN POINT FOUR POINT THREE
consisting of the U.S.S. FANSHAW BAY and VC-88; U.S.S.
GAMBIER BAY AND VC-10; U.S.S. KALININ BAY AND VC-3;
U.S.S. KITKUN BAY and VC-5; U.S.S. SAINT LO and VC-65; U.S.S.
WHITE PLAINS and VC-4; U.S.S. HOEL, U.S.S. JOHNSTON, U.S.S.
HEERMANN, U.S.S. SAMUEL B. ROBERTS, U.S.S. RAYMOND,
U.S.S. DENNIS and U.S.S. JOHN C. BUTLER

For service as set forth in the following

CITATION:

For extraordinary heroism in action against powerful units of the
Japanese Fleet during the Battle off Samar, Philippines, October 25,
1944. Silhouetted against the dawn as the Central Japanese Force
steamed through San Bernardino Straight toward Leyte Gulf, Task
Unit 77.4.3 was suddenly taken under attack by hostile cruisers on its
port hand, destroyers on the starboard and battleships from the rear.
Quickly laying down a heavy smoke screen, the gallant ships of the
Task Unit waged battle fiercely against the superior speed and fire
power of the advancing enemy, swiftly launching and rearming
aircraft and violently zigzagging in protection of vessels stricken by
hostile armor-piercing shells, anti-personnel projectiles and suicide
bombers. With one carrier of the group sunk, others badly damaged
and squadron aircraft courageously coordinating in the attacks by
making dry runs over the enemy Fleet as the Japanese relentlessly
closed in for the kill, two of the Unit's valiant destroyers and one
destroyer escort charged the battleships point-blank and, expending
their last torpedoes in desperate defense of the entire group, went
down under the enemy's heavy shells as a climax to two and one half
hours of sustained and furious combat. The courageous
determination and the superb teamwork of the officers and men who
fought the embarked planes and who manned the ships of Task Force
77.4.3 were instrumental in effecting the retirement of a hostile force
threatening our Leyte invasion operations and were in keeping with
the highest traditions of the United States Naval Service.

Enemy plane shot down

From the deck of Fanshaw Bay
Japanese shells strike another Taffy Three aircraft carrier

Leo Coulombe and the Elephant

Leo Coulombe

Your Grandma Lois and Grandpa Roy Garlock's family grew up in South Sioux City, Nebraska. Grandma Lois' mother, your Great-Grandma, was born Jessie Peck in 1884. Great-Grandma was married three times and had eight children.

With her first husband, Mr. Huffman, Great-Grandma had three children, Helen, Leo and Harold. I will tell you a little about Leo.

Great-Grandma's second husband was Mr. Coulombe, and though he was a step-father to Leo he raised the boy and Leo always used the last name Coulombe. With Mr. Coulombe Great-Grandma had two children, Louise and Donna.

Great-Grandma's third husband was Mr. Cotton, and they had three children, Darlene, Lois and Betty. That's your Aunt Betty and Grandma Lois, and Aunt Darlene who you have not met. Since Cotton was Grandma Lois' last name before she married, we know Great-Grandma by that name.

Great-Grandma Cotton

Aunt Betty was the last child born to Great-Grandma, and she and the older Uncle Leo became buddies. In 1943 Grandma Lois married Grandpa Roy and moved away while Aunt Betty and Uncle Leo still talked frequently.

I think I remember meeting Uncle Leo once when I was little, but our family moved from Nebraska to Pensacola, Florida where Grandpa Roy was stationed in the Navy, so I didn't really know him.

Uncle Leo was a house painter. In 1944, when he was much older than those drafted into the Army and as WWII was raging in Europe and the Pacific, he volunteered for the Army saying it was time for him "to do his part." That does not mean Uncle Leo was full of virtue, for his life was troubled with excessive drink, and while it would be fashionable today to classify him as a victim of a disease, I have enough common sense to know he did it to himself. Uncle Leo lost his children, lost his wife, and he went off to war.

What is an ordinary soldier's life like in war, what does he think? Most people cannot fathom, I believe, the mix of waiting, boredom, stupidity, fascination, anxiety, loneliness, fatigue, hunger, filth, disgust, noise and fear a soldier must endure. Uncle Leo was an ordinary soldier, older than most, and on his brief trip through hell he wrote a few thoughts in a pocket diary.

Through his troubles Aunt Betty remained his faithful and close friend, and years after his return from war he gave her his diary, telling her in a joking way some day it might be published. In 2001 Betty gave it to me.

I considered placing Uncle Leo's diary entries in the back of this book, in the Appendix, out of the way because they are long. But I decided to put them here because it is a tiny slice of history, it is a small window through which those who enjoy the comfort and safety of home while others go to war can take a peek to see what ordinary soldiers do for you. It is important.

Here are the entries in Leo's diary, just as he wrote them, misspellings and profanity and all, with a few less significant notes omitted. What he wrote will tell you a little of what was in his head, and maybe what he left between the lines is what was in his heart.

The WWII Diary of Leo Coulombe
"Dante was an Amateur"

1944

Dec 2	Left Italy aboard John P. Collier 1200 noon. Arrived Corsica Dec 3 1400.
Dec 5	Left Corsica for France. Trip uneventful.
Dec 6	Arrived in Marseille, France. Disembarked for staging area.
Dec 7	Air raid – ack-acks busy. No damage.
Dec 24	Christmas Eve. German paratroops expected to attack tonight. Battalion alerted and ready.
Dec 25	Attack failed to materialize. Still waiting.
Dec 26	Waiting. Wrote to Betty.
Dec 27	Waiting. Almost time for guard. Thinking of Betty-Jean.
	Dreamed of Darlene.
	Ack-ack busy blossoming high against the stars, 50 cal tracing eerie patterns through the night.
	2200 all is quiet. No damage.
	Retrospect – left the US Oct 12, crossed the Atlantic. Spain, Morroco, Africa, Gibraltar. Arrived in Naples Italy Oct 28, 1944. Isle of Capri.
Dec 28	Ack-ack again last night. No damage.
	Promised to write Louisa Ciccone at Bagdoli Napoli Italy. Have never done so.
Dec 30	Ack-ack exceptionally heavy last night.

1945

Jan 2	*Went to 7th hosp for dental work. Sgt Burr, Corp. Powers and myself are still in Marseille. Doing well. Muscatel plentiful. Paula gone. Where???*

Jan 2 *Went to 7th hosp for dental work. Sgt Burr, Corp. Powers and myself are still in Marseille. Doing well. Muscatel plentiful. Paula gone. Where???*

Jan 3 *Marseille on pass.*

Jan 4 *Paying the piper.*

Jan 5 *Guard duty tonight. Rumored Photo Freddie is a robot plane. Humrich gone to Marseille.*

Jan 6-7 *Getting everything ready to roll. Won't be long now.*

Jan 14 *Leaving in the morning for the front.*

Jan 15 *Left Marseille. Through Toul, Nancy.*

Jan 19 *15 kilometers from German border. Living in French apt house, badly shot up. Germans destroyed all bridges and rail heads in their retreat. 45 miles from Loonville.*

Jan 22 *Cold and snow last 3 days. Town all shot to hell. One baker stayed. Bought some bread. Good.*

Jan 23 *Into the front lines. Shooting for keeps.*

Jan 24 *Fire mission. Mission accomplished. I am operating Charlie S.B. radio out. Christ! I'm dirty. Lines went out twice yesterday.*

Jan 26 *We are still holding. Firing on targets of opportunity. Still cold and snowing. Damn German civilian wants us to save his spuds. Whata ya know. Schaufhausen G.*

Jan 29 *Battalion attacked German town. Entirely successful. Eight prisoners.*

Enemy firing on our O.P. Huge formation of planes went into enemy territory. One crippled and escorted by four fighters on return journey. Having a hell of a time keeping communication in.

Jan 30   *Mail came in last nite. Joan Stansberry sent me her picture. Letters from Betty and Darlene, Kathryn. Misting. Damn the war.*

Feb 2   *Flares over the lines. Men nervous. Tension becoming apparent.*

Feb 3   *Went up to our O.P. German bodies are free of snow and clearly visible. Laid wire through German town. Muddy and warm.*

Feb 4   *Operating S.B. Replacements came in. Pace gone to hospital.*

Feb 6   *Two men and jeep blown up by land mine.*

Feb 7   *Joe Schlitt and I go through German town. Nothing happened. People looking out the windows. Queer feeling. Sort of lost. Gun feels friendly.*
Chester was moving some rock from the kitchen door. Rolled a rock and found himself looking into the decomposed face of a dead German soldier. There's more of them there. They were caught by artillery fire. The heavy mist rising in the air gives away the position of the dead.
Battalion massed on German position. Concentration perfect. "Hitler, call out your burial party!"

Feb 7   *German agent wounded and captured. Threw hand grenade but it failed to explode. Sent to hospital.*

Feb 9   *Moving up tomorrow. 75 miles.*

Feb 10   *Moved along Loraine Valley. Now four thousand yards from German lines.*

Feb 11-13   *Heavy shelling continuous, night and day. Rain and mud, always.*

Feb 25   *Took Forbach last night. Artillery fire extremely heavy – going towards Germany. Saarbrucken next. Must cross Saar river.*

Feb 26   *Colder today. Firing continual.*

Mar 1   *Yesterday we was straffed by our own planes which was flown by German pilots. Gave them a warm welcome. They didn't come back.*
Oh, yes, we moved to our old position again. Mission accomplished.

Mar ?   *Lost track of day and date. Going back for 3 day rest.*

Mar 9   *Limbeck F. Everything quiet. A few Jerry planes now and then. Been trading everything we could find for eggs: at last we got ten. Consolidated all other items. 2 cans sardines, 1 can salmon, 15 spuds, 12 slices bread. And we had quite a feast.*
"Red alert" yesterday, nothing happened. A letter from Mom and one from Joan.

Mar 14   *The Big Push. Humrich, myself, Peelor and Schlite went to O.P. Jerry opened up on us with mortar fire. We hit the dirt. I lost my iron hat but later recovered the damn thing. Nobody hurt. We were lucky.*
Moved again. Jeep blown up. Post killed. Kittlo and Curtiss seriously wounded. Strafed continuously.

Mar 15   *The big push is on. We are part of spear head.*
Later. Mine fields and mud bogged us down. Artillery concentrations so heavy would shatter nerves of the dead.
Last night. Flares by the thousands over the lines. The front door of hell. Earth is shaking under me: din is terrible. Shells, like the scream of tornado rising to a high shriek and ending in the hell of explosions.

Sitting on a pill box of the old Maginot Line. A great bald hill in front. Thirteen tanks start up. Jerry knocks out one. One swings to left and blasts Jerry pill box. Doe boys fall in behind and advance on town at left of hill.

Can't see for flame and smoke. Firing still going on but town is ours.

No one came out of tank that was hit.

Air Force has been helping all day.

Moving ahead fast. Dead men and parts of dead lying all over the roads and fields. Like going down the throat of hell. Dante was an amateur.

Most of the dead are American. No time to pick them up. But there are lots of Jerries too.

Our M1 hit a mine. It's out. I'm in a fox hole now that was Jerrie's yesterday.

Mar 16-18   *Forward again. German artillery firing on us. Whole German army in front. We are in Germany heading for the Rhine. The road of the dead. I'm jittery as hell.*

Peeler and I digging a fox hole. 88s whine and I hit the dirt. They stop and we dig. They start and we dive. We cuss and start again.

J.O. hit in mouth by shell fragment.

Ziegfried line is holding us up but we'll get through.

Wish I had time to sleep somewhere without being shot at.

Betty Jean, this is a hell of a way to make a living.

Dead GIs all over. Christ, what a mine does to a man! The army don't pick up dead Germans, just let em lie. I think this is Sunday. No letters last two weeks. There comes the air corps, boy I'm glad to see em.

Mar 19   *Still trying to break through Ziegfried line. Maybe tonight.*

Zero dial on my radio makes GIs hunt their hole. Sounds like incoming mail.

Should connect with 3rd army in next few hours. Then we'll have them in a pocket. So says S2.

Knocked out two forts in Ziegfried line this AM.

Nothing to write on or I'd write home.

Mar 21-22 *Spear headed 7th army through Ziegfried line. Went 90 miles into Germany and stopped 8 mi from Rhine. Didn't stop for hell or high water. Moved continuously for 24 hrs. Supplies can't catch us.*
German prisoners streaming back. Through the towns every house put up a white flag. We sailed on through town after town leaving the rear elements to clean up. So damn far ahead of the infantry that I don't know where they are. Back of us somewhere.
German planes straffing. Wonder where in hell our air cover went. Haven't saw them since we started.
No eats. No sleep.

Mar 23 *5 mi from Rhine.*

Mar 24 *I personally take over Nazi home. It's a mansion. They have been operating a factory. We freed the slave labor. We move on.*

Mar 25 *Still on this side of Rhine. Patton closing in. We are 5 mi from Worms.*
No mail from home for a long time. Are you writing, Betty Jean?
It's quiet right now. Too quiet.
I'm in a culvert now. A German family crawled in with me while German artillery hit us.

Mar 26 *It "was" too quiet. Rhine crossed last night.*
Eggs for breakfast. Deer for supper. My God!
Shot down a Jerry plain.
German paratroops dropped behind us.
We are with 45th. Spear headed with 6th Armour.
Saw wagon hitched to dead horse, with a dead man holding the reins.

Mar 27-30 *Spear heading again. Chasing German army all over Germany. Many dead lying along the road.*
Stopped over night. On the way again soon.
Must write to Mom. Don't know how I'll mail it.

The tears are flowing back to their source, back to Germany.

Mar 31   *Spear heading again. Lost from rest of column. Wandered all over Germany. Was straffed and bombed by planes.*

Apr 1   *Found rest of outfit. We are still hitting into the Ruher. Have pushed deep into Germany. Far ahead of all American troops. Dead men and dead horses mark the trail we leave. We take no prisoners. Have no time.*
We are hitting hard and fast. Far ahead of Patton. Wish the infantry would get up here.

Apr 2   *Reached objective.*

Apr 3-4   *Strong opposition. Enemy tanks in woods. Got two. Two firing. German planes raising hell. Sure keep me hoppin.*

Apr 5   *Bastards throwing the works at us. Planes again, bombing us, straffing us. Mail coming in.*
Caught 7 prisoners inside our perimeter defense. At least they're prisoners now. Christ, a fox hole feels shallow when Jerrie's planes are on your tail.
This is a hell of a hot spot.

Apr 6   *Nothing around us but burned towns and dead Jerries. Plenty of both.*
Infantry hasn't caught up with us yet. Damn mud and rain.
Wish I could write to you Betty Jean.
Took about ten dozen eggs and two hams from a German house. Damn C rations.

Apr 8-9   *A little girl with her leg blown off. A GI split apart by a shell burst.*
Moving ahead slowly. Town is a hell of a mess. Two women on a horse and cart: wounded.

Apr 10-11   *Bombed and straffed by German planes. Hope our luck holds. Found some rare wine. Got drunk. Strong opposition here. Two guys arrested for rape.*

Apr 12   *Bombed again last night.*
German children have forgotten how to play: if they ever knew.
Bull chased me. I killed the bull.

Apr 13   *President Roosevelt died last night.*
We are on the move again. Going deep into Germany. Wish it was over. I'm tired of being bombed, straffed and shot at. Have a hell of a time staying alive.

Apr 15   *We attack castle on the hill, Nazi fortress. What a battle! We win. I duck 88s. Pinned down. Battle royal to our right.*
Tiger tank knocked out. Dead Sgt in the ditch.

Apr 16   *On the way again. SS troops are tough.*
Dog fight above. Jerry runs home.

Apr 17   *Liberated a ham and basket of eggs. Fighting from town to town. What the hell are they fighting for? There cause is lost. Even before it began.*
Prisoners are too numerous to mention.

Apr 18   *We have been farther ahead; some more fighting; done more fighting than any battalion in the 7th army. We have been commended by every outfit that we have supported.*
Enemy artillery around our ears.
Enemy infantry attack. We whip their ass.

Apr 19   *Moving forward 3 or 4 times a day. Fighting and ducking. Who in hell said the war is over!*
Lost my pipe. Damn it.
God damn tankers can't move into a town until we take it for them.
Germans shooting the hell out of us with artillery.

Position untenable, we move. Boy, that was a hot spot. And we're not out yet.

Apr 20-21   *I liberate a town.*
On the way again. I capture 2 non-coms from German house. Also 2 pistols. One was wounded in leg by shrapnel.

Apr 22   *German infantry in woods.*

Apr 23   *Infantry man with burp gun killed by sentry last night.*

Apr 24   *Plenty of mail going over.*
I acquire a camera.

Apr 25   *Casualties. Our own. I don't know why the infantry is called the front line. It takes them 3 days to catch up to us.*

Apr 26   *Straffed again. Casualties. Crossed the Danube. Three infantry and one Panzer division opposing us. Holy cats!*

Apr 27   *Christ I'm scared. Straffed. Plane down. 300 prisoners.*
Dog fight above 2 planes down.

Apr 28   *Am now with F.O. Another rat race in the offing.*
Nice girl. Had to leave.
Crossed river on railroad bridge. What an opportunity they lost. I felt like a duck in a shooting gallery.

Apr 29   *Stayed at German airport last night. Moving again. Airport was Landsburg.*

May 1   *Snowing. Alps just ahead. SS are dug in the mountains.*
Saw Jew concentration camp. We liberated the Jews. They were weak and starved, bearing the aspect of aged infirmity when their years were young.

> *Rice, Humrich and I throw out the Nazi mayor and put in a new one. A gun is a persuasive ballot.*

May 2
Into the Bavarian Alps after the SS.
Strong hold broken. The Luftwafe is through.
Hundreds of planes captured and destroyed.
What in hell do we do next? Almost in Austria.
Notes – We cracked the Ziegfried line at Mimback.
Two dead krauts on a load of spuds.
Bad-Aibling where planes and field was destroyed.

May 3
Humrich and I take over German shoe store. We give shoes to the slave labor we have freed. The town is Kolbermoor.

May 4
Skirted Chiem Sea, headed into Alps, slept in the clouds.

May 5
The lady's lips smile but her eyes are pure hate. Met part of French army yesterday.
Met SS troops high in a mountain pass holding a small village. Twice we went in and twice we drew back. Shot the hell out of it with artillery. Went in again and stayed. The smoke still rolling around me. Dead men and wounded. We are through the town and stopped by a road block on other side.
Still fighting when we get the news that war has ceased. But by God I've heard it for 3 weeks and still they shot at us. So what??? 5 PM
Lt Burke, Sgt Reid, Humrich, Marotto and I stay in Ruhpolding Agathe Kriegenhoffer. Nobody gets anywhere but Humrich.
Clara, a little Russian slave girl, said "I'm going to drink, dance, shake hands and go home."

May 6
Sitting in Agathe's kitchen. No comments.
Humrich and I liberate another pistol a-piece and a car load of guns. Nice goin.
Imagine, we haven't been shot at since yesterday!!!
Lt Burke liberates some wine, pens and lighters. We all get some.

May 7   *Through the mountain valleys on trail of SS and small groups.*

May 8   *A proclamation has gone out through the mountains for all German soldiers to lay down their arms and come in.*
We are waiting in Aschau high in the Bavarian Alps.
Creeping on again through the most beautiful valley I've ever saw; houses like miniature dwellings in a candy shop window, with gayly painted shutters picturing scenes from old Bavarian folk tales. And the people scurrying about with their bright colored dress. The mountains rising high on either side; and the water falls that tumble down the steep slopes, clear cold and laughing. I laugh too, because the war of Europe is over.
Later, Tall tuffted hills; the head dress of some proud savage, and the sun glowing red and strange above this land of hate and beauty.

May 9   *Crossed the Austrian border last night. This morning returned to Aschau.*
To Gaisburg. Everything OK.
AM at Viehausen Austria for 10 day rest. Its been a long time. Rape is getting to be quite a problem.

May 10-11 *Dug a 6x6x6. Think I'm getting plueresy again.*

May 22   *Still at Viehausen. Fraternization is getting to be a Court Martial Special. Keeps up the whole God damn army will be a prison camp.*
Looks to me as though the boys that won the war are paying through the nose.

May 27   *Three men fined $140 each for fraternization. What a laugh for the Germans! Lady, hold that light up! Let's see what we've been fighting for.*
The people are homeless and hungry. They are lost and forsaken by their leaders. But if a murderer can no longer strike, is he non-the-less a murderer?

Should the American soldier be punished for acting like a human being? Is hatred of the German to be instilled by a series of lacerations inflicted upon the mind of the American soldier? If he has no right to think and act for himself then what in hell is he fighting for?

Patriotism can be drowned in resentment. Nor is it a banner given to a chosen few to be rammed down the throat of lesser individuals.

Every American is born with the idea that he is free and equal to any man. That no matter how small his voice, the reverberations will be heard and understood. Hitler is dead. Let's keep his spirit out of America and out of the American way of living.

May 28   *Guard duty. Hospital at Zalsburg.*

Ration depot raided by hungry refugees. I'm sure that my gun would jam if a German ration depot is raided while I'm on guard. I can't picture myself protecting a former Nazi.

May 29   *Villagers kill and dress a horse for food. A few days ago it was a large dog. Winter will bring riot and revolution. The blood will flow again in Germany. And hunger and destitution will stalk hand in hand through Europe.*

Only the grace of God and the power of America and England will prevent a purge of German blood. The former slaves of Europe have not yet awakened to their own power. But come the day when a new leader shall raise his voice, they will be ripe to listen and to raise the banner of a new creed.

The victims of the concentration camps are no mere figments of the imagination. Like grim specters from hell they haunt the roads of Germany. Broken in mind and body. Living, bleeding sins of an insane people.

May 30   *I wonder if Viola has had her baby yet. Funny how the mothers presence is always required at child birth. Don't seem to make much difference about the father.*

I guess a rose is just as sweet who-so-ever sows the seed.

May 31   *The girls that got the boys fined $140 went to jail last night. They was out after curfew.*
This thing is beginning to get funny.
Raining again.
Looks like Gen'l Ike will need to get somebody straightened out.
Later. I wonder why I keep thinking of you. Could something be wrong? Or is it just C.B.I.

Jun 1   *Its too bad that liberating days are over. Then I lived on ham and eggs taken from the Krauts. Now I can't take anything. So eat C rations and stay hungry.*

Jun 2   *A German girl of eighteen. Almost beautiful. She came and sat by me, saying "My mother was an artist in Hamburg when the bombers came. Her arm was blown off. The Russians decapitated my brother. Now I'm alone. Allus kaput." Her eyes were pools of deep bitterness and her smile was like falling tears. I gave her a cigarette and we smoked in silence.*
These are Hitler's children. The children of the damned.
It's hard to understand or analyze a people nurtured in hell and all the evils thereof.
Hitler is to the younger generation what Christ was to the Christian. Retribution and inquisition won't change that belief. His death – if he is dead – won't change it. Hitler lost the war, but he never lost the people. Those that still live have been thoroughly educated to his ways. And it is only through the education of future generations that National Socialism will be weaned from Germany.

Jun 5   *In one half hour I start the long journey home. It is now 7:30*
Went through Munich where the ghosts of the Storm Troopers goose step amid the desolation of a once great city.

Stopping at Hiedelburg over night.

Jun 6   *On the way again. The long journey to the coast. The great industrial centers that have been systematically destroyed. House by house, block by block, street by street. And over all is the sickish sweet odor of the dead. The red poppy fields that splash through the countryside. The war ford of Mars has walked side by side with the master discriminator.*
The people grin foolishly at we who brought their empire crashing around their ears.
This town is Frankenthall. We stop at the Red Cross for coffee. I eat 7 donuts and 3 cups of coffee. Then on again. Through Mannheim and Worms and across the Rhine. Back over the same path where we so relentlessly pressed the fleeing Germans. Every bridge destroyed, highways blocked. Anything to delay the inevitable.
The Volksturm, created in desperation, and taught to fight the advancing columns. The Volksturm that refused to be sacrificed to a cause already lost. And retribution was sure and certain. A Volksturm that fled to the hills and hid in the woods. A Volksturm that killed their officers and trembled in fear. A people was weary and sick with the dread of past crimes who's evidence was everywhere. This was the vaunted Volksturm, the last ditch stand.

Jun 7   *Waiting in Worms for further orders.*
There are many things that for fear of capture I have not entered in this diary. Tom Knotts, our Comm Sgt lost his mind at Bagdalia Italy. Alphonse Pace was a mental case too. He blew his top at Lauderbach Germany. Kraft lost his nerve on hill 88. All 3 returned to the states. Our casualties I have never numbered.

Jun 9   *Left for La Harve France.*

Jun 10   *Still aboard train. If the damn thing was this slow in the states, it would have to pay squatters rights.*

Jun 11   *Arrived at La Harve.*

Jun 15   *Still waiting.*

June 16   *Humrich and me have the sleeves shortened on our ETO jackets. Price = 1 bar soap and 1 candy bar. Work done by French woman.*
Hope to ship out tomorrow.
Was talking to Lt from combat engineers. He said he wasn't going to send a telegram home, he didn't want the house all cluttered up with God damn relatives when he got there.
I've carried this God damn duffle bag over half the world. I'll throw the son-of-a-bitch in the drink.
Between Giesing and Eping 17 dead Germans scattered around and 3 American tanks. One tank was hit head on by an 88. It came in the front and went out the back along with the driver's head. Hell of a thing to be thinking about.
When I first landed in Italy, the first thing that I heard was a small boy on a Naples street corner. "Hey Joe, Hey Joe, piece a ass Joe, blow job, one pack cigarettes?" Italy, where the girls was lousy, dirty and willing, and the rest of the family was twice as willing.
Pompei with its obscene pictures, of what historical value I don't know. Perhaps for its' educational values in sexual extremities. But of course that's only one part of Pompei. And where's the GI that sex don't interest??
And then when we was racing through France on the tail of the German 19th army. The air corps caught them on the road and for 14 miles they cleared the dead men, horses and equipment from the high way with a bulldozer.

Jun 17   *Still waiting for a boat.*
Another shot, another short-arm. When I get out of here I'll get a picture of the darn thing and present it to the war department. Every time I see a medic now days it starts crawling out of my pants.

Jun 18	*Some simple minded individual loaded on the boat with a white phosphorous grenade in his duffle bag (taking it home for a souveneir). It went of, catching fire to the ship.*
	So we're still at La Harve. Waiting for a boat. What next????
Jun 19	*This damn camp must be an institution for the feeble minded. No body knows any thing or appears to want to. Guess they're afraid Uncle Sam will find out they're here and ship them to C.B.I.*
	My one amusement here at camp Herbert Terington is going to the Red Cross for coffee and donuts.
Jun 20	*Alerted again for over seas movement.*
Jun 21	*Left the port of La Harve, France at 1500 aboard the Isaac Sharpless, a slow freighter. Carrying 404 men going home for discharge.*
	Off the coast of England at 2200 hours.
	Weather stormy. Rough sea.
Jun 22	*Food is good.*
Jun 23	*Bought 4 cartons cigarettes. The boxes had a little gun practice.*
	Everybody playing poker or shooting crap. Lots of money changing hands.
Jun 24-25	*Heavy fog. Visibility limited to deck area.*
	Saw large school of porpoise this morning. None of em said anything.
Jun 26-30	*On June 27th at 1315 hrs passed from ETO into ATO.*
	What could be as monotonous as the sea?
Jul 1	*Still at sea. Probably arrive the 4th.*
	I wonder if I will find a job to my liking?? Shall I stay in So Sioux City?? Shall I go to the Pacific?????
	What shall I do.

Jul 2	*What has war taught me?* *That death is not to be feared, but evaded as long as possible. He's so damn final.* *That men killed in action most always fall on their face.* *That every war is the result of bad economics.* *Nuff said.*
Jul 4	*Land sighted 1455 hrs.*
Jul 5	*Laid in harbor all nite. Docked at 0730 hrs. Left for Patrick Henry.* *Had the best dinner I've had since leaving home.* *Sold my P38 for $50.00.* *Lored and me drink beer. First time for months.*
Jul 6	*Left Camp Patrick Henry Virginia for Levenworth Kans at 1900 hrs.*
Jul 7	*I'll be glad when this train gets out of Virginia. Red tape or instruments are equally painful. Poor Virginia.*
Jul 8	*Reached Fort Leavenworth Kans at 1100 hrs.*
Jul 10	*Discharged.*

* * *

After the war Uncle Leo did not find a job to his liking as he had hoped. He returned to painting and he returned to booze. He married Mary. He died in 1977 in a VA hospital.

Where does a man like Uncle Leo find redemption in our memory? Most people say redemption comes only from God, but I know different because I have found redemption for myself in the wide-eyed innocence of you, Melanie and Kristen. In the first part of The Long Story of the Elephant I told you when I look through Steinbeck's peephole at soldiers, though they may be scoundrels I see saints and angels, martyrs and holy men. That includes Uncle Leo, who took a trip into hell for your freedom and mine. He may not find redemption from anyone else, but he will find it from me.

A copy of Uncle Leo's diary now resides in the National D-Day Museum in New Orleans, and in the US Holocaust Memorial Museum in Washington, DC.

Who do you admire?

Leo Coulombe with wife Mary in 1946, after the war

John Harrah and the Elephant

Our family has many friends who have served in the US armed forces, and every one of them helped keep this country safe by building a strong deterrent against our enemies. Sometimes enemies persist and war cannot be prevented. I want to tell you about one of these friends who volunteered to endure the misery of war because it seemed the right thing to do for our country, but the country asked him to serve another way. He is an important friend of our family, especially so for Kristen. His name is John Harrah.

John, Jackie, Emily, Amy, Molly Harrah

In 1998 when we adopted you, Melanie, our adoption agency was Chinese Children Adoption International (CCAI) in Colorado, and they did a superb job for us. When it was time to start the adoption process for Kristen I had heard many good things about Harrah Family Services (HFS) in Texas, and had spoken to John several times. I asked HFS to handle our second adoption, and their service was even better than superb. John Harrah and his wife Jackie have themselves adopted three daughters from China. They were moved by their first adoption to start an agency to help others do the same, and they work together at HFS to treat their clients a little bit like family. We have become friends and I am pleased to include John's story in his own words below.

Who do you admire?

My War That Never Was
By John Harrah

The year was 1950. Ancient history to Emily (born 1995), Amy (born early 1996), and Molly (born late 1996). But 1950 was during my high school days and 1950 was a time of decision for me, John, otherwise known as Emily's, Amy's, and Molly's Dad. Along with most of the people in the USA I had never heard of the country called Korea when a United Nations police action erupted in newspaper headlines and on *radio* – there were few TVs at the time. High school girls probably had other things to talk about in 1950, but among the high school boys excitement raged over what we felt was finally going to be our war, and why in the world were some Americans calling it a *police action*, and where in the world was Korea?

A peninsula jutting out from China's Manchuria, Korea was a scene of death between the invading North Korean and defending South Korean armies in June 1950. To high school boys a war between any North and South of some country seemed to be a civil war. Our history teachers had been trying to force us to understand that even the USA had engaged in bloody Civil War battles long ago. My father, born in the late 1800s, told me of sitting in his father's hardware store and listening to stories told by veterans of the American *War Between the States*. So, in 1950, I turned to my father for explanations.

As much as I love my daughters and hope to always be there to guide them, these words may have to suffice since, after all, as this is being written in 2003 I am in the late 60s of my life. I have learned so much from my daughters, but my father was my first, best teacher.

Memories Emily, Amy, and Molly retain will mark my teaching abilities even if written words will never be enough.

By the time they are adults, Emily, Amy, and Molly will learn that soldiers have been fighting wars since before the first historical record. Learning that many wars have occurred does not answer the question of why wars occur. Mothers teach their children to not fight. As our girls already know, "It's not nice to fight." So, why are there wars? And why do people kill each other? And why do soldiers do what they do? And what is it that soldiers do?

William & Helen Harrah, 1916

Children's big questions may never be answered. This book tries to tell our children that we, as fathers, have been redeemed by their innocence, and in gratitude for our redemption we are trying to explain some of the *bad* things in life even though it is easier to speak of our love for our children and the beautiful world we have glimpsed through their eyes.

In order to talk about my war, strangely called a *police action*, I need to tell my daughters who I was, where I was, and what the world and I were doing so long ago in 1950 when my thoughts first turned to becoming a soldier.

The youngest of three sons with a sister three years younger than me, I lived at home in Chicago during high school with my mother and father. Mom explained that Dad was an engineer and had been an Army Engineer building fortifications in France during the first World War that ended in 1918. Many had hoped WW I would be *The War To End All Wars*. But my two older brothers served in the Army during the second World War, which ended with the birth of the atomic age in 1945.

With war in Korea on the horizon, I wanted to go with many of my high school friends who, with their parent's permission, had left school to enlist in the military. I was sure my first, best teacher would be able to guide me about becoming a soldier in a faraway land called Korea.

By the time I reached high school I began to understand my father often gave me much more than his words. He often cited words of others to make a point, and helped me understand what had been written. Much of my life has been spent discovering sources of the memorable words my father quoted.

When I asked my father what to do about my life and my war, I should have realized he was a much better teacher than one who only tells the way things are. My father always helped me see that events become the way they seem to be for many reasons and little in life is purely black and white.

After asking him what he thought I should do about the Army, my father spoke of the poem, <u>If</u> ,by Rudyard Kipling, a poem that outlines in deft wisdom the things mature men do, and that if a boy should do these things . . .

> ". . . Yours is the Earth and everything that's in it,
> And - which is more - you'll be a Man, my son!"

My father also spoke about how in his time young men basically chose either Army or Navy but now the USA had an Air Force, giving me at least three choices if I decided to enlist. I had been considering leaving high school early to enlist, and that did not mean I would have to forego college because there was the GI Bill to assist with education after my enlistment. I learned the Air Force could introduce me to technical fields of study, so I decided on the Air Force and I decided to first finish high school. When I enlisted I was selected for the field of electronics where I learned about airborne computers as long ago as the 1950s.

I expected to be part of the war in Korea because Air Force planes whose electronic bombing systems I was learning were then in Japan, being readied for battle in Korea. We received sad reports that several of my friends who enlisted in the Army had been killed in Korea by the time I was in service, but I was not deterred from doing my part in the Air Force.

John Harrah, Airman

I had little knowledge of international politics affecting this *police action* in Korea and the military operations surrounding the war. Planes I expected to support in Korea were instead transferred to France, as was I, to await political decisions about being engaged in Korea. While politicians played their silly games one of my friends lost both his legs in the far North of Korea because there was no air support as they battled soldiers who had entered Korea from China.

Bewilderment! There I was in France, learning French, with little understanding why Chinese and American soldiers were fighting each other in Korea where I wanted to serve my country. I started reading about Asia and learned that France was trying to colonize Indochina though hundreds of years before a mighty Chinese army failed to conquer that country, now known as Vietnam. China had conquered Korea hundreds of years before, and to this day South Korea's flag displays a symbol from China.

Yin and Yang show change in much the same way as night follows day, or women and men interact in their different ways. Sequences of events determine actions and inactions as influenced by powers outside themselves. No matter that my original intent was to fight in Korea and possibly fight soldiers from China. I have been guided by my father's words and have studied and will continue to study philosophies of China. Who knows? Somewhere there may be an explanation of how we were led to our daughters.

My life progressed from preparing for war, to teaching military students in Mississippi, to working for US computer companies, to teaching computers courses in California, to meeting Jackie who became my wife and led us to adopt our children from China. Our daughters have inspired us to help other friends become extended parts of our family as they also have been led to adopt children from China.

Emily, Amy, and Molly know that adopted sisters are real sisters. Someday our daughters will meet more of our friends who are also part of the greater family of those whose lives have been redeemed by the children they have adopted from China.

Whether or not I am still with them, Emily, Amy, and Molly will remember what I have taught them from <u>Desiderata</u> by Max Ehrmann:

> " . . . You are a child of the universe, no less than the trees and the stars; you have a right to be here. And whether or not it is clear to you, no doubt the universe is unfolding as it should . . . "

I have worn many uniforms, from the clothes of a child to the cool outfits of a high school gang, before proudly wearing the uniform of the US Air Force. I am most content with the uniform of just a Dad, in an old hat, t-shirt and jeans, with his wife and children in August of 2003.

John Harrah

John, Jackie, Molly, Emily, Amy, Harrah

Who Do You Admire?

As I told you about the elephant, I asked many times "Who do you admire?" You might think I ask that because I want you to admire me or the soldiers I served with in the Vietnam war. But that would miss the point.

Who you admire says a lot about you. If you admire the latest Rap star, Hollywood celebrity, the faces on the covers of teen magazines, the big names in sports this year or the cool kids at school, then you are like every other young person, being led by the nose by the popular culture. But if you admire selected and perhaps ordinary people for the virtues they reveal in their daily lives, you must be doing the hard work of thinking seriously for yourself and trusting your own sense of value.

Here are some of the people I admire.

I admire writer John Steinbeck. He never lost his wonder about how the human condition fits into the puzzle of nature, and labored tirelessly for just the right words to help us understand. He loved the company of common folk, and even when he became famous he would rather share a sandwich with a field hand than dine with celebrities.

I admire Martin Luther King, Jr. because he was right to take a stand against segregation laws and he had the courage of his convictions. The civil rights legislation that resulted from his work was long overdue to dismantle institutionalized discrimination in the South.

I admire Ward Connerly of the University of California Board of Regents, a black man who has taken a nationally publicized stand against affirmative action and racial preferences. He says those programs are wrong because they treat race as our defining characteristic, and they perpetuate racial strife. His stand affirms the dream stated by Martin Luther King, Jr. that all people be judged by the content of their character, not the color of their skin. I happen to agree with Mr. Connerly's position, but would admire him nonetheless if I did not because he, too, has the courage of his convictions. Black leaders all over the country have condemned him as a traitor to his race because they expect him, as a black man, to share their views. If you are thinking for yourself you might wonder "Gee, isn't that . . . racist?"

I admire the founding fathers of our country for their dedication and purpose, risking *their lives, fortunes and sacred honor* for the idea of democracy. Your schoolbooks might teach you these were rich white slave-owners, implying they do not deserve our respect. But even if flawed like the rest of us, they were remarkable men who changed the world for the better. Please read the Federalist Papers to understand how these men labored and negotiated and compromised to bring about the Constitution and the birth of the USA, something that very nearly did not occur.

I admire your mother for her unfailing and tireless devotion to you two girls, never thinking about a moment for herself.

Betty and Chris Christianson

I admire your Aunt Betty and her husband, Uncle Chris who died before he could meet you. They had a dream for Chris to become a Chiropractor, and though well past the age of most college students they both worked hard for years to put Chris through school. He became a doctor of Chiropractic, Betty ran their office, and by dedication to their practice and caring service to others they became a valued and respected part of their community. Chris always had a joke and a tease for kids; you would have loved him as we did.

I admire my mother and father, who grew up during the Great Depression, sacrificed during WWII, dedicated their life to their religious beliefs and served their church in many ways. When I grew up I made my own decisions about religion that differed with them, but I value the lessons they taught me, like being sure what you believe and then true to those values. I was too selfish as a child to realize the sacrifices they made for us, but now I know. I thought my father had too many rough edges, and understood him best only after he died when I had kids of my own. I wish he were alive to read this book.

Roy & Lois Garlock

Mel & Shirley Wollschleger

I admire your Grandma Shirley and Grandpa Mel for being the reliable source of help and advice friends and family turned to when they were in trouble. Their home turned into a gathering place for many who became close to them and knew they were welcome. I miss your Grandpa Mel quite a lot. He was my best friend from the time I married your Mom until he died. I think Mel had lots of best friends.

I admire career teachers like Melanie's First Grade teacher, Ms. Wiley, and college teachers like your Aunt Vicki. Teachers work for too little pay under counterproductive rules, and they endure far too many undisciplined students and inattentive parents. Teachers hold our future in their hands and deserve more resources and rewards than we give them.

I admire Euna Sumlin, my first mother-in-law, who taught me in my formative years by her example the meaning of unconditional generosity and kindness. She was the first to rise, the last to bed and forever tired because she had little rest. She was unfailingly kind and gentle to every soul she met no matter how undeserving they might be.

Euna Sumlin

Sisters Redeem Their Grumpy Dad

I admire Roger Brown in Salt Lake City, the most genuinely open and personable man in business I have ever known. Watching Roger helped me recognize that by nature I focus too much on tasks and technical matters, and could be far more effective by tending to the human side of business.

I admire Lee Nobles, my high school Spanish teacher who saw in me an under-performing student who could do better, and took the time to challenge me and help me discover the euphoria of achievement.

I admire Clifford Miller who worked hard every day as a plumber past his retirement age and long after his eyes failed him.

I admire you, Melanie, for how you turn everyone you meet into a friend, how you are compelled to wave and shout their name with an enthusiastic smile when we meet them in a store or drive past in the golf cart, and how you must hug each one of them and your teachers goodbye when I pick you up at school each day. That gift of open and spontaneous affection is one I never had, and I am proud of you because I think so many people care for you because they first felt that you cared for them.

I admire you, Kristen, though you have not yet begun to speak, for the way you have adjusted to our family just months after being a little frightened and withdrawn. You watched carefully, withheld your affections, gave your trust slowly only as it was earned, and have developed an increasing attachment to your Mom and Dad and Sister that is real and strong and resilient. Just recently you have begun to cry when Melanie gets in trouble, and to me that speaks volumes. You decidedly have a mind of your own. I like that.

I admire the men I served with in Vietnam, and the ones who fought there I don't know, for their skill and courage and determination to take one another home alive.

None of these are perfect people. They each have their strengths and flaws just like me. But in them I see something that earns my respect, something that has to do with their character and heart and nothing whatever to do with being popular or famous or wealthy. The people we admire help us set mental goals for our own behavior, and though I have fallen short many times I strive to be a better person like others I have observed.

I hope that you will think it through early in your life and decide for yourself who *earns* their place on your list of those you admire. If you choose well, ultimately the one most worthy of admiration will be you.

Do You Know Who You Are?

When you feel awkward as you morph from a child to an adult, when you are torn by inner turmoil and troubling questions flash through your mind, when the urge to escape to independence from your parents is overwhelming, remember this – it's a natural part of growing up, we all go through it.

For you girls there is an added dimension to growing up. Both of you joined our family by adoption and you are a different race than your Mom and Dad.

From the time of your first words we have taught you to be proud you were born in China, that adoption is a wonderful thing, that we don't know your birthmother and birthfather in China but we believe they loved you even though they could not keep you because of hard conditions, that we are your *parents* and our family is forever. We taught you these things because they are both important and true.

Nevertheless you may sometimes be troubled by certain thoughts or doubts. Kristen, as I write this you have not said your first words and we expect to hear them any day now. Melanie, when you were three you asked why your Mom and Dad are "banilla face" meaning our skin is a different color than yours. Just recently at six years old you told Mom you wanted a big nose like ours instead of your flatter nose, and you told me you wanted blonde hair like Barbie and Darby and Alex. These are natural questions and feelings.

As you get older your angst over racial difference is likely to be intensified as other kids tease you. Since man discovered fire kids have tormented one another about the smallest real or imagined difference, so do you think racial differences will be overlooked? Not a chance.

I remember during our first trip to China to adopt Melanie some Chinese people made fun of *me* because I was different. That's what happens all over the world, the local group differentiates themselves against *others* whether it's based on race or religion or country or even your grade or class at school. That's just how people are, and it's kind of silly when you think about it.

Sooner or later someone will taunt you about your different eyes or skin or hair, and it's inevitable even people who like you will say things like "Those aren't your *real* parents!" How do we protect you from this?

Some parents teach their kids all about racism, and how you need to band together with other kids of the same race to advocate for the rights of your racial group. Discrimination can take many forms and it is wrong, but I won't teach you to think of yourself as part of one group competing against the others because I think that's wrong, too. You will be encouraged by others to think of yourself as Chinese-American and advocate for that hyphenated group. I hope instead you will think of yourself as an American who happens to be Chinese, and advocate for everyone.

Race should be irrelevant because how we are physically different simply does not matter. How we *behave* matters. Segregating ourselves into racial groups perpetuates division and victimology. You are not a victim, you are an individual. If someone insults your heritage and your race and your family it doesn't make you a victim. But it does make them a dumbass, and I hope you will ignore it or take the dumbass to task, depending on the circumstances. More importantly, I hope you come to know who you are and not let dumbasses determine how you feel about yourself.

Who you are does not depend on your genes, where you were born, what you look like or anything physical at all. Who you are is in your heart, your character and values and beliefs, like pride in your Chinese heritage. Knowing who you are involves accepting yourself, knowing your own strengths and flaws, and not measuring yourself by what others might think.

Your mother and I often forget that you are Chinese. We don't forget intentionally, it's just that what's on the outside is not who you are, even though your Chinese features are beautiful. The person you have become inside is what matters, that's what we see in our daughters and that's what we love.

Learn to love yourself. There will always be dumbasses trying to make you feel bad about yourself, that's life and it happens to everyone.

But the dumbasses will fail if you know who you are.

Love, Life and Blood

Farmer's field in Melanie's home town of Diangdian, Anhui Province, China

Though you are US citizens and we are your parents, we have taught you to honor your birthmother and birthfather in your home country of China. It is important, we believe, for you to learn what you can about the country and the people who gave you birth. You have a love connection to your forever family, a life connection to the people of the USA and a blood connection to the people of China. When you think of yourself as richer because of those connections, perhaps that is when you are no longer a child, perhaps then you have grown up.

We have given you exposure to the Mandarin language, Chinese people and some of the culture, but our knowledge and ability to do so is limited. Ultimately, what you absorb about China is up to you.

As you grow from a child to a young adult it is natural for you to want to be just like your peers, resisting anything more than your Asian features to set you apart as *different*. I hope somewhere along the way you realize the differences among us are the spices that make life fascinating, and that such differences should be celebrated, not hidden or denied.

As you become old enough to read this, think it over and decide for yourself what is important to you. Learning to read, write, speak and understand the language of China will require commitment and determination on your part. Do you want it? Do you wish to find someone who lived most of their life in China to teach you what life was like there, the customs and holidays and traditions? If you learn the Chinese language and culture, you may find it useful in a professionally fulfilling way, opening opportunities to you. You may also find it personally fulfilling to build a connection to the people who gave you birth. You must decide. If you want it we will help you. But we will not force you.

Think about it and decide when you are young. Don't wait until your later years prompt you to look back, perhaps with regrets.

Kristen's home town of Yangjiang City, Guangdong Province, China

Your Music Will Soon Arrive

Every generation has their own music. It has to be different, it has to be new, and to be properly savored your music must shock your parents at least a little. It's kind of a rule.

Our music was rock and roll and the Beatles. Our parents were embarrassed at Elvis' bump and grind, rolled their eyes at songs like "A Hard Day's Night" and they declared their disgust over the Beatles' long hair. Therefore we loved them all the more, and still do.

Our parents were right to be concerned: our music did change our culture.

Your music has not yet arrived, and already I worry because your choice of music can affect your attitudes, friends, values and lifestyle. I worry because of the cultural decay spread by the current craze of Rap or Hip-Hop. Some would call me racist for my disdain of Rap because this so-called music originated in the black community. But I don't care where it came from, and it has quickly spread across all races everywhere.

I am one of the few remaining holdouts with an uncompromising opposition to Rap. However much the rest of the world disagrees with me, maybe if you consider my view it will make you think a little about your own choice of music.

Rap, or Hip-Hop, features young people strutting to a beat, looking *cool*, chanting or shouting or sneering semi-poetic and usually angry lyrics, acting very tough, indeed. And to enhance their tough appearance many have taken names like 2-Pac, Snoop Dog, Fifty Cent, Eminem, Ice Cube, L.L. Cool J., Puff Daddy, Big Daddy Kane, Big Ed, Big Kap, Big L, Big Mike, Big Noyd, Big Pokey, Big Shug, Big Tymers, Lil' Cease, Lil' Italy, Lil' Kim, Lil' Keke, Lil' Jon, Lil' Ric, Lil' Rob, Lil' Slim, Lil' Soldiers, Lil' Troy, Lil' Wayne, Lil' Zane, Dr. Dre, Beatnuts, Dead Prez, Three 6 Mafia, Mos Def, Busta Rhymes and Uncle Kracker, just to name a few.

My problem with Rap or Hip-Hop isn't the tough strut or cool name designed to impress kids so they will buy CDs. My problem is the immoral behavior taught by this music. *Gangsta Rap*, sought after by kids because it is violent and extreme, glorifies a lawless and immoral street and prison culture, portrays women as whores, treats cops as evil targets and, by the way, tramples the English language. If you wonder what I am talking about, flip the TV to an MTV Hip-Hop channel to spend a little time with way cool thugs, pimps and slut-chicks.

Maybe just because it shocks parents everywhere, kids of all races love it and buy Rap CDs by the millions. Spin-offs from Gansta Rap are more benign and some may not promote indecent behavior at all, but its' style mimics the indecent original and the genre of Rap has brought a new low to our youth culture.

Leave it to Hollywood and MTV to embrace the worst in our culture and promote Rap to make it mainstream. They did it well and are making tons of money. In deference to the young people who like Rap, much to my dismay officials everywhere have now accepted it and the immorality of Hip-Hop has spread throughout our culture.

The Oakland School District in California held a competition for students to translate Rap. Here is one small clip from the paper submitted by the student who won highest honors:

Assignment: Translate the selected lyrics from the song "One More Chance" by rapper Notorious B.I.G. (murdered in 1997 at 24 years old) from his album <u>Ready to Die</u>.

"She's sick of that song on how it's so long
Thought he worked his until I handled my biz
There I is - major pain like Damon Wayans
Low down dirty even like his brother Keenan
Schemin' - don't bring your girl 'round me
True player for real, ask Puff Daddy"

Student translation: Your current love interest no longer wishes to hear your fabrications about the length of your member. After I had sexual intercourse with your woman, she became enlightened as to the proper way it is supposed to be performed; violently and immorally. It would be in your best interest to keep your woman away from me as my sexual prowess is very strong. If you are unconvinced, ask Puff Daddy.

I'm sure it is titillating for young students to hear sexually charged lyrics. But what parent would let their children listen to this junk? What thinking taxpayers in Oakland would approve of their public school system promoting *artists* like Fifty Cent, who boasts of having been shot nine times? What teacher would add legitimacy to this music by participating in a translation exercise? Maybe it's just me who doesn't get it.

If you listen to this stuff will it help or hinder your intellectual and moral growth? I think you know the answer. I hope you reject every hint of Rap or Hip-Hop, its' strutting style, profane attitude, goofy dress and uneducated language. Don't reject it for me, reject it for yourself. Reject it because you are better than that, because you don't want to lower yourself to that level. If it helps, I promise to be shocked by any other music you select as your own.

Your music has not yet arrived, and already I worry. Could it be as bad as Rap?

Your music has not yet arrived, and there is hope, for there is time for you to think. I hope for you good music, deep music with a message that strikes an inner chord, strong music that wraps around you and thumps through your whole body and makes you jump and twist and move with abandon. I hope for you songs about life and love, sweet music that makes you stay very still with your eyes closed to blissfully absorb every note of the melody and harmony. I hope your music becomes for you and your friends a source of delightful binding together, a shared cultural center you can return to again and again for fond memories of youth. I hope you select music that makes you an even better person than you have already become. I hope for you good music.

Some day you may sit with your own children before their music arrives to shock you, listen with them and tell them with pride "This was our music." Choose well.

Who Will Decide For You?

Soon you will discover that Mom and Dad will not and cannot control your life. We will say no when we think that is best, we will insist on knowing where you are, who you are with, what you are doing and require you to be home by a set time. We will try to influence what you wear to convey a bit of morality in your appearance. But we won't always be there watching and sooner or later you can get away with anything.

The most we can do is teach you to look into your heart to know what is right, do your best, enjoy life and friends, stay away from smoking and alcohol and drugs, and resist all temptation to treat sex as a casual plaything. The most we can hope for is that you *want* to be a decent and strong person.

Who will decide for you?

When you're very young, especially in middle and high school, there is much peer pressure to do rebellious things, to act in new ways to shock your parents, to follow the lead of kids who are *cool*. It's nice to be popular and well-liked by the kids you want to be with, and so easy to be involved with a group that will lead you into trouble.

Who will decide for you?

If you watch TV or movies or read fashionable magazines, or just look around you at school, you will see a trashy pop culture encouraging young people to do all the wrong things. The pop culture mocks the kids with enough character to say "no" and take their own path because of what they believe to be right. In the long run some of the *coolest* kids emerge as the losers they are, and the kids who are true to themselves emerge as winners. Choosing the short run feels good right now, choosing the long run is good for you forever.

Who will decide for you?

Sex Means Commitment

Sex is one of life's wonders. The urges you will begin to feel very young are quite natural. But sex in a premature and casual way can be destructive, and if you are smart and strong you will use your brain to control your urges.

During your teenage years you might feel strong attraction to several different boys, but feeling that affection doesn't mean the time is right.

Sex is not proper until you are an adult. Sex is dangerous when you are too young because you risk disease, pregnancy and the emotional scars of relationships that do not last. It also discards the honor and dignity you own in your body.

But you will hear contradictory messages constantly. Your girlfriends and boyfriends may argue the cheap thrills of sex are just a rite of passage, merely what is expected of you in today's youth culture.

Will they decide for you?

Some parents teach their sons to treat girls honorably. But even the finest of young men have lusty thoughts flashing through their heads a hundred times an hour the likes of which their mothers will never know. Many women say "Men are pigs!" because the hormones jumping in our veins sometimes transform us unwillingly from Dr. Jeckle into Mr. Hyde. Some young men feel no duty at all to resist their urges, just erections with feet who will do anything, say anything, promise anything, overcome any obstacle to get into your pants, and many girls have embraced a culture of loose morals with surprising vigor.

Will they decide for you?

Some of your girlfriends at school will say they do it, why shouldn't you? Everyone does it, they say, because it's fun, they say, because it feels good, they say, oral sex isn't really sex at all, they say, giving little thought to disease, pregnancy or trading their dignity for the thrill of the moment.

Is that who should decide for you?

Deciding what to do might seem complicated when sexual urges and the popular kids pull you one way and your head or people who love you advise another way. But it can be simple, too; one girl's wise Mom told her "Any dog can do it, so save yourself for the best, dear!"

If the decision were mine, and I know it is not, your sexual activity would begin on your wedding night. But marriage doesn't solve everything because marrying a dumbass is even worse than pre-marital sex with a dumbass.

I hope you treat the matter seriously, know that the decision is yours alone and important. When you are an adult and decide to cross that bridge to responsible sex with the man of your dreams, you will discover one of life's greatest delights. Make very sure the man and the time are right, and then enjoy it.

But Daddy, What if I'm Gay?

Someone asked me "How will you react if one of your daughters is gay?" I didn't like the question at all, but when I stopped to ponder if *my* child is the one who turns out to be gay, well . . .

Here's my confession. The gay agenda that seems so fashionable today makes an old dinosaur like your Dad very uncomfortable. I don't understand being attracted to the same sex instead of the opposite sex. But that's not what bothers me because frankly I don't care what consenting adults do in bed behind closed doors, that's their business. What troubles me is that it should stay behind closed doors in my opinion, and broadcast pro-gay activism rubs me the wrong way, especially some of the exhibitionism and bizarre parades that resemble a freak show. Being gay should be no secret, but flaunting one's sexuality seems, well, unseemly.

I don't want you to be gay. But if that's how you are made, it won't be about me, it'll be about you.

I don't pretend to understand how being gay happens, though I seriously doubt it's a reversible *choice* as some churches would have us believe. But I do know this.

You are our daughter, and if you are gay that won't change. If you feel sexual turmoil in your youth, taking advice from your young friends or keeping it bottled up inside are the two worst mistakes you could make. The ones you should talk to are probably the least comfortable for you, your parents. Our highest priority is helping you find your way.

We'll have to find the right people to listen and advise, and you will have to be strong in a world that often won't understand or accept you. Maybe the hardest part will be learning to accept yourself.

But things will be pretty much the same at home. We'll still expect you to control your urges, treat sex as a serious matter of commitment, act responsibly and thoughtfully and wait until you are an adult. Your mother and I will always love and accept you, and anyone who doesn't like you for who you are can deal with me. If they're too tough for me I'll turn them over to your Mom.

Drugs Kill Dumbasses!

Don't be a dumbass! Drugs will kill you no matter how harmless some of it may appear because even the least lethal inevitably lead to more toxic drugs. Drugs easily become a habit, an addiction, a lifestyle. Any heavy user you meet never intended to go so far and ruin their life, they just meant in the beginning to have a little harmless fun. There is only one way to make sure you never become a junkie, and that is to never try it for the first time. Never.

No matter how much fun other kids appear to be having with drugs, note well those who use drugs, offer drugs to you and encourage you, for they are *not* your friends. Run from them and never look back.

Don't be a dumbass and don't let dumbasses decide for you.

Make Sure *You* Decide

Your friends and dates will push and pull and beg and plead to have you join them in the thrills of youth that could have lasting consequences. Whether it is experimenting with sex, drugs, smoking, alcohol, breaking the law, irresponsible driving, or any other way of expressing independence from parental control, the one who has to live with the consequences will be you. Will you let them in their weakness decide for you, or will you be strong and true to the one person you will look at in the morning mirror the rest of your life?

When you apply to the college of your dreams will you be able to present a clean record with pride?

When you meet the one you want to spend your life with, will you be able to openly talk about your past?

You have to live with the consequences of your actions, so make sure it is you who decides.

The Tricks and Traps of College

Your college experience will be a vitally important time in your life. There is an advantage to knowing in advance where the tricks and traps of college are hiding. Here is my version.

Hold Tight to Your Common Sense

You may see some strange things in college. My hope is by the time you arrive sanity will have returned to campus, but here is some unpleasant truth.

First, universities make much of diversity. That's nice when students really need to be educated about racial equality. But it is taken to extremes and some schools require students to attend sensitivity classes to teach moral relativism drivel like there is no such thing as right and wrong and all nations and cultures are equally valid. In some north African countries it is customary to mutilate the genitals of young women with a knife to prevent their sexual pleasure and thereby assure fidelity to their husband. Is that culture equivalent to our own? Not to me, and that's just one example. I don't accept as legitimate brutal regimes like Castro's in Cuba though you can easily find college professors who would disagree with me.

Second, to add irony to the notion of diversity, universities will never admit it but they reject diversity of political ideas. Most university faculties overwhelmingly lean to the left side of liberal, and there is little tolerance for conservative thought from professors. In some situations there is little tolerance in the classroom for conservative ideas on the part of students, which can jolt your mind when you still believe universities are bastions of free thinking. I don't know whether you will be liberal or conservative, but you should know where the trip wires are buried, and I hope you will always be tolerant of viewpoints different than your own.

Third, some professors are so radically liberal in the political notions they teach in the classroom that they border on anti-American, while a few are blatantly anti-American. And they get away with it.

Fourth, many universities have taken political correctness and sensitivity to absurd lengths that in the end are quite incorrect and insensitive. Committees construct lists of prohibited words or looks or expressions, lest some favored group be offended, with a serious intent that reminds me of George Orwell's <u>1984</u>. How they get away with this without free speech constitutional challenge is a puzzle.

Fifth, causes abound on the campus, whether it is anti-war, anti-big business, save the whales, the environment, animal rights or whatever. A young mind is a fertile field of enthusiasm.

All of which is to say our institutions of higher learning can be bizarre places if you aren't expecting any of this. And your education can be seriously sidelined if you get involved in these things.

But if you know to expect weirdness, you can ignore it, skirt it, stay under the off-beat radar screen in order to stay focused on your education. If your heart tells you to commit yourself to a cause, for example, I would advise you to stay focused on your education because in the long run a successful person can do much more to save the whales than a student carrying a sign and shouting slogans.

You will need to keep a tight grip on your common sense in college because on campus it may be tempted to abandon you.

Playing the Game to Win

The choices you make in college can either enhance or limit your career. As you prepare for college, consider this.

For many professions the top firms recruit from a short list of excellent universities, and they consider only the students at the top of the academic list to select for interviews and job offers. Those below the cut must look elsewhere.

To have the very best choices upon graduation, you need to be at the top of your class in an excellent school. How do you do that?

First, prepare for college with excellence in high school. If you have decided on your profession in advance, there are ways to find the finest schools for that profession. If you wanted to be a lawyer, for example, in Georgia one of the premier schools is Emory University School of Law. Excellent schools like Emory are expensive, parents' resources are not unlimited, and cost will be a factor when selecting the right school.

Wherever you go to school, how do you rise to the very top of your class in a competitive environment, so that recruiting firms compete for *you*, instead of you competing with other students? I learned how to do that, but to tell you how I have to bore you with the story of my own youthful academics.

I was a miserable high school student. Not only was I mentally lazy, my attitude suffered as my immature priority became breaking free from the control of my parents, with little thought to the consequences of my under-performance in high school. I barely graduated from high school and immediately left home for training school in the Merchant Marine.

Before I turned to college I married, spent a few years in the US Army and worked on Wall Street in New York City. When I entered college I was older than the average student and had some of life's experience to make me more serious. So while other students focused on beer, sex and getting by in the classroom, I focused on getting the job done quickly with the highest academic achievement. Here's what I learned.

Excelling in school is like a game. The rules of the game vary with the subject and the professor's style, and the trick is to quickly understand the unique rules in each class and then do a little more than what is required to assure an A grade. Whether the course is important or enjoyable is irrelevant, the *grade* is relevant.

For accounting classes the trick for me was hours of practicing debits and credits in increasingly complex transactions, and it made my head hurt but it got the job done.

For soft classes like Organizational Development in psychology the important thing was group participation and extra credit research.

For mathematics courses like trigonometry and calculus I found there was, for me at least, a very thin line between an A and an F. I either understood how it worked and how to solve problems or I didn't, and for me it involved nightly completion of extra homework problems to practice the classroom lesson that day. Falling behind would be fatal. It was not easy for me and many days I got stuck and chased down the professor in his office to ask questions so I would have time before the next class to rework the problems. Time after time the professor told me he couldn't counsel one student, please don't come back. The next day I would return to ask him for help again. I made As in these classes while many students failed or dropped. Sweat and persistence works.

For boring classes like macroeconomics I had to devise a method for memorizing. I underlined the important passages then read them into a tape recorder while wearing headphones, then listened to the playback while I read again and again. The combination of selecting relevant portions, underlining, reading, speaking and hearing with repetition was so powerful I can to this day visualize the marginal cost = marginal revenue chart on the lower right quadrant of the right hand page of the book. In some cases the answers to test questions were a mental picture on a specific page. It worked beautifully.

The important point here is not the specific technique I used because many things have changed since the 1970s. The important thing is the problem-solving approach to devising a method to win the game. Every professor was different, some were brilliant and some were dumbasses. Some subjects were important while others were frivolous. But to me the only thing that mattered was figuring out quickly how to win the A game in that particular course to enhance my grade point average (GPA). The attitude and determination mattered most.

While other students complained the professor was in a boring rut, or the subject didn't matter, or the workload was too heavy, or the grading system was unfair, I considered the class to be just one more game that I had to figure out to devise a winning strategy. Some courses were thoroughly enjoyable to me, like Geology, Zoology, and Business Finance, but while I enjoyed them I still played the game to win.

I learned those determined and willing to work are the ones at the top of the academic list, and it has nothing whatever to do with being naturally smart. Here's a case in point.

I had a friend in college who did not share my attitude and based his study on what he decided would be useful to him in the *real world*. As you might guess, his academic standing was not very good. We took an elective class together in Astronomy. He knew this was useless information to him so he didn't study much and gave me grief over my GPA as compared to his lower grades. He kidded me about being naturally smart, which I found ironic since that's how I had thought of the winners in high school. I talked him into studying with me, my way, for our final exam. He griped as I forced him to organize the data in a form friendly to memorizing, he bitched as I made him repeat questions and answers on Copernicus, Galileo and other pioneers, and he tried to quit every time I made him recite lists such as the color spectrum or planets in order from closest to the sun. He resisted when I made him explain concepts like black holes, quasars and supernovas. I made him do it not because I thought astronomy was important, but because winning the game was important to my GPA. We both scored an A on the final exam, but my grade was 95 while his was 100. He had a good lesson in winning the game but he never played again to win because we had different attitudes.

For my Associates degree I was learning these lessons the hard way, and I earned a high B GPA, 3.76 out of 4.0. For my Bachelor's degree I missed a perfect GPA by one point on one final exam and earned a 3.96 out of 4.0. For my MBA I achieved the GPA goal of 4.0, a perfect score. I completed this five year program in 3.5 years of hard work.

A Habit of Excellence

While I was focused on winning the game, I learned a great deal and acquired a habit of excellence.

Anyone who has attended college might tell you a B is perfectly OK, you don't have to have all As, and they are right. Anyone with common sense knows that academics don't measure the real value or potential of a person, there are many other factors like maturity, personality, character and people skills. But here's one 30 year old example how topping the academic performance list can matter.

In my final year of school I selected two excellent firms as target employers, but they had few interview slots and a very long list of students competing to interview. Both firms selected me to interview on campus because I was at the top of the academic list. One of the firms then invited me to visit their Kansas City office while the other invited me to visit their Dallas office, and both made me the job offer I was hoping for. I had excellent choices.

These particular firms had many other fine students to choose from, but they never considered most of them because they were below the cut on the list.

How much have things changed since this ancient history? Grade inflation has become rampant in the years since I was in school, but my guess is in the excellent schools top grades still mean something. You'll have to figure that out for yourself.

Here's the lesson if you're smart enough to listen. For me academic failure was a habit in high school. I discovered the habit of academic excellence first in US Army flight school, then in college. Every class was a game of quickly discovering what it takes to achieve an A and then doing just a little more. The end goal was having excellent employers competing for me instead of me competing with other students for interviews and jobs. Years after college my resume was always enhanced with academic excellence.

There are other important things in college, like developing contacts in the profession you are choosing, making strategic selections in your curriculum, and extracurricular activities to develop social skills and leadership. You can even have a little fun.

If you clearly identify the end goal and refuse to compromise in your determination to win, you will learn much from academic study, you will learn commitment, you will learn discipline, you will learn sacrifice as you study while your friends play, and you will develop a habit of excellence that will serve you well always.

Play the game to win to kick-start your career.

Tedious Thoughts of America

Julie and Melanie greet Chinese people in Hefei, Anhui Province, China

When we adopted you in China, Chinese people stopped us on the street to greet you, because like people everywhere they love babies. When these friendly people understood that we were adopting you and taking you home to the USA, they almost always said "lucky baby" and wanted to touch you. We didn't stop them because we knew luck plays an important role in Chinese culture, and they reached out to touch you to take some luck for themselves.

We considered ourselves the lucky ones that you would join our family and enrich our lives. But we knew these Chinese people envied your leaving China where the government controls where they live and work, their news, the size of their family and many other aspects of their lives, where the economic engine runs slow and constrains their opportunity, where criticism of their government might take them to prison, or worse. We could see from the look in their eyes they knew your life would be better in America, and that they wished they could take *their* family to the land of freedom and opportunity.

I have often thought of these people we met in China, who know only what little they discover from filtered news and limited contact with the west, and yet they seem to value freedom and opportunity more than many who are born in the USA and take what this country gives them for granted.

What does our freedom and opportunity in the USA really mean? Since I'm an old Grump with a sense of humor, maybe the best way to tell you about the beauty of America is to point out some of its' flaws and absurdities. This critical look might also make you think about the vagaries of life.

Democracy or Republic?

Winston Churchill once observed that democracy is the worst form of government, " . . . except for all the others." What he meant was the chaos and inefficiency of a democratic form of government can be maddening when you are trying to get something done quickly, but if power is efficiently concentrated in any one person or group that power will eventually be used to abuse the rest of us. Slowing down the process of change to a crawl seems to be an intentional part of the design of our system, which instead of a pure democracy is a democratic republic in which we elect others to speak for us. The republic form provides a deliberative buffer between the public mood of the moment and votes, to prevent hot emotions from squashing the few in a *tyranny of the majority*.

I have been involved in proposing legislation and I carefully watched as it was designed, drafted, *floated* and ultimately enacted. Waiting for others to act drove me nuts and the deal-making, compromising and negotiating nearly made me drop my lunch between my shoes. That's how the consensus wheels of a democracy turn, and it's tempting when you know what needs to be done to wish for a dictatorship where actions of the state are accomplished with the stroke of a pen, precisely what our founding fathers feared most.

Our form of government is messy and flawed, slow-moving and subject to horse-trading and self-serving arguments masquerading as debate. We like to claim our constitutional process is nearly holy, but in reality it is covered in warts and wrinkles. What makes our form of government desirable, and unique when this country was born, is that *we the people* decide what our government can do. In places like China, the government decides what the people can do. That small difference is everything.

All Men Are Created Equal . . . If They Own Land

The Declaration of Independence famously claims ". . . all men are created equal . . ." Of course what they really meant at the time was that people born to *royalty* should have no dominion over land-owning males. Today *all men are created equal* is assumed to incorporate everyone including women because the *men* in that phrase is seen as a metaphor for the human race, and some assume in error our founding fathers were thinking the same gracious thoughts. Nope. Women became voters in 1920 after 72 years of organized struggle.

What about slavery, the everlasting shame of America? There are bitter lessons here about human nature. The plantation economy of the American south thrived on slave labor in the fields, so the brutal inhumanity involved was overlooked. When you want to believe in something very badly, your mind works overtime to rationalize even something so evil as slavery, or the Nazi Party in 1930s Germany. Some of the founding fathers sought to end slavery at the same time a new country was founded because most of them agreed it was wrong, but they knew if they tried to end slavery they would never win the support required for a Constitution. So some of them held their nose and all of them proceeded with what they thought could be accomplished now and hoped the new country would deal with slavery soon, but later. *All men are created equal* didn't have quite the ring to it that was taught when I was a kid in school.

Treating people badly in the USA was not limited to slavery. In New York during the Irish immigration period advertisements for employment often said "Irish need not apply." Chinese labor was flagrantly abused to build the railroads to the west. Indians, or native Americans, were pushed off their land and their populations decimated in battles they had little hope of winning. As waves of immigrants arrived from Germany, Russia, South America, Asia and many other lands they found that most groups disdained and mistrusted the others. Religious discrimination was the same, as discovered by Jews and Catholics. But they all came for freedom and opportunity, and they were free to dislike one another.

This inter-group conflict is human nature, study *xenophobia*. In China today blacks are openly disdained, Caucasians like me are often ridiculed and the Chinese have despised the Vietnamese for centuries. When I was there the Vietnamese considered Cambodians to be an inferior race and they killed Montagnards in the mountains of their own country at every opportunity. Groups treating one another badly has always occurred all over the world, and the USA has been no exception.

Things are decidedly better today in the USA. Discrimination is not only illegal, it has become a social disgrace. In triumphant proof of their victory over past misdeeds, the professionally sensitive now tie themselves in knots trying to treat everyone precisely the same, which of course cannot be done in any rational way. In a twist that perhaps I alone find ironic, it is now acceptable to bash just one group – white males. Especially pre-sensitive dinosaur white males like me.

Free to be a Slug

Why do some people thrive on freedom and opportunity, overcoming all obstacles with hard work and determination, while others languish, squealing about their rights, endlessly complaining of their troubles?

Maybe this is the answer. You are free to succeed and free to fail, free to work hard and free to lay on the couch, free to develop your intellect and free to be an ignorant slug. The choice is yours, and you will find many ignorant, lazy slugs in the land of the free.

Rights and Responsibilities

While millions of people living in repressive countries would give *anything* for the freedom and opportunity we enjoy, many of our citizens fail to understand the rights we have. Please read the Declaration of Independence, Constitution and the Bill of Rights. Further, to understand the thinking and negotiating to get a consensus in the Constitution and Bill of Rights, you should read the Federalist Papers, and when you do you will be among a tiny percentage of citizens who have taken the trouble to consider what our country's foundation really means.

The Declaration of Independence says we have the right to life, liberty, and the *pursuit* of happiness, but it does not assure happiness and does not state any right to be happy, just a right to pursue it which we seem to do with limited success throughout life. The Constitution states a few rights, but the bigger notion can get lost if you don't step back for the big picture. The Constitution and its' amendments really are intended to specify *and limit* the rights of government, saying in essence here are a few things the federal government can do, and the rest we reserve for ourselves, or for the states to be more precise. It does enumerate some of our federal rights, such as a free press, safety from unlawful search and seizure, due process, a speedy trial by jury if charged with a crime, just compensation if government takes our property, and protection from cruel and unusual punishment. We are free to choose our religion, free to assemble peacefully, free to speak out against our government so long as we don't subvert it and free to own an arsenal of weapons if we choose. I may have missed a few, but you will find them if you read the documents yourselves.

As you read the Constitution and Bill of Rights please note there is no right to not be offended, no right to universal health care, no right of racial preference for any reason, no right to receive welfare payments, no right to being treated in a way one regards as *fair* and there are no guarantees that we will all achieve the same level of satisfaction or success. There is even no stated right to privacy, though the US Supreme Court stretched its' interpretation many years ago in *Roe vs Wade* to find a woman's right to an abortion within the Constitution's unstated right to privacy, proving once again the elasticity of legal argument to prove what you wish to be true.

Most citizens never read these foundation documents and never understand our founding fathers intended government's role to be limited. The same people who don't understand where their rights begin and end seem to want government to do everything for them, and the dumbasses they elect to represent them in Washington try to do just that.

I should explain that I call our elected representatives dumbasses for a few reasons. Too many of them don't know the basic foundation of our nation embodied in the reading I have proposed to you. The actions they take frequently contradict the limited government intent of our founding fathers as they pass new piles of laws and create new federal *programs* with abandon. Sometimes they become a little carried away with the importance of their office and need to be reminded, by humbling words like *dumbass*, they are just people like the rest of us and govern with our consent. Sometimes fellow citizens within my hearing need to be reminded these dumbasses are not royalty. Sometimes these dumbasses are faithful and hardworking and deserving of our respect, in which case dumbass is meant as sort of an endearment, and a reminder, to keep them on their toes! While our representatives see a steady stream of citizens at their office door lined up to kiss their fanny and talk about rights and beg for bigger government, maybe if I remind them they are a dumbass they will cause less trouble by occasionally shifting their focus from everyone's rights to everyone's responsibilities.

Somehow it seems those who bleat the loudest about their rights are the same ones who want the rest of us to give them a lifetime ride in the wagon, and the same ones who give little thought to their *responsibility* to share the load. Some seem to think there is some magical nanny in the sky with a bottomless purse to solve every problem life delivers. Calling *them* dumbasses requires no explanation.

Nanny State?

As pandering politicians make endless promises to buy votes, the dumbasses who vote for them seem not to understand that government help seems to almost always make a problem worse, and when it does no harm it does drain your pocketbook with little return.

On a TV program years ago a specialist in the US Department of Food and Drug Administration demonstrated to a TV interviewer how they poured different brands of catsup onto a slanted board and granted favorable ratings to the thicker catsup that flowed down the board more slowly. The interviewer politely asked if this was a worthwhile expenditure of government funds since we all pay this man's salary, and he answered with a question of his own – "Don't you want to know which brand of catsup is the thickest?" Of course there were hundreds of other FDA employees to test everything else in America's grocery stores.

Recently I watched a TV reporter interview two congressman about a $2 million government study funded to research native American homosexual activities. The opposing congressman lamented the waste of our tax dollars (bless him), and the other congressman defended his vote for the grant on the basis other people much smarter than him had recommended the study, and who knows what benefits might result?

The dumbasses we send to Washington to represent us too often lose sight of what should limit our government. They seem to think, as many reporters do, just because something is a good idea our government should do it. That's dead wrong, and that notion makes the spending pile ever higher.

Government spending is funded by taxation, the legal confiscation of money out of the pockets of our citizens. Every time a feel-good notion is considered for congressional funding it should meet this test: "Is this so important that we are compelled to forcefully take more money out of the pockets of our citizens to pay for it?" For national defense, roads and bridges and airports the answer is yes. For measuring how fast catsup flows and studying who sleeps with who on the Cherokee reservation, my answer is emphatically "NO!" But everyone forgets this test, so prepare yourself.

You're Buying the Fruit Loops

How does our government spend our money? Here's one way to think about it.

Picture yourself standing in front of a toilet bowl at home, lid and seat up, with a bowlful of Fruit Loops in your hand. Now imagine tossing the Fruit Loops into the air with one hand and trying to grab them as they fall with the other hand. You can munch on the Fruit Loops you catch, but those falling into the toilet are gone for good, well intended but wasted.

That's a pretty good approximation of how Congress spends your tax dollars. They mean well, but much of it goes down the toilet. Fear not, Congress tells us, some citizens have more Fruit Loops than others, Congress just needs to take more away from them to have more to toss into the air. So they toss and grab what they can, confiscate more and more Fruit Loops, and once a year on October 1 they flush the toilet to start over.

You're Also Buying the Clown Suit

OK, so it's not Fruit Loops, it's real money. Your money. But you wouldn't think so the way it's tossed around, promised to other countries and special interest groups. Why do politicians do that? To gain favor in hopes of receiving votes so they can keep their job. Simple, and disgusting.

So when Republican President George W. Bush promised on his recent trip to Africa to give those nations 15 billion US taxpayer dollars to help fight AIDs and develop their countries, how much was intended as altruistic help for the less fortunate and how much intended to buy the votes of black voters in the US?

If you scratch your head and wonder how he can give away *your* money, and use the event to buy *your* vote for *his* 2004 re-election, you're beginning to get it. Of course he has to persuade Congress to let the money go, and there will be much wrangling and deal-making, and maybe it will be reduced or even increased a little. I'm quite sure in the end we'll give ship-loads of your money to Africa because (1) the Republicans want to demonstrate to black voters they are an open and inclusive political party, therefore they cannot risk opposing their own party's president on aid to Africa, and (2) the Democrats won't risk alienating the black voter base they think they own. Of course both parties are assuming blacks in the USA vote based on the virtues of their own skin color at home and abroad, not what they consider best for their country. And neither party appears to be smart enough to know their assumption insults every voter who happens to be black.

Maybe if examined from a different viewpoint sending vast amounts of US taxpayer money to Africa is the right thing to do, but I have grave doubts about the motivation. And if you think Congress can flush your Fruit Loops down the toilet with abandon, just wait till the Africans give it a try.

The Tedium of the Truth

Remember being free to succeed or fail? Successful people overcome obstacles no matter what, and they accumulate more wealth than those who sit on their fanny complaining about their troubles. One would think there is virtue in hard work and financial success, but that idea might be shattered by this illuminating and perpetual political argument. I warn you it is tedious.

We have what is known as a *progressive* tax system, meaning not everyone pays the same percentage of their income in taxes; the higher your income, the higher percentage of your income is due in taxes. Liberal Democrat politicians generally argue taxes are too low because they believe the greater good is served by more government spending to help the lower income people. Conservative Republican politicians generally argue taxes should be cut to make government smaller, encouraging self-motivated people to work hard, build businesses, create jobs and make the economy grow for everyone.

Since the federal, state and local tax bite takes over half of every dollar you earn, which side are you on? Will you become a liberal Democrat or a conservative Republican? I don't know, it's up to you. Someone once observed "If you aren't liberal by the time you are 21 you don't have a heart, and if you aren't conservative by the time you are 35 you don't have a brain." I was a flaming liberal in my 20s and switched to conservative before 30, so maybe my flame just burned hotter than normal.

The problem, as I would describe it, isn't whether you are liberal or conservative, the problem is most people don't think things through to make intelligent decisions on where they stand. They react to the emotional manipulation on political issues like class warfare.

Consider the 2003 tax cut. Some marginal tax rates were reduced a couple of percentage points and the Democrats yelled *foul!* because the higher income taxpayers received more benefit. But how can the lower income taxpayers benefit the same when they pay little or no taxes, asked the Republicans? In fact, some pay no income taxes at all and receive what is called an *Earned Income Credit* payment since the Democrats don't want to call it welfare. Whether the Earned Income Credit is a good thing or not, it helps to start with the facts.

Here's where the real problem comes in. The lower income people don't pay income taxes, though some do pay payroll taxes, but there are vast numbers of them, and they vote. There are fewer high income voters and they pay the lion's share of taxes in the USA. So when there is a tax tug-of-war, how hard is it to persuade those who don't pay taxes to stick it to the ones who do pay taxes? When you have the chance to vote for taking money out of someone else's pocket and transferring it to your pocket, how will you vote?

When Republicans argue for tax cuts to unleash the economic engine, the Democrats say fine, lets cut taxes at the low levels where the virtuous low income people need it, not at the higher levels where those nasty rich people don't need it. And it sells, even though what they are really arguing for is more welfare at the low end, or transferring money from upper income citizens to lower income citizens. That might be a healthy debate if the Democrats would ever admit that is their objective. At the last measure in 2002 the Democrats demonized anyone earning over $50,000 a year, a cutoff apparently based on counting voters on their side of the line.

When the TV cameras come on the Democrats complain that tax cuts favor the rich but should go to the poor, and the Republicans counter that the poor don't pay any taxes so how could they be cut, and since the rich pay the taxes of course tax cuts favor them.

Both political parties seem to forget one notion. It's our money, not theirs. Both sides think in terms of confiscating our money and *then* deciding how to return part of it. Does it get returned to the one who paid it as the Republicans want, or to someone else who is more virtuous because they are poorer as the Democrats want? They never seem to think a tax cut is simply not taking the money out of someone's pocket in the first place.

Many people never see through this charade because these issues are tedious in the extreme. It's no fun to think through. The media rarely helps with perspective because, I suspect, it's hard to explain and perspective would discredit the Democrat side the media tends to favor.

Class warfare works because the truth is too tedious and the voter count makes it worthwhile.

As for my opinion, I would rather do away with all this nonsense and restructure the progressive tax system. I would rather see every citizen with income, no matter how low, pay some taxes however little so all of us have a stake in this country. The higher income levels could pay progressively more if it would get rid of the smoke, the lies, the manipulation and trickery of class warfare.

But what I believe to be the best tax structure is not the point. The reason I tested your patience on this subject is to illustrate the point that many things about our government, not just the tax class warfare game, affect your daily life and are not at all what they seem. You should pay attention, and you may not see the truth on the nightly news. To find what is true you must think, and you must dig.

Will you be one of the many blissfully ignorant, or will you be one of the frustrated and well-informed? You have to work for your frustration.

Whose Job is Your Job?

If you listen to politicians and the nightly news, you would think jobs are created in Washington. Not true. There is no big *jobs button* up there. Jobs are created by private industry, by what are often characterized as *evil corporations*. Furthermore, despite all claims to the contrary the President and Congress do not control the economy at all, the most they can do is take actions which make the long-term climate for economic growth better or worse. The news media's repetition of political claims and accusations about the President's record on the economy or creating jobs is further evidence of their failure to provide perspective to their readers and viewers.

The nightly news rarely tells you about the business cycle, that swings in interest rates and unemployment and economic activity are inevitable with the business cycle, and that no President has been able to stop or control the business cycle no matter how hard they try. The business cycle is caused by the combined actions of millions of individuals and businesses, often reflecting their mood or expectations, and when one recession is over and business is booming we all know the business cycle will bring another recession sooner or later. But the nightly news broadcasts the political nonsense the President is responsible for job losses or gains, and I often wonder if anyone in the news room gets it.

You will often see politicians making speeches and holding hearings and posturing for the cameras on the subject of jobs and corporate responsibility. A good example is the 2002 Enron accounting scandal, the excessive executive pay and contracts that paid Enron executives millions in severance packages when they quit, and the Enron employees who received nothing when their job disappeared and suffered more because their 401k was focused in company stock that became worthless.

The embezzlers and fraudsters in these and other corporate scandals should, indeed, go to prison, but not for the reasons implied on TV. The executives should be punished for their securities and fraud crimes, not because they were paid too much or because the employees lost their jobs and their 401k values disappeared.

Here's some tough truth. Politicians and reporters forget, every day it seems, the foundation of our capitalist system is the motivation of self-interest, the private pursuit of profit. People who have money and wish to make a profit invest to buy an ownership share of a corporation or its' equivalent, and they seek out the best executives to run it for them. They compete for the best executives with sweetheart compensation packages and golden parachutes, meaning they promise to pay them lots of money if they are fired, creating much envy among the rest of us. The executives' job is to *execute* the corporate mission; they buy assets like buildings and equipment, and they hire employees to do certain work. The employees are nothing more than part of the assets to make money for the corporation, and most of us spend our working lives as an employee.

But we lose sight of the fact we are just an asset with the purpose of making money for the shareholders. We get wrapped up in our career track, health care, accumulated vacation and sick time, pension plans, 401ks and other benefits designed to attract good employees just the way sweetheart contracts attract good executives. Somehow we come to think the purpose of the corporation is to protect and preserve our jobs, but that is not the case. If economic conditions turn, our job could disappear in an instant.

How is it, then, this country is so prosperous if the livelihood of its' people hangs by such a thin thread? The answer is the capitalist system thrives because the selfish profit motives and competition make a business seek to improve its' product, and consumers who earn money at jobs constantly seek to buy better products.

What about employees who lose much of their 401k retirement savings because the corporate stock it owns falls sharply in value? I can't sympathize very much. The most basic foundation of investing is diversification, reducing risk by not concentrating too much of your savings in any one security. Employees choose investment alternatives for their 401k money. When they get star-struck about the company they work for and decide to concentrate not only their job but their invested retirement funds in that company as well, if it fails they have nobody but themselves to blame.

Next time the news media interviews a crying worker who has just lost her job or her 401k disappeared because the company stock went south amidst a scandal, it is humane to sympathize with her predicament. But you might wonder if the reporter realizes there is only one person responsible for your job, your income and the wise investment of your 401k . . . you!

Capitalism works, even if most participants don't understand *how* it works.

The Search for Perspective

The news media is an advertising medium. That's right, the purpose of the newspaper and nightly TV news is to sell you soap. If the newspaper didn't carry paid advertisements, it might cost you $5.00 instead of 50 cents. Same for TV. The ads you see and read are the primary *dog*, advertisers pay for the medium, the news in the paper and the programming on the TV is the secondary *tail*. The *dog* wags the *tail*. That's not so bad when you understand how it works, but will rot your brain if you do not.

To make sure you see the advertising *dog*, you have to be enticed and intrigued by the news and programming *tail*. That's why reporters find titillating stories that will interest you, not important stories that *should* interest you.

For example, in early August 2003 four US soldiers were killed in Iraq when ambushed by loyalists of Saddam Hussein. TV news reports pounded on these sad losses with questions of getting *bogged down* in Iraq since there are still problems, ten whole weeks after the end of the shooting war. Ten weeks, when the President told the country, in case nobody had the common sense to know, transforming Iraq into a democracy would take some time, perhaps years. These reports of four deaths had legs, of course, because political opponents of the President can make themselves look good by criticizing his Iraq policies under the somber umbrella of casualties.

But there were no TV news reports that gave us real perspective on Iraq, no reports that hundreds of convoys were conducted safely while only a few were attacked, no reports that electricity and water flow had been restored to levels better even than before the war in many areas, no reports that an Iraqi government council is nearly prepared to begin their meetings to decide on the structure of the first Islamic democracy in the region, no reports that Iraqi students are back in school, no reports that most Iraqi people welcome their freedom, no reports that routine torture and execution have stopped in that country.

If you heard reports of those four casualties in proper context of 140,000 US troops doing a difficult and dangerous job that cannot be done quickly, what would you think? You might conclude we are doing the right thing in Iraq, or you might conclude we are wasting lives and resources on problems we either cannot or should not solve, depending on your viewpoint and values. But the nightly TV news told you what they wanted you to hear. To find perspective you'd have to read several excellent newspapers.

Those of us who found perspective on these four killed soldiers had to dig for more in-depth reports while the masses took the bait and began to complain about our role in Iraq. The primary reason I opposed the war in Iraq is the American public, led by the network news, has no stamina for a trickle of casualty reports. Any rag-tag insurgency group can make the life of the mighty US military miserable by blending into the population and killing one of our troops now and then. Our own TV cameras will do the rest for them. This is the classic insurgency strategy to drive a wedge between the dominant forces and the populace who support them. Our country should take on important and difficult tasks like Iraq, but the public is driven by the news cycle and the evening news is typically full of selected events with an agenda tilt but devoid of perspective.

The public took more bait a few days later when ABC news reported some 3rd Infantry Division soldiers were complaining about duty in Iraq and wanting to go home. If you ever needed proof some reporters are dumbasses, surely one who considers complaining soldiers to be news should make an irrefutable case. US soldiers have been incessant complainers since Washington's troops were cold at Valley Forge, and anyone with half a brain knows it . . . except a reporter and network wishing to slant the news to their agenda. When I was in the Army the standing joke was to worry most about morale when the troops were *not* complaining.

Whether our Iraq adventure succeeds or turns sour, we'll likely see from the network news just the juicy pictures and sound bites, not the big picture. Perspective means being able to put events in context, and our advertising-driven media is superb at showing us the *dog* and the *tail* it wags, but most fall short on perspective.

Some reporters are fine professionals. Those who rode into battle and risked their lives with our forces in Iraq, for example, made me proud of them, and I think they discovered many of the things I told you about the elephant. There just aren't enough of the fine reporters amidst the herd, and it's up to you to be skeptical enough to listen carefully and decide what to believe.

Blaming the media is easy, but if you do you have to blame yourself for being mentally lazy. That's because whether a reporter is a fine professional or a hack, they each have an agenda, and their agenda inevitably influences the selection of a story and the slant it takes. It's human nature, we all have an agenda, including you and me.

Many consumers of the evening news don't know they are seeing shallow news slanted by an agenda, and never realize what is missing. You have to understand the *dog* and the *tail* to realize why too many reporters have a keen sense for the *trivial* but no sense of the *substantial.* If you want perspective, you have to seek it out yourself by finding more in-depth reports. The bliss of ignorance, or working hard to find the truth; the choice hardly seems fair, but that's life.

The Blind Scales (or Guillotine) of Justice

If you ever find yourself in trouble with the law in the USA, don't listen to anyone who tells you there is nothing to fear if you have done nothing wrong. There is everything to fear. You don't get justice and truth from our legal system, you get . . . procedure.

Most of the time the procedure works and that's the virtue of the system. But if it doesn't find the truth you may be the only one who cares. Prosecutors are focused on whether they have enough evidence to win a case, to sell the jury, they don't want to lose because their measure of success and path to greater things is winning. If that coincides with the truth that's nice but hardly necessary. Prosecutors see so many lies every day they might be hard to convince you only *appear* to be guilty but are in reality innocent. Right doesn't always win.

Our justice system is not really a search for the truth at all. It is an adversarial system in which each side fights to win. Both sides use pieces of facts to craft arguments that often have no connection to reality, but what matters is who can sell their argument to the jury. That often means the most talented and high-priced lawyer wins. Truth often emerges as a happy accident, but the guilty quite often go free and once in a while an innocent person is convicted because truth lost.

I hope you stay out of trouble, but if you get into a jam exercise your right to remain silent, don't answer any questions until the very best lawyer advises you. You can advocate for reform of our system of justice later, after the smoke clears, after your high-priced lawyer wins.

You Can be Anything You Want . . . Except President

The US Constitution, Article II, Section 1, Clause 5 states "No Person except a natural born Citizen . . ." may be President of the United States. Since you were born in China and became citizens through a process called naturalization, you can't be President of the United States unless that provision is changed in the Constitution, a very unlikely proposition.

Why can't kids adopted internationally and who are faithful citizens become President? When our founding fathers were debating and pushing and pulling and negotiating and compromising over hundreds of matters to construct a new country, they feared most the intrusive power from their *oppressor*, the King of England, and that spread to a fear of *foreign powers* in general. Just to make sure those they feared from foreign powers could not become their President, they wrote into the Constitution the natural-born requirement and we have been stuck with it since then. Of course they gave themselves an exception by providing that anyone *already* a US citizen at the time the Constitution was written was eligible no matter where they had been born.

Is that fair? Well, of course not, but you may as well learn early that life is not fair.

Some parents who adopted kids born in other countries resent this prohibition and seek to change it. I consider it a blessing. Who in their right mind would want to be President, with the daily offensive and defensive finger-pointing mixed with posturing and butt-kissing required of a big-time politician? Not you, I hope.

Here's my advice. Never trust any person who actually *wants* to be President, and give thanks this insane office is not available to you for a reason that makes no sense whatever in today's world. If the Constitution is ever amended to open the office to you, and if anyone then ever mentions the possibility of your running for that office, I suggest instead you run for your life!

It's Up To You

The one constant in life is change. Which direction will change take our country? The USA has some magnificent virtues and some overpowering flaws. Will the problems be worked out? Who will tackle the tough ones, and if we don't will our nation survive in the long run?

As you look around to see who will save the day, glance in the mirror. Remember, you are free to succeed and free to fail, free to work hard and free to lay on the couch, free to develop your intellect and free to be an ignorant slug. If everyone chooses the couch maybe the national rot will become irreversible.

Whether change takes the USA to a better day or down the drain depends on individuals like you. Will you vote? Will you think? Will you educate yourself on the issues and take a stand for what you believe? Will you become involved and do your part? It's easy to assume someone else will do it, *they* will do it.

But there is no *they*, there is only *we*.

If you wonder what you can possibly do, consider the old man walking along a beach where millions of small starfish had been left to dry and die by the receding tide. The man would walk a ways and stop to pick up a single starfish and toss it back into the ocean. A little boy watching the man asked him:

"Excuse me, sir, why did you throw that starfish into the ocean?"

"So it would live." Answered the old man.

"But there are millions of starfish dying. How could you possibly make a difference?"

As the old man walked on to select the next starfish he said to the boy, "It made a difference to that one."

You don't have to run for national office to make a difference. You can volunteer, you can become active in your town, city or state , and if you help make life better for just one person, it will be you who will make a difference. You can simply be a good citizen, make your voice heard and vote.

Whether America prevails in the long run or falls victim to decay is up to future generations. I hope you learn from the mistakes my generation made when we lost many of our national virtues to the feel-good counter-culture starting in the 1960s. Maybe you can bring back the notion of doing what is right even when it isn't easy. Whatever your generation decides to do, I hope you leave your children fewer problems than we have left to you.

Now it's up to you.

The Magic of Consent

You might think from what I have written I must not like America very much. The truth is I love this country passionately despite all its' flaws and absurdities. Here we are free to realize our potential if we wish to spend the effort.

Many people think of the USA as a perfect place and then become disillusioned when they discover its' problems. By knowing the flaws in your country you can best understand how it really works and appreciate its' virtues because you have perspective, and won't be moved from your patriotism when human nature deals up a Joker.

The magic of our country is *the consent of the governed*. We call the shots at each election by selecting our very own dumbasses to represent us. Since they are just people full of flaws, like the rest of us, the job they do is full of flaws, and if we dislike our dumbasses we can yell at them and throw them out in the next election. This sounds like the worst way to run a country . . . except for all the others.

As you think of the people you are connected to by blood in China, maybe the very best you could hope for them is that some day they will be free to talk openly about the flaws and absurdities in their government, free to elect their own dumbasses, free to ridicule their elected dumbasses who surely will deserve it as much as our own, and free to throw out their dumbasses in the next election. We can only hope for them some day those who govern them must have their consent.

Speakers and politicians often declare the United States of America to be the greatest country, the only nation that could give us the freedom and opportunity we enjoy. But there are other fine and free countries, so I would prefer to say " God bless America. And may the people of China someday be free."

Trust Yourself

I hope to see you marry and have children of your own, but I may not live a long life. That's why I have written the things I want to tell you when you are older. I have bored you with my thoughts on many subjects not only to convey what I have learned, but to encourage you to think. If I'm not there to coach you, please do these things for me.

Trust yourself.

Consider what I have written seriously, but think for yourself and make your own decisions. The older I get the more I learn and the more I realize there is much I don't know.

Learn the discipline of intellectual honesty. Too many people aren't even honest with themselves.

Learn the enrichment of respectful conversation with someone who disagrees with you to understand their view and reconsider your own.

Be wary of those who have all the answers. There is nothing so certain as a small mind.

Never trust anyone who claims to speak for God.

Chart your own course in life with careful thought. Take the time to contemplate, recognize the tug of your own emotions to make sure they don't take you in the wrong direction.

Trust your own instinct and values, don't make decisions based on what others might think.

Don't drift along with the crowd, they might take you down a path you would not choose for yourself.

Step back from the daily turmoil and try hard to see through the veil of youth just how much your mother loves you. She has devoted her life to you.

Be a naturally happy person like your Mom and Grandpa Mel, enjoy life and don't let the dumbasses get you down. They're everywhere.

Teach your children the virtue of ordinary soldiers, and tell them your Dad showed you how to tell it true.

Appendix

Telling Melanie Her Adoption Story

When we brought Melanie home from China in 1998, like many others we wondered how we could tell her adoption story in a positive and truthful way, so she would accept the concept of adoption, a birthmother and birthfather in China, and be reassured that we are a family forever.

I developed a Powerpoint slideshow, with automatic transition to the next slide and narration in my voice. The hardest part was developing the text explaining why boys are favored in China. When it was done it took a mouse-click to start and it ran by itself. Melanie is now six years old, but has been watching her story since she was two. Some would argue that is too early, but it worked so well I will do it again with Kristen next year when she is two.

At first Melanie was just fascinated with her own pictures, but she gradually understood more and more bits and pieces.

Melanie was prompted by her story to ask questions like "Why didn't my birthmom keep me?" or "What's my birthfather's name" or "What does my birthmom look like?" or "How come I'm the only one in my class who is adopted?" The slideshow planted the seed that she should be proud to be from China, that adoption is a wonderful thing, we are her *parents* and our family is forever. Those things have taken deep root with Melanie. But her story isn't the end, it is just a beginning to start the conversations an adoptive parent should have with their child.

I know some adoptive parents who don't talk about this to their kids at all, waiting for them to bring it up. My guess is these questions or fears boil in our kids heads long before they talk to us about it.

I am including here the images and text of Melanie's adoption story, with a few updates as I have thought further about things like many birth mothers carrying forever the emotional scar of being forced to abandon their child. You might choose a different way, but maybe this will help you think about how you want to tell your child their adoption story.

Melanie's Adoption Story

This is the story of how you were adopted and came home from China with your Mom and Dad

China is an ancient and proud country. China developed one of the world's first written languages thousands of years ago.

A long time ago, emperors in China built grand palaces and temples . . .

. . . and a great wall built to keep out foreign invaders, one of the wonders of the world.

China has treatments and medicines, proven over hundreds of years, and we are just beginning to understand them.

Some Chinese people live in the crowded cities. Can you find the man with his little girl on his shoulders?

Others live on farms in the country where they must carry fresh water to their homes every day.

Some people live on boats . . .

. . . and others make a living taking goods to market on the waterways.

Did you know much of the world's tea comes from China?

Rice is a very important food in China. It's grown in water-soaked paddies, and is planted by hand.

Here's the rice paddies after the rice has grown to its' beautiful green. And China has lots of huge mountains like those in the background.

China has many large cities, jammed with people and buildings and cars and buses and bicycles.

Cars are very expensive, and there isn't enough room for everyone to have a car. So most Chinese save until they can buy a bicycle.

Places to live in China are very small, maybe without hot water. Finding a nice place to live is very hard because there are so many people.

Because apartments are very small, Chinese people like to relax in parks, like this one in Hefei, a northern city.

There are too many people in China, and Chinese leaders must carefully watch population growth, the food supply and many other factors related to such crowding.

The Chinese love children. but with so many people it is already difficult to build enough houses and apartments, and to provide enough jobs and food for everyone. If families have too many children, it would cause terrible problems.

So leaders in China made some laws allowing each family to have just one child. Most families are delighted with their one child whether a daughter or a son. But some families feel they must have a son since they can have only one child, and you might wonder why.

Chinese people in the countryside live a hard life where the manual labor of a man, and his sons, is very important. Daughters marry and move away with their husband, while a son remains with the family to care for his parents when they get old.

These Chinese boys will be expected to work hard on the family farm, and to take care of their parents in old age.

If this farmer and his wife have a child, they will likely hope for a son. But what if their only child is a daughter and not a son? They won't have help in the fields, and the daughter will move away when she marries, and they will have no son to care for them when they get old.

And so sometimes, even though they love their baby, the birthmother and birthfather feel they must secretly give up their daughter and try to have a son. Sometimes the birth mother doesn't have the money or the family support to care for a child. It makes them very sad to give up their baby, and they try to make sure the child will be safe and receive loving care.

This is part of your adoption story. You grew in your Chinese birthmom's tummy in a town named Dayangdian, in Anhui province near the capital city of Hefei, and you were born on April 5, 1997. We don't know your birthmom's name or who she is, and we don't know if her family needed a son or if she had no money or if she had no family support to care for a child. But we believe she loved you, and wanted so bad to stay with you. We don't know why, but she couldn't, and it must have broken her heart to let you go.

Your birth mother made sure you went to an orphanage where you would be safe and cared for until your forever family came to take you home. This is you with the director of your orphanage in Hefei.

Did you know, while you were growing in your birthmom's tummy, you were growing in your forever family's heart? At the orphanage, they took good care of you until China told your forever family they could come take you home.

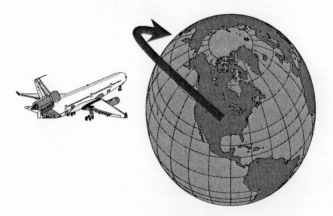

Your forever family came to China from far away on an airplane to meet you, halfway around the world.

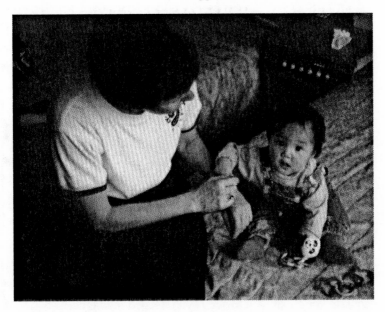

When you met your forever family, they adopted you. Adoption means they filed papers, and had meetings with officials . . .

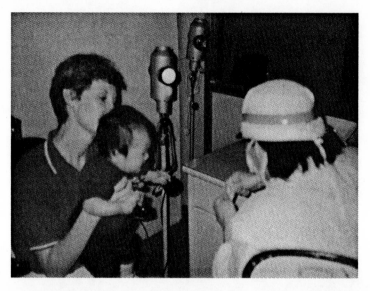

. . . and had a doctor check you to see if you needed medicine.

And then your forever family told everyone they know in China and at home that you are their very own daughter.

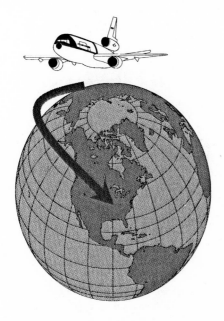

When the adoption was all done, you flew on an airplane with your forever family to your new home on the other side of the world.

Now, through a wonderful process called adoption, you are part of your family. This is your **REAL** family, the ones who take care of you.

And do you know how long you'll be part of that family? Forever, for your whole life, because that's what adoption and a forever family means.

That's the story of how you came from China to be with your forever family. We are so thankful China let us adopt you to be our daughter. We are very proud of you and proud that you are from China. You should be, too!

Printed in the United States
31644LVS00001B/170